The European Experience
A Historical Critique of Development Theory

D0870C75

DIETER SENGHAAS

The European Experience

A Historical Critique of Development Theory

Translated from the German by
K.H. KIMMIG

Berg Publishers
Leamington Spa/Dover, New Hampshire
1985

Berg Publishers Ltd
24 Binswood Avenue, Leamington Spa,
Warwickshire CV32 5SQ, UK
51 Washington Street, Dover,
New Hampshire 03820, USA

English translation © Berg Publishers Ltd 1985
Originally published as *Von Europa leren. Entwicklungsgeschichtliche Betrachtungen*
Translated from the German with the permission of the publishers
Suhrkamp Verlag, Frankfurt am Main
© 1982 Suhrkamp Verlag, Frankfurt am Main

British Library Cataloguing in Publication Data

Senghaas, Dieter
    The European experience: a historical critique
    of development theory.
    1. Europe—Economic conditions
    I. Title   II. Von Europa leren. *English*
    330.94'02   HC240

    ISBN 0–907582–17–6
    ISBN 0–907582–33–8 Pbk

Library of Congress Cataloging in Publication Data

Senghaas, Dieter, 1940–
    The European experience.

    Translation of: Von Europa leren.
    1. Economic development—History.   2. Europe—
Economic conditions.   I. Title.
HD82.S439713   1985   338.94   84–73482
ISBN 0–907582–17–6
ISBN 0–907582–33–8 (pbk.)

Printed in Great Britain by Billings of Worcester

Contents

For Eva and Tanja

Preface to the English Edition

The publication in English of my study *The European Experience*, which appeared in the Federal Republic of Germany in 1982, gives me an opportunity to explain how the book fits into the current development debate.

In the Federal Republic of Germany, too, the development debate of the 1950s and 1960s was informed by *modernization theory*. Of Anglo-Saxon, and mainly American, provenance, it was rooted in political science, sociology, social psychology and, above all, economics. Few of the products of this early development debate have survived; notable among them are the comparative-historical variants of modernization research (K.W. Deutsch, Reinhard Bendix *et al.*). From the mid-1960s modernization theory was challenged on two levels. The first challenge resulted from the growing discrepancy between the development predictions contained in modernization theory and the actual development process in the Third World. The second stemmed from the formulation of a new development paradigm, which, interestingly, did not originate in the highly industrialized societies of the West, the OECD (Organization for Economic Cooperation and Development) societies, but in parts of the Third World. I am referring to the *dependencia* theories elaborated in the Caribbean and Latin America, to the theory of peripheral capitalism formulated in Africa (mainly by Samir Amin), and to the continuing debate among Indian social scientists on the so-called 'colonial mode of production'.

This new paradigm, which I introduced into the political and scientific development debate of the Federal Republic with two publications in 1972 and 1974, has cast a new light on the problem of development and underdevelopment.[1] For the first time in the more recent development debate, the close link between the world economy and the development prospects of individual national economies was discussed explicitly, making it possible to identify the particular characteristics of dependent development in contrast with the development

1

processes in highly industrialized societies. Within development theory this led to the fundamental distinction between metropolitan and peripheral capitalism—metropolitan capitalism being defined as dominant economy (*économie dominante*, in François Perroux's terms), and peripheral capitalism as dominated economy (*économie dominée*).[2]

This discussion—like every new stage of the development debate—gave rise to the crucial policy question, how can delayed development still be conceived and put into practice within the context of an asymmetrically structured international society and economy? Conventional development theory argued for increased integration into the world market (associative development strategy), while the more recent paradigms cited above suggested a development policy of de-linking or dissociation. For my part, in a book on 'World Economic Order and Development Policy: A Plea for Dissociation', published in 1977, I have presented a development policy programme that identified *selective de-linking* as one of the indispensable prerequisites for successful delayed development.[3] So far as the history of ideas is concerned, I was able to go back to a German economist of the nineteenth century, specifically to the reflections by Friedrich List on development theory and policy.[4] The studies of List seemed to me especially relevant, because in the first half of the nineteenth century, when the Continent of Europe was facing the great challenge from the Britain of the Industrial Revolution, he posed a question for development policy which still appears quite topical: How can the continental societies successfully withstand the displacement competition emanating from the more efficient and productive British economy and avoid becoming peripheries of this forerunner of the first industrial revolution?

List advocated a limited period of selective de-linking, that is to say a development phase during which massive domestic development programmes would have to be planned behind deliberately erected protective barriers—programmes which, at the end of this critical development phase, would lead to the emergence of a competitive economy. Only after such a development phase based on the dynamics of the domestic market should the society in question open up to the world market and expose itself to international competition. In List's view the domestic economic development programme consisted of the systematic development of agriculture and industry, particularly the close intermeshing of both sectors. Without the mobilization of a society's agricultural potential, especially in the case of populous societies, the prospects for successful industrialization were considered only small. In this respect List was an adherent of 'balanced growth'. My book of 1977, which by way of dependency theory and dissociation strategy introduced Listian considerations into the current development debate, has led to an extremely lively discussion on the pros and cons of such a programme.[5]

At an early stage in this debate on 'free trade or de-linking' I found the lack of a historical perspective a drawback. It also seemed increasingly important to find out how European societies actually developed in the nineteenth and early twentieth centuries. Over the past thirty years conventional development theoreticians and, above all, practising politicians, have constantly argued that free trade is the key to development. My knowledge of List's arguments against the British free-trade school made me sceptical. These doubts led to a research project resulting in the present book on European development. As I have pointed out in the preface to the original German edition, this book presents a deliberate eurocentric viewpoint. I wanted to know how European societies responded to the British challenge and which development paths they followed. I was particularly interested in finding out why some parts of Europe developed while others turned into peripheries displaying all the symptoms of contemporary Third World societies.[6]

In calling the book *The European Experience*, I wanted to draw attention to the lasting lessons provided by European development history. However, the book does not deal exclusively with Europe. It also contains some historical diagnoses of non-European societies which are now highly industrialized. In addition, it includes reflections on non-European societies which, in different political and socio-structural conditions, could easily have become part of the highly industrialized world, but whose development potential remained blocked. The book contains, too, a chapter on the question as to whether Far Eastern development is following in Europe's footsteps. This question is becoming increasingly relevant, since the Far East and the Pacific basin are widely held to represent the new dynamic growth pole of international society and the world economy for the twenty-first century.[7] There is also a chapter on the role of socialist development policy, whose empirical frame of reference extends beyond Europe.

Despite these forays into non-European regions, the book's main focus is on an analysis of the varied European development experiences and their relevance to the current development policy debate.

Acknowledgments

The author wishes to thank the publishers of the following journals, in whose pages earlier versions of certain chapters have appeared: Chapter 1, *Economics* 21 (1980); Chapter 4, *Economics* 26 (1982); Chapter 6, *Bulletin of Peace Studies* 3 (1981); Chapter 7, *Economics* 18 (1978).

Foreword

Like its predecessor, *Weltwirtschaftsordnung und Entwicklungspolitik. Plädoyer für Dissoziation*,[1] this book takes as its starting-point topical questions of development theory. Although, unlike its forerunner, it is mainly concerned with the history of development, it seeks to contribute to the current debate on development policy. In contrast with the earlier book, its perspective is in three ways *eurocentric*.

Reconsidering Europe

In the first place, the present volume is eurocentric in drawing empirically, though not exclusively, on the history of European development in the nineteenth and twentieth centuries. The development debate of the past three decades has centred on the Third World, not Europe. Both the theory of modernization and that of peripheral capitalism have taken for granted the development of Europe (usually meaning north-western and central Europe), and of some overseas settler colonies, into highly industrialized societies. There seemed to be no reason, therefore, to make Europe itself the object of the development research. In the debate on development policy that has taken place within Europe, the European experience itself has thus remained largely disregarded.

When I refer to Europe in the following pages, it is not simply to north-western and central Europe, where highly industrialized societies have developed, nor just to the present area of the European Community,[2] but to north-eastern, eastern, south-eastern and southern Europe as well. Most of the following observations relate, therefore, to the whole of Europe, developed and underdeveloped, from Iceland to Romania and from Finland to Portugal. Non-European development

5

experiences are taken into account only where the argument seems to require it. Current development trends in the Third World are touched on but marginally.

Fascination with the history of European development springs from the remarkable diversity of its development patterns. In parallel with the rise of highly industrialized societies which developed gradually over decades (almost all the OECD countries), there occurred the formation of typical enclave economies or peripheries, mainly in southern, south-eastern and eastern Europe as well as in Ireland. In addition, until the early twentieth century, there existed backward, undeveloped societies, as in large parts of the Balkans (e.g. Albania). Inward-directed development paths can be found alongside export-orientated ones. Some countries possess abundant, others only scanty resources, success or failure to develop not being clearly deducible from such different starting-points. Europe provides an illustration not only of capitalist but of peripheral-capitalist and, commencing with the present century, of socialist development paths.

Apart from the practical-political reasons for dealing with Europe (as supplied by the debate on the southern enlargement of the European Community and the problems of intra-European regionalism[3]), this diversity of development experiences alone ought to be reason enough to make European development over the past 150 years the object of comparative historical research. Fortunately, there have been some recent contributions which, in contrast with earlier studies, focus not only on certain regions but on the whole of Europe.[4]

The present book is eurocentric in another respect. The issues dominating the development debate over the past thirty years were, as a rule, formulated in the developed world and projected on to the Third World. Rarely have they been projected back on to the developed world itself.[5] Some striking examples may illustrate this state of affairs.

While, over the past two decades, the Third World has been constantly advised to integrate into an 'unrestricted world economy' on the basis of free trade, it has hardly ever been questioned whether, during its initial development stages in the nineteenth and early twentieth centuries, Europe itself had developed in such a way. And rarely have the repercussions of free trade in different societies been properly examined. Forced industrialization remained for decades the development prescription for the Third World. The ultimate consequences of industrialization without prior improvement in agricultural productivity, as witnessed in the European context, were not considered. Even today autocratic-corporatist regimes in the Third World are frequently regarded as 'inevitable·agents of modernization'. But where did development in Europe lead to when taking place in such political and institutional conditions?

Critical contributions to the development debate, too, were usually formulated without regard to the European experience. In the book mentioned above my own analysis of peripheral-capitalist society resulted in a programmatic 'plea for dissociation' (de-linking). But what part did dissociative policies play in the European process of development, if in fact pressure for peripheralization was present in the development of European societies?

Finally, the present book is eurocentric in its intention to draw lessons from the varied recent history of European development.[6] To this end I focus on some of the important questions raised by the current development debate. For example:

— How did the gap in development between advanced societies and latecomers inherent in the structure of the world economic system affect the development chances of *European* societies, especially of export-orientated economies? What part was played by free trade and/or de-linking? To what extent were external or internal factors responsible for development success or failure?

— What relationship can be observed, in the history of European development, between a given social structure and the direction and extent of the development of the productive forces?

— What is the position of agriculture in the development process?

— What is the connection between distributive equity, growth and development?

— What are the political conditions that promote or hinder development?

— Are there any verifiable links between resource endowment, the mobilization of knowledge and skills (human capital) and the likelihood of development success or failure? Did cultural factors play a major part in them?

— What were the general conditions for metropolitan-capitalist development—that is, for the formation of efficient economies? What were the causes of the development dynamics of peripheral-capitalist societies in Europe? What place does socialist development policy in Europe occupy in the history of development?

Centred as it is on Europe, a book such as this one is bound to meet objections that have to be taken seriously. Does it not resurrect the very eurocentrism whose disastrous role has just been recognized in the recent development debate?[7]

The kind of eurocentric approach that elevates the operating prin-
ciples of highly industrialized societies into a model for universally valid
development patterns and distils them into prescriptions for societies
which are still predominantly agrarian, should indeed be criticized.
Development projects based on this kind of thinking and planning were
bound to produce results other than those intended.[8] But, as will be
demonstrated, it is this very type of eurocentrism that disregards
decisive lessons from the history of European development. To take
them into account does not mean advocating a new suspect eurocentrism. Of course, this book would not have been written, had I not
considered some of these experiences useful for development policy.

The cultural critique of European development, which is currently
popular and widespread, by no means undermines such an assessment.
Those who, turning their backs on Europe, claim to discover new
horizons of development policy elsewhere (e.g. in China),[9] would be
surprised to learn that many of their alternative policy recommendations can be traced back to the European development experience.
There were, for instance, a great many treatises in eighteenth-,
nineteenth- and early twentieth- century Europe discussing natural
methods of improving agricultural efficiency—a consequence of many
practical, small-scale experiments and of increasingly productive agricultural units. Agriculture-based industrialization, on a manageable
scale, is not a new invention, and some of the recently discovered
'intermediate technologies' formed, only a few decades ago, standard
practices in European agriculture and industry. It is precisely the
export-orientated development patterns of European societies that
demonstrate the practical relevance of the concept of 'self-reliance' in
the history of European development.

If the varied development experience of European societies provides
positive lessons, does not a reconsideration of the history of European
development suggest itself? This book attempts to contribute to the
belated revision of a problematic image of Europe still dominating the
development debate. If, moreover, it stimulates an investigative interest in European development, concerned with questions of theory and
policy, an additional purpose will have been served.

The Neo-Listian Problem: Foreign Economic Policy Conditions and Autocentric Development

In *Weltwirtschaftsordnung und Entwicklungspolitik* the discussion of development theory and practice ended, as already noted, with a 'plea for

dissociation', which provoked a wide debate on development policy.[10] The starting-point was provided by the examination of non-European peripheral societies and economies, for whose analysis the concept of peripheral capitalism seemed useful. As is well known this concept revolves around a number of serious structural deficits of peripheries:[11]

(*a*) inadequate integration of agriculture and industry (lacking forward and backward linkages);

(*b*) insufficient depth of production—that is, a lack of integrated economic circuits;

(*c*) constriction of the internal market, rooted in the social structure, even in the case of populous societies; and

(*d*) as a rule, growing cleavages in society and economy.

In order to overcome these defects of dependent reproduction I suggested, in contrast with the prevailing interpretation, a dissociative development policy, not expecting any lasting solution for the problems of Latin America, Africa and Asia from a further integration into a world market already characterized by considerable development differentials. Differences within the group of peripheries, which are now being intensely debated in science and politics,[12] were at that time already apparent, but largely ignored, the emphasis being placed on comparable structural deficits of various peripheries. The resource endowment, along with the history and the development stage of different countries, was disregarded, and so the plea for dissociation remained abstract and general, focusing on three imperatives of development policy:

(*a*) de-linking of Third World countries from the world economic system dominated by industrialized capitalist countries;

(*b*) broad-based development of national domestic markets; and

(*c*) cooperation with other developing countries (collective self-reliance) and, if necessary, strictly selective cooperation with other more highly developed societies.[13]

In analytical and programmatic terms, *Weltwirtschaftsordnung und Entwicklungspolitik* had a clearly discernible reference system, without being able at that point to flesh it out with historical evidence. It was probably this weakness that led, in the ensuing debate, to the misapprehension that the terms 'dissociation' and 'autocentric development' were identical, despite the fact that I had always referred to three different requirements of development policy and their combination.

It is to be hoped that the investigations into development history presented in the present volume will help to clarify the historically variable role that associative and dissociative strategies (including mixes of the two) have, respectively, played in autocentric development processes.

To this end, Part I presents a historically based typology of auto-centric development. The aim is to identify the different associative or dissociative development paths that can be observed in recent European history. In addition to this typology, Part I discusses important general reasons for the success or failure of such development paths, above all the role of agricultural advance in the development process, which I consider to be a fundamental one.

In Part II, in contrast, the analysis concentrates on only one section of the typology elaborated in Part I—on export-orientated (i.e. tendentially 'associative') development. The intention is to throw into relief the conditions in which integration into the world market has led to autocentric societies in the past.[14] The Scandinavian development pattern is presented as an example of export-orientated and, at the same time, autocentric development. Some causes of autocentric development or peripheralization are pin-pointed in an illustrative comparative treatise on small, predominantly agrarian, export economies. Some of these evolved into mature industrial societies; others, despite comparable positions in the world market, into peripheries.

These two sections on development history make it possible to outline essential aspects of an export-orientated and autocentric development scenario, and to ask questions about the development chances of societies attempting to transform themselves, in present conditions, into 'mature' industrial societies by means of forced export growth.

In the present book the political relevance of the arguments based on the history of development are demonstrated only through the topical examples of Taiwan and South Korea and their export-orientated development path. To extend this kind of analysis to other export-orientated 'newly industrializing countries' is a task for further investigation.[15] Equally important for the current development debate would be a study of the populous, more internally dynamic, 'newly industrializing societies' (Brazil, Mexico, etc.) in the light of the general political diagnosis of Part I.[16]

The broad historical discussion in Part II of the conditions for successful export-orientated development should not give the impression that this book contains, if not explicitly, then by implication, a plea for such development. It should be clear from the argument in Part I that this would mean drawing a rash conclusion from a limited diagnosis of development history; especially, since in recent attempts at delayed development, the historical trend seems to indicate an increase in dissociative components, and since successful export-orientated development paths require socio-structural preconditions that are rarely encountered. If such favourable conditions were to appear, however, there would be no fundamental reason preventing successful export-orientated development from happening even today. But the exceptional case of the Israeli development pattern after the Second World War shows how improbable this is.[17]

Part III of this book illuminates the place of socialism in the history of development. The thoughts presented there tie in directly with *Plädoyer für Dissoziation*, for, in the history of development, socialism has had a strategic function for dissociative attempts at delayed development. The experiences resulting from these attempts enable us to judge the achievements and shortcomings of socialist development policy. The discussion concludes with a dialectical judgement. The achievements in surmounting typical structural deficits of peripheral-capitalist societies are indisputable, but the instruments employed in this process prove, in the long run, to be obstacles to self-sustaining economic growth and dynamic development. As is demonstrated by the present crisis of socialist development in *all* the socialist countries inside and outside Europe, it is not only stagnation that threatens, but a relapse into conditions of real deprivation and an intensification of social problems leading in the same way as in peripheral-capitalist societies to an increasing militarisation of politics, society, the economy and culture. There can be no doubt, after all, that one of the main causes of the growing development defects within these societies lies in the neglect of some basic experiences from the history of European development—above all, underestimation of the importance of agricultural development and at the same time promotion of a disproportionately large sector of heavy industry. Both inevitably prevent a balanced development of the potential internal market and result—as in all cases in recent history—in development blocks.

The discussion of socialism in Part III also results in a revision, based on the history of development, of the traditional theory of socialism.

Like *Weltwirtschaftsordnung und Entwicklungspolitik* the following discussion centres on the question, posed in classical theory by Friedrich List, of how delayed development is possible in a world economy characterized by growing development differentials.[18] This line of enquiry, however, by no means excludes other aspects of research into the history of European development so far as they are relevant to development policy.[19] In my previous book, which dealt with the present problems of the Third World, I gave reasons why the transition from economic peripheries to autocentrically developed societies was

improbable and suggested, therefore, a dissociative development path.
However, following List, a reintegration into the world market ought to
have taken place in the long run. The present book shows the whole
span of possible relationships which can be observed, in development
history, between associative and dissociative external economic conditions, on the one hand, and autocentric development or peripheralization, on the other. I shall discuss:

(*a*) societies that have developed autocentrically despite, or because
of, their integration into the world market;

(*b*) societies that have developed into peripheries in the course of
their integration into the world market, and have remained so to the
present day;

(*c*) societies that have experienced a breakthrough in development
during periods of more or less pronounced de-linking from the world
market; and

(*d*) societies that have remained peripheries despite more or less
pronounced de-linking.

The location and sequence of these cases (and of some mixed
versions) in the more recent history of European development are
discussed in Part I.

The diversity of the development paths that can be observed in
Europe suggests a comparative historical approach.[20] Such an approach can generate insights that do not flow easily from otherwise
indispensable investigations into single cases or points of detail. The
value of such an approach does not, however, depend primarily on the
intention behind the method, but on the validity of the results of the
analysis. If these can help to elucidate some aspects of the present
development discussion, my reconsideration of the European experience of development will have served its purpose.

1 Autocentric Development despite International Competence Differentials: Problem and General Diagnosis

Throughout the history of mankind development differentials have existed between societies, between civilizations and between entire continents. During the early Middle Ages north-western Europe, later to be the site of a developmental breakthrough that shaped world history so decisively, was totally underdeveloped and marginal, com pared with the great civilizations of the ancient world and the non-European empires.[1] But such differentials remained of no consequence for development policy; exchange relationships came about by way of long-distance trade, the content and extent of which generally left the internal dynamics of the trading societies untouched. As is demonstrated by the changing history of the trade routes, long-distance trade played a much greater part in shaping the destiny of those trading nations that specialized as intermediaries than in the development of societies that produced the traded commodities, mainly exotic and luxury goods.[2]

A qualitative leap over and above mere long-distance trade occurred only when a more or less world-wide division of labour emerged, which happened, at the latest, in the early modern period. It should be remembered that, initially, the traded products comprised mainly precious metals and other luxury goods, less frequently raw materials and rarely foodstuffs—that is, not, as yet, goods for large mass markets[3] which, because of the low development level of the productive forces and of transport, did not exist. The then emerging structure of a world economy based on the division of labour is, in the more recent debate on development theory, rightly regarded as the starting-point of the world economic order that shapes international society today.

For many years attempts have been made, in the context of the

13

so-called 'world system approach', to trace the familiar features of the present world economic order, such as the gap between highly indus- trialized societies (metropoles) and the Third World (peripheries), back to the early modern period.[4] It is beyond dispute that relation- ships based on the division of labour between core societies and periph- eries already existed at that time. What is in dispute, not surprisingly, is how to explain the emergence and extent of such relationships at the end of the Middle Ages and the beginning of modern times. The further the discussion advances, however, the clearer it becomes that at that time patterns were set which continued to determine the development paths of individual societies and entire continents well into the nine- teenth and twentieth centuries.[5] It is not only the diverging develop- ment paths of Europe and the extra-European continents that can be traced back to the late medieval and early modern periods; the diverg- ing development patterns within Europe itself during the nineteenth and twentieth centuries—for example, in northern and north-western Europe, on the one hand, and southern and eastern Europe, on the other—have, viewed from the present, a 'pre-history' of at least 400 to 500 years, during which the course was set for diverging development paths.[6]

Recent studies have nevertheless shown that as late as the eighteenth century the overall development differential within Europe was still in the region of 1:2. The pronounced development differences within Europe and, to an even greater degree, between the developing regions of Europe and the other continents, emerged only during the nine- teenth and twentieth centuries.[7] Several factors were at work here.

Competence Differentials and the Pressure towards Peripheralization

The primary factor was undoubtedly the development breakthrough achieved by England in the eighteenth and nineteenth centuries as a result of an agrarian, industrial and commercial revolution. Why it was England which first achieved this breakthrough in Europe[8] and not, for example, France, is a subject frequently discussed among historians. But this question is much less relevant for an understanding of long- term development than a discussion of the inevitable repercussions for Europe and the world after a qualitative leap in development had taken place in just one country, England.

What sort of breakthrough was it? Put simply, it resulted from a marked improvement in the efficiency of the English economy. Discus-

sion of the Industrial Revolution in England tends to focus on technological breakthroughs and new production methods.[9] However, the
industrial revolution in England was preceded by a no less important
agricultural revolution, by the expansion of the national and international trade networks, by the diversification of the infrastructure, and
by the extension of political and legal institutions which consolidated
the rule of law and increased, though only gradually, the opportunities
for popular participation.[10] That the Industrial Revolution was much
more than just an *industrial* revolution, is demonstrated by later, not
very successful, attempts to engineer development breakthroughs 'artificially', solely by means of forced industrialization.[11]

A second reason for the widening gap between divergently develop-②
ing societies is to be found in the facilitation of, and increase in,
international communication and traffic. Even though the dramatic
change in this respect, the so-called 'transport revolution', occurred
during the second half of the nineteenth century, as a result of new
transport technology and drastically falling costs, England's early
capacity to penetrate foreign markets with mass-produced products,
machinery and expertise reflects the improvement in communication.[12]
For without an increase in international communications the development breakthrough of one or more societies would create relatively few
problems for the rest of the world. The combination of the two, a
localized development breakthrough and increasing interdependence,
was bound to produce a tendentially *world wide*, specific development
problem ('delayed development'). Its political relevance has been
growing constantly since the early nineteenth century. On the one
hand, because the gap between leaders and laggards in development
grew wider and relationships increased between different societies; and
on the other, because the development problem became truly world-
wide, leaving no society untouched. For some considerable time now
there has been no effective 'protection by distance'; nor do 'development reservations' exist any more. Even the very societies that de-
couple from the world economic order, in an attempt to follow their
own development path, bear witness to its power.[13]

What, then, is the nature of the international development problem
that results from development differentials? When societies at different
levels of development come into contact, the more highly developed
society and more productive economy unleash a process of *displacement
competition* within the less developed and less efficient society and
economy.[14] This competition is directed not only against the traditional
trades that are no longer competitive, but influences social institutions
and people's motivation. For if the challenge is overwhelming, the

cumulative superior competence of the more highly developed and
more productive economy has a discouraging effect on the less developed society.[15] If the superior society can produce more goods, if it can
produce them better and cheaper, if it floods the market with new
products and new production processes, if it dominates technological
progress and distinguishes itself by special organizational competence
(management), then it requires massive efforts on the part of the less
developed society not to be pushed towards the periphery of the world
economy. Modern history, especially since the early nineteenth century, has shown that, by means of displacement competition, superior
competence is easily translated into the peripheralization of the less
developed society, if the latter does not consciously counteract the
competence differential and resist the pressure towards peripheralization. In this context, peripheralization usually means not only a falling
away from the level of development already reached, but often entails a
functional downgrading of the less developed society into an outpost of
the more highly developed one; in extreme cases into a monocultural
exclave for food production and the extraction of raw materials. Such
peripheries of the world economy possess an unmistakable structural
make-up, leading in the more recent discussion of development theory
to the distinction between *metropolitan* and *peripheral* societies.[16]

If one looks at international society as a whole, it becomes all too
apparent that, beginning with the first Industrial Revolution in England,
the major part of the world suffered peripheralization in the above-
mentioned sense, with only a few societies managing to resist the
pressure towards peripheralization and achieving self-reliant delayed
development ('autocentric development').

For a long time there has been a tendency in the development debate
to take the development of the highly industrialized societies for
granted, and to regard underdevelopment as the problem—that is, as
the phenomenon that demands explanation. In view of the development history of the past 250 to 500 years, however, it would seem more
sensible to regard *peripheralization as the norm and successful development as
the exception*. This conclusion is supported, on the one hand, by the
quantitative distribution of the two groups of cases and, on the other, by
the considerable difficulties confronting even the present highly industrialized societies in the early stages of their own development *vis-à-vis*
more advanced societies. The history of individual developed societies suggests it is reasonable not to regard their successful development as
predetermined. The majority of the developed countries have been
through *critical development phases* during which a slide into the status of a
peripheral region was certainly possible but did not happen. On the

other hand, it is possible to identify phases of development in some peripheries (though not in all of them) during which a final slide into peripheralization could still have been prevented.[17] But in most cases all practical attempts in this direction failed, making further development towards peripheralization inevitable. From a comparative viewpoint it is, in any case, useful to consider the history of the development of European and non-European societies in a counterfactual perspective: what constellations would have been necessary and what factors would have had to be effective for development to occur and peripheralization to be avoided?[18] Without arguing idealistically, such a methodological approach skirts the facile assumption that there existed no alternatives to the development patterns actually observed. Despite this methodologically reasonable and pertinent circumspection, the empirical diagnosis is inescapable: *peripheralization remained the normal reaction to international competence differentials and autonomous development remained the exception.*

Nowadays it is rarely disputed that growing international competence differentials create special problems for those societies which are trailing in development, the so-called latecomers. In too many cases potential peripheralization has been translated into actual peripheralization. These facts are also confirmed by literature which does not use the terminology employed here. But has the problem of imminent peripheralization existed ever since the development breakthrough in England? Has pressure towards peripheralization always been a virulent problem for development policy? Was this pressure noticeable in the early development stages of the present OECD societies, or were these societies privileged to be able to develop in a relatively autonomous way, free from the external pressures that have been described? If the latter had been the case, the development problem that has been formulated retrospectively with regard to the early development history of societies which are now highly industrialized would have been wrongly posed—a non-problem, indeed.

Several observations tell against such a special historical position of today's highly developed societies—for example, the OECD countries.

(1) General treatises on the history of European development contain numerous scattered references to the actual displacement competition caused by English products in the rest of Europe.[19] What is more, industrialization in the main development regions of Europe often proceeded with the help of English machinery and occasionally even with the participation of English expertise, skilled labour and capital.[20] No single reference to the textile, mining and engineering industries can, however, describe the gap that separated England from all other

Table 1:   *Index of the industrial potential of selected European countries,*
           1860 (absolute figures)

England	=	100
France		22–27
Germany		13–16
Austria/Hungary		8–10
Belgium		7–9
Russia		7–9
Switzerland		4–6
Spain		3–5
Sweden		3–5
Italy		2–3
Netherlands		1–3
Norway		1–2
Denmark		0.5–1
Poland		0.5–1
Greece		< 0.5 }

Source: Paul Bairoch, *Commerce extérieur et développement économique de*
            l'Europe au XIXe siècle, Paris, 1976, p. 172

European societies even as late as the mid-nineteenth century—that is,
one hundred years after the onset of the Industrial Revolution.[21] Some
generalized figures, relating to the whole of the Continent, may convey
a clearer picture of the development gap existing at the time. They
document the pre-eminent position of England within the European
and world economies in the middle of the last century.

According to more recent calculations, England in 1860 accounted
for 45 per cent of world industrial production while comprising 2 per cent
of the population.[22] Taking only the 'modern' sectors of the first
industrial revolution into account, the comparable figure for cotton
manufacture and iron and steel production amounts to 50 per cent of
world output. One-third of the world's commercial fleet was English,
as was one-quarter of world exports and one-third of world imports.

Even if the data are related only to Europe, England's pre-eminent
position becomes apparent. With 10 per cent of Europe's population in
about 1860, England produced 55 to 60 per cent of European manufactures; 58 per cent of the iron production of Europe (including Russia)
originated in England. England accounted for 55 per cent of European
energy consumption, while 59 per cent of the cotton imported into
Europe found its way into English factories. England owned more than

Table 2: *Index of the industrial potential of selected European countries, 1860 (per capita figures)*

England	=	100
Switzerland		55–65
Belgium		45–55
France		17–22
Germany		10–15
Sweden		8–10
Austria/Hungary		5–9
Spain		5–8
Italy		2–4
Russia		0.5–1

Source: Bairoch, op. cit., p. 174

45 per cent of Europe's commercial shipping. She accounted for 30 per cent of European foreign trade and for 45 per cent of the trade in finished products. Table 1 above (which relates to the industrial potential of the modern sectors of textiles, iron, steel, coal, chemicals, but excludes craft-based industrial production) shows that in 1860 the English industrial potential surpassed the combined figure for the fourteen countries following. Calculated on a per capita basis (Table 2 above), England's leading position can be clearly demonstrated. In 1860 England led the 'industrial nations', followed by Switzerland and Belgium, both countries with a small population and a relatively large industrial potential, which were followed in their turn by France and Germany, both populous economies with a still relatively low *average* level of industrialization but with individual regions that were well on a par with English, Swiss or Belgian industrial development. As is shown in Table 3 below, England exported manufactures to the tune of $650 million in 1860, an unrivalled position in Europe. According to other data, between 1850 and 1890 England's share of world exports was 25 per cent, while France accounted for 10 per cent and Germany for 9 per cent. During the same period the United States accounted for only 8 per cent, although she was to catch up quickly later.[23]

The England of 1860 has been called an overwhelming economic power (*puissance économique superdominante*),[24] a judgement that is well founded according to the data presented above and despite the fact that average figures (e.g. for per capita industrial production) imply a levelling of heterogeneous economic areas. In reality, industrialization in all European countries was a highly regionalized process,[25] with the

Table 3:   *Exports of manufactures, selected European countries, 1860*
           (millions of 1960 US dollars)

England	650
France	250
Germany	120–150
Switzerland	60– 70
Austria/Hungary	40– 60
Belgium	30–35
Italy	25–30
Spain	15
Sweden	11
Russia	5

Source: Bairoch, op. cit., pp. 171–2.

main industrial regions on the Continent trailing not so far behind
England as the averages would suggest. Nevertheless, the observation
on regionally concentrated economic growth applies equally to England. The quoted averages therefore paint a reasonably correct picture
of the development differential that existed in Europe in the middle of
the last century.

Other data tend to reinforce this picture. In 1860 England displayed
a sectoral composition in her economy that was achieved by other
currently industrialized countries only decades later. As early as 1846
only 22 per cent of the economically active population were still
employed in agriculture—a proportion reached by Denmark, Sweden
and Norway in about 1950 and by Finland in 1970! In France 51 per
cent of the economically active population were still employed in
agriculture in 1860, in Sweden the figure was still 50 per cent in 1910,
while Finland reached this threshold as late as 1945.[26] England had,
therefore, not only a large industrial potential and a high per capita
industrial output, but an economy which had undergone unparalleled
qualitative and structural change by the middle of last century. The
size of her internal market, in conjunction with her pre-eminent
position in world trade, facilitated an increasing division of labour in the
production of consumer and investment goods. It opened the door to
mass production and economies of scale—the basis of successful displacement competition *vis-à-vis* traditional trades and proto-industries,
both in England herself and abroad.[27]

However appropriate it may be to emphasize the dominant position
occupied by England in the world economy in the middle of the last

century, and to focus on the competitiveness which emanated from that country, it should not be forgotten that during the second half of the nineteenth century a new front of international displacement competition was opened up by the flooding in of cheap grain from overseas. This was due to the opening up of agriculturally productive areas in the United States, Canada, Australia, New Zealand, Argentina and Uruguay and was a consequence of the transport revolution. As is well known, this challenge led to the great agricultural crisis of the 1870s and 1880s and provoked a widespread protectionist reaction.[28]

It should also be remembered that displacement competition originated not only from the leader of the world economic hierarchy, England, but was exerted to an increasing extent by successful or half-way successful laggards on to economies which were falling still further behind and becoming peripheries. Thus, at the turn of the century, Italy was under pressure from the superior competition of more highly developed societies while herself trying to export simpler manufactures (like textiles) to even more backward, still less developed areas like the Balkans and the Middle East. *Over long periods, pressure towards peripheralization became cumulative. The later an attempt at delayed development was made, therefore, the more difficult it became.*

That those European societies which are presently members of the OECD did not develop automatically into highly industrialized societies and that there existed a real challenge from the more advanced English society is corroborated by the fact that not all societies in Europe, not even all those in north-western Europe, the original area of the Industrial Revolution, followed the English development path. With regard to the present OECD societies this succession is taken for granted, but, as will be shown in detail in the following pages, it was by no means clear from the beginning that Denmark and the Netherlands, for instance, would establish a metropolitan development pattern and that Ireland, Hungary and Romania would end up with peripheralization. The same applies to the European settler colonies (Australia, New Zealand, South Africa, Argentina, Uruguay, Chile, the United States, Canada) which, in the long term, developed very differently, despite an identical position in the world economic system. This phenomenon will be analysed in detail later.[29]

(2) England's superior competence after industrialization was matched by the resolve of some of the threatened European societies to protect themselves against being flooded by cheap English goods. Continental Europe reacted to the English challenge in the same way as England had countered sporadic challenges from the Continent in the hundred years prior to her Industrial Revolution: by means of

protectionist measures, mainly protective tariffs and import bans.[30]

Just as England had not developed on a free-trade basis it was, as a rule, impossible for the societies in continental Europe to respond to the greatly increased English post-Industrial Revolution challenge in an open fashion, based on free trade. If proof is needed for the actual displacement competition that emanated from England and that was perceived as a deadly threat on the Continent and by the rest of the world, it lies in the varied (dissociative) protective measures that can be observed everywhere during the first six decades of the last century, even though the depth of response differed in individual cases.

If one studies the nineteenth century, one finds that the majority of European countries adhered to the principle of free trade only during the few years from 1860 to the second half of the 1870s. Prior to that, up to the middle of the century, England edged closer and closer to a free-trade position, which finally gained the upper hand with the repeal of the Corn Laws in 1846 and the Navigation Acts in 1849. In the period up to the First World War, England stuck to a free-trade posture even though the majority of European societies had switched to a protectionist policy in the late 1870s in reaction to the agricultural crisis. *England's own stance from the middle of the century, therefore, was by no means representative of the whole of Europe.* In this respect, as in many others, she occupies a special position. In the rest of Europe the periods of protectionism outweighed the few years of a generalized free-trade system after 1860.

The lively debates on the advantages and drawbacks of free trade and/or protectionism that took place in Switzerland, a country which, in the end, was to adopt a coherent free-trade stance, show, furthermore, that the superiority of England presented her rivals with a more than casual threat.[31] In the case of protectionist measures it is necessary to differentiate between those for 'infant industry' and those for the safeguarding of older industries. While the former were concerned with the welfare of newly emerging production units which, without protection and support, would have been helplessly exposed to superior English competition, the latter were geared to the safeguarding of traditional sectors which were no longer competitive. In reality, the elements were often indistinguishable, although selective industrial promotion tended to follow the 'infant industry protection' line. In contrast, agricultural protectionism from the late 1870s onwards was conceived as protection aimed at the preservation of ageing economic structures. Both were directed, though with different motives, against imminent displacement competition: in the one case with a progressive bent, aiming to become competitive through the creation of efficient production units; in the other, aiming to guarantee the survival of uncompetitive sectors by means of protection.[32]

A third observation suggests itself for discussion: the struggle in the history of ideas between the free-trade school and the proponents of development through protectionism. Looking at the literature on international trade and development that has appeared over the past two decades, the reader could be left with the impression that only variants of one single school, geared towards free trade and the international division of labour, have ever existed, and that opposing positions have never been convincingly presented or fought for in the political arena. The impression is created that the present OECD societies have always developed on the same free-trade lines as those pursued since the mid-1950s. Any recourse to protectionist measures—as happened in response to the world economic crisis of the late 1920s and early 1930s—is regarded as a political mistake inviting disaster. In this connection it is overlooked that, with the exception of Switzerland and the Netherlands, none of the present highly industrialized countries has developed in conditions of continuous free trade; not even England did so during her take-off phase up to the middle of the last century.[33]

Nor is it acknowledged that there have always been schools of thought which deviate from the free-trade position and are motivated by considerations of development policy. The fact that in England the free-trade school, with its cosmopolitan bent, emerged victorious, is intimately connected with England's pre-eminent position within the world economic system. The high level of productivity, a result of the Industrial and Agricultural Revolutions, made the prospect of competition between English goods and less efficiently produced foreign commodities look attractive. Consequently, an aggressive free-trade stance accorded with English interests.[34] However, for industrial latecomers, trying to establish infant industries, a protectionist posture seemed equally appropriate. Accordingly, the academic and political debate on delayed development despite English superiority took place initially in those countries in which the conditions for such development were still relatively favourable. Later on, this debate can be observed in countries which had fallen considerably behind and in which special efforts were required to stand up not only to England but to those societies which had by then successfully caught up with England and—as in the case of Germany and the United States—were well on their way to overtaking her.

It is significant that alternatives to the dogma of free trade, which were gaining ground outside England during the nineteenth century, were formulated by authors who were academics as well as practical politicians.[35] There were not many of these, and most of them no longer figure in the current textbooks on economics and development theory. Some are forgotten, a few are vaguely remembered. Who now recalls Alexander Hamilton's plea for the establishment of indigenous industry in early America, aimed at rejecting the division of labour imposed by England, between a North America producing agricultural goods and raw materials and a Great Britain producing manufactures? Did not Friedrich List's systematic contribution to the problem under discussion remain completely neglected until a short time ago?[36] And is it not the case that science and the debate on development policy have still not succeeded in fairly assessing the value of his contribution?[37] The Romanian Manoilesco is forgotten for many reasons, some political; but in the 1930s he nevertheless wrote the most important and systematic study on the possibilities of delayed development since List's principal work had appeared in 1841.[38]

That North Korean contributions to the same problem have remained practically unknown is certainly not due solely to the fact that only sparse information reaches us from this relatively isolated country. It is a result, too, of prejudice against a development path which is in many respects an interesting one.[39] It was in North Korea that—not unlike the debate in post-war Romania—List's classical development theorems were applied to the relations between *socialist* societies at different development levels. That that very problem has still not been solved is borne out by the continuing development differentials among the members of COMECON (Council for Mutual Economic Aid).[40]

What, then, do the alternatives to the free-trade school have in common? They are all opposed to a world economic system that forces economies at different development levels into a process of unfettered competition which necessarily leaves the less-developed economies by the wayside. They argue against an international division of labour between societies, some of which command a decisive development lead in practically all the relevant industrial sectors, while the others regress to mere food producers and suppliers of raw materials. Despite the stringency of the plea advanced by the free-trade school for a sensible division of labour between a cloth-producing England and a wine-producing Portugal, the real development of both countries since the eighteenth century has shown that the promised levelling of the development differential between them has not occurred because of the particular circumstances. This fact had already provoked biting comment from Friedrich List. Again, it is significant that even today the history of this stock example, designed to prove the validity of the free-trade prescriptions, has still not been critically investigated by

economists. Nevertheless, the diagnosis emphasizing the peripheralization effects of the English–Portuguese division of labour, which was
presented by List almost 150 years ago, has retained its validity to the
present day in the same way as similar critical judgements which
appeared in Portugal in the mid-eighteenth century.[41]

While Hamilton, List and Manoilesco categorically rejected the
prescription that little-developed societies should lay themselves open
to unfettered and unlimited free trade, they expressly advocated a
broad-based domestic development of the productive forces in agriculture and industry. They regarded a policy of de-coupling (dissociation)—which could be more or less forceful according to circumstances—as
the external precondition for viable domestic development efforts. It is
significant that the advocacy of a dissociative development policy grew
more radical as the international development differentials widened.
While initially one found only limited and sporadic pleas for the
protection of individual infant industries (e.g. in the case of Hamilton),
the recommendations became more sweeping only a few decades later,
until finally, in the case of societies such as those in south-eastern
Europe which lagged behind in industrial *as well as* in agricultural
development, broad-based and comprehensive dissociation in the face
of multiple pressure towards peripheralization (in both agriculture *and*
industry) was considered indispensable.[42]

The preceding reflections on England's 'super-dominant' position in
the nineteenth century world economy, on the strategic function of
widespread protectionist measures in the development process, and on
schools of thought engaged in resistance against the pressure towards
peripheralization, indicate that the syndrome of international competence differentials, displacement competition, imminent peripheralization and the fight against it was already endemic in the development
process in nineteenth- and early twentieth-century Europe. It would
therefore appear unreasonable to assume that those societies which
were later to industrialize successfully occupied a special position
vis-à-vis the above-mentioned development problem.

If this is the case, the very questions which are, in view of the
growing disparities within international society, part of the present
development debate, must be relevant to an analysis of the early phases
in European development from the end of the eighteenth to the first
part of the twentieth century. Empirical studies underpinning the
recent theory of peripheral capitalism have, for example, diagnosed a
multitude of peripheralization processes which have resulted in deformed reproduction structures. Against the background of these studies, one has to ask why some societies, having suffered the same

pressure towards peripheralization, have nevertheless achieved self-reliant development. Many societies assumed a free-trade posture during decisive stages in their development process and ended up as peripheries. Why did they not reap the positive development rewards postulated by orthodox theory while a handful of other societies enjoyed them?

These questions, only touched on here, have been covered systematically and in greater detail elsewhere.[43] To pose them means looking at the early phases of the European development experience from the viewpoint of the present debate. As will become clear in the following paragraph, it has to be taken into account that, in some cases, such early phases are not located in the nineteenth century, much less in the first half of it, but in the first half of the twentieth century as well. With the exception of Switzerland and Belgium this applies, for example, to all the smaller export-orientated societies in Europe, notably to Finnish development history, which will be discussed in Part II.

Responses to Pressure towards Peripheralization

There were several types of response to the English challenge, depending in each case on a multitude of factors. Four factors appear to have been of special importance:

(1) The type of reaction depended crucially on the development level attained by the challenged society at the time of imminent displacement competition. A plausible thesis would be that the challenge was the more likely to be taken up and met constructively the higher the development level and the more the autonomous development dynamics was geared towards a modernization of the society in question. As will be shown later, the development attained depended on the extent to which traditional feudal structures had disintegrated and on the advance of broad-based agricultural modernization, broad-based industrialization and general commercialization.

(2) A second factor shaping the kind of response—without, however, determining it—was the size of the challenged society. Within Europe England counted among the populous territorial states. It had, however, a greater domestic market potential than other continental societies of comparable size (France, Germany, Austria–Hungary), since the modernization process was much further advanced in England than in those countries, not to mention Russia, the population giant of Europe.

Populous territorial states are protected by their very size, for the larger the population the smaller the relative GDP share of foreign trade.[44] The absolute amount of foreign transactions can still reach considerable proportions compared with the export figures for smaller societies, which tend to be large in *relative* but small in *absolute* terms. Such a natural protection factor operates irrespective of whether protectionist policies are or are not pursued. It would, however, be wrong to conclude that such a size and the concomitant protection make successful development highly probable. In nineteenth-century Europe, Russia provides the best example of the absence of a direct link between a populous and vast territorial state and a high level of development. This also applies to medium-sized societies like those of Italy and Spain.

On the other hand, it is clear that small countries, unless they remain isolated and backward, are from the very beginning especially exposed to the competence differential between more and less highly developed societies. In their case, the analysis of the resulting pressure towards peripheralization is particularly interesting, and more generally instructive. After all, in order to develop, they are compelled by their sheer size to turn towards the world market while at the same time having to fight against imminent peripheralization. This makes them the focus for the comparative study of response patterns to pressure towards peripheralization.[45]

(3) A further factor determining the reaction to imminent peripheralization was the point in time at which delayed development was attempted. The later this attempt occurred, the wider was the gap that separated not only the original forerunner, but those which had managed to catch up with England, from the remaining laggards. This is not to say that an early response was necessarily more promising despite still limited competence differentials. Historical experience does not support such a clear link, demonstrating once more that, despite the aggravating circumstances hampering a late attempt at delayed development, other factors were more decisive in shaping the course of development.

(4) Basically, associative and dissociative development strategies are available in response to imminent peripheralization.[46] An *associative* response means openly accepting the challenge and adapting to the superior economy through division of labour. This amounts to the free-trade position. A *dissociative* strategy accepts the challenge by attempting to develop the domestic economic potential in the shelter of more or less far-reaching protectionist measures, international competitiveness *not* being the guiding criterion for development promotion.

The preceding reflections suggest that, in the case of an associative response, the danger of peripheralization was bound to be especially acute, above all in the case of small export-orientated economies. Conversely, it can fairly be assumed that large populous territorial states with a relatively high development level could afford to take an associative posture, their development emphasis resting in any case on the dynamics of the domestic economy. Furthermore, dissociative cases ought to occur generally at a late historical stage and in populous societies. In small societies a dissociative development strategy ought to be more the exception than the rule.

Which forms of response to the English challenge (and to the challenge of its successful imitators) can be observed empirically in the European and extra-European history of development?

Disregarding for a moment the most widespread reaction, actual peripheralization, and concentrating on the cases of attempted and reasonably successful delayed development, one can observe, in historical order, the following patterns of response—namely, different types of autocentric development.[47]

Type I: Dissociative development based on the dynamics of the domestic market

Among the early developers whose industrial revolutions occurred only a few decades after the English one, was Belgium, pursuing, in her early development phase (from 1830 onwards), as the only country with a small population (in 1860, 4.6 million inhabitants), a development path directed towards the opening up of her domestic potential.[48] Naturally, Belgium was soon forced to conquer foreign markets: in 1890 Belgian per capita exports topped the European league. But the first decades were used for developing the domestic economic potential, above all the development of an infrastructure, notably the extension of the most comprehensive railway network in Europe. Such a development course was by no means inevitable, for Belgium, whose political basis remained unstable until 1830, could easily have become an exclave for the export of raw materials to the surrounding territorial states (England, France, Germany). The necessary resources were abundant; they could have been used quite differently. For the very reason that small countries with abundant mineral and energy resources tended to turn into exclave economies and peripheries, Belgium's early self-reliant development, which, after the middle of the century, turned into a dynamic export offensive, is all the more remarkable.

What sets the Belgian development path apart from late cases of Type I development is also the early preponderance of basic goods, capital goods and engineering sectors in manufacturing industry. In the other societies of this type—without exception populous territorial states—consumer goods industries were initially of far greater importance than heavy capital goods and equipment industries.[49] Within Europe dissociative development based on the dynamics of the domestic economy occurred in France, Germany and Austria-Hungary. With certain qualifications, this also applies to the United States—in reality three different, easily identifiable economic regions with differing internal structures—during the second half of the nineteenth century.[50]

The above-mentioned societies in continental Europe—France, Germany and Austria–Hungary—shared a marked bias towards the development of the domestic economy. In view of the size of these countries and the politically determined external economic conditions, their development can be characterized as more or less dissociative; more markedly dissociative in the case of France and Austria-Hungary. In both countries protectionist measures directed against higher developed neighbours played a more decisive role than they did in Germany, where the benefits and the impact of the Tariff Union (1834) still remain a topic for debate.[51] In all three development patterns the emphasis was on *private economic activity*—that is, on investment by private entrepreneurs and on consumption of equipment and goods for mass consumption by private households. Even though there was public investment and public demand as well as agricultural and industrial promotion by the state, they played—compared with later instances of autocentric development (Types IV and V below)—only a supportive role in development processes already under way. Foreign trade, while of course taking place, did not shape economic growth to the same degree as, for example, in the development cases of Types II and III. In the case of France and Austria-Hungary the relevant studies generally emphasize the slow and gentle pace of development—in other words, the lack of phases in which a dramatic breakthrough occurred. In Germany, by contrast, the construction of the railways in the middle of the nineteenth century gave the development process a lasting dynamic impetus.[52]

This type of autocentric development path has frequently been termed the 'textile path',[53] a characterization appropriate in the sense that it highlights the role of light industry with its linkage effects. This term would, however, become problematic were it to obscure the fact that—as in the English case—as early as the first development phase various industries emerged without which the first industrial revolution would have been unthinkable, notably in vast countries rich in resources: coal and ore mining, ore smelting, iron processing and, finally, engineering.[54] The term 'textile path' is nevertheless useful in view of the gradual shift of emphasis from the textile to the capital goods industry that occurred in the course of the development process.[55]

The pertinence of the label 'dissociative development based on the dynamics of the domestic market' is finally demonstrated by the course of American development in the second half of the nineteenth century. Not only did the population treble after the Civil War (increasing from 31 million to 93 million in 1910), but industrialization advanced behind much higher protective barriers than existed in other countries of this development type, either at the same time or before.[56]

Type II: Associative export-led development

In this instance we are dealing with the classical case of a Ricardian development path. National economies are supposed to develop by integrating into an international division of labour according to the principle of comparative advantages. Export activities are promoted, often without the domestic market having been developed. Crucial, however, is the fact that the whole economy, export industries as well as sectors geared towards the domestic market, was fully exposed to competition in the world market. As a rule protectionist measures should therefore not be of any importance: at the most one could conceive of selective tariffs for the short-term protection of infant industries, in order to reduce temporarily the level of the external challenge and with it the difficulty in countering foreign competition. In the exemplary ideal-type case, however, this type of development path would be built on unfettered free trade.

In the present official debate on development policy such a posture represents the dominant opinion. In development history very little convincing supportive evidence is to be found: to be precise, just the two cases of Switzerland since the late eighteenth century and the Netherlands since the late nineteenth century. Together with England and Belgium, Switzerland[57] belonged to the first generation of industrial nations and, throughout the nineteenth century, the country retained an eminent position within Europe in terms of its per capita industrial potential (cf. p. 19). The Swiss case is also remarkable for the fact that the country was exceptionally disadvantaged with regard to its natural resource endowment: the raw materials of the first industrial revolution had to be imported; as early as the eighteenth century there existed a trade deficit in agricultural commodities; Switzerland was land-locked; the connections with European waterways and railway networks were not established until well into the nineteenth century.

What is more, until the mid-nineteenth century Switzerland remained politically fragmented. In some respects, the country embodied almost the opposite of what classical theory on European development had postulated as the precondition for private-capitalist development, namely the formation of an administratively and infrastructurally unified territorial state as a basis for economic growth and an evolving market economy.

In spite of these unfavourable starting conditions, the Swiss development path (import of grain and raw materials, use of domestic cheap labour for the processing of high-quality manufactures, export of these products to foreign markets in the face of strong and growing competition) proved successful. A detailed analysis—presented elsewhere[58]—reveals, however, that after the lifting of the Napoleonic continental blockade, pressure towards peripheralization was especially acute in Switzerland, with the result that the free-trade stance remained by no means unchallenged.

The second development path of this kind, the Dutch one, shared common ground with the Swiss: neither country had any sizeable energy and raw material resources available during the first phase of the Industrial Revolution.[59] In contrast with Switzerland, the Netherlands possessed, however, a considerable agricultural potential. Her export commodity basket consisted of highly processed agricultural goods and special products (like bulbs). But apart from that, the Netherlands, too, was forced to import raw materials, processing them locally in order to sell manufactured foods profitably in foreign, competitive markets.[60]

Both societies had small populations. In 1860, Switzerland had 2.5 million inhabitants, the Netherlands 3.3 million. That the outlined development path was not inevitable, however, is evidenced by other small European societies like those of Ireland, Portugal, Greece and the Balkan states, which experienced quite a different development course, namely peripheralization.

Swiss and Dutch development correspond with the Type I pattern in so far as, to an even greater degree than in Type I cases, economic development started from *private* initiative and was geared towards *private* demand. In both countries the sequence of light industry and engineering was even more pronounced than in the Type I cases mentioned, if only because other intermediate steps—like the establishment of *broad-based* basic goods and capital goods industries—were excluded through lack of natural resources. In order to be competitive in certain niches of the world market, the engineering industry, like the consumer goods industries, had to concentrate on a limited number of highly specialized product ranges. This required a highly trained and qualified population.

Type III: *Associative-dissociative development*

Development of the associative-dissociative kind began with an upswing in export growth (a predominantly associative phase), the agricultural, silvicultural and mineral resources of the societies in question being devoted mainly to exports. In a later phase a dissociative development policy was pursued, corresponding with the well-known pattern of industrialization through import substitution: the substitution by local products of, at first, formerly imported consumer goods, and later, of basic, capital and engineering goods. In the long term, development of this kind led to a comprehensively associative free-trade posture, which, however, was not adopted until decades after the start of modern development, for the most part not until decades after the Second World War.

Amongst the positive cases were Denmark, Sweden, Norway and Finland as well as Canada, Australia, and New Zealand. Like the Type II cases, these are all countries with relatively small populations, however different their resource endowments. As with Types I and II, private economic activity had precedence, though the extent of state intervention in setting the external economic conditions for the domestic industrialization process (dissociative phase) was considerable.

Like the cases of Type II, those of Type III are especially relevant because their development proved successful despite the fact that it started with the export of *unprocessed* foodstuffs and raw materials. They will, therefore, receive special attention in two chapters of Part II.

Societies of this type seized export opportunities according to the doctrine of comparative advantages (and, in this respect, they do not differ from the representatives of Type II). If one examines individual cases in relation to the content of their export orientation, the following subtypes can be distinguished,[61] some overlap in characterization being inevitable:

Type IIIa: Cases with an emphasis on so-called staple goods (timber, ores, grain); an emphasis often retained for decades so far as the content of the commodity basket is concerned. Export growth starts with the export of staple goods and displays this commodity profile for a relatively long period. This subtype would include Australia, New Zealand and Canada as well as, initially, Norway and Finland, the first two cases retaining a high export share of unprocessed, or only partly processed, raw materials even today, while the last-mentioned cases have managed to shift markedly their export profile in the direction of processed products.

Type IIIb: Cases where, initially, agricultural staple goods (e.g. grain) are exported. Later, however, a transition to agricultural processing takes place, resulting in an increasing export of *processed agricultural* commodities. The classic case was Denmark, comparable to the Netherlands and New Zealand so far as the export of processed agricultural commodities is concerned.

Type IIIc: In addition to the characteristics mentioned in Types IIIa and b, this subtype is characterized by the export of *finished manufactures* (in this respect comparable to the Swiss example), based on locally available raw materials which are initially exported unprocessed and then, to an increasing degree, as semi-processed and finished goods. In this context attention should be drawn to the role of ore mining, iron ore exports and the connected engineering industry in Sweden.

Type IIId: In the case of this subtype, an integration into the world market is achieved—in addition to the strategies listed under Types IIIa, b, and c—by means of *international services* (transit traffic, passenger and freight shipping, etc.) Such elements are manifest in some Type II cases (the Netherlands and Switzerland), but above all in Norway which, in 1880, had the third largest merchant fleet after Britain and the United States (between 1865 and 1914 her income from shipping amounted to about 40 per cent of total export revenue and more than 10 per cent of the national income).

Type IV: Dissociative state-capitalist development

Like the cases of Type I, Type IV cases are characterized by the primacy of the dynamics of the domestic economy. But in contrast with Type I cases, the dynamic impulse did not derive from autonomous private economic activity and growing private demand for consumer goods and equipment, but to a remarkable degree from public industrial promotion, mainly through investment in heavy industry and engineering, through state demand for armaments and through the establishment of an infrastructure. The state did not limit itself to supportive economic measures, but made a massive contribution by way of investment and demand. As the emphasis lay on heavy industry, this development path has appropriately been termed the *steel path*.[62] Foreign trade did, of course, take place. In contrast with the external trade of Type I countries, it did not, however, reflect the development level of local manufacturing industry; its sources were either agricultural products, raw material deposits or products of traditional craft industries, but not modern manufactures. Japan after the Meiji restoration certainly represents the most noteworthy case. In Tsarist Russia, development took a similar course, though unsuccessfully, as the fundamental preconditions, like the modernization of agriculture that took place in Japan, were lacking.[63] To a certain extent this type includes Italy after 1890, though in that country production for expanding private consumption was indeed relevant to the development process.[64]

The fact that societies like that of Japan had a large population, and that their development process began relatively late, allowed the *dissociative* bias of development policy to continue for a long time, in contrast with the Type I countries. In the case of Tsarist Russia it evolved into the socialist development policy of the Soviet Union after 1917/18; and in that of Japan, it was abandoned only in the course of the general liberalization of the highly industrialized countries after the end of the reconstruction period following the Second World War.[65]

All cases of the four types of development path were confronted, to varying degrees, with substantial pressure towards peripheralization in the face of growing international development differentials following the Industrial Revolution. The *limited dissociative* development strategy based on the dynamics of the domestic market (Type I) aimed in the long term, emphasized as always by the theory of *temporary dissociation*, at a free-trade posture. In this case, *dissociative* policies were therefore intended to contribute to the establishment of industries which, as early as possible, would be able to export competitive manufactures and machinery to unprotected foreign markets not yet taken over by monopolies. Consequently, exports were bound soon to reflect the mature profile of the domestic economy. This, by the way, also applies to Belgium, which, early on, had specialized in the production of a mixture of semi-finished goods and machinery.

In the case of the continuously export-orientated development path of Type II, success was assured only if, from the very outset, competitive high-quality products could penetrate foreign markets. By contrast, the development path of Type III cases was more gradual. It started out from the export of unprocessed goods. Then, locally available resources were processed and, step by step, a general diversification of the industrial structure was promoted by means of dissociative protectionist measures, notably in sectors unable to develop without protection.

Forced dissociative state-capitalist development (Type IV) emphasized to a lesser degree the establishment of internationally competitive industries. These were not necessary, as the potential domestic markets were very large. The export of products from traditional economic sectors served the auxiliary purpose of earning foreign exchange for purchasing equipment in order to establish domestic industrial complexes. There was no reason, therefore, to export goods that would have reflected the increasing maturity of the domestic market. In view of the low development level existing at the start of Type IV development, a dissociative development policy was bound to acquire much greater momentum and become an end in itself. In contrast with Type I and especially Type II cases it could, to a far lesser degree, be conceived as a selective instrument for achieving a limited end.

Type V: Dissociative state-socialist development

The above-mentioned Types I–IV involve variations of capitalist development. In Types I, II and III cases private economic activities were dominant, while public measures of industrial promotion were of secondary importance. The Type IV development path can be termed state-capitalist, because the state not only intervened to protect and promote private economic activity but itself became the development agent.

The latter function became even more pronounced in the case of Type V development paths. This type includes developing societies which—having originally been relegated to the status of peripheries in the traditional world economic system, or having remained relatively isolated and undeveloped (as, for instance, Albania)—for a variety of reasons had de-coupled from the reproduction mechanisms of the capitalist world economic system during the course of this century. Among the causes of this de-coupling are the ruin of the respective societies in the wake of both world wars and civil wars, as well as revolutionary upheavals, military occupation, and—often—a mixture of all these factors.

The Soviet Union and Mongolia represent the earliest cases of this development path. After the Second World War they were joined by China, North Korea, Albania and Cuba as well as the eastern and south-eastern European region—for the most part, former peripheries like Poland, Hungary, Bulgaria, Romania and Yugoslavia.[66]

In the case of these developing societies dissociation is not seen as a short-lived instrument for the promotion of domestic development. On the contrary, it is a relatively persistent concomitant of the development process when confronted with general under-development. This does not mean, however, that in practice there were no economic relations with the surrounding socialist and capitalist world. But these links were, and still are, particularly between the socialist countries themselves, highly selective. They are regarded as a limited tool for promoting further domestic development. Especially in contrast with the historical experience of Type I–III cases, the domestic development dynamics is not integrated into the world market, at least not during the first few decades. In other words, it takes place without regard to market-orientated investment assessments and to the profitability rationale underlying such assessments.

Type VI: Delayed development in the case of newly industrializing countries

Is delayed development of peripheries possible within the existing world economic system without de-coupling from the world market? The current discussion on development theory and policy is split on this issue. On one side a repetition of delayed development under capitalist auspices is considered improbable; on the other, there are theoretical positions regarding such development as a real possibility. In addition, some 'semi-industrialized' countries (like Taiwan) already call themselves 'developed countries with relatively low per capita income'.

Type VI is included here because it raises the question of the newly industrializing countries, even though a final judgement concerning the above-mentioned controversial debate on these countries is not yet possible. But even if only few peripheries succeeded in shedding the typical characteristics of peripheral societies and economies, these cases would represent a great challenge to the debate on development theory.[67] Those development theories arguing that such delayed development is probable would then have to explain why the experience of a few peripheries cannot become generalized.[68] And those theories, according to which comprehensive delayed development is improbable but for a break with the capitalist world market, would have to be revised. In these circumstances, those newly industrializing countries would represent a particular challenge, where delayed development by means of export-orientated integration into the capitalist world market could be observed (Taiwan, South Korea, etc.). For, in line with the above-mentioned considerations, they would be exposed to much greater pressure towards peripheralization than would quite populous and large countries (Spain, Brazil, Mexico, etc.), even though in the latter cases, too, such pressure has long been internalized by being introduced into those societies through the establishment of foreign production units *within* their domestic markets ('internationalization of the domestic market'), normally in reaction to protectionist measures taken by individual countries for the purpose of safeguarding a planned strategy of import substitution. In such circumstances pressure towards peripheralization operates in two ways: from the outside and from the inside.[69]

The Types of Delayed Development in Historical Perspective

Taking for granted Britain's role as the earliest 'forerunner' of development, a clear sequence in the types of response becomes apparent in the case of the 'latecomers'.

Type I included Belgium which, together with Britain (and Switzerland), became one of the forerunners of industrial development in continental Europe. The other representatives of Type I were all large territorial states whose development process evolved gradually over the whole century.

Switzerland, as the typical representative of Type II, belonged to the early developers. Her position was characterized by early specialization within the international division of labour.

In their first prolonged upswing phase the development of the cases representative of Type III can be understood only in relation to the preceding dynamic development of Britain. Over many decades the exports of those countries were directed to Britain (at a later stage also to the large dynamic territorial states in Europe and to the United States). In this sense, the Type III countries were initially outposts of the flourishing British economy, which had a growing demand for agricultural and mineral raw materials. Import substitution industrialization started as a reflex of successful export orientation and advanced after the latter had moved into a deep crisis caused by world economic factors (as towards the end of the 1920s).

From a comparative historical perspective it can be observed that at the same time as the representatives of Type III embarked upon their export-led upswing, the forced growth dynamics of the representatives of Type IV began, notably in the case of Japan and Russia.[70] A strong state turned into the decisive agency of modernization, as it were, as a substitute for such non-existent, development-promoting local conditions and social forces as were present to a relatively large extent in the populous territorial states of Type I. The development of Type IV cases was, to a high degree, politically motivated. Japan wanted to modernize in order to escape the fate of a China increasingly penetrated by imperialism.[71] In Tsarist Russia varying efforts towards an accelerated and forced modernization of the country were connected with the traumatic experience of the Crimean War.

While such political factors did not play a comparably eminent role in the cases of Type I, II and III, they were much more important in those countries where comprehensive dissociation occurred. These cases of state-socialist development (Type V) historically succeeded the cases of state-capitalist development (Type IV). They are all located in the twentieth century, predominantly after the end of the Second World War.

Chronologically, this development path will possibly be succeeded by the delayed development of a few or more newly industrialized countries (Type VI). If they take place at all, these development processes will do so in the second half of the twentieth century and state bureaucracies will play a major part in them.[72]

If one considers the historical succession of these varying typical reactions to increasing international development differentials and mounting pressure towards peripheralization from the early nineteenth century up to the present, one reaches the inevitable conclusion that delayed development became increasingly difficult, and to a growing extent a political matter, the further one proceeds from the period of the first industrial revolution to the present day. And does not the current debate on a 'New International Economic Order' also testify to the increasing *politicization of the development question*? One hundred and fifty years ago it still seemed possible to develop more or less independently alongside Britain (Belgium), or to engage in direct competition with Britain (Switzerland). A hundred years ago some countries still found it possible to develop by initially adopting the role of a kind of exclave for the advanced British economy (Type III) in order to differentiate and deepen their own internal structures by means of gradual import substitution industrialization at a later stage. These were, typically, countries with a relatively small population, while at the same time large territorial states with less favourable internal preconditions for delayed development already followed a different option: state-capitalist development directed from above. In the past sixty years not a single country has succeeded with delayed national-capitalistic development. Those managing to overcome the stark characteristics of peripheral economies pursued a more fundamental dissociative development policy that went beyond the state-capitalist case (Type V). How many so-called newly industrializing countries will successfully change from peripheries into developed countries in the coming decades is a controversial question that cannot yet be decided empirically.

The long-term development trend over the past 200 years is unmis-takable: *the salience of dissociative conditions for delayed development has become more pronounced*. While initially the probability of autonomous delayed development—parallel to the British process and/or induced by it—was relatively strong, development became, the closer one gets to the present, the object of purposive promotion initiated and coordinated by the state.[73] In this process the social agents of delayed development changed. Initially these were private enterprises that opposed tradi-tional state intervention inspired by mercantilism while at the same time demanding selective, supportive protectionist measures for them-selves. At the later stage (from Type IV onward) the state apparatus itself became the agent of delayed development; in Type V cases initially in combination with the urban proletariat (Soviet Union) and later, after the Second World War, in combination with the peasantry and rural population (China and others).

On account of the trends over these last 200 years there can be no doubt about the close link between the outlined economic development problem and the political conditions in which development took place in each case. The development processes in Britain and in countries of Type I, II and III, which were based on private activity, were associated with the typical institutions of the liberal state. It would, therefore, be reasonable to assume a close elective affinity between industrialization based on consumer goods and the characteristics of the liberal state. On the other hand, in the later development cases there was a close link between industrialization forced by an autocratic state apparatus and heavy industrialization characterized by high capital expenditure.[74] Characteristically, intermediate positions can already be found in Type I countries, notably in the case of Prussia-Germany. But the real chasm is the one that separates Britain and the cases of Type I, II and III, on the one hand, from the cases of Type IV and V, on the other. In the case of the newly industrializing countries, the autocratic bias of political institutions is no less marked than in the historical cases of Type IV and the contemporary cases of Type V. Up to now Type VI cases have confirmed rather than refuted the long-term development trend towards autocratic structures.[75]

Free Trade as a Special Case

The long-term development trend outlined above reflects the growing difficulty in developing autocentrically within a world economic system characterized by increasing development differentials. Despite this trend having already been diagnosed by historically orientated development research, though not yet in its comprehensive typology, the insight gained has until now had no impact on the received doctrine of official development policy in the industrial countries. Free trade is regarded as the most promising principle for successful delayed development. This doctrine is, however, contradicted by historical experience in several respects.[76] Britain, the nursery of free-trade thinking and policy, for example, adopted a free-trade stance only after having successfully modernized her agriculture and attained a leading position in industry. Among all the societies which achieved delayed development, those of Switzerland and the Netherlands were alone in following such a free-trade path more or less consistently, thus marking the exception and not the rule. In the case of the large territorial states of Europe, the free-trade orientated development phase was relatively brief (1860–75/80). And in the case of the small export-orientated societies of Type III, a non-free-trade posture played a major part in the broadening and deepening of the industrialization process. In the development cases that occurred at a still late stage (beginning with Type IV), a free-trade orientated foreign economic policy was completely out of the question. In the case of the newly industrializing countries, only the coming decades will show whether such a policy can once more successfully sustain delayed development.

Moreover, it is significant that at any given time the leading economies in the capitalistic world market, once Britain and now the OECD club, should adopt a free-trade stance, because such a posture matched their 'natural' interests. For in international competition leading economies stand the best chance of penetrating foreign markets successfully.[77] Lagging economies are not successful in doing so, and former leading economies which have fallen back into a second- or third-ranking position are progressively less successful at it. The development of Britain is a case in point. As long as Britain did not yet occupy a leading position but stood a good chance of winning one, she embraced a protectionist attitude. After she had attained a leading position, she turned to free trade and, in the face of the declining competitiveness of many sectors, she tends, like other highly industrialized societies, to resort once again to protectionism, at least in certain areas. Like List one hundred years earlier, Kitamura came exactly to the point when, in 1941, in a study on the theory of international trade, he wrote the following:

The principle of free trade was . . . proclaimed by the country with superior production technology in order to sustain or to increase its lead. The main reason for this was that free trade is no leveller but on the contrary exacerbates the differences in wealth. Free-trade theory, understood as a political demand, thus attempted to maintain and reinforce the existing inequality. Its aim was the English supremacy. When List criticized the school [of free-trade theory, D.S.] on the grounds that it did not recognize different development levels, it was less a theoretical than a political argument in the fight against this supremacy. . . . Free trade operates, in this respect, on the same level as the protective tariff; both are only different weapons in the pursuit of one and the same aim: the strengthening of one's own fighting position in competition.[78]

In order to attain such a fighting position, the chance of being able autonomously to determine the external economic conditions of domestic market development processes was of the utmost importance. This becomes especially apparent in the case of smaller export-orientated societies exposed to the world market where, apart from differences in their internal structures, great discrepancies in the degree of political sovereignty existed. Where sovereignty had been achieved, it was possible purposively to counter pressure towards peripheralization (as, for instance, in Scandinavia and the handful of settler colonies which developed into highly industrialized countries). Where such sovereign control was lacking (as, for instance in Greece, the Balkan states and other societies which could be forced into unequal treaties), development-retarding domestic conditions combined with the inability to hold out successfully against external pressure towards peripheralization. The importance of such sovereign control can be gauged above all from those cases where initially few favourable conditions for autonomous development were present. This applies to Norway around the turn of the century, where the task was to maintain or regain national control over natural resources, notably the cataracts which were essential for generating hydroelectricity. Luxembourg, too, which had 260,000 inhabitants in 1910, should be mentioned here.[79] This country (as well as Belgium) could easily have developed into a raw material (iron ore) exporting exclave of its rapidly industrializing neighbours, if the local processing of locally produced raw materials had not been encouraged as a result of sovereign political decisions. The danger of imminent peripheralization as a result of exclave-like dependency was averted by decisive political counter-action. Comparable processes can be also observed, despite a pronounced export orientation, in the successfully developing settler colonies like Australia, New Zealand and Canada. In many respects these politically motivated measures for promoting development did, at the time, spring from the same considerations that nowadays inform the demands for a 'New International Economic Order'. These centred and still centre on the right to national control over domestic resources and the demand for the mainly local processing of local raw materials in order to secure for the national economy a larger share in the value added.[80]

Apart from the theoretical debate on free-trade versus protectionism it should be stated, in purely empirical terms, that free trade and protectionism produced widely varying results according to the different internal structures from which they sprang and upon which they acted. In Britain, from the second half of the 1840s onwards, the free-trade stance thus translated itself into high rates of economic growth which could still be sustained during the phase of general free trade in Europe between 1860 and the second half of the 1870s.[81] In contrast, it can be shown that the continental European countries enjoyed higher economic growth during the protectionist phases before 1860 and after 1875/80 than during the free-trade period. The same holds true, incidentally, for Britain after her trading partners had turned protectionist and she adhered almost unilaterally to free trade.

How is this experience, that runs counter to the common view on the repercussions of free trade and protectionism, to be explained? The reason for the different repercussions lies in the differing internal structures of Britain and the remaining European societies, including those whose development had advanced furthest at the middle of the last century. In 1846 only 22 per cent of the economically active population were still working in agriculture (as mentioned above, p. 40), while 37 per cent were employed in industry. In view of the internal structural change that had already been accomplished, free trade for Britain at the middle of the last century meant the continued and accelerated shedding of labour by agriculture and its transfer to industry, where average productivity was higher. For the countries in continental Europe with their large agricultural sectors, free trade after 1860 entailed first of all the displacement competition between British goods and their own manufactures. The situation was, however, aggravated by the displacement competition between cheap foreign grain and locally produced grain. This competition reduced the purchasing power of the peasantry, with negative consequences for local industrial production. In Britain, by contrast, the cheapening of foodstuffs owing to the import of inexpensive grain and processed foods (cheese, butter, etc.) made possible a rising standard of living of the urban-industrial population and with it a widening of the domestic market for manufactures. During the nineteenth century, in the free-trade period, the levelling of the development differentials as predicted by free-trade doctrine did not therefore take place.[82] Demonstrably, a levelling occurred rather during the protectionist phases when higher economic growth rates of the continental economies produced a noticeable shift of the working population towards industry. European development history shows furthermore that, in times of accelerated growth, which were also times of protectionism, the foundations for a *future* intensification of intra- and extra-European trade were laid, so that, retrospectively, domestic growth served as the engine for trade rather than trade as the engine for growth. This relationship can, incidentally, be palpably demonstrated by the example of export economies, for these have conquered different shares of world trade according to the degree of their domestic economic diversification—as will be shown in detail in Part II.

A free-trade response to the British challenge was thus not typical of other European countries, nor have the development effects predicted by free-trade doctrine occurred outside England during the free-trade phase. As explained, the exact opposite of the doctrine's contentions can be observed.

What lesson is to be drawn from this experience offered by development history? *Free-trade doctrine obviously refers to a special case.* The results predicted by it can materialize only if countries entering into trade relations with one another are at a comparable development level and have already modernized their internal structures as far as possible— that is, if the process of agricultural modernization and industrialization has advanced to the point at which more people are engaged in industrial and quasi-industrial activities than in agricultural fields, and at which agriculture has itself become part of industry. This, however, applies only at the later development stages. Seen from the experience of the nineteenth century it is, therefore, not surprising that generalized free trade should not happen until years after the Second World War, since only then did the highly industrialized societies acquire an internal profile that made free trade as an external economic posture, with beneficial internal repercussions, look promising.

It is characteristic that, so far as the development policy proclamations of these countries towards the less developed ones are concerned, their own historical experience has been repressed and, as always in recent development history, free trade has once more become the ideology of the leading economies—nowadays because it best suits their economic interests, at least during phases of economic growth, in the same way as it was to the special advantage of Britain *vis-à-vis* the Continent of Europe in the few decades of generalized free trade.

Periphery Development as the Most Common Reaction to Pressure towards Peripheralization

In a global perspective, pressure towards peripheralization emanating from the dominant economies has translated itself into actual periphery development. The latter resulted, on the one hand, from the voluntary integration of less developed societies (like Latin America since the beginning of the nineteenth century) into a world economic system based on division of labour.[83] However, in the majority of cases political pressure, economic constraints, use of military force, or a mixture of these factors, played a significant role in reshaping European and extra-European societies into exclave economies. Since such an external bias was profitable for peripheries, particularly during the period of industrial upswing in the advanced industrialized countries after 1880, it generally prevailed over competing forces. Its basis was mostly a local power alliance, backed by foreign countries, between a landed oligarchy and commercial capital.[84] Where alternative paths were tried, their embryonic social agents, notably the still rudimentary sectors of the national bourgeoisie, were defeated.

In view of the voluntary and/or enforced external bias, the displacement competition emanating from the dominant economies was bound to hit local industry and lead to its ruin. When the influx of cheap grain from overseas into Europe carried displacement competition into even the rural sectors of European peripheries, protectionism by means of protective tariffs became an inevitable reaction. In a later phase, a conscious transition to industrial protection as a basis for mainly state-directed local industrialization by means of import substitution can be observed in all the peripheries of southern, south-eastern and eastern Europe. Such industrial promotion by protection was based on the conviction that—in early twentieth century terminology—'proletarian nations' (peripheries) had to protect themselves against the 'plutocratic nations' of north-western Europe (dissociation), unless they wanted to end up as the poor-houses of Europe and the world.[85]

The problem facing such a dissociative development policy, conceived in the peripheries as a reaction to persistent pressure towards peripheralization, lay in the task of having to build on traditional agricultural and craft structures that were blocking autonomous development. For, in all the peripheries, the agrarian structures remained unchanged during decisive development phases, and where agrarian reforms were implemented—mainly from above—they tended to buttress the power of the traditional landed class. Spain, southern Italy and Romania offer ample illustration for reforms which turned into 'counter-reforms'. The domestic market remained, therefore, limited even in the larger peripheries; the fragmentary industrialization led to large industrial over-capacities and was bound to be wasteful and inefficient on account of the narrowness of the domestic market rooted in the social structure, even if industrial growth often showed remarkable increases.[86]

If one looks at the internal structures of precisely those European peripheries, notably at their ossification and structural disseverance, their development-retarding old and new power alliances (the old ones between landed oligarchy and commercial capital, the new ones between landed oligarchy, finance capital and state bureaucracy), it becomes clear why, in the face of persistent pressure towards peripheralization, corporatist and dictatorial development solutions appeared tempting and prevailed. For in the face of the internal contradictions characterising periphery development, development dictatorships commended themselves as a lever for delayed development. What could be observed in the Third World in the 1960s and 1970s had intellectual and practical forerunners in the shape of the diverse development dictatorships on the peripheral southern and south-eastern fringes of Europe before the Second World War. Salazarism, Francoism, Italian fascism and the diverse corporatist regimes in the Balkans, south-eastern and eastern Europe aimed—in terms of development policy—by means of an appropriate agricultural and industrial policy to overcome the structural defects of their societies which had turned into peripheries.[87] The attempt to encourage development efforts by way of concerted action, as laid down in corporatist doctrine, reflects the fact that a continued integration into the existing world economic system could not prevent further peripheralization and that free play of world economic forces was bound to accentuate peripheralization. Such doctrines, therefore, propagated solidarity across class boundaries and nationalism as a basis for tendentially dissociative-autarchic industrial development. Nationalism and corporatism were regarded as complementary and progressive. The 'individualistic and anarchic capitalism' in western Europe was considered objectionable; an educative dictatorship was considered inevitable if the development differential between 'plutocratic and proletarian nations' was to be overcome.[88]

From the standpoint of development policy, all the corporatist development dictatorships of the European periphery have failed, as they were not able to overcome the heterogeneity of traditional society—in contrast with the proclamations of their doctrine. As traditional power structures were retained, development processes remained blocked. In some peripheries, as in south-eastern Europe, it was left to a socialist development dictatorship to eliminate the old class structure and to initiate forced industrialization. It is by no means misleading to argue—as, recently, with regard to the Romanian development path— that after 1945 the socialist development dictatorships realized those very aims which had been envisaged but not attained by corporatism, because it left the traditional class structures untouched.[89]

Such an interpretation is also supported by the close connection between nationalist, corporatist and socialist movements in the peripheries as early as the first decades of this century.[90] The 'revisionist' definition of socialism as a means of *delayed* development of the productive forces in backward and peripheralized countries that gradually emerged there proved, in historical perspective, more far-sighted and in practice more far-reaching than concepts of socialism which regarded socialism as a development stage beyond mature capitalism. Such a concept of socialism emanating from practical political movements was, moreover, not limited to the experience of the European periphery. Blended with revolutionary nationalism, such a doctrine of socialism can be traced back to Sun Yat-sen, to Ataturk's Kemalism, African and Arab socialism, and to the socialisms of many other decolonization and liberation movements.[91] In all these cases the traditional metropolitan definition of socialism was rejected as orthodox; the heretical definition aiming, for reasons of development policy, at an immediate realization of socialism. This definition was economic in that it argued for forced capital accumulation, technological progress and massive growth as a means of overcoming underdevelopment.[92]

The Strategic Importance of Agricultural Modernization in the Development Process

In the preceding paragraphs different responses of potential development laggards to the pressure towards peripheralization that has existed since the first industrial revolution have been outlined. How can it be explained then that, within Europe and outside, a number of societies have succeeded with delayed development (autocentric development) while vast economic regions of international society have actually been peripheralized?

Societies wanting successfully to counter English displacement competition had to repeat what had led to England's development breakthrough: *a combination of broad-based agricultural revolution and industrial revolution.* A review of European and extra-European development history during the nineteenth and early twentieth centuries shows a clear correlation between agricultural modernization and successful industrialization, or else between the lack of agricultural moderniza-tion and the failure of industrialization.[93] This close relationship derives from the varied macro-economic functions of agriculture in the early phase of industrialization, and also from industry's growing contribution in raising agricultural productivity.

Disregarding imports and exports, the size of the industrial sector depends directly on agricultural productivity.[94] If agriculture succeeds in producing a sufficient amount of food for a growing urban-industrial population, and sufficient quantities of raw materials for industrial processing at the same time that it is shedding labour, industry can develop and the rural areas can become markets for industrially produced consumer goods and equipment. The more efficient is agri-culture, the closer the potential interrelationship between agriculture and industry and the greater the chance of a gradually emerging dynamics of intra-industrial linkages which become—against a back-cloth of growing agricultural productivity—the basis for self-sustaining economic growth.[95]

If a close relationship exists between agricultural efficiency and the prospects of the industrialization process reaching the stage of self-sustaining growth, one should be able to observe *different relationships between agricultural and industrial development,* depending on the level and direction of agricultural modernization.[96]

(1) Persistent subsistence agriculture and industrialization would have to be mutually exclusive, according to the considerations outlined above. Notably in Europe, the development history of the Balkans provides evidence for the close connection between a stagnating agri-culture (in this case mainly smallholdings with low productivity) and the improbability of a more than embryonic industrialization.[97] But even in a country like Russia, which exported sizeable quantities of agricultural commodities,[98] there was a close link between low agri-cultural productivity and a low level of industrialization. At the start of this century *agricultural output* per head of the Russian population employed in agriculture amounted to just over 4 per cent of the per capita output in New Zealand, to 8 per cent of that in England and to 30 per cent of that in Bohemia/Moravia—the last figure being con-siderable, but still at the lower end of the countries industrializing on a broad base. Per capita *output of manufactures* in Russia amounted in 1913 to only 10 per cent of the figure in England and to less than 15 per cent

of that in the oceanic settler colonies. Per capita income amounted to roughly one-third of that of the advanced European and extra-European industrial societies. Though the industrial potential of Tsarist Russia at the start of the First World War was, in absolute terms, indeed considerable (she occupied sixth place on the continent of Europe), its relative size on a per capita basis indicated the overall backwardness of the country.[99]

(2) In contrast with the above-cited borderline case, one should be able to observe particularly dynamic industrialization processes in societies with a highly productive agriculture. Taking once again per capita agricultural output and per capita production of manufactures as the measure, the surmised relationship becomes especially evident in the case of the four settler colonies: the United States, Canada, Australia and New Zealand. At the beginning of this century New Zealand held first, Australia second, the United States fifth and Canada seventh place in the world with regard to per capita agricultural output. In per capita output of manufactures the United States took first, Canada third, Australia fourth and New Zealand sixth place in 1913. The combination of high agricultural productivity and advanced industrialization consequently translated itself into a high-ranking position with regard to per capita income: the United States had the lead, followed by Canada (second place), New Zealand (third place) and Australia (sixth place).[100] The close link between an efficient agriculture and industrialization is all the more remarkable, since all the named settler colonies counted among the big exporters of agricultural commodities and were all, with the exception of the United States, geared to exports. The importance of the link outlined here is not reduced by the fact that in the above-mentioned thinly populated settler colonies fertile soils could be exploited extensively over a long period, for this exceptionally favourable condition existed equally in the less successful settler colonies.[101]

(3) If there is a close link between agricultural and industrial development, early and forced agricultural modernization would have to translate itself into early and forced industrialization. The latter would have to be relatively unbalanced, because labour set free by agricultural modernization can be absorbed by industry and services only with a time-lag. This connection is evidenced above all by English development history, which contrasts sharply with the development history of other countries where a close link between a slow and steady industrialization can be traced.[102] The development of France is relevant in this context, and also that of other regions on the Continent. Thus, as late as the end of the nineteenth century, agricultural small-

holdings were dominant in France, followed by tenanted and subtenanted farms, while in England 7,000 owners controlled more than 68 per cent of the land. In France, agricultural activity took place mainly in small family-operated units with a low degree of specialization, since they produced—in contrast with the large farm units in England which were based on a division of labour—mainly a range of products for their own consumption and only marginally for the market. Population density in rural areas was higher in France; therefore, in contrast with England, even marginal land was cultivated. In England, such land had been given over to pasture at an early stage. Consequently, the proportion of stock-farming and pasture land was higher there, and more organic fertilizers per acre as well as draught-animals were available. In French agriculture the scope for capital formation was smaller; capital intensity per acre and per person employed lagged behind that in England. Surplus income raised by agriculture was bound to remain limited. Eighteenth- and nineteenth-century travellers were well aware of the different structural make-up both societies: the dominance of large-scale capitalist farming in England contrasted with the agricultural smallholding in France, whose position was consolidated by the French Revolution.[103]

Comparison between cases of early forced agricultural modernization with others of later and rather gradual growth in agricultural productivity does not imply a preference for the first as opposed to the second type. For, viewed from the present, both types of society have successfully developed. The discussion is therefore solely about divergent development rhythms in the face of different institutional conditions.[104]

(4) A particularly close connection can be observed in the case of Denmark, where agricultural modernization emanated from viable and well-consolidated, family-operated units, and where the industrialization process evolved in unmistakably ideal-type stages.[105] Increasing productivity in (export-orientated) agriculture was followed by industrial production of simple consumer goods and equipment, whereby the local informal sector was gradually displaced by growing industry. Consumer goods industrialization was followed by the production of more complex equipment and by engineering, until an agrarian society lacking all industrial raw materials had finally developed into a highly industrialized society. Balanced agricultural development was matched by parallel industrial development, less rapid than in the English case and more broad-based than in the case of France and of other Type I societies.

(5) During the nineteenth century the populous and large territorial states of Europe could not yet be regarded as integrated economies. All

of them were still segmented into definable regions often straddling national borders.[106] The link between agricultural and industrial development that is postulated here should therefore be evident in different regions within one and the same territorial state. In France, impulses for industrial growth issued from those regions in the north and north-west where agricultural modernization had greatly advanced, compared with other regions—for example, in the south and south-west. A positive correlation between agricultural modernization and industrial development appears within Spain in Catalonia and the Basque country, in northern as opposed to southern Italy, in the English-speaking part of Canada in contrast with the French-speaking part, and in Germany to the west of the Elbe.[107]

In this respect the Austro-Hungarian monarchy resembled a microcosm embracing all variants of interrelationships. The regions with advanced agricultural modernization, such as Lower and Upper Austria, Bohemia, Moravia and Silesia, developed into industrial growth poles, while the remaining parts of the monarchy (e.g. Galicia, Bukovina, Hungary and Transylvania, Carinthia, Istria, Croatia and Dalmatia) lagged behind agriculturally and industrially, which also applies—despite all the export success—to the Hungarian agricultural economy with its extensive production methods.[108] While the north-eastern regions pushed ahead, turning, though with delay, into industrial regions in the western European mould, the south-eastern regions were and remained, even after the disintegration of the Austro-Hungarian monarchy and up to the end of the Second World War, problem regions of development policy—a piece of the Third World in Europe.[109]

(6) Has there ever been industrialization except in the wake of agricultural modernization? And have there been cases where industrialization failed to materialize after successful agricultural modernization? If the answer to either of these questions is in the affirmative and if the postulated link between agricultural and industrial development is valid, we should be dealing with *special cases.*

As for the first question—possible exemplars are Switzerland and Norway.

In contrast with her image abroad, Switzerland is by no means endowed with particularly favourable natural conditions for agriculture.[110] Her development resulted from an early integration into the international division of labour. Basic foodstuffs and industrial raw materials were imported, and raw materials were locally processed into finished goods, which were then sold abroad pending development of the domestic market. In the early phase, the basis of Switzerland's agriculture lay therefore in foreign countries which were able to produce surpluses. However, it should also be emphasized that at a later stage alpine dairy farming in Switzerland herself was exploited for the production of processed goods (condensed milk, chocolate, etc.)

In the case of Norway, agriculture cannot be regarded as the developmental stimulus. The impetus for industrial development derived from foreign investment, by means of which newly developed hydroelectric energy resources were to be exploited. The result was a typically dualistic economic structure: capital-intensive industrial enclaves side by side with a relatively stagnant agriculture. The Norwegian example also demonstrates, however, that swiftly following agricultural modernization can successfully counteract the injurious manifestations of peripheralization resulting from dualistic structures. This was due to the fact that most of the land was cultivated by independent farmers.[111]

As regards the other question—concerning the lack of industrialization after agricultural modernization—there seems to have been only one society in Europe whose agriculture occupied a leading position without its sparking off early industrialization: the Netherlands. An early and broad-based agricultural modernization accompanied, since the end of the nineteenth century, by a belated industrialization, represents a paradox of development history. But when the industrialization process, which was overdue, finally took off, it could quickly develop against the backcloth of an efficient agriculture. It seems appropriate to surmise that the paradoxical Dutch development path goes back to that country's exposed position during the sixteenth and seventeenth centuries, when it successfully conducted an entrepôt trade in exotic merchandise, staple goods and manufactures. Its success as a trading nation had, at least temporarily, turned into a development obstacle at the transition to industrial society. Without agricultural modernization the Netherlands could have become a peripheral economy no different from that of Ireland.[112]

Such a danger is documented by the two settler colonies with efficient extensive agriculture, Argentina and Uruguay, which developed into actual peripheries in contrast with the successful settler colonies mentioned above (the United States, Canada, Australia and New Zealand). With regard to per capita agricultural output, Argentina and Uruguay occupied the third and fourth place in the world (after New Zealand and Australia)! But their per capita industrial production was insignificant at the turn of the century. In both societies a favourable agricultural potential was exploited, without its being utilized for the whole economy—in contrast with the United States, Canada, Australia and New Zealand. As will be shown in detail later on, this was due to the different institutional and social conditions in which the production of export-orientated agricultural commodities took place. The high agricultural productivity with which both societies were endowed by nature was not qualitatively improved by progressive agricultural modernization.[113]

(7) The development history of those export-orientated agrarian societies in Europe where considerable growth in agricultural exports could indeed be observed, without, however, agricultural modernization or dynamic industrialization taking place, point in the same direction, even if on the basis of a far less favourable natural endowment. In this connection the export regions of Russia, Spain and Italy spring to mind, as well as the societies specializing in agricultural exports: those of Ireland, Portugal, Romania, Hungary and Poland. What were their common characteristics with regard to the postulated link between agricultural and industrial development?

It is certain that the volume of agricultural output increased in these countries, in contrast with the stagnating agrarian societies of Greece, Albania, Bulgaria, Serbia and the other areas of the western Balkans.[114] However, this was not as a result of agricultural modernization based on intensification and mechanization but because of extensive growth *within the traditional institutional framework.* The fact that the volume of agricultural output increased, had nothing to do with a development-promoting increase in agricultural efficiency. Higher output resulted from increased pressure on the peasantry to expand production on new and old land without any sizeable productive investment. While, at the turn of the century, Romania accounted for 8 per cent of world grain exports, the rural population lived at or below subsistence level. The high world market share should therefore not obscure the catastrophically low agricultural productivity—one of the lowest in Europe—and a rural penury of frightening proportions.[115] And Romania serves here only as an example of comparable export-orientated agrarian societies in and outside Europe which developed into peripheralized growth economies.

The lesson to be drawn from these observations on positive and negative development experiences is obvious. In the positive case, industrialization was certainly stimulated by various impulses; but nowhere has industrial development reached the stage of self-sustaining growth unless an increase in agricultural productivity *preceded* or *accompanied* industrialization. In other words, attempted industrialization without agricultural modernization was bound to end in blocked development. This relationship can nowadays be observed all over the Third World, but it also determined the development history of Europe.

The response of European and extra-European societies to the pressure towards peripheralization emanating from Britain was predetermined by the given development level of each pre-industrial agrarian society and by the type of agricultural modernization. Societies with autonomous processes of agricultural modernization experienced a smooth transition to industrialization and, consequently, to a constructive response to the English challenge. The step to competitiveness and competitive superiority—the basis for successful displacement competition against the challenger—was then only a question of time. Societies not generating any endogenous impulses towards agricultural modernization faced the alternative of either turning into exporters of foodstuffs and raw materials on the basis of extensive production, which led to periphery development, or of temporarily remaining marginal and undeveloped, with the result, nevertheless, of turning into peripheries at a later stage.

In order to explore the causes of different development paths, particularly of *successful*, *misdirected* and *failed* industrialization, one is well advised to assess the development level of the productive forces in agriculture *before* the onset of industrialization. Decades, if not centuries before the English challenge, the course was gradually set for guiding the development process in the direction of either autocentric development or peripheralization.

In this sense European development history provides an object lesson in development policy. *In the cases of successful delayed development, industrial growth was preceded by a redistribution process,* usually labelled defeudalization or decomposition of feudal relationships of production.[116] In each case to a different extent, this process facilitated *agricultural modernization*. There was, therefore, *distribution before growth*, in complete contrast with the prescriptions issued by conventional development theory over the past thirty years. As is well known, these followed the motto 'growth first, redistribution later'. Only recently have relevant present-day development experiences (e.g. Taiwan) led to the realization that European development history teaches a lasting lesson in this respect.[117] For all agrarian societies that did not go through a process of redistribution (agrarian reform) before the onset of industrial growth, ended up as peripheries. Particularly bad cases of periphery development can be observed where proclaimed agrarian reforms led to an even more unequal distribution of land and power than had existed prior to the reform—that is, where agrarian reform had been turned into *counter-reform*.[118] What could be observed in many parts of the Third World from 1950 onwards in this respect had already happened in Europe during the nineteenth century, as for instance in

Portugal, Spain, southern Italy, parts of Greece and Romania. The outcome then was no different from today: the deepening of the internal disseverance of the affected societies.

Types of Agricultural Modernization and the Maturing Process of Market Economies

In all cases of agricultural modernization at least two different paths must be distinguished, the difference being due to the varying population density of agrarian societies. In *thinly populated* agrarian countries, agricultural modernization took a different path from that of overpopulated ones. Since the difference between the two had (and still has) a major impact on the industrialization process, it will be outlined in the following pages.[119]

Densely populated agrarian countries, which include the European agrarian societies,[120] start off with a low land-population ratio: scarce land is met by an abundance of labour, while little capital is at hand in the initial stages of agricultural modernization. Agricultural modernization started here with the disintegration of feudal relationships of coercion, and it aimed at overcoming the development blocks inherent in feudalism (arbitrary laws and legal insecurity, the burden of dues resting on the producer and the unproductive consumption of the surplus by the ruling feudal class, the subjection to monopoly rights, fragmentation of landholdings, absence of stimuli for institutional and technological innovation, etc.). Together with the move towards sensibly sized farm units (enclosures, field clearance), guaranteed access to land and legally guaranteed scope for individual initiative and freedom of disposition—that is, the establishment of security of ownership and tenure, (property rights)—belonged (and still belong) among the fundamental prerequisites for the production of an increased agricultural surplus.[121] With new institutional conditions for growth, productivity per acre improved despite the existing scarcity of land, though in the presence of an adequate labour supply. The intensification of agriculture manifested itself in relatively high yields per acre. Labour productivity, however, remained relatively low at this stage of development. Only the growing scarcity of agricultural labour, a by-product of advancing industrialization, and the ensuing rise in wages, induced increasing farm mechanization. Rising productivity per acre (intensification) was compounded, with a time-lag, by increasing labour productivity (mechanization). The combination of the two produced an agricultural sector whose share in the GDP dropped to a few percentage points, which could, however, fulfil its positive macro-economic function all the better.

This type of agricultural modernization thus passed through the following stages. From an agriculture with low labour productivity and modest yields per acre grew one with high yields per acre and high labour productivity. Labour-intensive agriculture turned into a capital-intensive one, while low agricultural purchasing power, low wages and high industrial production costs were supplanted by high agricultural purchasing power, high wages and low industrial production costs. In this way a domestic market, which had initially been lying fallow, was gradually opened up.

The modernization process in *sparsely populated agricultural regions* (settler colonies) was characterized by a different sequence. An abundance of land combined with scarcity of labour to ensure that agricultural modernization had to be geared towards increasing efficiency through the use of labour-saving and labour-easing machinery and transport equipment (mechanization). This enabled a relatively small agricultural population to achieve high yields on the basis of an initially extensive agriculture, which differed, however, from the extensive production in peripheral economies where productivity per acre *and* per person employed was low. In thinly populated agrarian societies a relatively low productivity per acre combined with high labour productivity, based on early agricultural mechanization which stimulated the growth of a local industry for agricultural machinery. It was only when, in societies with a favourable land-population ratio, the supply of land gradually diminished, that improved means of production combined with better seed, improved rotation of crops and more efficient soil cultivation, began to be applied. Along with the production of agricultural machinery, chemical industry (fertilizers and herbicides) gained in importance. In this case, in contrast with densely populated agrarian countries, intensification followed mechanization, and the early mechanization necessary for agricultural modernization produced, together with high and increasing wages, considerable impulses for the growth of a local consumer and capital goods industry.

Faced with ample reserves of land and a labour shortage, agricultural modernization in thinly populated agrarian countries thus started out from low productivity per acre and high labour productivity. But in this case, too, *in the long run* ever higher labour productivity coincided with high productivity per acre, owing to a process of agricultural modernization based, initially, on mechanization, and later, on intensification (Table 4 below).

Table 4:   *Types of agricultural modernization*

| | | **Mechanization** | |
		plus	*minus*
Intensification	*plus*	Developed societies	European agrarian ←]economies
		↑	
	minus	Settler colonies (USA, etc.)	Peripheries

As thinly populated agrarian countries are rare, the process of agricultural modernization taking place within them can be observed less frequently than that in densely populated agrarian countries. In the former cases, however, *the maturing process of market economies* manifested itself over and above the agricultural sector both earlier and more clearly than in the latter ones. What does this process consist of? Highly productive agriculture, in these cases, made for high incomes, and scarce labour resulted in high wages. High wages favoured agricultural mechanization directed towards increased labour productivity and induced early labour-saving investment in industry. In this way a capital goods sector, whose size and dynamics indicated the maturity of the respective economies, emerged alongside the consumer goods sector brought about by rising incomes. The settler colonies had the advantage of carrying through agricultural modernization and industrialization without having first to overcome feudal structures. In societies with a feudal past, the process of capitalization depended upon the extent and speed of the disintegration of feudal structures.[122] The longer capitalist production had recourse to pre-capitalist economic regions, the longer the maturing process of capitalist society was delayed, since in conditions of retarded capitalization and of cheap labour which could be continuously recruited from pre-capitalist economic regions, incentives for a deepening of the productive structure (vertical diversification, capital intensification) were weak or non-existent. While it is true that, in the early stages of industrialization, pre-capitalist economic regions support capitalist industrial production by means of cheap labour, cheap food and cheap agricultural raw materials, as well as unfavourable exchange relationships between industry and agriculture,[123] it is also true that such a symbiotic relationship becomes fatal for the maturing of capitalist societies in the long run. For in such circumstances the domestic market remains limited, and above all a pool of cheap labour remains in existence. But the latter is bound to dry up if rising costs and competition, spreading across the whole potential domestic market, leave capitalist enterprises no alternative to accumulation by way of innovation—that is, to labour-saving investment and an efficient use of the available resources.[124] Only in such conditions do the capital goods industries and their upstream sectors become the dynamic growth pole of the economy. A differentiated capital goods industry is, however, necessary if the level of productivity throughout the economy is to be raised.

This very mechanism, indispensable for the maturing of a coherent and competitive economy, is lacking in peripheral economies. There the absence of agricultural modernization, together with asymmetrical integration into the international division of labour, limited industrialization; and the industrial complexes, which were artificially grafted on to stagnating agricultural development, did not develop autonomous impulses towards capital intensification. Consequently, peripheries usually lack the self-reliant capital goods sector[125] which, in the course of the development process, has become the industrial backbone of highly industrialized societies.

Development Factors in Different Development Configurations

In the preceding section an attempt was made to elucidate the conditions in which the response to pressure towards peripheralization, emanating from Britain, led either to autocentric development or to peripheralization. The common denominator of those development paths successful in the long run was broad-based agricultural modernization with its interrelated industrialization, both of which supplied the basis for an opening up of the domestic markets—notably in small countries. In this way, originating from a few regional growth poles, ever-expanding economic regions and, after many decades, fully consolidated economies ('national economies') emerged, characterized by a *highly integrated and coherent domestic economy* (homogeneity). In their case, a development potential was tapped that is basically latent in every society and which can be realized by means of agricultural modernization and industrialization. In this connection, the different development paths of European societies throw two aspects into relief:

(1) In view of a varying resource endowment in each concrete case, autocentric development paths were constructed from different build-

ing blocks and different combinations of them, even if after many decades they have ended up with the very same (OECD) profile. This observation applies not only to the development paths grouped into main types above, but to the various development paths within one and the same type.

(2) Whether individual factors promoted or retarded development depended crucially on the socio-structural and institutional context within which they operated (= development configuration). The basic experience is that the same factors which were development-promoting within an autonomous process of agricultural modernization and industrialization did not usually promote development in a context unfavourable to agricultural modernization.

Both aspects will be illustrated briefly below, without any attempt to verify exhaustively the various observations in empirical terms.

Without question, abundant *natural resources* like coal and ore deposits have shaped the development path of Belgium. In the same way, ore mining has determined the development course of Sweden. But, quite apart from the fact that both these societies could well have become peripheries, the development paths of Denmark, the Netherlands, Finland and Iceland show autocentric development to be possible even without such energy and mineral resources. Among populous societies, the development of Japan is especially relevant in this connection. This contrasts with Spanish development, where plenty of resources were available throughout the whole territory but failed to make any positive contribution towards the broad-based development of that country. Their mobilization was frequently directed towards the outside world, the dynamic impulses and linkages resulting from them remained limited to enclaves, and the whole economy remained disjointed. Obvious potential linkages, for instance between the coalfields in Asturia and the ore deposits in the Basque country, remained unexploited.

A large *population* can be a significant development factor, as is evidenced by the development of Britain, France, Germany and the United States. As is shown by the example of Tsarist Russia, the population giant of Europe in the nineteenth century, however, there is no direct correlation between size of population and development prospects. It is frequently argued, though, that small countries with limited populations enjoy particularly favourable development conditions if they integrate into the growth dynamics of populous societies by means of an export-orientated strategy. This kind of conclusion is certainly confirmed by Scandinavian development, although contradicted by the experiences of Portugal and southern Europe. The Belgian case demonstrates, moreover, that small countries need not always develop on an export-orientated pattern. In appropriate conditions the option of dissociative development based on the dynamic impulse of the domestic market followed, at a later stage, by an (associative) export orientation, is also conceivable.

Nation states territorially consolidated at an early stage, like France, seem to have had better development prospects than those remaining unconsolidated, like Germany and Italy. However, the unsuccessful development history of Portugal, one of the first European territorial states, would contradict such an assumption, in the same way as would the development history of Switzerland, where the industrial revolution took place at the same time as in England, at a moment when the territory remained considerably fragmented politically and economically. The rise of Finland occurred in the first five decades of the present century, even though neither its international political status nor its internal political affairs were really settled. These conditions have made Finland's development more difficult but not impossible.

Let us consider the role of *infrastructure*. The comprehensive road and canal network in England, Belgium and parts of France had made possible the development of a market economy earlier than in territories less well endowed with transport facilities. But the gain derived from the development of an infrastructure varied widely from case to case, as is evidenced above all by the construction of railways. In northern and north-western Europe railway construction produced considerable macro-economic linkage effects and, after its completion, the new transport network facilitated the movement of goods in an increasingly tight-knit market economy. Where broad-based development processes were already under way, the contribution of railway construction to the homogenization of initially fragmented and regionalized economies was considerable. Where the former did not take place, the early construction of a railway network proved a white elephant. For the freight capacities remained unused and the intended economic advantage of transporting goods faster and cheaper with the help of the railways evaporated, both because there was often nothing to be transported, and, what was transported, had to be moved at high cost in view of excess capacity.

Contrasting examples spring to mind: for example, railway construction in Sweden as opposed to that in Spain. The former was integrated into a gradual process of industrialization and advanced this process by opening up new linkage potentials (local production of locomotives, carriages, etc.).[126] In the Spanish case, railway construction was grafted on from outside without its stimulating essential inputs from the domestic economy.[127] In the Balkans, railway construction executed by foreign capital produced even fewer linkage effects. Where military considerations did not dictate the logistics of the rail routes, economic considerations, foreign capital interested in the extraction and transport of raw materials, did so. In those cases where railway construction was not part of an autonomous development process, it became, in view of considerable debt repayments, a growing drain on already weak public finances. Limited resources would often have been better employed in broad agricultural modernization. For through their foreign debt the countries in question became dependent on foreign interest groups and lost their already fragile political sovereignty.[128] What stimulated new spurts of growth in cases like Sweden, Belgium and Germany, leading to micro-economic linkage effects and structural change, proved in unfavourable starting conditions to dissipate scarce resources and consequently to be a wasted investment.

A comparable picture presents itself in the case of *foreign investment* and *technology transfer in general*.[129] In societies where agricultural modernization and industrialization progressed autonomously, exogenous injections of capital, purposive adoption of foreign technology and selective employment of foreign experts have, as a rule, introduced dynamic impulses into the economy. The development of new industries and the modernization of old ones were thus facilitated. In the case of Types I, II and III countries, these transfers from more highly developed Britain played a most useful role. By contrast, Type IV cases and those of societies that have become peripheries, show, however, that the *technology* of more highly developed societies can be usefully absorbed by latecomers only if the necessary conditions are present and if the ability of industry, state bureaucracy and science to choose foreign technology and to employ it locally has been purposively promoted.

In this connection, Japan after the Meiji restoration is constantly, and justifiably, quoted as a positive example. But Scandinavia, too, refused to be swamped by foreign technology and found, as a result of considerable efforts of its own, a middle way between the adoption of foreign technology and the promotion of locally developed technology. In contrast, the example of Hungary after 1890 shows how the adoption of technology and even the local development of certain niche technologies (in this case, milling and the production of electric motors for public transport) remained isolated because the average technology level of the rest of the economy remained low. In a society like that of Hungary, characterized by latifundia, advanced technologies in just two industries were of little use—despite their ability to compete world-wide. A comparison with Dutch development after 1880 suggests itself. Against the backcloth of an efficient economy and a relatively homogeneous domestic market came the late development of specific industries dedicated to the construction of specialized ships, diesel engines, light bulbs, and so on, whose growth impulses had positive spill-over effects across the whole Dutch economy, because of the latter's rising average development level. A similar case can be observed, though to a lesser degree, in the economic region of northern Italy after 1895, where new industries for the production of typewriters, typographic equipment, bicycles, cars, and so forth, became part of an already advancing process of agricultural and industrial development, into which they were able to inject substantial dynamic impulses.

The varying importance of free trade and protectionist *foreign economic policy* in different socio-structural and institutional contexts is evident. Portugal's free-trade stance, maintained over decades, led to that country's peripheralization in just the same way as it led to the peripheralization of Spain and south-eastern Europe. Within the Austro-Hungarian monarchy, which was protected by import duties from the outside world while practising free trade internally, Hungary's monocultural position as grain exporter was consolidated. But the transition from free trade to protectionism during the nineteenth century by no means led to development breakthroughs in all the cases *without* a preceding agricultural modernization, because the export-orientated agrarian interests favoured by free trade were now able to buttress their traditional political and economic power position with protective barriers.[130] In both cases, structures injurious to development were therefore consolidated.

While in the context of autonomously advancing, broad-based development, protection—*in line with the Listian prescription*—was useful for safeguarding infant industries, it had, notably in the case of export economies based on extensive production methods, retrogressive effects. It is remarkable how in export-orientated cases, where industrialization was paralleled by agricultural modernization (Scandinavia, the settler colonies), a clever mix of free trade and protectionist policies was pursued, making possible, on the one hand, an integration into the world market and, on the other, the necessary protection of local import substitution industrialization (Type III societies). In Canada, the United States, Australia and New Zealand the protectionist measures employed were surprisingly tough for export economies, as they were for an economy with a sizeable export sector, as in the United States.[131] Free trade and/or protectionist external economic policy instruments must, therefore, be seen in their specific development context. Outside such a context one cannot ascribe any development-promoting or retarding effect to them except in purely abstract terms.

Finally, what about the much-cited role of *cultural factors*? Rarely has a statement been taken up as frequently as the Weberian thesis on the connection between the Protestant ethic and the spirit of capitalism. At first glance the evidence for this thesis seems to be overwhelming, for it is above all Protestant societies that have developed successfully, like Britain, Scandinavia, the respective regions of Switzerland and the English-speaking settler colonies. In Canada the development of the Catholic part of the country is lagging spectacularly behind that of the Protestant areas. But how is such a theory to explain the successful development of other countries and regions not dominated by Protestantism? Was the Catholic culture of northern France, in the Spanish Basque country, in Catalonia, in northern Italy and in the development regions of Upper and Lower Austria less development impeding than the Catholicism in the remaining parts of the countries mentioned? Predominantly Catholic Belgium belonged to the early industrializers, while the Netherlands with a pronounced Protestant culture was a late industrializer. And how does the development of Bohemia and Moravia, not only within the Austro-Hungarian monarchy but after 1919, fit the thesis on the connection between Protestantism and capitalism? Countries like Ireland and Portugal, as well as Greece, the Balkan states, Poland and Russia would, however, seem to support the thesis, were there not the contrasting examples—and more recent developments.

For in this connection the current debate on the role of Confucianism in south-eastern Asia becomes relevant to development history. For one thing, the Confucianism postulate clearly undermines a narrowly formulated thesis on the positive correlation between Protestantism and capitalism. But even if a connection between Confucianism and the increased chance of successful delayed development could be proven, one would have to reflect upon the fact that the Far Eastern countries concerned (apart from Japan), which are today credited with a special development talent,[132] did not develop at all differently from the other societies in their Asian vicinity *prior* to the Second World War. Did not changed socio-structural and institutional conditions for growth after the Second World War play a greater part in these cases (as well as in the cases of successful Catholic development societies) than Confucianism itself? As, for example, the fundamental revolutionary changes in Chinese and North Korean society after the Second World War, as well as a thorough agrarian reform in Taiwan and an agrarian reform in South Korea, both of which were far less half-hearted than in other countries of the Third World. Where institutional development blocks existed, Catholicism and Confucianism, and also

Protestantism (take Germany east of the Elbe), retarded development. Where these blocks were overcome (as happened relatively early in Japan), traditional cultural orientations had little chance of holding back the forces of development freed from their institutional strait-jacket.

Conclusions

To summarize:

(1) The development differential between 'front runners' and 'laggards', which is under scrutiny in the current development debate, is not a phenomenon of only the past few decades; nor is the development problem stemming from it confined to the relations between the highly industrialized societies of today and the Third World. In the face of an increasingly intermeshed world economy, differences in the competence levels of more highly and less developed societies translate themselves into a displacement competition between the more developed and the lagging societies. As early as the nineteenth century this competition became tendentially world-wide. Beginning at the latest with England's breakthrough to the Industrial Revolution, the less developed societies, even in Europe itself, faced the threat of peripheralization. Then it was not simply those European countries that have actually developed into peripheries which were candidates for peripheralization, but the presently highly industrialized societies as well. With regard to the currently debated development problems Europe had, therefore, no special position. Consequently it makes sense to project current questions of development theory and policy back on to the development history of Europe.

(2) Basically, the English challenge could be met with associative and/or dissociative responses of varying degrees. At least five different responses can, in fact, be observed in the nineteenth and twentieth centuries:

(*a*) dissociative development based on the dynamic impulse of the domestic market (Type I), which is usually to be found in the case of populous societies already advanced in development to a certain degree;

(*b*) associative export-orientated development (Type II), which represents the ideal type of development path integrated into the world market, though in reality it can be documented with only two cases;

(*c*) associative-dissociative development (Type III) where, usually in the case of smaller export-orientated societies, a clear sequence from initial export-orientation to the opening up of the domestic market by means of agricultural modernization and industrialization can be traced;

(d) dissociative state-capitalist development (Type IV) in cases where populous territorial states without favourable institutional conditions for growth made late attempts at catching up in development; and

(e) dissociative state-socialist development (Type V), which took place outside the capitalist world market.

Variants of dissociative policy can thus be observed more frequently than free-trade approaches and, viewed over a long period, the dissociative components became more pronounced as repeated attempts at delayed development were made. An undiluted free-trade response to the English challenge was in every respect the exception. Only when the development levels had been more or less equalized—that is, after qualitatively comparable economic structures had been established in the trading countries—could free trade become generalized. To achieve this state of development it took almost a hundred years between the mid-nineteenth and mid-twentieth centuries.

(3) In conditions of free trade, displacement competition in societies still dominated by agriculture led to reduced growth. In such conditions the levelling of development differentials, as postulated by free-trade doctrine, could not occur. Economic history has vindicated the political scepticism shown by the opponents of the free-trade school.

(4) The most frequent reaction to threatening peripheralization was actual periphery development. Whether attempted delayed development led to autocentric development or peripheralization depended, apart from other secondary and tertiary factors, essentially on the development level of the challenged society. If, in the history of individual societies, an autonomously advancing process towards broad-based agricultural modernization, embryonic industrialization and increasing commercialization can be observed, the prospects for successful delayed (autocentric) development were usually good. In contrast, the kind of societies in Europe (and overseas) which seized growing export opportunities within the emerging world market without prior or concurrent elimination of traditional oligarchic social structures, have become peripheries. In those countries where attempted land reforms turned into counter-reforms, thereby leading to the retention of unproductive agrarian structures and to the marginalization of the rural population, the ground was prepared for peripheralization. In these cases, export success further consolidated social structures already injurious to development. In contrast, in those countries where export orientation and

industrialization were preceded by a redistribution of the resource most important in agrarian societies, namely land, the probability of broad-based industrial growth was increased.

(5) Societies in Europe (and overseas) have reached the high development level of mature industrial societies only through opening up their own domestic market potential. This statement also applies to small export-orientated countries. Crucial to the maturing process was a persistent rise in agricultural and industrial productivity, a diffusion of productivity gains across the *whole* economy and a rise in the average income of labour in *all* economic sectors.[133] Where productivity was stagnant, development as a whole remained stagnant. And where productivity gains were only sectoral—confined to certain industrial complexes or economic areas without being diffused across the *whole economy*—dualistic structures hostile to the opening up of the domestic market emerged. The maturing process of capitalist societies required favourable conditions for accumulation and an increasing domestic demand. This connection appeared first in the successfully developing settler colonies; later it could be observed in the cases of all the present OECD societies. Together with a long-term development of labour shortages, the rise in *mass* incomes, which had been achieved by political means, played a decisive role. Both developments encouraged capital intensification, a process that advanced the maturing of capitalist economies.

(6) The direction of both European and non-European development was determined by the social structures and existing institutions that had evolved during the course of history. If these were conducive to broad-based agricultural modernization and industrialization, growth-retarding factors became less important and a lack of natural resources could often be compensated for by an above-average mobilization of knowledge and skill.[134] This, more than anything else, explains the secret of the rapid success of many small European countries with specific and limited resources. In conditions hostile to agricultural modernization and subsequent industrialization, not even factors that usually were particularly development-enhancing could enable a society to achieve a development breakthrough. A comparative analysis shows, moreover, that particular development-enhancing factors can be present in different strengths and become relevant to development at different points in time. Development is, in K.W. Deutsch's words, the result of a non-synchronized assembly-line process with long waiting lines, based on various determining factors, the sequence of which can vary from case to case according to the laws of probability.[135] Only the starting condition for successful delayed (= autocentric) development is likely to be clearly defined: an agriculture capable of achieving broad-based productivity gains.

Europe from a Eurocentric Viewpoint?

At this point a possible objection to the preceding arguments must be considered. Can one make any sense of European development history in the nineteenth and early twentieth centuries through an analysis focused solely on Europe? Are not colonialism and imperialism consti-tuent parts of European development history, and is an approach that excludes what was then the Third World not bound to distort the whole picture? Does not the more recent literature on development theory, guided by the so-called 'world system' approach,[136] emphasize the formation of a *world economy* within which, beginning in the late fifteenth and early sixteenth centuries, north-western Europe came to determine the direction of development and the rest of the world became the periphery of Europe?

The following observations make an analysis of development history focused on Europe seem less problematic than might appear from the viewpoint of the current discussion on development policy.[137]

(1) The external economic links of European societies were mainly of an intra-European nature.[138] During the nineteenth century, for example, 70 per cent of total European exports were directed towards Europe itself, while 65 per cent of European imports originated in Europe. Roughly 80 per cent of the total foreign trade of European societies was with the developed regions of the world economy (Europe, North America, Oceania). Hence trade with that part of the international economy now called the 'Third World' amounted to around 20 per cent of European foreign trade. In 1830 this corre-sponded to roughly 1 per cent and in 1910 to roughly 3 per cent of European GDP.

With regard to the percentages quoted, it has to be taken into account that they include the combined imports and exports of Britain and continental Europe. Yet Britain's foreign trade profile differed markedly from those of continental European societies. Between 1830 and 1930, 80 per cent of the foreign trade of continental Europe was directed towards Europe itself, a further 10 per cent was with North America and Oceania, and the remaining 10 per cent with the 'Third World'. Europe's share of British trade, in contrast, was always much smaller (between 1860 and 1910 about 35 per cent of total exports), and the trade with North America and the Oceanic settler colonies much greater (around 25 per cent of exports). Britain's trade with the

'Third World' amounted to 40 per cent of total foreign trade—in sharp contrast with the links that continental Europe maintained at the time with the 'Third World'.

For the development of Europe, and especially continental Europe, the growing mutual interlacement of those societies nowadays called highly developed was of much greater significance than the quantitatively far less important links with the 'Third World'. And even in the case of Britain's external economic profile, which was atypical of Europe as a whole, the data on foreign investment in 1914 point in the same direction: almost 50 per cent of capital investment took place in the United States, Canada, Australia and New Zealand.[139]

The tendency to overemphasize the role of the Third World stems from the fact that a great many authors have dealt with Britain, not continental Europe, and that some of the influential studies were written in the historically limited periods of increasing interlacement with the Third World (e.g. around the turn of the century) without longitudinal trend analyses having led to a later revision of misconceptions.[140]

(2) Seen in connection with other fast developing societies, like North America and Oceania, nineteenth-century Europe was, except in cotton, self-sufficient and not dependent on the supply of foodstuffs and agricultural and mineral raw materials from the Third World.[141] With regard to cotton, the question arises as to whether its export from the southern states of North America can be regarded as an export of an industrializing country (the United States) or as an export of a plantation economy with a Third World character. For at the start of the American Civil War in 1861, 77 per cent of Europe's cotton imports originated from the United States, the rest coming mainly from India and Egypt. In the case of wool imports there is no comparable problem, for around 1900 slightly more than 80 per cent of English wool imports came from Australia and New Zealand, countries which were, at the time, already in a process of comprehensive development.

If, apart from cotton, no other essential raw materials from the 'Third World' were fed into the first long phase of industrialization in Britain and Europe during the nineteenth century, what then did Europe import from those overseas regions that turned into peripheries?

Apart from cotton, the imports consisted mainly of those goods already brought in from overseas in the seventeenth and eighteenth centuries: sugar, tea, coffee, spices, tobacco, silk, china, rare timbers, natural dyes, and so on. As in the three centuries preceding the Industrial Revolution, most of these commodities were not products for mass consumption but luxury goods, some of which became only gradually articles for mass consumption. They were, moreover, not essential inputs of industrial production. The latter required commodities which were, always with the exception of cotton, produced in sufficient quantities in Europe itself during the nineteenth century—for example, coal, the main energy source, iron ore and non-ferrous metals. Only towards the end of the nineteenth century did imports of fats and oils, leather and wood, raw rubber and a limited number of minerals from the Third World increase,[142] without, however, greatly affecting the import structure described above. In the course of the twentieth century, Third World resources have become increasingly important for the further industrial development of Europe, though in some sectors (such as energy) it was not until the end of the Second World War that their significance became apparent.

What was of rather limited importance for the industrial reproduction of industrializing European society could produce considerable distortions in the Third World in view of its fragile pre-colonial and colonial structures. In the light of the present situation it may seem strange to regard the emergence of monocultures in the Third World as reflecting Europe's high degree of self-sufficiency in locally produced goods.[143] But if the Europe of the first industrial revolution had achieved a lower degree of self-sufficiency, probably a much broader and more massive claim on the resources of the remaining world would have been necessary in order to sustain the same rhythm of industrialization. In particular the supply of mineral raw materials remained extremely limited: as late as 1913 only 11 per cent of the overall modest exports of tropical countries consisted of minerals—a reflection of the Third World's low share in world raw material production at the time.[144]

That the Third World also failed to secure a higher share of Europe's agricultural imports is due to the fact that its agricultural production could not compete with the prospering agriculture of the settler colonies.

Notably in the case of Latin America, which had become independent at the beginning of the nineteenth century, small export achievements did nevertheless add up to an export orientation which formed—in combination with a hardly changing subsistence economy—the basis of dualistic exclave economies and led in the wake of export growth to the emergence of heterogeneous societies. If at the time broad-based agricultural modernization had complemented the production and export of the commodities that were in demand in Europe, the prospects for delayed industrialization would have been neither more nor less favourable than in comparable cases in Europe itself.[145] A comparative analysis of different development paths of export-orientated societies (see Part II) would, in any case, suggest such a conclusion.

(3) It is beyond doubt that, since the end of the fifteenth century, a

world economy based on division of labour has gradually emerged, and it is indisputable that European societies have plundered other continents, even if to a varying extent. There is, nevertheless, still no theory to explain how, in the developed countries, robbery and pillage have translated themselves into the *institutional framework for a sustained dynamic development impulse on the basis of constant innovation and productivity gains.*[146] For it is not only since the beginning of modern history that robbing and looting have tended to go hand in hand with opposition to innovation. It is, moreover, much more difficult than is often assumed in general theories to reconstruct convincingly in empirical and historical terms the transition from commercial capital, based on the realization of trading profits, to industrial capitalism.[147] Explaining the transition from an incipient agrarian capitalism to industrial capitalism presents, in contrast, hardly any comparable analytical difficulties, and historical experience suggests, as is shown in this chapter, a symbiotic link between the two. As opposed to the case of commercial capital, the social agents of agrarian and industrial capitalism had either to survive or perish in conditions of competition, and hence progressively in conditions of *accumulation by means of innovation*. Transfers from the rest of the world could at best facilitate accumulation already under way; but in no circumstances could they provide the basis for innovation favourable to accumulation. If the case were different, it would be particularly hard to explain why those parts of the world that entertained especially close trade links with Europe (like North America and Oceania) developed and did not turn into peripheries themselves. The very same question arises in the case of Europe, where some export economies ended up as highly industrialized societies, others as peripheries.

PART II Export-led Development

2 Growth and Equity: the Scandinavian Development Path

In the more recent discussion on development theory the specialization and over-specialization of economies with regard to the export-orientated production of foodstuffs and agricultural as well as mineral raw materials is usually regarded as the main obstacle to *autocentric* development. In this connection the mineral-based exclave economy and the agricultural monoculture in overseas countries—both outposts of higher developed industrial countries—are considered but extreme cases of dependent and *deformed* growth economics.[1]

Based on this discussion, several historical cases of extensive world market-orientated specialization (Type III societies) will be illuminated in this chapter: cases in which the export-orientated production of agricultural, forestry and mineral commodities did not lead to the emergence of typical exclave economies but paved the way for a broad-based and well-proportioned (i.e. autocentric) opening up of the domestic market. If specialization played a major part in the formation of distorted reproduction structures in the Third World, an analysis of 'deviant' historical cases with a high degree of specialization but without comparable deformation is important for the further differentiation of development theory and for the debate on development policy. Basically this involves two groups of societies: on the one hand, the Netherlands and the four northern European countries of Scandinavia (Denmark, Norway, Sweden and Finland); and on the other, the successful settler colonies (Australia, New Zealand, Canada and the United States). From the first group, only Scandinavia will be discussed in the following pages. A study of several settler colonies and of the Netherlands will be found in a later chapter.[2]

Finland's Remarkable Development as an Example

The questions of development history and theory to be discussed here could be explored through the example of each of the four Scandinavian countries.[3] In this respect the choice of Finland is an arbitrary one. It can essentially be justified by the fact that, among the four Scandinavian countries, Finland had (apart from Norway) the worst starting conditions for delayed development—not only with regard to the economic resource endowment, but because, as late as the first decades of this century, her political, cultural and social identities were by no means settled. Besides, in the second half of the last century, when export-orientated specialization in the above-mentioned sense nourished the growth of the gradually emerging national economies in all four Scandinavian countries, Finland was the most backward in terms of development. From the perspective of the current development debate it seems surprising that this latecomer, which was surrounded by the other rapidly advancing Scandinavian countries and by the large industrializing territorial states of Europe, did not, like many other countries at the same time, turn into a periphery economy, even though many prerequisites for a monocultural exclave economy based on forestry products were present. No less remarkable is Finland's extraordinarily dynamic growth and development process in recent decades, which has led to a considerable diversification of the domestic production structure. A few data will illustrate these observations.

According to Colin Clark's calculations, Britain's average real per capita income surpassed that of Finland by 200 per cent between 1925 and 1934 (1,069 international units compared with 380).[4] A glance at the *World Development Report 1979* issued by the World Bank shows that in 1977 Britain's per capita income was 30 per cent smaller than that of Finland ($4,420 as opposed to $6,160).[5] The same sources show that the gap between American and Finnish per capita income, which amounted to 264 per cent at the end of the 1920s, has now narrowed to 38 per cent. In the case of such a statistical comparison between highly industrialized societies, the kind of distortion to be found in Third World statistics should not be of any importance; the figures quoted do, more or less, reflect the real state of affairs. Why, then, was Finland, whose economic development in this century rested for decades on the *export-orientated* production of forestry products, able to overtake Britain, the European forerunner of industrial development, and impressively narrow the gap with other capitalist industrial societies, both with regard to the other Scandinavian countries, which have always been more highly developed, and with respect to the large territorial states of central and western Europe? This question arises all the more, as other societies, whose average real per capita income between 1925 and 1934—according to Clark's figures—was roughly equal to that of Finland (Greece, Hungary, Poland, Italy, Yugoslavia), have not yet achieved a position that is in any way comparable. Japan, which was then at the same level as Finland, is the only noteworthy exception.

The remarkable distance covered by Finland in just a few decades can be gauged from the data given below.[6]

One hundred years ago Finland was among the most markedly agrarian countries in Europe. In 1870, 85 per cent of the population were employed in the primary sector (agriculture, forestry, fishing), and at the end of the Second World War this share was still as high as 50 per cent of the labour force. Not until thirty years later, in 1975, had this figure fallen to 14 per cent. The persistent predominance of the primary sector was mirrored in a slow development of the secondary (industry, mining, construction) and tertiary (commerce, transport, banking, general services) sectors. Only since the late 1960s and early 1970s has the internal structure approached the typical profile of highly industrialized societies without yet having fully reached it: in 1977, 14 per cent of the economically active population were employed in the primary, 38 per cent in the secondary and 48 per cent in the tertiary sectors. The late and very slow shift of the economically active population from the primary sector to industry and services is exceptional even for Scandinavia. In Denmark, Norway and Sweden less than 50 per cent of the economically active population were employed in the primary sector even before the First World War (Denmark, 36 per cent; Norway, 39 per cent; Sweden, 49 per cent), while in Finland a comparable proportion could be observed only after the Second World War. For decades this sectoral distribution of the labour force was reflected in a relatively low degree of urbanization: in 1910 just over 10 per cent of the population lived in urban centres, and only since 1970 has the share of the rural population fallen below 50 per cent.

If one looks at the composition of foreign trade, the predominance of the *timber and paper industries*, which dates from the turn of the century, becomes obvious. Shortly before the First World War their combined share in total foreign trade was around 80 per cent. In the inter-war period this share remained static, and only since the early 1970s has it gradually fallen below 50 per cent. Finland thus *is one of those countries whose export commodities' basket remained for decades relatively little diversified, but which has nevertheless achieved a high per capita income.* Since mono-export structures tend to be present in typical peripheries, partially diversified export commodity baskets in semi-peripheries and broadly diversified ones in metropoles, the extraordinary combination of mono-export structure and high per capita income calls for an explanation.

Finland is a country with a low population density and, as shown by the data on urbanization, the larger urban conglomerations have emerged only since the Second World War. If, in conditions of low density and wide dispersal of population, a *national economy* is to emerge, above-average infrastructural investment is required. A country with the structural profile described above is, however, unlikely to command abundant and easily accessible capital.

The natural wealth of Finland lies in her forests. She has no coal and few other minerals—that is to say, hardly any of the prerequisites of the first industrial revolution that are usually considered important.

Finland's total agricultural area is also limited. In the 1930s it amounted to no more than 12 per cent; while 74 per cent of the country was covered by forest, the remaining 14 per cent consisted of lakes and could not be cultivated. Agricultural modernization started rather late and was originally confined to the south-western regions. In the famine year 1867/8, 137,000 people (8 per cent of the population) died, and not until the end of the 1930s was Finnish agriculture productive enough to be able to guarantee the food supply of the population. Only then could the export of a small number of processed agricultural goods (such as dairy products), which had begun at the end of the last century, be considerably increased.

If, on top of this, one considers Finland's political history, the picture which, from the perspective of development policy, is already less than promising, begins to look even bleaker.[7]

It is difficult to judge at what point Finland became an internally consolidated nation state. When in 1809 the Finnish population was separated from the Kingdom of Sweden and subordinated to the Russian Tsar in his capacity as 'Grand Duke of Finland', a Finnish national identity did not yet exist.[8] The gradual awakening of Finnish nationalism in the second half of the nineteenth century indicates a belated process of nation-building. The élite of the country had always been orientated towards Sweden and spoke Swedish. The conflict over the Finnish language and the struggles at the turn of the century over the constitutional rights of the autonomous Grand Duchy of Finland within the Tsarist monarchy supplied for the first time a focus for the emerging national consciousness. But even at the time of her independence at the end of the First World War, Finland was still not a nation in the true sense, as is documented by the immediate onset of the civil war between 'Whites' and 'Reds' and the then ensuing decade-long struggle between conservative and bourgeois Centrists on the one hand

and Social Democrats and Communists on the other.[9] Compared with these socio-political lines of conflict, which have by now been overcome, but at the time cut very deep, the geographical division which is at present apparent between urban agglomeration centres in the south and south-west and a 'marginalized' Finland in the north and northeast appears politically far less dramatic than regional planning studies would suggest.[10]

The above-mentioned domestic lines of conflict were to a varying degree tied up with the fragile international status of Finland *vis-à-vis* both Tsarist Russia (or the Soviet Union) and the Western powers (especially Germany, Britain and Sweden). As for her relations with the West and Russia, it is only in the past fifteen years that Finland has found a *modus vivendi* more or less respected by all the parties concerned. Within the framework of certain self-imposed foreign policy limitations, Finland is autonomous. With regard to her internal structure, she remains part of the Western capitalist world, while taking into account the security interests of the Soviet Union (the 'Paasikivi-Kekkonen line').[11]

The Finnish Development Path

The development of Finland, like that of the remaining Scandinavian countries, can be understood only in the light of her world market links. Furs, tar and timber were the staple goods tying Finland to the dynamic centres of the world market within the framework of the mercantilistically structured Baltic trade. Until the end of the seventeenth century it was the export of furs; in the seventeenth and eighteenth centuries it was mainly tar, which was traded for salt and tobacco; later it was timber, which was first cut by hand and then in sawmills located on rivers in the interior.[12] Exports based on wood did not, nevertheless, achieve a breakthrough until the 1860s to 1880s. A number of world economic and domestic political factors contributed to this breakthrough. Owing to technological innovation in shipping, the freight rates for bulk goods fell during this period (the 'transport revolution'). Britain's final transition to free trade improved the export opportunities of the Scandinavian countries, which were able to satisfy part of the growing British demand for food and raw materials. In Finland mercantilistic restrictions were lifted (e.g. in 1867 the ban on steam-powered saws). The elimination of the guild system (1868) and the introduction of freedom of trade (1879) laid the institutional foundations for a local, though still largely craft-orientated, industry. 'Modern' factories, however, were also founded: for example, in 1885 the first cellulose factory; in 1895, the first rubber factory for the production of galoshes; in 1912, the first veneer factory; and shortly before 1913, the first cement factory. The upswing in timber exports stimulated rafting, created a demand for steam tugs, led to the construction of canals and spawned as early as the final decades of the last century wood-processing activities on the river estuaries, where an export-orientated sawmill industry, using an ever-increasing amount of steam-power, had found a favourable location.

In 1870, 52 per cent of all exports went to Russia, but at the start of the present century the export statistics of the Grand Duchy reveal a shift towards Western countries. This shift was caused on the one hand by the growing interest of Western countries in Finnish wood-based goods, and on the other by the tariff revision in Tsarist Russia (protectionism), which made it more difficult for Finland to sell simple processed goods from her food, textile and metal industries to that country. When the Russian market contracted or when it was temporarily lost, as happened after 1917, the goods formerly sold there could not be diverted to Western markets, where they were not competitive. The preponderance of wood products in Finland's export commodities' basket, which was already excessive at the turn of the century, was bound to become even more marked as a result of increasing orientation towards the West. The small labour-intensive local consumer goods industry began to depend almost exclusively on the domestic market, where purchasing power derived for a long time mainly from export income. In the present century the Finnish economy was based for decades on a functional mechanism typical of peripheries: concentration on export-orientated exploitation of local resources (in this case wood); incipient import substitution industrialization; importation of foreign machinery for the export sector (sawmill equipment, i.e. whatever was not produced locally) and of locally unavailable raw materials and semi-finished products for the import substitution industry; and dependence of the internal economic development dynamics on the cyclical movements of the world economy.[13]

The 1937 statistics on Finnish industry provide a first hint as to why the country did not become a periphery after all. Wood-processing industries accounted for 41 per cent of net industrial production at the time, but the share of the woodworking industry as such had fallen to only 18 per cent, with the paper industry being responsible for 24 per cent of total net production. Thus, at an early stage, the Finns knew not only how to fell, raft and process trees into sawn timber, but how to aim at *higher levels of processing*—for example, at the initially mechanical, later chemical, production of cellulose and wood-fibre, of paper-pulp, cardboard and paper, and of even more highly processed goods based on these products.[14] In the mid-1930s, 43 per cent of exports were products of wood-based industries, 40 per cent products of the paper industry. The roughly 7 per cent export share of industries based on the domestic market seems, by contrast, extremely low (textile industry, 1.5 per cent; leather industry, 0.3 per cent; metal goods industry, 2.8 per cent; stoneworking industry, 1.4 per cent; remaining domestic market industries, 1.2 per cent). The share of agricultural commodities in exports certainly rose again to about 10 per cent from the middle of the 1930s, but this scarcely counteracted the preponderance of wood products in exports and the pre-eminence of wood-based industrialization.

There are two factors which have decisively shaped the long-term development dynamics of Finland. First, the distribution of the essential natural resources of the country—forests and agricultural land; and second, the further industrialization after the Second World War, which became necessary for the settlement of reparations.

Although detailed data are lacking, there can be no doubt that the distribution of forest ownership in Finland did not show any gross inequalities but, rather, moderate disparities. In the case of export-led growth, the difference between the two is crucial: *in an export economy whose social structure is characterized by high property concentration, export earnings are translated into an income concentration that is macro-economically fatal, as it impedes a broad-based opening up of the domestic market.* In the Finnish case a 'counter-factual' development scenario could easily be imagined. In identical world economic conditions, but in the case of highly concentrated forest ownership (a kind of 'forest latifundism'), the income from the timber exports would have gone to a small forest-owning oligarchy, which would most probably have allied itself—like the agrarian oligarchies in Latin America—with a numerically small, but politically influential, comprador bourgeoisie. Despite a small population (in 1890, 2.4 million; 1938, 3.7 million; 1975, 4.7 million) and a backward agriculture, which, according to traditional investment criteria, seemed—but only *seemed*—to offer little scope for development, there would have been few incentives for investing, at an early stage, in the establishment of a local import substitution industry. Any economist would have maintained that productive investment in the manufacturing and equipment industries was bound to founder on the 'narrowness of the domestic market'. The sophisticated consumer demand of the small but wealthy upper class could have been easily satisfied through imports. Against this kind of socio-structural background Finland would have turned into a typical peripheral capitalist society!

The fact that the inherited distribution structure was unequal, but that this inequality was limited, has helped Finland to avoid such peripheralization. Finnish economic historians describe how the proceeds from timber exports were translated into a *gradual rise in rural incomes* which, together with step-by-step agricultural modernization, provided the long-term foundations for *broad-based* import substitution industrialization.[15] That the resulting industry was not internationally competitive has by no means taken away from its success.

The second important factor in Finnish development was the diversification of industrial production into metal-working and engineering industries, which began slowly at the end of the 1930s and continued immediately after the Second World War.

The Finnish metal-working industry emerged after the Second World War out of the necessity of the country's having to pay war reparations to the tune of $300 million to the Soviet Union, more than 70 per cent of which had to be rendered in the form of goods. These comprised ships, railway wagons, machinery, cables and other goods from sectors of production which in Finland, at the time, either did not exist at all or existed in only rudimentary form. 'The Finns quickly conjured up the industries needed for fulfilling their obligations. The reparations were settled on time by 1952.'[16] In 1975 the share of the metal-working industry in *industrial* net product amounted to 25 per cent; by 1977 the share of the metal-working industry in the export of manufactures had increased to 27 per cent, while the share of the wood-processing industry had fallen to roughly 40 per cent. In the late 1970s, 37 per cent of the industrial work-force was employed in the metal-working industry (including the basic materials industry)—data which indicate a marked maturing process.

Before the Second World War Finland had already produced machines for wood-processing and paper-making. The development of additional production capacity, required for reparation purposes, supplied the impulse for the extension of the product range and for the introduction of new technology. In the manufacture of cranes and lifts, for example, Finland is today a leading producer in Europe. The electrical engineering industry produces power generators, transformers, high-voltage cable and powerful electric motors which are used in the production of transport equipment, such as locomotives and ice-breakers. Like other small countries, Finland is orientated towards a *high degree of specialization in technological niches*. Finnish ice-breakers are said to have no competition at the moment. Finnish shipbuilding has, moreover, secured a large share of the market in the construction of luxury liners, ferries, container ships and ships for timber transport. The country is a competitive producer of oil-rigs. The development of new technology facilitated the construction of specialized ships, such as ships for the transport of liquefied gas. An industry for the production of basic materials has also been established. Half of the iron can be drawn from local deposits. In addition, nickel, copper, zinc, chromium, cobalt and vanadium are produced. In early 1972 Finland started to develop a petro-chemical industry.

At the same time as the Finnish metal-working industry became an important part of the national economy, agricultural modernization advanced. The share of agriculture and forestry in the Finnish GDP has by now fallen to scarcely 10 per cent. The share of employment in this sector fell from 50 per cent at the end of the Second World War to 13 per cent in 1978. Today agricultural production centres on milk and meat products: 45 per cent of the agricultural net product derives from milk products, 30 per cent from meat production, 10 per cent from cereals and 5 per cent from eggs. Among the main agricultural exports are butter, cheese and dried milk, as well as certain special products like crispbread.

Agricultural modernization has entailed a reduction in the number of smallholdings (6–25 acres), but the family-operated farm with 25 acres of arable land and 85 acres of forest still predominates. Its output has risen, while the numbers employed in agriculture have fallen. Thus, in the post-war period, Finland achieved the final breakthrough to an economic structure differing only to a small degree from the economic structure of other OECD societies which had industrialized decades earlier than Finland.

Is Finnish Development Exceptional?

Colin Clark's data on average real per capita income between 1925 and 1934 show that the figures for the remaining Scandinavian countries—Denmark, Sweden and Norway—stood at 50 to 65 per cent of the British level. According to the statistics contained in the *World Development Report 1979*, the per capita income of Denmark is 82 per cent, that of Norway 100 per cent, and that of Sweden 109 per cent above the British one. All three countries have edged closer to the former leading economies (the United States and Canada) or have overtaken them. In the light of these data Finland's development seems by no means exceptional; it is representative of the long-term development dynamics which can be observed all over Scandinavia.

Development in Finland has been portrayed in some detail because around the turn of the century she was the most backward country in Scandinavia. While in 1910 80 per cent of her economically active population was still employed in the primary sector, the corresponding percentage for the 'agrarian country' Denmark was only 36 per cent. Sweden's secondary sector employed 32 per cent of the labour force in 1910—a figure not attained by Finland until sixty years later, just before 1970! Despite such contrasting starting conditions, the profiles of the production structure in all four Scandinavian countries have greatly converged over the past decades and have by now become almost identical, at least with regard to economic aggregates. This development is all the more remarkable because the development paths of all four Scandinavian countries had initially only one thing in common: dynamic growth based on exports. For the individual Scandinavian countries differ greatly in their resource endowment. Hence the question which we have attempted to answer in the Finnish case must also be applied to Norway, Denmark and Sweden: Why did these countries not become peripheries despite the export-led growth?

The Norwegian development path

For 400 years Norway was under Danish colonial rule, from 1815 until 1905 she was subordinated to Sweden.[17] This past has contributed to the emergence of a tendentially dualistic social structure. The peasantry, which was widely dispersed and tied to subsistence agriculture, was facing an urban population whose prosperity depended on foreign trade. The latter had been controlled for centuries by foreigners: first, by the Hanseatic League; then, after 1560, by Danes, Dutch, Scots and Germans. In terms of transport links the country was scarcely developed. In 1860, 90 per cent of its exports consisted of timber, fish and iron products. If one includes in the export earnings the income from Norwegian merchant shipping, statistics show that between 1860 and 1914 at least 40 per cent of the export income was usually earned by the Norwegian merchant fleet operating on a world-wide scale! In terms of tonnage Norway was, after the United States and Britain, the third largest shipping nation, and this internationally orientated service sector supplied the Norwegian economy with one of its most important growth engines.

Norway's export structure suffered from the disadvantage that the production of the major export commodities caused few linkage effects in the rest of the economy. Merchant shipping, too, produced few repercussions in the domestic economy. In the field of wood-processing Norway was at an early stage exposed to competitive pressure from Sweden, Finland and Russia. In the manufacture of iron products competition from the expanding Swedish iron industry could be felt. By Swedish and Danish standards, agricultural modernization in Norway at the turn of the century was negligible. At that time no interconnection between an emerging industry and an agriculture in the process of modernization could yet be observed. This vital basis for a dynamic development impulse which would affect the whole economy was still lacking.

By using abundantly available hydraulic power for the generation of electricity Norwegian industry has, however, expanded massively since the turn of the century. Hydroelectricity supplied the basis for new industries depending on cheap energy, primarily electro-chemical plants (for the production of fertilizers) and electro-metallurgical industries (for the production of aluminium and copper). Although autochthonous Norwegian inventions played a part in the development of hydroelectric power stations and electro-mechanical production technology, these new industries were initially but exclaves of the larger European industrial societies. Foreign companies invested massively in the acquisition of cataracts and hydroelectric power stations as well as in the newer industries, with the result that the Norwegian parliament found itself compelled to pass, between 1905 and 1910, restrictive investment laws, mainly with regard to the further construction of hydroelectric power stations by foreign capital. Since the technology employed in the new industries was capital-intensive and imported from abroad, the repercussions on other industries remained at first limited. Only gradually did certain multiplier effects emerge, promoting the development of the metal-working and engineering industries. Between 1900 and 1915 traditional industries achieved increasing growth rates, notably the woodworking and textile industries. The fish-processing industry began to modernize; the—by international standards, belated—transition of the Norwegian merchant fleet from sailing-ships to steamships accelerated.

In spite of these developments at the start of this century, the Norwegian economy was by no means a coherent 'national economy'. That the structural defects existing at the time could be overcome in the following decades, is—seen in the long term—due to the belated modernization of agriculture, the emigration of a considerable part of the labour force and the further diversification of the secondary and tertiary sectors. In 1977 agriculture accounted for 6 per cent, industry for 35 per cent and services for 59 per cent of the GDP. Of the economically active population, 8 per cent were employed in agriculture, 37 per cent in the secondary sector and 55 per cent in the service sector. The diversification of the Norwegian economy that has by now been achieved also manifests itself in the present export structure. In 1977 machinery and equipment exports amounted to just over 30 per cent and exports of finished goods to 50 per cent of total exports. The share of energy exports has increased to 19 per cent in the past decade. When considering this figure one should, however, take into account the substantial rise in oil prices since 1973/4. Minerals and metals comprised 18 per cent, while the share of food exports remained stable at around 10 per cent in the last twelve years or so.

At 30 per cent, Norway's export/GDP ratio is today the highest in Scandinavia. Despite her continuing high export dependency, Norway has succeeded in overcoming the dualistic social structure which formerly characterized the country.

The Danish development path

Denmark, too, has followed a typically 'Scandinavian' development path characterized by pronounced export-orientation and gradual diversification of the production structure.[18] In the eyes of many foreigners Denmark is still an 'agrarian country' even today, but over the past few decades she has, of all Scandinavian countries, constantly had the lowest proportion of economically active population employed in the primary sector. While in 1910 this proportion was still more than 80 per cent in Finland, 49 per cent in Sweden and 39 per cent in Norway, it amounted to no more than 36 per cent in Denmark. In 1977 it had fallen to 8 per cent. In the same year 37 per cent of the labour force was employed in the secondary and 55 per cent in the tertiary sector. In 1976 the GDP showed the following composition: 7 per cent agriculture, 36 per cent industry, 57 per cent services. The profile of the Danish economy consequently matches that of highly industrialized societies.

The starting-point of Danish development in the second half of the nineteenth century differs from that of the two previously examined Scandinavian countries, Finland and Norway, despite a comparable role of the export sector as a growth engine for the whole economy.

Denmark's image as an agrarian economy is, of course, not unfounded, for Danish development originated primarily in the modernization of agriculture. Apart from the provision of international services (trade, shipping) Denmark had—when faced with her one-sided resource endowment, no alternative but to develop her agriculture. The country has no mineral deposits, but 75 per cent of its total area is potential farmland. If Danish development were to follow an export-orientated pattern, agriculture had to supply the foundation, at least during the initial stage. It did indeed play a leading role comparable to Finnish wood-processing and Norwegian shipping.

Until the European agricultural crisis of the 1870s Danish exports consisted mainly of grain. Cheap grain from overseas led to a reduction in Danish competitiveness. Denmark did not respond with agricultural protectionism. On the contrary, Danish farmers switched to animal feed production, animal husbandry and the processing of animal products—that is, the production of dairy and meat products.[19] An expanding cooperative sector supplied the institutional basis for the growing efficiency of Danish agriculture. Agricultural modernization and the transition to an agricultural *processing economy* (food processing) resulted in a parallel *industrialization of agriculture*.

Judging from the export figures, the conversion of Danish agriculture from cereal to meat production and dairy farming was highly successful. Processed agricultural products accounted for slightly less than 90 per cent of the total exports in 1910; they consisted mainly of meat, butter, eggs and cheese, with butter taking the largest share.

Denmark's early industrial development is intimately connected with agricultural modernization. Characteristic is the wide geographical spread of industrial plants despite the fact that in 1914 almost 50 per cent of the industrial work force was concentrated in Copenhagen. Initially the secondary sector produced mainly for the domestic market—a reflection of its low international competitiveness because of the initial preponderance of craft-orientated production and the only gradual emergence of large-scale industry. Statistics on the composition of the GDP in 1915 highlight above all the following sectors of production: sugar and margarine factories, breweries, tobacco-processing and weaving, clothing industry and wood-processing, the graphical industry, ceramics and glass industry, iron smelting, and the engineering and capital goods industries (mainly shipbuilding). Danish industry was built around import substitution. The share of its products in total exports remained for a long time limited, while on the other hand it was efficient enough to supply from local production around 70 per cent of the manufactures consumed in Denmark in 1914. Its dynamic impulse derived mainly from the domestic demand for agricultural equipment and simple consumer goods. Such domestic demand was stimulated by export receipts, as family-operated farms of a reasonable size predominated in Danish agriculture and export receipts were as a result quite widely spread.

The statistics on Danish economic development point to four periods during which the industrial growth rate greatly surpassed that of the whole economy. The first two periods, 1890–7 and 1905–13, were part of the stage of early agriculture-based industrialization already outlined. The third period, 1932–9, must be seen as a response to the world economic crisis and the growing protectionism among Denmark's important trading partners. During the fourth period, 1956–67, the GDP share of the primary sector fell within ten years from 18.8 per cent to 9.4 per cent, while the share of the secondary sector increased from 46.0 per cent to 50.5 per cent. The later two periods mentioned have witnessed a considerable structural diversification of industrial production, which also manifests itself today in the composition of exports. In 1977, 54 per cent of exports were finished goods, half of these machinery and equipment. The share of agricultural products in total exports continues to be relatively high (in 1977, 34 per cent), but the whole export structure no longer bears any comparison to that of the early phase of industrialization.

The statistics on Danish economic development throw into relief the early preponderance of the tertiary sector. In 1900 it accounted for slightly less than 44 per cent of the GDP. Between 1930 and 1976 its share climbed—first with fluctuations and then steadily—to 57 per cent. The early data on the size of the tertiary sector reflect the considerable commercialization of agriculture, the growing intermeshing of agriculture and industry, and the spatial interlacement of urban and rural areas as well as the great importance of international services.

Denmark's development thus began with *agricultural modernization* linked to an *agriculture-based industrialization*. Despite a considerable export bias and despite Denmark's trade being excessively concentrated on Britain, the *domestic economic development potential* was progressively exploited from the very beginning. In Denmark, the disruption of the regular external economic links during the world-wide economic crisis at the end of the 1920s and beginning of the 1930s resulted in a further industrialization impulse which led to the *diversification* and *intensification* of productive capital. The post-war economic boom accelerated this process and resulted, by the end of the 1960s, in a structural profile which is metropolitan in every respect.

The Swedish development path

At least with regard to its starting-point, Swedish development since the second half of the nineteenth century stands midway between that of Denmark, on the one hand, and that of Norway and Finland, on the

other.[20] While the Danish economy was built on agricultural modernization and agriculture-based industrialization, and while in Norway
and Finland forestry, mining and international services became the
growth engines rather than the agricultural sectors, which were structurally extremely weak, Swedish development is characterized by a combination in one and the same country of all the activities mentioned.
Swedish industrialization, which experienced a considerable upturn in
the second half of the nineteenth century, was preceded in some parts
of the country, notably the south, by a remarkable *agricultural modernization*. During the first half of the nineteenth century Sweden was a net
importer of grain; in the second half food exports and imports balanced. For a long time Sweden exported mainly oats to Britain; a part
of agriculture then switched to the production of meat and dairy
products. As in Finland and Denmark, butter exports increased considerably at the end of the century.

   Swedish industrial development between 1870 and the start of the
First World War is mirrored in the distribution of industrial labour.
Around 1870 the iron mines, together with the iron and steel industry,
employed slightly less than a quarter of the industrial labour force, the
wood-processing industry slightly less than one-fifth, and engineering
already a little over one-tenth. In the above-mentioned period the
share of labour employed in the wood-processing industry grew for a
time, only to fall back to slightly less than one-fifth in 1908. The share
of labour employed in ore mines and in the iron and steel industry
declined to 14 per cent, while the most remarkable development was
the increase in engineering employment to 19 per cent. A similarly
remarkable expansion occurred in the paper and paper-pulp industry,
whose share in industrial employment doubled from 4 per cent to 8.4
per cent. The same applies to the stoneworking industry, in which an
increase from 6 per cent to 13.4 per cent took place.

   During the above-mentioned period Swedish industrialization was
thus characterized not only by a considerable quantitative expansion of
industrial activity. More important in the long run was the speedy
growth of *capital intensification* in the above-mentioned areas, which
resulted in *higher processing levels*, *greater efficiency* and the building up of
new dynamic sectors of industry (engineering). Even before the Second
World War this structural change manifested itself in the export
statistics: 26 per cent of exports consisted of wood products, while
exports of paper and paper-pulp already accounted for just under 18
per cent. Exports of pig iron, which were resumed at the turn of the
century, reached 8 per cent, but iron and steel products more than 9
per cent. Grain exports had practically ceased, while butter exports

increased to 6 per cent. Engineering exports amounted to just under 3 per cent in 1880; afterwards they gradually increased, reaching 10.5 per cent in 1911–13. From the statistics on the sectoral distribution of the economically active population in the Scandinavian countries in 1910 Sweden emerges—notably in comparison with Denmark and Norway—with a relatively high share of just below 50 per cent still tied to agriculture. Compared with Denmark and Norway the proportion of the labour force employed in the tertiary sector was surprisingly small, namely 19 per cent (in contrast with 36 per cent in Denmark and Norway), while the share of secondary sector employment was higher than in both the above-mentioned countries. These figures reflect Sweden's marked *early export orientation* with regard to *industrial exports* and only a *subsequent opening up of the domestic market*. Crucial to Swedish development was the *early international competitiveness of the capital goods sector*, in which in the final decades of the last century some remarkable inventions were made (milk centrifuge, turbines, electrical machinery, gasometer, ball-bearings, safety matches, etc.). In his early comparative study on industrialization processes, Walter Hoffmann has emphasized the important position of the capital goods sector within the Swedish industrial structure.[21] The massive railway construction in the 1870s and the development of hydroelectric energy as an input for the electro-metallurgical and electro-chemical industries strengthened the solid position of engineering in Sweden and accentuated the trend towards import substitution, notably in the capital goods sector.

In Sweden the decline in the agricultural population was slower than in Denmark and Norway, but considerably faster than in Finland. As late as 1950, 20 per cent of the economically active population was employed in agriculture and forestry; in 1977 this figure was just 5 per cent. In the same year 37 per cent of the labour force was employed in the secondary and 58 per cent in the tertiary sector. In 1977 agriculture contributed 4 per cent, industry 33 per cent and services 63 per cent of the GDP. These data add up to the well-known structural profile of metropolitan economies (OECD).

Explanation of the Scandinavian Development Path

The preceding exposition was intended as a description of the *secular development trend* of the Scandinavian countries. A more detailed study would have to take into account a number of important factors not included here—for example, population growth, the impact of both world wars and of the world economic crisis, the considerable growth of the public sector, the effect of foreign economic policy measures, the long-term consequences of the welfare state for international competitiveness, the growing internationalization of industry by way of foreign investment and technology transfer (notably in the Swedish case), and so on. The connection between political development (the role of labour parties and social democracy, alliances with agrarian parties) and economic development would also have to be highlighted. Failure explicitly to discuss such factors does not mean they are underestimated. Some will be discussed in detail in the following chapter in the context of these or other examples. In this section, however, the question will be examined as to how the above-outlined economic development of the four Scandinavian countries can be understood in the light of development theory.

In the preceding case-studies the importance of the *export sector* for Danish, Norwegian, Swedish and Finnish development was emphasized. Retrospectively it makes little sense to contemplate which course Scandinavian development would have taken without such exogenous growth impulses mediated through exports. The export activities did, in fact, provide the dynamic growth impulse—often at a time when sufficient local growth impulses were still lacking in the internal market. But this point of departure is by no means typically Scandinavian. It applied, after all, to all the smaller countries which at that time tried to ride on the expansion of large national economies by means of the *export-orientated* production of foodstuffs and agricultural and mineral raw materials. Their growth dynamics are correctly characterized as *exogenously determined* and *dependent*. All the countries in question— Denmark and Ireland, Finland and Portugal, Sweden and Spain, Norway and Romania, among others—tried to profit from such an association with the forerunners of industrial development. The important question in terms of development theory is why some have succeeded in developing—in Britain's footsteps—from suppliers of foodstuffs and raw materials into *mature* capitalist *national* economies, while others degenerated into peripheries of the capitalist world economy despite high export growth rates. In this context the distinction between European and non-European countries is by no means decisive, as is proven by the example of Ireland and the cases of export-orientated southern, south-eastern and eastern Europe. In the temperate zone of the southern continents, too, development experiences differed widely, as is shown by Australia and New Zealand, on the one hand, and South Africa, Argentina, Uruguay and Chile, on the other. The following considerations, however, will focus on the Scandinavian countries.[22]

The reasons for the *successful development* of Scandinavia are certainly varied, and their chronological sequence and correct weighting in the context of the typical Scandinavian development scenario remain—as is only to be expected—a moot point among scientific experts.[23] This applies above all when the analysis focuses on short periods. If, however, one tries to understand Scandinavian development since the second half of the nineteenth century and to explain why, despite differing starting conditions, all the Scandinavian countries have acquired a *more or less identical structural profile* in the 1960s and 1970s, a few macro-theoretical considerations focused on long-term development processes could be helpful. These are not invalidated by the fact that they require differentiation and specification for each individual case and particular period.

An important reason why the Scandinavian countries in contrast with most European and non-European developing countries have not turned into peripheries—even though export-orientated growth started on an *enclave-like* pattern—lies in their relatively early switch from the production of unprocessed staple goods such as grain, wood, fish, iron ore, to the *first stages of processing*, which finally resulted in their no longer exporting mainly unprocessed goods but semi-finished and finished manufactures. The conversion of Danish (and also Swedish and Finnish) agriculture to the production of meat and dairy products is equally typical of this process, as is the progression of the Finnish (and also Swedish) wood-based industry from the export of uncut timber to the export of sawn timber, then to the export of paper and paper-pulp, and in recent times to the export of furniture and household products, glass products, ceramics and jewellery of typical Scandinavian design—that is, to products for an up-market foreign demand. In the wake of the transition from raw material exports to exports of semi-finished and finished manufactures, the production of the respective goods lost its enclave character within the domestic economy. While in other parts of the world, monocultures and mining enclaves emerged, the increase in local wealth resulted in Scandinavia in Hirschmanite *linkages*.[24] In this way the export-orientated sectors could be integrated into a gradually evolving *national* economy. Yet the linkage potential of the typical Scandinavian staple goods was, with the exception of mining products, by no means particularly favourable. As is well known, the potential forward and backward linkages of the food-processing industry are much more limited than those of the textile industry; iron-processing has a greater impact on upstream and downstream industrial activities than wood-processing.

Sweden thus had special advantages over the other Scandinavian countries. Probably crucial for Scandinavian development as a whole, however, was the fact *that the production of initially unprocessed staple goods reached a really significant scale in the relatively small domestic economies*. In the specific socio-structural conditions of Scandinavia the dynamic impulse emanating from this kind of production was strong enough to trigger off *relatively broad-based* growth. This observation applies to Denmark, whose institutional and technical agricultural modernization coincided with industrial development. In the long run it also applies to Sweden and Finland. Initially it applied least of all to Norway, which was characterized, as is emphasized above, by a relatively dualistic social structure.

Apart from the structural repercussions (linkages) outlined above, the transition to processing had another positive effect: generally favourable, even if cyclically fluctuating, external terms of trade. The Scandinavian countries were able to import raw materials and cheap goods for mass consumption and profitably to export processed goods, semi-finished goods and raw materials required by Britain and, at a later stage, by the other metropolitan countries for their growing economies. In this way they avoided what is frequently postulated by traditional development theory but is by no means continuously operative, namely deterioration in the terms of trade between producers of agricultural and mineral raw materials, on the one hand, and producers of finished consumer goods and capital goods, on the other. The challenge from more highly developed and productive countries, which were able to produce some goods more cheaply than Scandinavia itself, did not result in regression but in *innovative responses* triggering off new growth and development impulses and safeguarding international competitiveness. The conversion of agriculture, as described earlier, is an important but by no means exceptional example of such a *world market-orientated strategy for survival*. If implemented successfully, this becomes at an early stage a kind of strategy for wealth creation, based not on the colonial exploitation of other societies (foodstuffs and raw materials were usually imported from other successfully developing countries like the United States and Canada) but on *domestic productivity gains*.

The backward and forward linkages outlined above were, however, not limited just to the export-orientated sector of production. Directly and indirectly, export receipts were translated into an *import substitution industrialization* based on a growing demand for equipment and consumer goods. This *export receipts effect* is crucial for an understanding of Scandinavian development. It resulted from the fact that, in contrast with typical exclave economies and monocultures, the distribution of natural resources and productive capital was only moderately uneven, and certainly much more uniform than in the case of typical plantation economies or economic structures characterized by the coexistence of latifundia and minifundia. Where ownership of land, fishing rights, forests and mineral deposits is highly concentrated, a *broad-based import substitution industrialization* cannot get off the ground.[25]

The Scandinavian development scenario therefore presupposed foreign demand, as a result of which domestic and foreign investment was guided into the export sectors in search of profits. But this is just one aspect of this development path. The other lies in the linkage effects that extended beyond the export sector and created a local industry responding to local needs. In this way Scandinavia avoided what became a chronic structural problem in the Third World in conditions of colonial rule: the emergence of export economies with crippled domestic markets.

Such a development scenario has—as can be imagined—specific *socio-structural* and *institutional* prerequisites. Among them are:

(*a*) an agrarian structure that did not impede *agricultural moderniz-ation* (few large estates, prevalence of medium-sized farms open to innovation, eradication of village penury, openness of landowners and tenants towards institutional reforms and technical innovation);[26]

(*b*) a *moderate* rather than gross *inequality* in the distribution of important resources;[27]

(*c*) an income distribution, which facilitated macro-economically relevant *saving* directed towards productive investment, and fuelled a sufficiently large demand for additional as well as new equipment and consumer goods as to make an impact on the domestic economy;

(*d*) a *high* average *level of education* of the population (high literacy level, growing enrolment in institutions of advanced education such as vocational training schools, secondary schools, technical colleges, tech-nical universities and polytechnics);[28]

(*e*) *private enterprise prepared to invest*, facing the risks of capitalist competition and backed by an expanding banking system;[29]

(*f*) *a peasantry politically organized* (cooperatives, agrarian parties) and an industrial working class organized in trade unions and *labour parties* as a counterweight to industrial and state bureaucracies;[30]

(*g*) the spread of *technical innovation* in all sectors as a basis for sectoral and macro-economic productivity gains as well as inter-national competitiveness;[31]

(*h*) a *stable political framework*, resulting from an increasing democra-tization of political institutions and from the growing political power of new social movements; and

(*i*) the building up of an infrastructure as a basis for and a consequence of intra- and inter-sectoral differentiation, especially the inter-meshing of agriculture and industry and the emergence of urban agglomerations.

Not all these factors were simultaneously present in each individual Scandinavian country; but where they were initially lacking or of little weight, they gained in importance during the first decades of development. In Norway agricultural modernization started later than in Denmark. The building up of infrastructure in Finland did not take place until Denmark and Sweden had already completed the infra-structural development of their economies. A stream of Swedish inventions emerged around the turn of the century, at a time when in Finland the first hesitant steps were taken towards the establishment of an engineering sector, and so on.

Which traditional development theories are able to explain, at least partially, the long-term development process of the Scandinavian countries? Hirschman's linkage theory has already been referred to above. By means of it, the macro-economic development *potential* of export-orientated production can be explained. However, in order to interpret the transition from export growth to domestic economic expansion, a complementary sociological approach is required, as is evidenced by the preceding enumeration of *socio-structural factors*. And even then the question would still remain unanswered as to why Scandinavia has attained its present high development level. For an answer, Lewis's theory on the development dynamics of dualistic economies with unlimited labour supplies is useful.[32] As postulated in Lewis's general and abstract model, two economic sectors existed in the Scandinavian countries: the export-orientated and the subsistence sector. For decades the supply of labour exceeded demand. Wage increases could therefore be limited, especially as in the first stage the demand came from abroad. Investment in the export sector, and later in the import substitution industry, consequently produced a relatively high return. The high propensity to invest was translated into growing employment in the secondary and tertiary sectors. Considerable emi-gration resulted in a thinning out of the labour reserves.[33] The growing scarcity of labour induced by growth and emigration increased its political weight and with it the income opportunities of wage-earners. The resulting cost pressure led to labour-saving investment, which raised the average productivity level of the Scandinavian economies.[34] In Scandinavia the drying up of the *unlimited supply of labour* ushered in the interplay between increasing real incomes and enforced productiv-ity gains—an interplay that presupposed an institutionalized settle-ment of conflicts between capital and labour. The emergence of such a conflict resolution mechanism was hastened by the dominant political influence of the Scandinavian social democratic parties. The resulting social achievements are today accepted by all the influential political groupings, even if in times of world economic recession certain adjustments seem inevitable.[35]

Hirschman's theory predicts that in certain specific conditions export growth will produce domestic economic linkage effects. Lewis's theory predicts the transfer of large numbers of people from low productivity to high productivity jobs. In the socio-structural conditions of Scandinavia both processes have opened up a *development potential*, whose size and content could *not* have been predicted one hundred years ago by a static analysis of the existing factor endowment and a concomitant assessment of comparative advantages. Scandinavian development documents the fundamental difference between the optimum allocation of a given factor endowment, calculated in the short term, and the realization of a *dynamic development potential* which in parts has yet to come into being.[36] This also constitutes probably the main difference between the Scandinavian development path and typical peripheral-capitalist development.

Development resulting in the peripheralization of the Scandinavian societies was not impossible from the outset, though the socio-structural factors outlined above provided at an early stage effective counterweights. When describing the Finnish development path, we referred to a hypothetical *counter-factual alternative scenario*. We assumed that highly concentrated ownership in Finnish forestry would have given rise to a typical *exclave* economy. Such alternative development scenarios can also be conceived with regard to the other Scandinavian countries. If a manorial agrarian structure, atypical of the rest of Scandinavia, had not been eliminated in Denmark during and after the second half of the eighteenth century, an eastern European development path would have become probable in Denmark.[37] In the case of Sweden, some sort of combination between the Balkans and Romania—that is, a mineral-based enclave economy and latifundism—is conceivable if an agriculture *and* industry based on solid medium-sized units had not prevented such an unfortunate development. If one looks at the situation in Norway at the turn of the century, certain development trends in the Balkan economies of the nineteenth and early twentieth centuries come to mind: economic enclaves based on mining and hydroelectric power and developed by foreign capital; an infrastructure geared to these enclaves and financed by foreign capital; a meagre agriculture which remained meagre; international services (passenger and freight shipping) without impact on the domestic economy (as, for example, in the case of Greece), and so on.[38] It is no accident that in the first decade of this century laws for the protection of local resources were passed in Norway which bear considerable similarity to the 'Charter on the Rights and Duties of States' demanded by the Third World in 1974/5 and later, and finally passed by the United Nations.

Sovereign Norway could implement such restrictive laws. Many so-called exclave economies were not sovereign, but forcibly integrated into colonial empires. Without being forced into it, many sovereign societies hoped to draw considerable benefits from their integration into the world market on the basis of a division of labour and their comparative advantage. In both cases the basis for political, economic and cultural self-determination was undermined. Being so different from Scandinavian development, the very experience of the dependent Caribbean, of politically emancipated but economically dependent Latin America, of colonial Africa and Asia, reveals that *gaining a separate political, economic and cultural identity* is a decisive factor in the local processing of growth impulses emanating from the world market.[39]

Concluding Remarks

In the current debate on development policy it is, in particular, the more recent World Bank studies that have led to the rediscovery of the development-promoting role of a moderate degree of inequality at the start of forced growth.[40] The latest motto of development policy is therefore 'growth with equity'; meaning that in conditions of moderately unequal distribution of resources and incomes, forced growth does not necessarily have to result in the further absolute impoverishment of the lower social classes. Even in present conditions the development implications of forced growth processes depend obviously on the *socio-structural conditions* prevalent *at the onset* of economic growth. But even in conditions of only moderate inequality there is no automatic connection between growth and the lack or elimination of absolute poverty. On the contrary, what is required—especially in conditions of private capitalism—is considerable political control over domestic and external economic processes, in order to prevent export growth from making society more oligarchic and producing a sort of rentier capitalism.[41] If historical proof of these recent insights produced by the international development debate were needed, it would be quite appropriate to point to the Scandinavian development path. It represents an instance of delayed development despite integration into a world market characterized by productivity and competence differentials. The successful development of Scandinavia was based on a secular increase in the overall productivity of its economies. The Scandinavian social structure has helped to prevent the emergence of structural heterogeneity. In the same world market conditions, but different local circumstances, Scandinavia could have became a kind of south-eastern Europe, a part of the Third World.[42]

3 Alternative Development Paths of Export Economies

What circumstances led to export economies, not or no longer colonies, becoming peripheries within the capitalist world economy during the nineteenth and early twentieth centuries? And in what conditions did they develop autocentrically?

This question will be tackled in the present chapter by means of a comparative analysis of relevant cases. We shall exclude those cases where the political autonomy of local élites was eliminated as a result of colonial and imperialist penetration and where, consequently, there was no scope for independent decision-making in the domestic and external economic spheres. We shall look for cases where we can assume at least relative political autonomy.[1] We shall label those countries *export economies*, whose growth began initially with the export-orientated production of agricultural and mineral staple goods (grain, cotton, timber, minerals, etc.).[2]

The Contrasting Development Paths of Two Small Agricultural Exporters: Denmark and Uruguay

For the purpose of illustration, in the following pages we shall discuss the fundamental questions in greater detail against the backdrop of two cases with more or less comparable starting conditions but sharply differing long-term development dynamics: Denmark and Uruguay. This choice is at the same time accidental and deliberate. In place of the two cases mentioned we could have chosen other examples, such as Denmark and Ireland, the Netherlands and Portugal, Norway and Greece, Sweden and Spain, Finland and Romania (in the European area alone). The two cases mentioned lend themselves to a comparative analysis for the following reasons: both countries are relatively small in area and population. Around the turn of the century Denmark had a population of 2 million; in 1977 it was 5.1 million. At the turn of the century Uruguay had slightly over 1 million inhabitants; by 1977 the number had increased to 2.9 million. Both societies have an extremely one-sided resource endowment based on agriculture. In the presence of relatively favourable climatic conditions a high percentage of their land area can be used for agriculture. Denmark has no mineral resources, Uruguay only a few (iron ore, silver, gold, lead, copper, manganese, lignite, talcum), which are, however, not yet developed and were therefore irrelevant to economic development in the past hundred years.[3] *Small countries with such a one-sided resource endowment are usually considered to have no chance of development.* Such a diagnosis is often backed with the widespread thesis that the export-orientated development of economic formations of the named kind and size would, in the context of an increasingly hierarchical world economy, result in peripheralization—particularly if foreign trade is characterized by high partner concentration and an export commodities' basket composed of only a few goods (high commodity concentration).[4] Both characteristics, high partner and commodity concentration, were present in both Denmark and Uruguay from the middle of the nineteenth century at the latest. *In both cases the first substantial growth impulse resulted from the export-orientated production of agricultural goods, which were for decades sold mainly to Britain.*

In view of the outlined circumstances, the theoretically relevant question arises why, in comparable world economic conditions, the export-orientated growth dynamics of Denmark resulted in the emergence of a typical metropolitan society and economy (autocentric development), while the export-orientated growth dynamics of Uruguay resulted in that country's peripheralization within the capitalist world economy. Choosing Uruguay as an example has, incidentally, a special attraction, since this small Latin-American country was long regarded as an exception within Latin-American development, as 'Latin America's Switzerland', as 'Latin America's first welfare state', and as the only relatively advanced bourgeois democracy with parliamentary institutions that had developed in Latin America at an early stage.[5] Uruguay belongs furthermore to those Third World countries where, at an early stage, illiteracy had been considerably reduced and where, compared with other Latin-American cases, a relatively high social mobility could be observed within the urban agglomeration of Montevideo. The fact that Uruguay has by now become 'Latin Americanized' despite these differences, renders the analysis of this case all the more interesting, especially as, for a long time, it was considered unrepresentative.

In the following section we shall first outline several marked contrasts in the development paths of Denmark and Uruguay. The analysis will centre on those factors which, according to the interpretation offered above, were responsible for Denmark becoming a country with a typical OECD profile: in 1977 the per capita income stood at $8,040; and while typical peripheral structures evolved in Uruguay, her per capita income was $1.430 (see Table 5, p. 115) and was thus in the top range of the 'middle income countries', in the same bracket as Brazil ($1,360; not shown in the Table) and Argentina ($1,730). How can the present discrepancy between Uruguayan and Danish per capita income (which is in the order of 1:6) be explained, in view of their comparable starting-points?

The following section begins with a characterization of the Danish development path. Next, we shall outline the various characteristics of the development of Uruguay. Finally, by means of further case-studies, we shall attempt to answer the question whether the observations on the contrasting development dynamics of Uruguay and Denmark can be generalized and possibly fashioned into general statements of development theory.

The Danish development path

The economic development of Denmark in the second half of the eighteenth century and first decades of the nineteenth century is characterized by extensive de-feudalization—that is, the emergence of a free peasantry and interlinked nascent agricultural modernization.[6] Both processes have recently been described in the following terms:

> The agrarian reform in Denmark, the first in Europe, progressed very gradually, extending over a period of about a hundred years, even though the decisive steps were taken in the period between 1788 and 1807. The results were varied and quite different from those of most European countries. In England, the process resulted in the extensive dislocation of the rural population and in large-scale farming by a landed aristocracy and/or capitalist tenants. In France, it resulted in the emergence of a diverse sector of smallholdings; in Russia, the 'obscina' based on shared obligations was maintained despite the abolition of serfdom; and Prussia, the fourth type, witnessed the survival intact of the manorial estates and emergence of a new rural class, the cottagers, called upon for farming the estates. In Denmark, the separation of peasant land and manorial land led to a reduction in the size of the estates—which were henceforth farmed with the help of labourers and cottagers—and to the emergence of a substantial sector of medium-sized

farms, whose fragmentation was prevented by the ban on any further partition of an inheritance. An eviction or proletarianization of the peasantry—as, for example, in England—did not occur. In the middle of the nineteenth century two-thirds of the farms and half the cottager plots were privately owned. Only about 10 per cent of the cultivated area was tenanted. An equally important result of the agrarian reform was, however, that the disintegration of communal land tenure and field clearing facilitated the transition from the three-field system to a ten- to eleven-year cycle of crop rotation, which in turn resulted in considerable productivity gains, even though agricultural modernization started on the large estates where it could be financed from compensation payments.[7]

From the middle of the nineteenth century until the great European agricultural crisis of the 1870s and early 1880s Denmark can be characterized as an *agrarian export economy*. If one compares the 1820s with the 1870s, the rising share of grain production in total agricultural output and the rise in the agricultural exports share become apparent. The latter tripled from 12 per cent (1820–4) to 36 per cent (1870–4), with the grain exports share rising from 33 per cent to 54 per cent, intermittently topping even 60 per cent. 'This disproportionate rise in agricultural exports indicates that, from 1851 onward, the agricultural upswing was based mainly on grain exports, with live cattle and butter also playing a role. The country was well on its way to becoming a cereals monoculture'.[8]

In the 1850s, 1860s and early 1870s Denmark's export offensive was so pronounced that the country was visited by several commissions of foreign experts whose reports provide an insight into the state of Danish agriculture at the time. But, despite her undeniable export success, Denmark too was confronted with difficulties on account of the European agricultural crisis that started in the mid-1870s. For the agriculture of Denmark could not successfully compete in her major export market, Britain, with the cheaper agricultural imports from overseas (initially chiefly from the United States). Russian grain, too, became a serious threat undermining the dynamic export growth of Danish agriculture. Denmark's political and agricultural response to this world economic challenge constituted a momentous move which protected the country from regressing socially and economically to a periphery of Europe (possibly in the mould of Ireland and Romania). Instead of retreating into agricultural protectionism, which could be a quite rational response for large and populous territorial states,[9] a *process of structural change* occurred in the export-orientated sectors of Danish agriculture which led away from export-orientated cereals production towards a processing economy—that is, animal husbandry and local processing of meat and dairy products destined for export.[10]

By switching from a grain exporting economy to an export-orientated processing economy, Danish agriculture tried to conquer a new position within the world economy against a backdrop of comparative advantages which had yet to be achieved. Comparative cost advantages demanded that feed grain (and bread grain) which could be produced more cheaply overseas, should be imported, that these imports should be used for human consumption and for the rearing of livestock, and the resulting agricultural raw products should be processed locally so that they could be sold competitively as *processed* agricultural goods (meat, bacon, ham, butter, cheese, etc.) in markets previously supplied with grain. Such a reorientation of large parts of Danish agriculture was by no means without problems, and only the cyclical recovery of the large European economies (such as Britain and Germany, Denmark's two major trading partners), which started in the 1890s, made this structural change a success. Between 1875 and 1927 animal feed production tripled in Denmark. Grain production, which had originally been dominant, declined from 78 per cent to 45 per cent of the total agricultural output, mainly as a result of the absolute decline in bread grain production. Forage plant production, on the other hand, rose from 68 per cent to 84 per cent, indicating not only an expansion in the area of forage plant cultivation but the conversion of grassland to beet cultivation. In the 1920s imports of feed grain and pellets amounted to 13 to 15 per cent of domestic feed production. 'The desire to profit from the fact that world market prices for animal feed were declining faster than the prices for animal products, and to exploit the possibility of building up, at relatively low cost, stock farming beyond the potential of local forage plant production, accounts for the free-trade orientation of the Danish peasantry.'[11] The conversion process is also evidenced by the change in the number of livestock between the 1870s and the 1930s. The number of cattle doubled to more than 3 million, that of pigs grew sevenfold to 3.6 million, and that of chickens grew from 4.6 million to 22 million. The number of horses remained static and declined with the onset of mechanization. Sheep farming, originally the most important branch of stock farming in terms of numbers, declined from 1.5 million to just below 200,000.

What were the consequences of this switch from a grain exporting economy to an *agricultural processing economy*? In the long run, the following factors were important:

(1) The above-mentioned reorientation towards increased specialization resulted in a renewed *modernization impulse*, evidenced by the intensification, scientific penetration and increased mechanization—in short, advancing capitalization—of the agricultural sector. According

to the comparative studies by Colin Clark, Denmark still led Europe in agricultural productivity in the 1920s.[12]

(2) In the agricultural sector, *densely intermeshed* structures emerged which would nowadays be characterized as an expression of auto-centric sectoral development. Menzel has described these mutually intermeshing and interlinking micro-cycles, which resulted in the consolidation and growing productivity of the agricultural sector, thus:

> While previously, in addition to cereals production, domestic work with all its varied aspects—animal husbandry, milk and fodder production, the growing of vegetables and potatoes, food preserving, slaughtering, baking and even the home production of textiles—had been in the centre of agri-cultural activity, with a division of labour occurring only inside the family, these activities were now largely abandoned in favour of well-planned specialization. Well-planned in the sense that the mix of arable and live-stock farming was not arbitrary, if one were aiming at maximum profit-ability, but depended on the availability of family labour. The production of grain for sale was supplanted by the production of animal feed (cereals, beet, forage plants) for farm-based consumption. Instead of exporting grain, feed grain and feed supplements like oil cake and bran were imported. The increased feed supply enabled the farmers to keep additional cattle, pigs and poultry, increasing in turn the output of organic fertilizers, which were supplemented by imported artificial fertilizers, increasing in turn forage plant production. Cattle farming concentrated on the export of live animals. Dairy farming was dedicated to the production of milk which, in its turn, was the input for butter and cheese production. First butter and later, to a smaller extent, cheese, became important export commodities. The by-product of butter production, skimmed milk, served as an important input for the fattening of pigs. Within the framework of rational economic organiz-ation the expansion of pig farming was therefore largely tied to dairy farming for supplies of skimmed milk. . . . Pig farming itself was geared to the production of a further export product, 'bacon' (= de-gutted and salted halves of pork). The offal and innards from pig-slaughtering were used as additional feed in poultry farming. Pig farming itself was, apart from the raising of broiler chickens, mainly devoted to the production of eggs for export. This resulted in—even by the standards of modern agriculture—an extraordinarily high proportion of output being marketed, estimated for the heyday of the processing economy at 94 per cent of agricultural value-added.[13]

(3) The modernization of agriculture was founded on and resulted in growing linkages with local craft-based production and an *agricul-ture-based industrialization*. In view of the dispersed location of the family-operated farms, this agriculture-based industry was also dispersed relatively widely across the country and directly geared to the needs of the agricultural sector. The growing mechanization of agriculture sparked off the production of agricultural equipment, starting with sim-ple implements but quickly progressing to relatively complex equip-

ment for farms, dairies, abattoirs, and so on.

(4) Danish statistics on the sectoral distribution of the economically active population in the period 1890–1940 reveal a relatively high proportion of tertiary sector employment: 36 per cent in 1910 (compared with 19 per cent in Sweden and 8 per cent in Finland).[14] Obviously this high share resulted in part from the international operations of the service sector (shipping, etc.) but to a large degree also from the high degree of commercialization achieved by agriculture on account of the above-mentioned developments.

The question arises, of course, as to what were the *prerequisites* for the structural transition from a grain exporting agriculture to an agricultural processing economy in Denmark. In other European countries the same world economic challenge resulted in the restoration of a no longer competitive agriculture under a protectionist premise (Spain, Portugal *et al.*).[15] In the case of Denmark, the prerequisites for an innovative response to the world economic challenge included above all the following factors:

(1) As early as the middle of the last century the Danish population was distinguished by a relatively high *level of education*. General schooling was introduced in 1814. In the mid-nineteenth century illiteracy was confined to 10 to 15 per cent of the Danish population—a percentage achieved in Europe at that time only by Sweden, Norway, Switzerland and Germany. The comparative figure for England and France was still 10 to 15 per cent.[16] Around the turn of the century illiteracy had been practically eradicated and a broad-based elementary education of high quality was in force. A special role in the extension of elementary education and technical expertise was played by the *folk high schools* and *agricultural schools* which sprang up in rural areas after the middle of the last century, teaching agricultural skills and developing—above all in the case of the folk high schools—the consciousness necessary for the institutional and political self-organization of the independent peasantry. Without such education, which was also provided by specialist institutions like technical schools for dairying, the productivity gains achieved by Danish agriculture from the 1880s onwards would probably not have materialized. For these gains were based on the growing emphasis on science in agricultural activity—for example, the systematic observation of livestock (breeding programme, feed input, rearing techniques).[17] That, for instance, the yearly butter output per cow rose from 44 kilograms to 131 kilograms between 1871 and 1930, presupposed the accumulation of 'intangible capital' (knowledge, competence, expertise).[18]

(2) One of the prerequisites for the success of Danish agriculture

since the 1870s was the high degree of political and economic *self-organ-ization* of the independent farmers.[19] This organization was institutional-ized in a differentiated and multifarious *system of rural cooperatives*. The cooperatives had an economic and political function within the agricul-tural sphere as well as a general political role.

If the medium-sized family-operated farm was the building-block of Danish agriculture, the cooperatives fulfilled the economic function of integrating the family-based farm into wider economic networks, in order to contribute through economies of scale to cost reductions. They also helped to standardize products, improve the quality of products, organize the buying of equipment and inputs, and the sale of agricul-tural produce—in short, to increase the economic efficiency of the family-operated units in crucial areas.

In terms of agrarian politics the cooperatives had the function of strengthening the position of the independent family-operated farms *vis-à-vis* the large landowners who, though numerically weaker, wielded initially substantial political influence. These cooperatives acquired a general political function to the extent that the political system of Denmark gradually became open to new interest groups on account of their lobbyist pressure, giving them direct access to political and administrative decision-making institutions (parliament, the govern-ment, etc.). The latter function gained in importance when other newly emerging social groups—as, for example, the large number of cot-tagers, and later, the industrial working class—were able to organize themselves politically and to influence national decision-making (cot-tager organizations, trade unions).

The Danish farmers' cooperatives are also of special interest, be-cause they combine individual initiative and self-reliant economic activity (private enterprise), on the one hand, with an institutional integration of these decentralized family-operated farms, on the other. Within the cooperatives the leading personnel were appointed in democratic elections. Every member had an equal vote and profits were shared according to performance. In this way a *combination of smallholding and large-scale production* emerged, which greatly increased the efficiency of the farms. This institutional arrangement—that is, the combination of family-operated farms and a large number of cooper-atives—should be regarded as an autonomous *innovative achievement* in the rural sector of Denmark, as an instrument of successful adaptation to external economic change.[20]

(3) The ability to implement broad-based agricultural moderniz-ation and innovation is rooted in socio-structural conditions. In order to understand Danish agricultural development (and, in the final

analysis, the Danish development path as a whole), it is vitally important to have a knowledge of the distribution of domestic economic
resources. We have already indicated above that in the course of the
de-feudalization of Danish agriculture *viable medium-sized farms* emerged,
coexisting with, on the one side, a relatively small number of large
estates, and, on the other, with a relatively large number of smallholdings. In 1919 more than 55 per cent of farms were in the middle
category (12 to 75 acres); roughly 55 per cent of land belonged to farms
of between 35 and 150 acres. Large estates, though existent, did not
play a dominant role. Smallholdings under 12 acres were numerous
and linked to the large estates, but had nevertheless a certain degree of
independence on account of their being integrated into agricultural
cooperatives.[21] With the exception of about 10 per cent of them, farms
were owned by the farmers themselves, with the result that the additional income derived from agricultural modernization found its way
to the family-operated units—increasing in turn the propensity to
invest and innovate further.

The consequences of broad-based agricultural modernization and
agriculture-orientated industrialization have already been emphasized
above. Agriculture, however, required not only equipment, and agriculture-orientated industry processed not only agricultural raw materials.
As real incomes increased on account of productivity gains and growing exports of processed goods, the real income of the rural population,
including that of the cottager sector which had been consolidated by
state measures, rose too. These increases in real income were translated
into a broad-based demand for mass-consumption goods, stimulating
over the years *import substitution industrialization* in Denmark. The first
industrialization thrusts of this kind can be observed in the periods
1890–7 and 1905–13, and thus they were reflexes of the above-mentioned
agricultural modernization. The share of craft-orientated production in
the secondary sphere remained remarkably high, and only in 1914 did
industrial output in the narrower sense of the term begin to exceed
craft-orientated production within the secondary sector.[22]

A more comprehensive *import substitution industrialization* started with
the crisis of the 1930s. In the conditions of the world economic crisis,
export dependency was bound to produce negative repercussions in the
Danish economy and society, for the drift towards a variety of protectionist measures among the major trading partners forced the Danish
economy into a difficult situation. It was overcome by a state-
interventionist development policy, which was directed towards promoting a further differentiation of the domestic market, coupled with
exchange controls which were used as an instrument of development

policy. The new policy amounted to import substitution and an increased orientation towards the domestic market; externally, trade protection and, internally, public stimulation of the economy became inevitable.[23] This change, resulting from the world economic crisis, forced Denmark to abandon her previous liberal trade policy in order to pursue a protectionist economic policy and to develop a purposive industrial policy coupled with an agricultural policy which aimed at the stabilization of rural incomes. The abandonment of the gold standard in 1931 implied a devaluation of the Danish currency. The burden of adjusting to the new world economic situation was therefore placed on the whole economy and not just on the agricultural sector (as would have been the case in the absence of devaluation). By means of purposive exchange controls, only the most vital goods were allowed into the country, thus creating incentives for the local production of all the remaining goods. The Danish government's measures had astonishing success. While economic growth averaged only 1.5 per cent between 1920 and 1932, it increased to an average 6.5 per cent in the period 1932 to 1939. Menzel talks in this connection about a kind of 'second take-off', a diagnosis backed by the observation that the real industrial breakthrough and the decisive shift in the economic centre of gravity occurred simply in the period after 1933. Only then did the GDP contribution of the secondary sector exceed that of agriculture. This *second industrialization impulse* was based on an above-average expansion of the textile, engineering, transport equipment, electrical, chemical, printing, and paper industries. Of special importance, as in every development process, was the substantial employment growth in the engineering and transport equipment industries. In Denmark this increase was mainly related to a further specialization in agricultural machinery and machine tools, diesel engines and ships, as well as equipment and machinery for cement factories, dairies, cold stores and food processing. Among the new sectors were, notably, chemicals and electrical engineering—industrial sectors without a local raw material base. In the areas of specialization noted above, the export of machinery had acquired a considerable importance; as early as the 1930s 30 to 40 per cent of the machinery output was exported.

A further industrialization thrust between 1956 and 1967 brought about an even more far-reaching diversification in the structure of industrial production, this time again in conditions of free trade, until, by the 1970s, a typical OECD profile had emerged: in 1970, 8 per cent of the economically active population produced 7 per cent of the GDP in the primary sector, 37 per cent of the work-force 36 per cent of the GDP in the secondary sector, and 55 per cent of the labour force 57 per cent of the GDP in the tertiary sector. It is remarkable that the share of engineering, electrical engineering and transport equipment in industrial value-added to 26 per cent at the time in question.

The first industrialization thrust before 1910, and the further development up to the reorientation of Danish economic and development policy in response to the crisis, were accompanied by *gradual shifts in the internal power structure*. While, during the last decades of the nineteenth century, the Danish political system witnessed a stalemate between the Right (representing large landowners, industry, civil servants, the self-employed and white-collar workers) and the Left (representing independent farmers and cottagers), increasing democratization, as regards the chances of participating in government, resulted from 1901 onward in so-called 'governments of the Left' (Venstre). This period also saw the rise of trade unions and social democracy. Denmark had a unitary trade-union movement: as early as 1900 50 per cent of the work-force was organized, and in 1906 two-thirds of the male work-force. In 1899 the so-called 'September accord' instituted an agreement between employers and trade unions, recognizing the union movement as a legitimate political force and guiding the struggle between capital and labour into a reformist-pragmatic direction. In 1924 the first social democratic government emerged, and through an alliance between the Social Democrats and Venstre the crisis of the late 1920s and early 1930s was resolved, not without problems but with circumspection and a radical Keynesian approach.

Characteristics of the Uruguayan development path

In a brief description, Dieter Nohlen has outlined the beginnings of the Uruguayan development path[24] thus:

'From the outset Uruguay found herself in a special dependency situation. The dependency did not surface in the displacement and deformation of existing economic and socio-political structures by European expansion, but in the development of a society in response to foreign demand. This form of dependency did not necessarily imply underdevelopment or backwardness. So long as the natural local conditions of production, soil and climate guaranteed comparative cost advantages, the only prerequisite for a flourishing agricultural export economy was adaptation to the demands of the foreign market. During the nineteenth century this was successfully done with great efficiency and flexibility. While from the end of the eighteenth century onward Uruguay had exported leather, skins and horn, as well as live cattle and salt beef, European demand for raw wool stimulated in 1860 the import of sheep and, within just one decade, their increase to 20,000 head. In 1835 the territory was already totally devoted to livestock farming.

A rapidly growing population, which expanded from about 30,000 in 1810 (mainly indigenous people) to more than 1 million in 1890, enjoyed an increasing standard of living owing to export receipts. In these conditions, as early as the start of this century a representative political system became established, based on the dualism of two political parties, which determined, without intervention by the army, the political fate of the country. Because of her political and social development, Uruguay was regarded as a 'special case' among Latin-American countries.[25]

The foundation of the Uruguayan state in 1828 was a result of political struggles taking place in the La Plata basin during the wars of independence of the states in that region, and occurred after the latter had gained their political sovereignty.[26] Britain had an interest in the new state, as Montevideo provided a good staging post and base for the economic penetration of this part of Latin America. Before 1830, however, the lack of internal political stability in Uruguay hampered such penetration. Although the anglophile élite dominated the government of the young republic and pressed for Montevideo to be made into a staging post and Uruguay into a British sphere of influence, this urban élite, orientated towards trade and trading profit, was opposed by the stock farmers of the interior. Like their counterparts in Argentina at that time, the latter were not prepared to let the traders in the coastal towns and their foreign allies monopolize the benefits flowing from newly won independence. They therefore fought for a national development path in preference to economic dependency. In Argentina, Rosas was the protagonist of this opposition, made up of stock farmers, gauchos, craftsmen from the interior who were threatened by British displacement competition, small urban entrepreneurs and members of the lower classes, as well as conservative and Catholic enemies of European liberalism. The Argentine domestic political constellation had a considerable impact on Uruguay, where similar political fissures developed.

At the beginning of the 1840s, Rosas and his Uruguayan allies had gone on the attack, while in the whole La Plata region the supporters of European influence and economic as well as political liberalism were on the retreat. One should bear in mind that during this same period the opening up of China was enforced, for example, and that, from the British viewpoint, it was imperative to eliminate the political obstacles to the expansion of free-trade imperialism. Nevertheless, this part of Latin America was obviously not interesting enough to Britain at the time to warrant a massive military intervention by her. Offers from the Uruguayan anglophiles to transform the country into a British protectorate were rejected by London.[27] In 1846 Britain aborted minor attempts to intervene and tried to reach an agreement with Rosas. According to Winn, this first phase of Uruguayan development provides evidence that Britain could not enforce 'cooperation' on the lines of free-trade imperialism where the position of local collaborators was too weak and insecure. This domestic situation was to change in the space of less than two decades.[28]

After an interlude between 1830 and 1864, when Uruguay came under Brazilian influence—a subordinate position which did not satisfy the political and economic élites in Uruguay—a renewed political and external economic alignment with Britain came about. From the mid-1860s onward, Britain in her function as lender and trading partner, filled the gap caused by the decline in or rejection of Brazilian influence. This decade also saw Uruguay being linked to Europe by cable and steam. Under British leadership sheep farming and meat processing were established—two industries aimed at the European market that, by the outbreak of the First World War, had come to dominate the Uruguayan economy. A military dictatorship after 1876 created the stability and favourable investment climate necessary for further British investment and a certain modernization of livestock farming. Between 1872 and 1889 the forced fencing of pasture land resulted in the shedding of around three-quarters of the work-force previously employed in stock farming. Stock farming, already dominant, expanded still further—with a parallel rise in export receipts. Uruguay became the country with the highest per capita livestock population in the world. In order to supply the British dinner-table (meat) and British textile factories (wool) with sufficient produce, Uruguay seemed to lack only railways and capital. Despite the development crisis of the 1880s and early 1890s, at the turn of the century Uruguay became, on account of increased borrowing and growing investment, a genuine part of the so-called 'Atlantic economy' whose function, in the case of Uruguay, was to supply foodstuffs and agricultural raw materials to Britain and, in return, to develop and secure Uruguay as a market for British goods and an investment sphere for British capital. In 1881 the representative of the British government in Uruguay wrote proudly to London: 'All the industrial enterprises of this country which are of any importance are in English hands. Railways, tramways, banks, docks and . . . gas and water supplies have been established by English capital, and are managed by Englishmen.'[29] In 1890 the President of Uruguay compared his position to that of the 'manager of a great ranch, whose board of directors is in London'.[30]

At the turn of the century the economic infrastructure of Uruguay was concentrated in British hands and the British informal empire had become a fact of life. British capital and enterprise dominated transportation, communications, utilities and insurance, and occupied the leading position in banking, meat processing and ranching. Uruguay had 1,100 miles of railway and all of it was British. All seven of the international loans Uruguay had contracted during the preceding four decades had been floated in London, and Uruguay was linked to England by the highest per capita debt in South America. The note issues of British banks provided a large part of the circulating medium of the country and British bankers controlled much of Uruguay's domestic savings. British exports to Uruguay were greater than the sum of her two closest competitors, and Uruguay sent close to 2 million to London annually in repatriated profits. What diplomatic interference and military intervention had failed to compel in the era of free trade, British economic superiority and Uruguayan collaboration had secured in the era of the 'new imperialism'. By 1900 Uruguay was England's.[31]

As pointed out by Nohlen, the problem of the Uruguayan agricultural export economy stemmed from the fact 'that the export surplus was not converted into larger production capacities, but mainly into imports of consumer and luxury goods for a social minority, whose behaviour was orientated towards Europe. Uruguay imported the whole range of goods, even those whose production required little capital and no specialized labour'.[32] Winn regards the Uruguayan élite's readiness to collaborate as decisive in creating the opportunities for British penetration in the late nineteenth century. According to his account, parts of the old Uruguayan élite had been eliminated in the conflicts and civil wars of the mid-nineteenth century. They lost their property and often found themselves forced to sell their land and their companies to a rising new commercial and livestock farming élite of recent European extraction (immigration).

Denuded of economic power, the old Uruguayan élite was transformed in the late nineteenth century into the lawyers, managers and agents for the mostly British economic interests which replaced them at the top of the Uruguayan economic hierarchy. Deprived of an autonomous economic base, they became a dependent political élite, promoting and protecting the British interests with which they had identified their own fortunes and futures.[33]

The alliance with Britain was meant to guarantee stability and prosperity and finally also to safeguard the geopolitical position of Uruguay in the La Plata region. 'Lastly, the Uruguayan élite saw an alliance with British capital as a strategy to finance its imitation of European life-styles, restore its family fortunes and secure the economic influence its own diminished resources could no longer command.'[34]

In the study cited above, Winn has shown that in three vital areas, railway construction, banking and meat processing, British influence and British capital made no contribution at all to the emergence of a diversified economy. In his view, railway construction financed by British capital resulted in the consolidation and further entrenchment of the *status quo*—that is, a system of livestock farming based on extensive production methods. The task of the railways was to transport agricultural products as quickly as possible to Montevideo for export, and to move in return English goods beyond Montevideo into the hinterland. In view of the high freight costs, those goods continued to be produced whose costs in large estates based on extensive farming methods were particularly low. This integration of Uruguayan stock farming into the Atlantic economy prevented diversification towards a more intensive agriculture, limiting population growth and productivity gains. Social mobility in this sector remained low, especially as Montevideo provided a haven for the population displaced from the land, producing one of the highest urbanization ratios. The high land concentration was translated via export receipts into a high income concentration, creating among 'luxury consumers'[35] a demand for British not Uruguayan goods. The repatriation of profits, particularly from British capital invested in railway construction, prevented infrastructural diversification—for example, the planned but never executed construction of canals, from which an agriculture based on intensive production methods could have benefited.

British capital was engaged above all in financing the relatively low-risk import-export business. *It was geared for commercial activity and not for unlocking the development potential of the economy as a whole.* In view of the dominant British influence, it is not surprising that the displacement effects witnessed in other parts of Latin America occurred in Uruguay too. Local capital tended to flow into the buying of land, the acquisition of large estates, and into British banks. Long-term investment was discouraged in view of the opportunities for reaping short-term 'windfall profits' through the import-export business. The industries favoured by British capital, for example meat processing, remained a sort of *enclave* without broad-based linkage effects. Even the processing of by-products from abattoirs—potentially a local activity—took place initially not in Uruguay but Britain. Hides for example, were dried in Uruguay in order to be shipped to Europe. They were not processed into shoes in Uruguay, and all the remaining leather processing was done also in Europe.

The role of British railways, finance, banking and meat processing in Uruguay during the late nineteenth century was to integrate Uruguay into the Atlantic economy as a specialist in the production of certain pastoral commodities required by Europe and as a customer of European manufactures. In this task, they were assisted by a Uruguayan élite which equated social status with the conspicuous consumption of imported luxuries, financed by pastoral exports and British credits. The cultural imperialism of British influence had economic consequences. Mill and Spencer may have introduced liberal and positivist ideas into the salons and academies of Montevideo, but the conspicuous consumption of British imports that accompanied the spread of English definitions of progress was the despair of the Uruguayan entrepreneur and the graveyard of local initiative. At the turn of the century, with the exception of foodstuffs, Uruguay imported most of what it consumed, with England by far the largest supplier and greatest gainer. On the eve of the First World War, Uruguay was still an import-export economy, and even that ubiquitous cliché of early industrial development—the textile industry—was conspicuous by its absence, although wool had been Uruguay's leading export for decades. As late as 1910, only 0.01 per cent of the 40 million kilograms of wool produced in Uruguay was spun locally, and the vast bulk of the wool left Montevideo without any processing. Although Uruguay today produces some of the finest woollen textiles sold in England, in 1900 it was Britain that manufactured the fine woollens sold in Uruguay. Even the Uruguayan army, an obvious market for an infant local industry, wore uniforms cut from English cloth. British capital and enterprise may have been important in the integration of Uruguay into the Atlantic economy, and Uruguayan interests associated with the export economy may have benefited from the process and the special relationship, but the English economic predominance contributed little to the diversification of the Uruguayan economy or to the generation of a sustained and autonomous economic growth.[36]

England's penetration of the Uruguayan economy was accompanied by the consolidation of the political system in Uruguay. The following steps were crucial to this consolidation: the victory of central government over the centrifugal power of local *caudillos*; the transition from military rule to civilian government and from a recurring resort to force to parliamentary rule; and the transition from élitist politics to some sort of mass politics.

In Uruguay, as elsewhere, the export economy had political consequences—particularly in the one disproportionately large urban centre, Montevideo—making it seem advisable for the export and agricultural interests, allied with each other from the 1860s and 1870s onward, to offer material concessions to an urban population, within which social discontent was building up. The comparative advantages, on the basis of which Uruguay's economic élite ran an agricultural export economy in alliance with Britain, were obviously of such magnitude as to facilitate, in the first decades of this century, a political compromise between the representatives of the rising urban classes and the traditional export and agrarian oligarchy. While the *status quo* in the agrarian sphere remained untouched, the urban population could be placated by means of state-financed urban reforms (welfare measures) and modern populist policies.

In the period from 1900 to 1930 one can observe, in the above-mentioned circumstances, an expansion in the production of manufactures for the domestic market, an expansion in the meat-freezing industry, now mainly on the basis of American investment, and increased economic activity on the part of the state in order to create the necessary conditions for the expansion of the domestic market—for example, through the nationalization of parts of the infrastructure, public investment with labour market repercussions, the expansion of public services, relatively progressive social laws and, not least, through a tariff policy designed to protect manufacturers against foreign competition. The agricultural export economy had thus induced considerable social change, not in its core sector, extensive cattle-ranching, but indirectly in the large urban centre, Montevideo; social change that resulted in new domestic battle lines, even though it did not entail fundamental structural reforms. This process found expression in the so-called *Batllismo*, named after the then leading political personality who advocated political reform, economic nationalism and a political solution of the 'social question'.

But despite this political and social change, despite an expansion in—particularly small scale—manufacturing in Montevideo, the overall economic structure of Uruguay remained relatively unchanged. The dynamic impulse of the whole economy still derived from agricultural exports, and international economic crises were bound directly to affect the whole Uruguayan economy in an adverse way. This became apparent in the world economic crisis of 1929, resulting (as in the rest of Latin America) in forced 'import substitution industrialization' as the engine of growth. 'In the period 1926–55 the value of industrial output increased by a yearly average of 6.5 per cent. Manufacturing activity, stimulated and accelerated by the world economic crisis, brought about the political hegemony of the industrial sector but remained essentially limited to satisfying the demand of the domestic market, which was too small for the application of modern technology. Only 10 per cent of its output was exported.'[37] Between 1930 and 1960 the urban work-force trebled. Within twenty years the number of state employees trebled too.

The slowing of inward-directed economic growth and, finally, the stagnation after the middle of the 1950s, ushered in the crisis of bourgeois democracy in the economic system of peripheral capitalism. Industrialization on the basis of import substitution had reached its inherent limits of growth. At the same time, the export of agricultural products no longer provided growing surpluses once the Korean War boom was over (quadrupling export prices after the period 1940–50). For an expansion of agricultural production, however, the existing pattern of land ownership and land use would have had to be changed. This overtaxed the socio-economic innovative capacity of the existing system. The distributive activity of the state, which had previously provided a social and growth regulator, declined continuously after 1956. The extensive welfare provisions, especially the inflated public bureaucracy . . . deprived the state of investment funds. All social groups, from the upper middle class downwards, suffered a painful decline in real incomes and standards of living, accompanied by growing disparities in the distribution of income. Because of the shrinking material base of the welfare state, the distribution conflicts acquired increasingly violent overtones. This 'Latin Americanization of Uruguay' went hand in hand with the growing political organization of the working class, the rebellion of the petty bourgeoisie and the middle classes, and the demise of parliamentarianism and rule of law. Because of the armed struggle by the Tupamaros against the system, as well as the electoral success of revolutionary socialist parties, the threatened social groups holding positions of economic power took refuge in a repressive dictatorship which was installed by the military in a *coup d'état* in 1973/4.[38]

Denmark and Uruguay compared

The intention of the preceding account was to demonstrate that highly divergent development patterns can evolve from quite similar starting-points. In Tables 5 to 8 below (pp. 115–18) the outcome of these different development paths is illustrated by means of aggregate data. While in the late 1970s the difference in the size of population and work-force between Uruguay and Denmark was in the region of 1:2, the discrepancy in the absolute size of GDP was 1:10, and in per capita income 1:5.6. The difference in export volume was 1:20, and the difference between the Uruguayan and the Danish share in total world trade was 1:25.

Such considerable differences cannot be attributed to different 'natural' resource endowments. These were, after all, initially rather similar in both cases, as shown above. Nor can different export opportunities within the world economy explain the diverging development patterns of the two countries. For if any country was initially in a disadvantaged position, it was Denmark—a position of vulnerability within the international division of labour that could be counteracted only by a shift in Danish agriculture towards stock farming and food processing, as described above. Moreover, with regard to the two main products, wool and meat, Uruguay occupies an excellent position within the Third World. UNCTAD (United Nations Conference on Trade and

Development) statistics, for example, show Uruguay—with 14 per cent of Third World meat exports in 1979—in second place just behind Argentina.[39]

The main difference between the two development paths lay in the contrasting positioning of the primary sector in both economies. The restructuring of Danish agriculture, which resulted in densely inter-meshed micro-economic cycles within agriculture itself, evolving straight into agriculture-based industrialization and gradually into general import substitution industrialization, did not take place to a comparable extent in Uruguay.[40] Stock farming, which started with extensive production methods, remained basically extensive over dec-ades and did not on the whole lead to any diversification of agricul-ture, was bound to prevent the emergence of an agriculture-based industry of Danish quality and density.[41] That Uruguayan society had experienced a certain degree of growth which is still reflected in a high average per capita income by Third World standards, was in the past and is still due to the low-cost production and export of agricultural commodities (wool, meat and, later, rice) whose respective share in the country's total exports in 1975 was 24 per cent, 22 per cent and 9 per cent.[42]

From the standpoint of extensive stock farming, agriculture-based industrialization was not necessary. The deliberate integration of Uruguay into the classic division of labour between Britain and Latin America eliminated for a long time any incentives for autonomous industrialization. Nor did attempts, dating from the period of *Batllismo*, to pursue a more nationalistic economic policy (including welfare measures), change the traditional economic structure to a sufficient degree. The successful sale of wool and meat in the world market provided a dynamic impulse which resulted in quite considerable social change (rise of a working class, of a broad middle class, etc.) without leading to a fundamental shift towards a mature industrial-capitalist system. Social change was sufficiently significant to make an impact on the domestic political situation without, however, forming new struc-tural patterns. *Batllismo*, a variant of Latin-American populism, was able to flourish and survive for a relatively long time because it was supported by the continuing trade success of a *mono-export economy* which was profitably integrated into the world market. To the extent that the growth potential of this agricultural export economy based on exten-sive production methods became exhausted owing to lack of investment and insufficient diversification, the rest of the economy was bound to be adversely affected, as it depended on the export sector. Populism and its concomitant, bourgeois democracy, were bound to fail, being grafted on to an economic structure which lacked the solid foundation necessary in the long term to support them both.

Seen from this perspective, the thesis that Uruguay was once the 'Switzerland of Latin America' is thoroughly misleading, since Uruguay's economic structure suffered from the very beginning from the same typical peripheral-capitalist defects as the other Latin-American countries.[43] Uruguay was, however, exceptional in the sense that, on the basis of a relatively prosperous agricultural export economy, she succeeded for a long time in preventing these conflicts from becoming economically and politically virulent. In structural terms, Uruguay was 'Latin American' like all other Latin-American economies.

As already mentioned, this process has nothing to do with Uruguay's 'natural resource endowment', which a comparison with Denmark will show. Table 5 (p. 115) contains some basic data on the structure of production in both countries, namely on the compositon of the GDP and on the sectoral distribution of the work-force. At first glance the data convey a deceptive picture indicating relatively similar distribution patterns. The aggregate figures do, however, hide qualitative differences. Denmark's agriculture is run on *intensive lines*, Uruguay's on *extensive* ones. The Danish infrastructure is highly *diversified*, the Uruguayan infrastructure is diversified to only a small degree and, as can be gleaned from other data,[44] is considerably *undercapitalized*. Uruguayan industry is based on a plethora of *small firms*, each employing only a small number of workers. The size of the tertiary sector in Denmark results from a relatively diversified structure of agricultural and industrial production, while that of the Uruguayan tertiary sector has its origins in the political history of that country since the *Batllismo* period: Uruguay's tertiary sector was inflated excessively through state action.[45] A qualitative difference, which can be quantified with data, shows up in the different share of the sector, comprising engineering as well as the manufacture of transport equipment and electrical machinery, in total net industrial product (Table 8, p. 118). The size of this industrial subsector is 3 per cent in Uruguay and 26 per cent in Denmark, a very respectable figure by OECD standards.[46]

The contrasting internal structure of the two countries can also be highlighted by means of Table 6 (p. 116), which deals with the structure of exports. In both cases Table 6 shows a relatively high share of food and agricultural raw material exports in the total exports. In 1977 both these export goods combined amounted to 39 per cent in Denmark and 66 per cent in Uruguay. The proportion of agricultural raw material exports, however, is much lower in Denmark than in Uruguay (5 per cent compared with 21 per cent), and the processing levels of foodstuffs are quite different, as described above. UNCTAD

115

Table 5: *General statistical data on the cases discussed (1977)*

	Population ('000,000s)	Per capita GDP (US $)	Distribution of the GDP %			Distribution of the labour force %		
			Agriculture	Industry	Services	Agriculture	Industry	Services
Denmark[a]	5.1	8,040	7	36	57	8	37	55
Uruguay	2.9	1,430	12	36	52	12	32	56
New Zealand	3.1	4,380	12	31	57	10	35	55
Netherlands	13.9	7,150	4	34	62	6	45	49
Ireland[a]	3.2	2,880	16	37	47	21	36	43
Israel	3.6	2,850	7	40	53	8	37	55
Thailand	43.8	420	27	29	44	77	8	15
Spain	36.3	3,190	9	38	53	19	42	39
Argentina	26	1,730	13	45	42	14	29	57
Australia	14.1	7,340	5	32	63	6	35	59
Canada	23.3	8,460	4	31	65	6	30	64
South Africa[b]	27.0	1,340	26	38	35	30	30	40

[a]1976   [b]1975

The countries are listed in the order of appearance in the text

Sources: UN 1978 Yearbook of National Account Statistics, New York, 1978, Vol. 1, p. 1103
World Development Report 1978, New York, 1978 (World Bank), table 3
World Development Report 1979, New York, 1979 (World Bank), tables 1, 3, 19

Table 6: Data on the export sector of the cases discussed (1977)

	Volume of exports (billions of US $)	Exports as a % of world exports	Per capita exports of manufactures (US $)	Exports by category (%)							
				Foodstuffs	Agricultural raw materials	Fuels	Minerals Metals	Finished manufactures	Chemicals	Others	Machinery Equipment
Denmark	9.9	0.98	994	34.1	5.0	3.2	3.2	54.1	7.1	19.7	27.3
Uruguay	0.5	0.04	62	44.5	21.4	—	0.8	33.4	1.4	29.6	2.4
New Zealand	3.1	0.23	169	47.7	29.8	1.3	4.9	16.3	3.2	10.0	3.2
Netherlands	43.6	3.94	1,563	21.7	3.6	18.2	6.5	49.5	14.5	16.3	18.8
Ireland	4.4	0.36	545	40.1	1.9	0.7	2.7	49.5	9.8	24.4	15.3
Israel	3.1	0.22	522	15.0	3.8	—	2.1	78.2	10.6	57.6	10.0
Thailand	3.5	0.24	13	59.9	12.1	—	9.4	16.5	0.4	13.6	2.5
Spain	10.2	0.86	165	21.2	1.8	3.7	9.7	63.5	6.4	31.5	25.6
Argentina	3.9	0.33	38	68.2	6.1	10.5	2.6	22.6	3.6	8.6	10.4
Australia	13.1	1.31	189	31.3	13.3	13.5	23.9	15.6	7.1	4.1	4.4
Canada	41.3	3.64	807	11.7	11.7	12.5	15.6	48.4	4.1	11.5	32.8
South Africa	4.5	0.6	66	32.5	8.0	1.1	25.2	25.3	4.2	15.2	5.9

Sources: UNCTAD 1979 Handbook of International Trade and Development Statistics, New York, 1979, Tables 4.1, 4.3 World Development Report 1979, New York, 1979 (World Bank), Tables 1, 12.

Table 7: *Data on the wages share in national income and the structure of demand with regard to the cases discussed*

	Wages and salaries as a % of national income (1975)	GNP by category (1977)(%)					
		Public consumption	Private consumption	Gross domestic capital formation	Gross domestic savings	Exports of goods and services	Resource balance
Denmark	60	24	56	23	20	29	−3
Uruguay	34	12[a]	75[a]	14[a]	13[a]	20[a]	−1
New Zealand	66	17	58	28	25	28	−3
Netherlands	73	18	58	23	24	54	1
Ireland	68	19	65	25	16	52	−9
Israel	66	37	56	23	7	36	−16
Thailand	32	11	68	26	21	22	−5
Spain	65	10	69	23	21	15	−2
Argentina	46	77[b]		19	23	13	4
Australia	68	16	59	28	25	16	−3
Canada	73	20	57	23	23	24	—
South Africa	66	—	—	—	—	—	—

[a] 1976 [b] no separate data available

Sources: *UN 1978 Yearbook of National Account Statistics*, New York, 1978, Vol. 1, part 3, in each case Table 2
World Development Report 1978, New York, 1978 (World Bank), Table 5 *World Development Report 1979*, New York, 1979 (World Bank), Table 5

statistics show considerable differences in the composition of the export commodity baskets. The Danish basket is relatively diversified: the first fifteen commodity groups account for 52 per cent of total exports, while in Uruguay exports of wool, meat and rice alone amount to 52 per cent of total exports. Discounting the fifteen major commodity groups listed, there remains, in the case of Uruguay, a residual figure of 18 per cent, indicating the low level of diversification of the export commodity basket.[47] The *UNCTAD Handbook* lists the present number of export commodities in the case of Denmark as 171, and in that of Uruguay as 85.[48]

Of great qualitative importance is the export share of machinery, transport equipment and electrical appliances, indicated in Tables 6 and 8. In 1977 half the exports of finished goods, which amounted to 54 per cent in the Danish case, consisted of machinery and equipment (27 per cent). In Uruguay, the total exports of finished goods amounted to 33 per cent in 1976, only 2.4 per cent of which consisted of machinery

Table 8:   *Data on the capital goods sectors with regard to the cases discussed (1977)*

	Mechanical and electrical engineering products and transport equipment as a % of industrial value-added	Mechanical and electrical engineering products and transport equipment as a % of total exports
Denmark	26	27.3
Uruguay	3	2.4
New Zealand	12	3.2
Netherlands	22	18.8
Ireland	12	15.3
Israel	26	10.0
Thailand	8	2.5
Spain	18	25.6
Argentina	24	10.4
Australia	25	4.4
Canada	26	32.8
South Africa	17	5.9

Sources: UNCTAD 1979 Handbook of International Trade and Development
             Statistics, New York, 1979, Table 4.1
             World Development Report 1979, New York, 1979 (World Bank), Table 6

and equipment. There was a less drastic discrepancy in the export of chemicals.

In so far as the present differences between the economic structures of Denmark and Uruguay can be conveyed by means of such aggregate data, they should have become clear in outline through the tables mentioned above. The real discrepancy would be brought out, above all, by a comparative *input-output table*, which, however, is not available. Such a table would reveal the high degree of structural interlacement in the case of Denmark and the continuing structural deficits of Uruguay, deficits typical of peripheral capitalism.[49]

Another discrepancy between the structure of Denmark and that of Uruguay is illustrated by Table 7 (p. 117). This contains figures on the percentage share of wage labour income in the total national income. In the past twenty years this figure has been around 60 per cent in Denmark and 34 per cent in the case of Uruguay. Both figures are not directly comparable, since the percentage share of wage labour as opposed to the proportion of self-employed is certainly lower in Denmark than in Uruguay, where the large number of craft-based production units and small industrial firms reduces the amount of wage labour.[50] Despite this statistical distortion it would be plausible, however, to assume that, even after taking these different proportions into account, the relative share of wage labour income in terms of national income is considerably smaller in Uruguay than in Denmark and that, despite this likely distortion, the share of wages must therefore be much lower in Uruguay than it is in Denmark (possibly by about 15 per cent).

Table 3, which also illustrates the disposition of the GDP, reveals that the investment share in Uruguay amounts to about half the Danish figure. The same applies to public consumption of goods and services, while the share of private consumption in Uruguay exceeds that in Denmark by one-third. If on the distribution side of the GDP the wages share is at least 15 per cent lower in Uruguay than in Denmark, while on the use side investment and public consumption are only about half as high as in Denmark, when at the same time the share of private consumption is disproportionately high, then such a profile corresponds with what could be called 'rentier capitalism'. This is characterized, on the basis of quite considerable foreign exchange receipts from export earnings, by a combination of a low propensity to invest and a spectacular propensity to consume ('conspicuous consumption'), which will be described in detail later on.[51]

These data reveal the difference between a society which, like the Danish one, has experienced *broad-based competitive-capitalist development*, including a thorough capitalization of all economic sectors, and a society which, as in the case of Uruguay, remained characterized, despite populism, by a persistent *oligarchic structure*, which was never affected by comprehensive competitive-capitalist capitalization. In the economic history of Uruguay, oligarchic and persistently extensive export-orientated stock farming resulted in *polarized internal structures*. In Denmark, the transition to intensive agriculture, with its related local industry and the further step towards broad-based import substitution industrialization despite continuing export orientation, resulted in the emergence of an internally intermeshed, coherent economy. *The two development paths are set against a backdrop of markedly different social structures.* These differences show up in exemplary fashion in the distribution of land, which was initially in both countries the most important factor of production. The available data on land tenure show in the case of Denmark a relatively *even distribution*, with a core of consolidated and modernizing family-operated farms,[52] while in the case of Uruguay the disparities in the size of landholdings and in land ownership are on a 'Latin-American' scale.[53]

These different degrees of inequality implied different development potentials of the domestic markets in question. In Uruguay, a highly unequal structure resulted in import-export activities on the pattern of the classic division of labour between metropoles and peripheries.[54] In a later phase, import substitution industrialization started, which, as always in these cases, ran out of steam more or less quickly, and which, against the backdrop of an oligarchic structure, has still not resulted in the emergence of an internally consolidated *national economy*.[55] The contrast with Denmark is obvious: there a moderately unequal ownership structure translated itself into widespread income growth on account of growing export receipts and into productivity gains which supplied the basis for a really broad-based development of the domestic market— despite her relatively small population. If in the evolution process of an export-orientated national economy completely new areas of production and exports are developed—as, for example, in the engineering and capital goods industries for which a 'natural' factor endowment is lacking— then a qualitative and quantitative increase in per capita export production and a rising share in world trade seem, even in the case of small national economies, possible after all. The present difference in the per capita exports of manufacturers of the two countries in question, which is in the range of 1:16, speaks for itself and indicates, like other data, the fundamental contrast between the development paths illustrated in Table 6.

The two case-studies show clearly that small countries with small populations, which are moreover characterized by a one-sided agricultural resource endowment (good soils and a favourable climate), can advance along highly divergent development paths. *Smallness as such does not have to result in a narrowness of the domestic market*. The latter emerges only in the specific circumstances of a markedly unequal resource distribution. The Danish example demonstrates that a country with a small population and without mineral resources is able to develop a *coherent* domestic economy, including a capital goods sector[56] which is always disproportionately important for the overall dynamics of successful economic development, and which, if it is to survive in small countries, must be internationally competitive at an early stage.

Where a large population is lacking and only limited resources are available, the development of 'invisible capital'[57] can make all the difference. The early and remarkable spread of literacy, a broad elementary education, the increasing importance of vocational schools, technical on-the-job training and technical universities have allowed Denmark to compensate for those resources that were lacking in its natural factor endowment. A wide spread of competence contributed to the high transformation and innovation capacity of Danish society, and indeed provided a counterweight to pressure towards peripheralization. Even though Uruguay, too, was characterized by relatively early and widespread literacy, her educational institutions, especially those in the area of higher education, were from the start biased towards the arts, philosophy and law rather than pragmatic-technical subjects.

Without doubt the two examples demonstrate the importance of social *core structures* that have evolved over a period of time.[58] But for the successful political implementation, from the middle of the eighteenth century onwards, of de-feudalization, Danish development would have taken a different course from that outlined above. If big estates had retained a larger presence and greater political influence, agricultural development on the pattern prevailing east of the Elbe would have been more likely than an agricultural system based on family-operated farms and an economically independent peasantry.[59] The landowners would have been able to fall back on a sufficient number of small farmers (cottagers), with the result that, at least after the European agricultural crisis in the mid-1870s, high growth in grain exports accompanied by rural poverty would have taken place.[60] How the large landowners would have responded to the agricultural crisis is difficult to guess. They would probably have tried to implement a protectionist policy—which was indeed demanded by them in Denmark at the time. However, in view of the developments in the world grain market, such protectionism would not have been practicable for a small country like Denmark without considerable income losses for the big landowners. Here the contrast in size between the Danish and German or French domestic economies would have made all the difference.[61]

In the same way as successful *de-feudalization* marked a decisive socio-structural watershed in Denmark, the emerging *oligarchic structure* shaped the development dynamics of Uruguay during the whole of the nineteenth century, its influence persisting well into the twentieth century. The contrasting cases of Denmark and Uruguay show clearly that such social core structures are obviously over-determined.[62] (Structures are 'over-determined' if, despite changing individual factors, the core structure remains relatively unaffected, with the result that past development trends continue unbroken.) On the surface, Uruguay was some sort of exception in Latin America on account of the relatively high standing of her export commodities. But despite the fact that a high rate of literacy was achieved at an early stage and that the populist *Batllismo* movement led to an early implementation of welfare measures, and even though Uruguay developed at an early stage the typical political institutions of bourgeois society (parliamentarianism), the traditional *oligarchic* social structure, especially the agrarian structure, has to this day prevented a breakthrough to a mature, highly industrialized society and economy.

The export success of Uruguay benefited her oligarchy. By leading to *overspecialization*, whose concomitant symptom was a *lack of domestic economic diversification and coherence*, it damaged the development of the economy, preventing the emergence of a *national economy*. Like other wool- and meat-exporting economies, that of Uruguay was exposed to *the very same* cyclical fluctuations within *one and the same* world market.[63] Her dominant classes grasped the export opportunities offered by the world market. Like all export economies they were confronted with bottlenecks, whenever world economic downturns reduced the demand for their main export commodities, meat, wool and hides. In certain other societies, however, the first foundations for viable national economies were laid as a result of profitable export activities. Not so in Uruguay. Nor can her future development prospects be considered promising, considering the previous hundred years of misdirected development. In a recent assessment Nohlen voiced the following opinion, one that is shared by other observers of the Latin-American scene:

> It is difficult to see how the existing development deadlock can be remedied other than by means of structural reforms in agriculture. Only a reform of land tenure, combined with a shift away from extensive production methods and with an increase in agricultural output and productivity, can create an opening for development. Without such incisive intervention in the socio-economic structure, the target figures of development plans are not worth the paper they are written on. As long as she is guided by the traditional agricultural export model on the basis of an unchanged system of land tenure and by the political model of a regime of terror, Uruguay really has no development prospects.[64]

Further Illustrations

New Zealand—another small agricultural exporter

The preceding paragraphs were based on the twin examples of Denmark and Uruguay. Can the observations and interpretations derived from these two examples be substantiated by other case-studies? One looks for countries with small populations and a one-sided agricultural resource endowment. New Zealand comes relatively close to such a profile.[65] In 1900 her population was around 300,000. In 1977 the country had 3.1 million inhabitants,—that is, slightly more than Uruguay and 2 million less than Denmark. In 1977 agriculture provided 78 per cent of her total exports, 30 per cent of which were still agricultural raw materials. On the basis of aggregate data, New Zealand today ranks between Uruguay and Denmark. In 1977 her per capita GDP was $4,380, as compared with $1,430 in Uruguay and $8,040 in Denmark. In 1975 her share of world trade was 0.23 per cent, as compared with Denmark's 0.98 per cent and Uruguay's 0.04 per cent (see Tables 5 and 6). How can this intermediate position be explained?

The development of New Zealand can be understood only in the context of her integration into the world economy. As in the case of both the above-mentioned countries, it was *agricultural exports* that provided the crucial growth impulse for New Zealand's economy. Initially, the agricultural export economy was founded on sheep farming, which took place on very large landholdings and which, from the middle of the last century, provided the basis for *wool exports*[66] With the reduction in freight costs and the introduction of refrigeration technology, transport to England of frozen meat and later of dairy products became possible from 1882 onwards. For both 1892 and 1910, statistics indicate that sheep farming contributed 55 per cent of the total exports. Of these, 43 per cent were wool exports and 12 per cent exports of frozen meat, the share of wool exports falling to 38 per cent and that of meat exports rising to 17 per cent by 1910.[67] As in the two cases examined above, New Zealand's external economic condition was characterized by an extreme concentration of trading partners (Britain) and a considerable concentration of export goods. And as in Uruguay, the exports of agricultural commodities were counterbalanced by imports of British manufactures and equipment, and especially British capital, at least during the first decades of export growth until the 1890s. How, then, has New Zealand avoided following in Uruguay's footsteps despite such an external economic structure and despite a kind of 'latifundist' system of land tenure? The following factors are relevant. Until the 1890s the distribution of land ownership was heavily tilted in favour of large holdings. In 1891, 2 per cent of the farms occupied 54 per cent of the land, while smallholdings constituted 58 per cent of all farms but were confined to 4 per cent of the land. The proportion of medium-sized farms was 40 per cent, occupying 42 per cent of the land.[68]

In the wake of the agricultural crisis of the 1870s and 1880s, which also hit New Zealand, and in view of the agrarian situation outlined above, a progressive-liberal party defeated the Conservative Party, dominated by large landowners, in parliamentary elections in the early 1890s—a victory that resulted in the formation of a government under its leadership. From 1892 onwards this political grouping attempted by means of various Land Settlement Acts to prevent the further expansion of large landholdings or even to 'eliminate large landholdings altogether'.[69] By means of a progressive land tax, the buying of land by the state and the purposive sale of unused Crown land, the medium-sized farm sector was successfully expanded and the sizeable sector of large landholdings reduced. Initially, the process certainly did not result in an agriculture built on family-operated farms comparable to the Danish case, for in 1914 the sector of large estates was still of considerable size. Crucial for New Zealand's development was, however, the fact that the rural and urban groups which were politically opposed to the large landowners, succeeded, through government and public administration, in establishing an effective political counterweight in tune with their own social and economic interests.[70] Only on this basis could the policy of a deliberate *internal colonization* be implemented, for such an attempt had previously been blocked by the large landowners owing to their control over land and political power.[71] By diminishing the large landholding sector and establishing smaller, though by European standards still very large, farm units, it was also intended to lay the foundations for an *intensification of agriculture* ('closer settlement'). With regard to the export sector this implied, above all, promoting and strengthening the dairy industry whose products, butter and cheese, could be exported to a growing English market once suitable refrigeration technology had been developed. The dairy industry was based mainly on the production of *high quality* goods which were subjected to quality control by public bodies before being exported, a necessary measure in view of the strong international competition, mainly from Canada, the United States and Denmark. Between 1891 and 1911 the value of New Zealand's cheese and butter exports grew more than tenfold; their share in total exports was 2.5 per cent in 1891 and 13 per cent in 1911. Parts of agriculture turned to dairy farming slightly later than in Denmark, but their export success occurred during the same two decades before the First World War. As a result of these developments, New Zealand ended up with an agriculture that operated differently in different sectors. Sheep farming, based on *extensive* production methods, remained vitally important for the production of wool and frozen meat—wool exports providing the largest share of total exports. Sheep farming retained its importance because the low costs and the relatively stable, and even increasing, export earnings rendered this sector especially profitable. The fact that part of agriculture adopted *intensive* farming methods, producing for export (dairy products) as well as for the domestic market (fruit, vegetables, honey, etc.)—combined with the shift in domestic political power from the Conservatives to the progressive Liberals—has saved New Zealand from falling into the structural trap that caught Uruguay.

This difference surfaces also in the treatment of industry. While

Uruguay, as described above, subordinated herself to the typical division of labour between metropoles and peripheries, and while Denmark practised considerable tariff protection against imports of manufactures from as early as the 1860s, the mixture of world market integration and *selective dissociation* was even more pronounced in New Zealand than in Denmark. This tariff policy, part of a *deliberate development policy*, was also implemented by the progressive-liberal government after 1895 and especially after 1900. The protection was geared above all to the establishment of agro-industrial enterprises, tied to agriculture by forward and backward linkages, as well as for the import substitution industry.[72] As a percentage of the value of imported goods the tariffs on textiles, leather goods, glass, clocks, metal goods and steam engines were 20 per cent, on cloth and hats 25 per cent, and on garments 10 per cent—to name but a few.[73] Remarkably, economic statistics from the turn of the century indicate a surprisingly low proportion of the work-force being employed in the primary sector (in 1891, 28 per cent; in 1906, 24 per cent), while the share of the industrial work-force was 28 per cent in 1981, rising to 31 per cent by 1906.[74]

New Zealand's later development history up to the present is characterized by a further *equalization of land ownership*, the continuing *intensification of agriculture* by means of technology and motorization, the application of new scientific procedures in animal husbandry and soil cultivation, the use of artificial fertilizers and the successful fight against the rabbit plague.[75] As a result of these developments, agriculture achieved a considerable degree of diversification. At the same time internal colonization made further progress. Between 1941 and 1970 alone, more than 1,600,000 acres were developed by the state in New Zealand and divided into roughly 4,000 farms. Agricultural productivity grew more than six and a half times between 1938/9 and 1969/70. In large parts of New Zealand the output per acre is low, though very high in the case of intensive cultivation, but labour productivity in agriculture is exceptionally high everywhere. According to comparative statistics in the 1920s, New Zealand had the highest per capita agricultural output in the world, followed by Australia, Argentina, Uruguay, the United States, Denmark, Canada and the Netherlands.[76] The differences in the agricultural structures concealed by such data are thrown into relief by a comparison of the cattle stocks in New Zealand and Uruguay. While cattle stocks in Uruguay have remained more or less stationary since the first decade of this century (about 8 to 8.5 million cattle, with sheep stocks declining from 26 million to 19 million), the majority of the roughly 65,000 farms in New Zealand (1979) derive their income from an expanding sector of livestock farming. 'Owing to

increasing intensification, the number of livestock has grown to about
60 million sheep and 8.8 million cattle [1970], and has thus nearly
doubled since the Second World War.'[77]

A deepening of New Zealand's economic structure occurred as a
result of the development policy measures adopted in response to the
world economic crisis of the 1930s. The fall in world market prices
reduced export earnings by 40 per cent between April 1929 and April
1930, with the result that national income dropped by one-third. In
1935 the first Labour government came to power. Its measures as
regards incomes policy (the creation of public employment, introduction of the forty-hour week and of a high minimum wage) resulted in
increased mass-purchasing power and increased employment. Like
Denmark, New Zealand adopted a clearly *protectionist* and *state-
interventionist* economic course.

Tables 5–8 alone give an outline of the present structure of New
Zealand's economy. Salient features are the still relatively high share of
the agrarian sector in the production of the GDP and the relatively
small proportion of exports of finished goods (16.3 per cent), including
machinery, equipment and electrical engineering products (3.2 per
cent). By the standards of other OECD countries, this industrial
subsector is relatively small. This applies also in relation to Australia,
whose exports comprise only a relatively small proportion of capital
goods, while the industrial subsector has attained a quite considerable
size within the domestic economy, namely one-quarter of the industrial
net product (Table 8). Statistics on the use of the GDP reveal, on the
other hand, a distinctly metropolitan profile. In contrast with Uruguay,
the share of investment is relatively high (28 per cent). Consumer
demand accounts, as in Denmark, for slightly more than 60 per cent,
the state demand for goods and services being rather low. The share of
wage income in the GDP amounts to 66 per cent. These figures make
up a profile which could be considered the opposite of the rentier
capitalist profile examined in the case of Uruguay (Table 7).

In terms of per capita income and share of world trade, New Zealand
occupies an intermediate position between Uruguay and Denmark.
The development of Denmark resulted in a broad, comprehensive and
coherent diversification of her internal structure, while Uruguay remained on the whole characterized by a peripheral-capitalist structure,
despite the fact that intermittently she presented a different outward
appearance. New Zealand escaped peripheralization on account first of
her political, then of her economic *de-oligarchization* , without having as
yet attained a degree of structural diversification and coherence comparable to Denmark's.[78] A simple but telling indicator of the structural

differences between Denmark, New Zealand and Uruguay is provided by their capital goods sectors' varying contributions to the GDP and to exports (Table 5). The varying share of the capital goods sector in net industrial output (26 per cent in Denmark, 12 per cent in New Zealand and 3 per cent in Uruguay), as well as the different contribution of capital goods exports to total exports (approximately 27 per cent in Denmark, 3 per cent in New Zealand and 2 per cent in Uruguay) reflect in quantitative terms, though at a high level of abstraction, the different degrees of maturity attained by the three economies in question.

The Netherlands and Ireland: two further examples

The present analysis can be extended by means of further relevant case-studies. The central selection criteria remain the same as in the cases discussed above: a relatively small population, an overwhelmingly agricultural resource base, growth impulses derived from agricultural exports, export-led integration into the international division of labour, climatic-geographical location in the temperate zone and relative political autonomy. Among the countries which, on this basis, have experienced an upturn in development comparable to the Danish one,[79] is the Netherlands. In Ireland, by contrast, peripheral-capitalist development can be observed. In this connection Iceland could also be cited as a positive case. According to World Bank statistics her per capita income amounted to $7,070 in 1977; her export commodity basket comprises 77 per cent foodstuffs, mainly fish and processed fish products. Since 1968 her share of metal exports (aluminium) has risen from 0.5 per cent to 16 per cent. As in the case of Norway since the turn of the century, these exports are based on the processing of imported raw materials with the aid of local hydroelectricity and the exploitation of geysers.[80]

So far as the long-term profile is concerned, Dutch development provides the closest approximation to the Danish experience.[81] Despite all differences in detail, their historical progression is on the whole comparable: increased modernization and intensification of agriculture in the wake of the European agricultural crisis of the 1870s and 1880s, leading to growing specialization in dairy and meat products as well as in an expanding cultivation of vegetables; a high degree of specialization in certain agricultural niches such as the growing of flowers and the production of bulbs; agriculture-related small-scale industrialization and, between 1890 and 1910, the development—though to a much more limited extent than in Denmark—of new dynamic growth industries like the electrical, chemical and petro-chemical industries. In many respects Dutch development since the middle of the last century can be understood only in connection with the development of the Rhine and Ruhr area. Its coupling with this dynamic growth pole of Germany intensified the economic links between the two countries: on the part of the Netherlands mainly through increasing supplies of foodstuffs, through labour commuting across the border and, above all, through an expanding transit trade by road, river and rail. It is not surprising, therefore, that in 1913 services contributed 57 per cent of the Dutch GDP,[82] and that the size and the quality of the Dutch communications network reflected this situation. Several factors have probably contributed to the fact that the Dutch domestic market developed more slowly than the Danish one. For example, high population growth from the middle of the last century onward, a smaller proportion of economically independent farmers and widely fragmented landholdings, relatively high productivity per acre, coupled initially with low labour productivity, relatively high capital intensity in the new dynamic sectors, and so on. Despite such factors, Dutch growth has followed a relatively balanced pattern, which is due not least to the rise of the food-processing industry. The latter processed not only local agricultural raw materials (production of powdered and condensed milk, processing of potatoes into glucose and starch), but products from the colonies (sugar refining, the making of cocoa powder, chocolate and margarine). In 1913, 28 per cent of the labour force produced 16 per cent of GDP in the primary sector, 35 per cent produced 27 per cent in the industrial sector, and 38 per cent produced 57 per cent in the service sector.[83] In 1977 per capita income amounted to $7,150; 6 per cent of the labour force was employed in the primary, 45 per cent in the secondary and 49 per cent in the tertiary sector. The composition of the GDP was 4 per cent, 34 per cent and 64 per cent respectively (Table 5). The contribution to the net industrial product of mechanical engineering, electrical engineering and the production of transport equipment amounted to 22 per cent (Table 8). Exports of foodstuffs constituted 21.7 per cent of the total exports, agricultural raw materials 3.6 per cent and finished manufactures 50 per cent, the latter figure comprising slightly less than 20 per cent of machinery and equipment (Table 6).

Irish per capita income is at present about half-way between those of Uruguay and New Zealand ($2,880) (Tables 5–8).[84] Statistics on the distribution of the work-force and the composition of the GDP reveal a remarkably high proportion of the population still engaged in agriculture (21 per cent in 1977 producing 16 per cent of the GDP), and, on the other hand, a rather low share of services. An initially surprising fact that emerges from the statistics on the composition of net industrial product is the 12 per cent share of mechanical and electrical engineering and the production of transport equipment. According to export statistics, the share of agricultural exports amounts to 42 per cent; exports of finished manufactures account for 49.5 per cent, comprising a high proportion of machinery, electrical machinery and transport equipment (15.3 per cent). The data on the exports of finished manufactures and their relatively high capital goods content are, however, no more indicative of a high average productivity level of the Irish economy than is the relatively high share (12 per cent) in net industrial output of engineering and the manufacture of transport equipment. They are a result of foreign investment in *industrial enclaves*, whose production is sold in the world market. The data on an agricultural sector, which is palpably overmanned, and on an insufficiently developed service sector, can therefore be easily reconciled with the observations above. If the relatively high share of the capital goods sector (compared with Irish per capita income) were to show up in the average productivity of the *whole* economy—as, for example, in the case of Israel, which has a population of 3.6 million and a per capita income of $2,850—a generally advanced productivity profile would have to be expected (Table 5). The relatively high share of industry, especially the capital goods sector, in the GDP and exports thus obscures the peripheral-capitalist core structure of the country, which has evolved in the course of history.

The history of Irish development is a prime example of emerging peripheralization.[85] When she was politically united with Britain, but separated economically, Ireland had an economic structure that was relatively diversified by the standards of pre-industrial societies (from about 1660 to 1820). Coupled with the import of cheap industrially produced finished goods from Britain, the subsequent integration of the Irish agricultural export industry (meat and live cattle) led to the emergence of a classic division of labour between metropole and periphery. In Ireland this development amounted to a regression of the whole economy and later of the whole society, as indicated by famines, emigration and a shrinking population (in 1841, 6.5 million; in 1971, 2.9 million).[86]

The expanding Irish cattle-exporting industry, by supplanting other agricultural enterprises with a higher output per acre, caused a decline in demand from the land-intensive export sector. Simultaneously, competing imports were depressing non-export industries. The combined effect was greatly to reduce total demand, the scale of operations, and hence overall efficiency in labour and capital-intensive industries in Ireland. Unit production costs in industries other than the expanding cattle industry became greater as the scale of the industries decreased, and industries not initially threatened by imports or by diversion of land to cattle in time also became vulnerable. More and more cottage industries were forced out of business, and the non-agricultural work-force of southern Ireland declined even more rapidly than the agricultural work-force. Reducing wages did not stem the process. As wages dropped and famine became chronic in Ireland in the decades following George III's death, employment in labour and capital-intensive industry declined, the urban population declined and more and more people competed with increasing cattle stocks for possession of land. Wage reductions . . . had two serious shortcomings. First . . . they caused a massive rise in the death rate, in Ireland in the 1840s, as in western Europe in the 1340s. Second, wage reductions, by depressing local demand, reduced the scale and so the efficiency of local industry.[87]

Not even Ireland's political separation from Great Britain in 1922 resulted in the elimination of the peripheral-capitalist core structure that had evolved during the nineteenth century. Though a food-processing industry emerged, it remained structurally weak. The separation from Britain led, moreover, to an immobilization of the Irish agrarian structure. The latter is based on about 300,000 farms, 150,000 (50 per cent) of which comprise less than 50 acres, a further 130,000 with less than 100 acres, and 20,000 large estates.[88] In Ireland commercially successful farms coexist with highly fragmented 'minifundist' units. Broad-based industrialization, with a high capacity for absorbing labour freed by agricultural modernization, did not happen. Industry remained orientated towards certain limited sectors and too insular. Even the more recent attempts to attract foreign investment for the export-orientated production of manufactures have resulted only in industrial enclaves without the necessary macro-economic spill-over effects.[89]

Conclusions for Development Theory

Overall, the examples cited above demonstrate that it was neither the quality of soils nor the climate, nor the world economic conditions in which these export economies evolved,[90] which were responsible for the success or failure of development paths, but *socio-structural and institutional* factors which channelled political decision-making into different directions during *critical phases of development*.[91]

What conclusions should be drawn for development theory from the preceding discussion of individual development paths?

Where successful development could be diagnosed in the preceding analysis, it depended—in the socio-structural, institutional and political field—on the initial distribution of resources and on a shift of political power towards new economic groups in the course of the development process; and—in the economic field—on an increase in the overall productivity of the economy in question. In the following pages these factors will be re-examined.

Increasing overall productivity in the development process

In the successful development processes analysed above (Denmark, the Netherlands, New Zealand), the *overall productivity* of the respective economies has increased as a result of the secular transfer of the mass of the labour force from the primary to the secondary and tertiary sectors, and as a result of the modernization, diversification and intermeshing of these sectors.[92] The particular characteristics of these development paths stemmed from their *specific initial profile*, which was characterized by a small population, a predominantly agricultural factor endowment and orientation towards agricultural exports.

The process of raising the overall productivity of the economies in question began without exception in the sector that offered the best chances for development on the basis of existing resources, namely, with the *modernization and diversification of the agricultural economy*. Such a process provided the bridge to agriculture-related industrialization, based initially on small-scale production. Once this process attained greater momentum, it led to the emergence of agriculture-related industrial complexes. The latter included enterprises for the processing of agricultural products and raw materials as well as industries that produced a growing proportion of the equipment required for agricultural modernization. This *agro-industrialization*, which was initially geared to small-scale production of simple goods, gradually achieved greater economies of scale and turned out increasingly complex products. The development process evolved, therefore, relatively organically.

At a later stage in the process of raising the overall productivity of the economies in question, the establishment of *consumer goods industries orientated towards the domestic market* (import substitution), and the subsequent establishment of certain *heavy and capital goods industries*, played an important role. This stage in the development process amounted to a progressive opening up of the domestic market, as demonstrated by Walther Hoffmann as early as the beginning of the 1930s.[93] In each case the emerging domestic industries became internationally competitive at different moments and to different degrees. In the Netherlands, for example, the early competitiveness of modern sectors is striking, while in Denmark the import-substituting consumer goods industry remained uncompetitive for a long period, in sharp contrast with specific products of the capital goods industry—for example, Danish milk centrifuges.

The sequence—agricultural exports, agriculture-related industrialization, import-substituting consumer goods industrialization, import-substituting capital goods industrialization—is predetermined by the initial resource endowments of the economies in question. Some remarks on contrasting examples of economies with small populations, but with different resource endowments, may help clarify this theme.

Belgian development[94] in the first half of the nineteenth century, for example, was—after the end of the Napoleonic continental blockade and an intermittent period of stagnation—protectionist and inward-directed from 1830 onward. The dynamic impulse that shaped overall development stemmed from energy generation, heavy industry and the production of semi-finished goods rather than from the production of textiles, which remained craft-based for a long time, or from agriculture, which was less than flourishing. The prerequisite for such a development path was provided by a resource endowment which differed substantially from that of the other cases discussed in this chapter by being based on coal and ore deposits. Only in a second development phase, from about 1860, did Belgium engage in an export drive, overtaking Switzerland as the European leader in per capita exports in 1890. It is only afterwards that the broad-based and dynamic development of the domestic market, by means of a real increase in the demand for mass consumer goods and the capital goods required in their production, can be observed.

The second example, the Swiss development path,[95] also indicates the strategic importance of the initial resource endowment for the industrial development sequence. As Switzerland possessed on the whole neither mineral resources nor—as was often supposed abroad—an especially favourable agricultural potential, her development path was characterized by the following sequence: broad-based proto-industrialization before the Industrial Revolution; importation of raw materials from abroad and their processing into finished goods (to begin with, mainly into high-quality textiles) for export; gradual industrialization of the export sector, including the establishment of an engineering industry; highly export-orientated specialization in the production of a limited number of agricultural products of special quality (dairy products, chocolate, stock cubes, etc.); and a gradual opening up of the domestic market. In contrast with the Belgian case, this development path was essentially free-trade orientated. It was in the main locally accumulated competence that was exploited, since this constituted Switzerland's real resource endowment on account of the country's historical development since the late Middle Ages. This basic orientation has remained unchanged until the present day.

In the cases of successful development that are analysed in the present study, the increase in overall productivity depended also on the *technological capabilities* acquired in the development process. These relate to the capacity efficiently to employ foreign technology locally—that is, to adapt it to local circumstances—and, crucially important in the long run, to invent new technology, even if only in niche areas, to introduce it into the domestic economy, and to market it competitively abroad.[96] This has been achieved by the Netherlands and Denmark, while in Ireland and Uruguay—both cases of periphery development—no breakthroughs of this kind occurred.[97] The diffusion of technological skills and knowledge is, however, indispensable for an economy, in the interests of attaining high standards of productivity in *all* sectors—and, consequently, a mature, typically metropolitan, profile.[98]

If an *economy* initially *biased towards agricultural exports* is to attain high overall productivity, it has to reduce—by whatever means it can—its *bias towards agricultural exports*, but without, in view of the small population, being able to overcome a *bias towards exports* as such. Crucial aspects are: the *transition from a mono-export structure to a diversified export structure* as well as the emergence, despite the export orientation, of a *diversified internal structure* and a concomitant *opening up of the domestic market*. In the course of this process the sector that might become a structural trap through the export of unprocessed or little processed agricultural commodities, declines in importance and the export commodities' basket becomes economically more profitable to the extent that the internal structure of the whole economy diversifies and attains a higher level of productivity.[99]

The strategic role of the initial distribution of resources in the development process

It is precisely the analysis of small countries geared to agricultural exports that has revealed the crucial importance of socio-structural, institutional and political factors in the development process. In countries with a mainly agricultural resource endowment, the course of the development process depended on the *initial distribution of the main resource—namely, land*. The conclusion drawn by Morawetz from an analysis of the development processess between 1959 and 1975 is certainly confirmed by the present comparative study:

It simply may not be possible to 'grow first and redistribute later', because
the structure of growth may largely fix the pattern of distribution at least
until much higher developed-country levels of per capita income are approached. That is to say, if greater equality of incomes is to be an objective
in the medium term, it may be necessary to tackle it as a first priority by land
reform, mass education, and whatever other means are available, rather
than leaving it until after growth has taken place.[100]

Finland, whose development has been discussed in the preceding
chapter,[101] knew—like Norway and Sweden (apart from southern Sweden)—no feudal structures in her pre-industrial period. Denmark under-
went a process of de-feudalization. In the Netherlands about 50 per
cent of the farms were owned by economically independent farmers,
the remainder being tenanted in conditions of relatively high contrac-
tual security. New Zealand experienced a process of de-oligarchization.
By contrast, the persistently oligarchic agricultural structure of Uruguay
and the dichotomous structure of Ireland stand out.

The *broad-based development of an infrastructure and communications network, as well as the abolition of institutions and rules hindering the mobility of
capital, labour and technological progress*, became as important for the
process of increasing overall productivity as the initial distribution of
land resources. A propensity to innovate developed to the extent that
socio-structural and institutional conditions rendered such initiatives
promising, which depended essentially on factors like the establishment of the rule of law and opportunities for individual gain as well as a
positive correlation between risk-taking and profit chances (property
rights).[102]

Shifts in political power during the development process

Economic growth in the leading sectors, as well as in their up-and
downstream areas, together with the gradual broad-based diversification of the whole economy, induced social change, which showed up
in horizontal and vertical mobility. This social change gave rise to new
social classes and interests which became politically aware of their
situation, organized themselves into pressure groups and made their
weight felt in the domestic political struggle. The more broad-based the
process of socio-economic development, the greater the *politicization* of
society and the more pronounced the shift in political power away from
the traditional power groups (large landowners, monopolistic commercial capital, etc.) towards the representatives of new interest groups

(small and medium-sized farmers, private entrepreneurs, the proletariat, the new bourgeois and intellectual middle classes and public administrators). The result of such a gradual power shift, which tended to accelerate in periods of acute crisis caused by world economic cycles, was by no means predetermined, in the sense that a slide into peripheralization would have been impossible.[103] This observation is corroborated by the conflict over Danish tariff policy in the 1870s and 1880s between large landowners, on the one hand, and small and medium-sized farmers, on the other. It is also confirmed by the conflict between industry, the urban middle classes, the farmers and the proletariat—by then organized in trade unions and the Social Democratic Party—over the response to the world economic crisis of 1929 and initiation of a new development phase in the 1930s, a policy that was born out of a tactical alliance between social democracy and the farmers' representatives. As for New Zealand, the conflict between large landowners and the groups interested in an *intensive* agriculture ('closer settlement') was described in an earlier section. In this case, the direction of development was not clearly predetermined as regards power relationships, but was on the contrary the result of intense internal political struggles that were decided in favour of the progressive Liberals, and later in favour of the Labour Party,[104] and thus in favour of an autocentric development path.

An analysis of the gradual emergence of high overall productivity in successful economics must—in the same way as the diagnosis of development blocks in defective development processes—take into account the interlacement of political, institutional, socio-structural and economic factors. Such factors are relatively closely intertwined and, as already evidenced by the cases mentioned above, their combination is by no means coincidental. They reinforce one another cumulatively, as elaborated by Myrdal in the case of peripheralization processes as well as in autocentric development paths.[105]

The Cuban development path—a current example of attempted agricultural export industrialization

All the development processes in the cases discussed above began in the second half of the nineteenth century at the latest. The development dynamics tending towards autocentric development or peripheralization therefore spans about a hundred years. But are there any *current* examples of autocentric development in spite of an initial dependence on agricultural exports? An interesting example in terms of development theory is provided by the Cuban development path after 1963. In a comprehensive study, Fabian has recently examined the programmatic basis of the Cuban development path and its attempted implementation.[106] In this connection his analysis is of paradigmatic importance.

Until 1959 Cuba was in every respect an exclave-like sugar monoculture, which combined an export monostructure with a social and economic monoculture. After the successful revolution of 1959 the new leadership aimed during the first few years at the immediate broad diversification of agriculture and industry while neglecting the sugar sector and sugar exports. In view of the one-sided natural resource endowment (soils of tropical quality and as yet undeveloped nickel deposits which were, in any case, not all that abundant), this 'Soviet development path' pursued by the Cubans (in spite of Soviet criticism) led after only a short time into a blind alley. Because of a shortage of foreign exchange and an increasingly precarious food situation, a fundamental revision of the development course became inescapable. Surprisingly, the course that has emerged after 1963 corresponds *programmatically*—and to a certain degree already also in reality—with the model of successful autocentric development on the basis of an initial bias towards agricultural exports, as portrayed in the preceding discussion.

In contrast with the interim period from 1959 to 1962, export-orientated *sugar-based agriculture* again became the hub of the development strategy. This decision was initially based on short-term static considerations of comparative advantages, but reflected also the intention to secure in the long term *new dynamic comparative advantages* for the Cuban economy. The crucial task in terms of development planning was that of having to maintain a sugar-based mono-*export* structure for the acquisition of foreign exchange, while at the same time eliminating the sugar monoculture that had dominated the social and economic structure of pre-revolutionary Cuba. In response to this task, development planning was based on the following considerations:

(1) Use of the *sugar sector* as the starting-point for a gradual *(incremental) diversification* of Cuban agriculture and industry. The incremental approach contrasted with the earlier attempt to achieve immediate broad structural diversification while neglecting the sugar sector.

(2) *Selective concentration* on certain key areas: in the first place the modernization of sugar-orientated agriculture through the attempt to establish linkages between the sugar sector and a *diversified agriculture*, yet to be created, outside the sugar sector—that is, in the area of animal husbandry (cattle-rearing). Utilization of the waste products of the sugar sector as animal feed.

(3) Establishment of a *sugar-related industry* (e.g. sucro-chemical pro-

duction) and of an engineering industry orientated towards the sugar sector. Manufacture of *equipment* for sugar-cane production, (e.g. combine harvesters and, ultimately, complete sugar-mills).

(4) Establishment of *selective growth poles* outside the sugar sector, using other available natural resources. Gradual further diversification emanating from these *secondary* growth poles, based—as in the sugar sector—on an incremental approach, selective promotion of key sectors, *concentric* development processes, aiming at the gradual *intra-sectoral* and *inter-sectoral interlacement* of the Cuban economy, resulting in the elimination of the traditional monoculture and the establishment of a Cuban *national economy* despite a continuing bias towards exports.

(5) Gradual *diversification of the export structure* as a by-product of an increasingly autocentric internal structure. Reaping of *dynamic comparative advantages* through increased overall productivity in the domestic economy.

The development strategy espoused by Cuba fits precisely the historical experience in those cases diagnosed in this study as successful export-orientated development paths. Whether the Cuban leadership will successfully implement its project is beyond the scope of the present discussion. What it has been necessary to point out are the parallels between the historical experiences of small export economies that were initially geared to agricultural exports, and the current development programme and its attempted translation, however difficult in present conditions, into concrete practice in the case of Cuba.

The Cuban development path after 1963 is also of special interest, because most cases of successful delayed development in socialist conditions tend to conform to the Soviet pattern of forced industrialization rather than to the Cuban example.[107] This applies to the south-eastern European countries, Romania and Bulgaria, as well as to Hungary and Poland. And it applies especially to Norlth Korea and, with certain qualifications, also to Yugoslavia and Albania. Development in North Korea was not centred on the export of her abundantly available mineral resources but on the promotion of heavy industry and on the unlocking of the agricultural potential that initially lay fallow. In Romania and Hungary, too, it was not grain production that re-emerged as the 'leading sector' but heavy industry, in exactly the same way as in Yugoslavia and Poland. In Albania the export of the few available mineral resources provided the foreign exchange necessary for the establishment of an import substitution industry and, in a later phase, a small sector of heavy and capital goods industry.

The reference to other examples of delayed development in socialist conditions was designed to highlight Cuba's exceptional approach, at least since 1963, to the practice of delayed development—a practice that appears especially interesting in the context of historical case-studies. For just as Danish farmers tried to link cattle-rearing, dairy farming and the raising of pigs and poultry, and just as they succeeded in creating agriculture-related technological and institutional innovations (milk centrifuges, cooperatives), so Cuban development planners are obviously trying, despite severely limited pasture land, to develop animal husbandry by using sugar-cane waste products as feed input, to breed for the first time indeed highly productive tropical dairy cows and cattle for meat production (which until now have not existed), to build cane-harvesting combines in order to meet a growing scarcity of labour, and to link sugar-cane agriculture with a sucro-chemical industry. All of which has led—as in the case of Danish, Dutch and New Zealand's agriculture and Finnish forestry—to the elimination of monocultures in the domestic economy and in the export sector as a result of diversification and increasing productivity, that is to say to the emergence of a national economy.

Some Further Observations Based on the Analysis of Larger Export Economies

Can the observations that have been made in the preceding paragraphs be *generalized* to cover cases other than those discussed? Up to this point the analysis has been based on small countries with a limited population and few resources, since it is they that face the most obstinate prejudice from development theory. But what determines the development chances of larger, more populous export economies that are richer in resources? We are looking for cases where growth impulses resulting from agricultural export activities could have played a considerable part in economic development, and where at least relative political autonomy existed. Which examples would supply the answer?[108]

One would certainly have to number Hungary (as part of the Austro-Hungarian monarchy), Romania, Argentina and the American Midwest states among the large food exporters in the nineteenth and early twentieth centuries.[109] Among the large exporters of agricultural raw materials were the southern states of the USA. Export commodity baskets containing foodstuffs, agricultural raw materials and minerals can be observed in the case, for instance, of Spain, Australia, Canada and South Africa.

The question that arises is, what was the *overall economic development potential* that was unlocked by staple goods exports in the above cases? All the examples listed confirm the observations derived from the preceding case-studies. Crucial for the unlocking of the development potential created through export earnings was, as regards agricultural exports, the agrarian structure underlying agricultural production, and, as regards mineral exports, the way in which the mining sector— which initially always had an enclave-like structure—was linked with the rest of the economy. The way that export opportunities were processed within the export economy was crucial for overall development in both these areas.

The large agricultural exporters in eastern and south-eastern Europe, Hungary and Romania, were characterized by extremely latifundist structures. In Hungary, for example, just 0.2 per cent of the farms of more than 1,000 jochs (1 joch – 1/2 acre) controlled—in 1895—32 per cent of the agricultural land, while just under 55 per cent of the farms under 5 jochs occupied slightly less than 6 per cent of the area.[110] Romanian agricultural statistics for 1907 convey a similar picture: 30 per cent of the farms under 5 acres occupied 4.3 per cent of the agricultural land; 0.6 per cent of the farms over 250 acres controlled 40 per cent.[111]

Development blocks rooted in latifundism: Hungary and Romania

Hungary presents an especially interesting example in this connection, since the agrarian élite enjoyed relatively extensive political autonomy after the compromise with the Habsburg monarchy in 1867, while on the other hand a large domestic market, protected against foreign competition, existed within the Austro-Hungarian monarchy whose population numbered 35 million in 1860.[112] Moreover, Hungarian development was not exclusively orientated towards agriculture. While in the textile industry integration into the Austro-Hungarian monarchy resulted in displacement competition from more highly developed regions (Bohemia, Vienna, Lower Austria), mining, iron and steel production and engineering contributed as early as the turn of the century a full 30 per cent of industrial output.[113] Industrial diversification, however, did *not* reflect an organic relationship between agriculture and industry—which would have resulted in productivity gains in cereal farming and a gradual opening up of the Hungarian domestic economy. The extension of the transport network by way of railway construction and shipping actually reinforced the latifundist structure of the grain exporting economy, which was successful in spite of its low productivity. Only the integration with flour milling created a few linkage effects, but these remained necessarily limited. With a different agrarian structure, Hungary (within her 1918 boundaries) could certainly have achieved diversified national-capitalist development, for the necessary agricultural potential was available, as were minerals. And, not least, Hungary had considerable technological competence at her disposal—even though this was concentrated in Budapest—which resulted in important inventions in electrical and mechanical engineering even before 1914.[114] But the social structure that emerged in Hungary from the sixteenth century onward (second serfdom) proved the major obstacle to a full mobilization of the development potential. Thus the advanced periphery structure that could be observed in Hungary before 1914 was the same as was to emerge in Latin America several decades later in the wake of import substitution industrialization: a structural disseverance (heterogeneity) between the politically dominant sector of large landowners and the sector of smallholders; a disseverance between capital-intensive, highly concentrated and monopolistic large-scale industry, organized in trusts, and undercapitalized local cottage industries; and a growing gulf between town (Budapest) and country, as well as between the aristocracy and agrarian capitalists, on the one hand, and a pauperized rural population, on the other. Average real hourly wages of industrial workers were less than one-third of those of British workers and less than half of those of their German counterparts.[115] As later in Latin America, the impact of the grain-exporting economy induced social change in Hungary (migration from agriculture, increased urbanization, increased productive investment by foreign capital and its mobilization effects). But this social change was not translated into structural change as the basis for *national* economic development. Rather, it reinforced, as could be observed all over the Third World a few decades later, the structural heterogeneity that was a hallmark of traditional society.[116] Hungary provides one of the earliest and clearest illustrative examples of how oligarchic and rentier-capitalist classes and social structures prevent an *existing development potential* from being realized, and how in such conditions a relatively successful export activity leads to the typical profile of peripheral capitalism with all its symptoms.

Romanian development was of identical pattern, though less dynamic than its Hungarian counterpart.[117] The agrarian reforms that were implemented in the nineteenth century (1831 and 1864) amounted to what Ernest Feder has called 'counter-reforms' in the Latin-American context.[118] Despite existing labour shortages, they contributed to pressurizing the mass of the rural population into offering themselves as cheap labour to the large landowners—with force and brutality as the stock method of repression. While the Hungarian economy had experienced a certain degree of diversification, Romanian export agriculture—which, after all, accounted for 8.3 per cent of world wheat exports between 1911 and 1913—resembled a classic periphery exporting foodstuffs and importing manufacturers. In the existing political conditions unfavourable terms of trade—owing, for example, to the fall in grain prices after the European agricultural crisis of the 1870s—could be compensated for only by extending and strengthening the repressive forced labour system.[119] It is hardly surprising that, confronted with such an extremely unequal agrarian structure and poor productivity, agricultural exports did not provide any strong development impulses for the rest of the economy. In contrast with other agrarian societies with a 'frontier' (e.g. the United States), internal land colonization in Romania has not led to the emergence of viable farms owned by an economically independent peasantry, but to the expansion of large landholdings based on extensive production methods and the growth of repressive forced labour practices. In spite of the relatively large population (in 1913, 7.2 million) and the oil reserves, which later could have become a source of more diversified development, the traditional agrarian structure could not provide a basis for broad-based industrialization. In Romania, too, a traditional social and class structure has prevented the development potential from being realized.

Comprador policies—another cause of development blocks: Thailand

The two examples from eastern and south-eastern Europe—which, for all their minor differences resembled the Uruguayan development path—could convey the wrong impression: namely, that in the case of an agriculture-orientated export economy, only an agrarian structure fragmented by the split between large and small estates would prevent the emergence of a national economy. That this is not the case is evidenced by the example of the Thai rice export economy since the middle of the last century. This example is especially interesting, as the export commodity in question was at the same time the main subsistence food, only the rice surplus exceeding local food requirements being exported. As was common in Asian irrigation farming, cultivation took place along labour-intensive horticultural lines, based on small farm units.[120]

From the middle of the last century, when the export trade in rice started, until the turn of the century, the terms of trade between rice exports and imports of finished goods (mainly textiles) were favourable for the rice economy.[121] The cultivated area was extended and rice exports increased. But, at the same time, small-scale local production of processed goods contracted on account of the increased importation of manufactures. Moreover, real wages fell while the price of land rose.[122] After 1910 these developments were accompanied by falling land productivity in rice cultivation. The bulk of rice exports was produced by farmers owning small farm units, but a proportion of the paddy-fields belonged to landowners living in Bangkok who employed tenant farmers in their cultivation.[123] As so often in the case of agricultural structures with a low degree of ownership concentration, the marketing of the export commodity by local or foreign trading companies—often with the participation of the state—gave rise to the oligarchic deformation of what was to begin with a moderately unequal distribution of wealth in the rural sector.[124]

If such a structure is coupled, as in the case of Thailand, with the opening of the country to free trade, more or less enforced by England, the share of income concentrated in the hands of the rural and urban elites increases while, on the other hand, foreign displacement competition destroys local small-scale industry, resulting in the emergence of periphery structures.[125] In Thailand this happened between 1850 and the turn of the century or, rather, 1940, in a society that was never formally a colony, yet whose dominant class behaved 'like a colonial government'.[126] In contrast with the Romanian and Hungarian élite, the Thai leadership was certainly under greater foreign, namely British, pressure, its freedom of action being patently more circumscribed than that of the dominant groups in the two aforementioned countries. Recent studies on Thai development between 1850 and 1940, however, have highlighted the considerable discrepancy between the dominant group's quest for micro-economic profitability and the macro-economic necessity to invest in desirable infrastructural projects (irrigation systems, construction of canals), which would have raised productivity but remained untackled.[127] Strategic considerations, too, obviously played an important part in the decision to invest in railway construction and military projects rather than in irrigation systems. 'Railroad investment improved public administration and Bangkok's control of provincial and local governments, while the development of the military also served national security goals.'[128] Moreover, the government was prepared to invest in irrigation projects only when these promised an immediate profit for the dominant class (absentee landlords).

As long as the export commodities can be profitably sold in the world market, or as long as falling prices can be compensated for by increasing the exploitation of local labour or by extending the area of cultivated land, there is nothing to force a dominant class in societies like those of Hungary, Romania and Thailand to invest in broad-based agro-industrialization. Favourable conditions for the export of primary goods indeed provide an incentive for neglecting modernization measures that would increase productivity in the long run. Many examples of periphery development point to a direct link between export success and the emergence of export-orientated monocultures, for favourable profit opportunities usually provided a strong incentive for not diversifying the agricultural sector, for not intensifying the cultivation methods, and for neglecting the links between agriculture and an industrial sector yet to be created. In this way peripheralization was furthered as a consequence of *deliberate* policy decisions and in defence of the interests of the dominant class (agrarian oligarchy, comprador bourgeoisie).[129] Again, the example of Uruguay springs to mind, though it is no more unique than the other three cases mentioned here, but is representative of European and non-European economies whose dominant rentier-capitalist classes defended their own interests by advocating specialization in the production of a small number of export-orientated staple goods.

Rentier-capitalism versus capitalism: the southern states of the USA

A theoretical debate relevant in this connection, parts of which will be retraced here, has recently flared up around the case of the cotton producing and exporting southern states of the USA.[130] Despite minor differences, slavery in the southern states shared many characteristics with oligarchic agrarian societies. Socio-economic reproduction was based on extensive land use; varied forms of forced labour were prevalent; land and labour were used in an extensive and wasteful way—that is to say, when exhausted, they were simply replaced by new resources (land lying fallow or not yet developed, slave-trade, etc.); production was structured on monocultural lines and orientated towards international demand; fast growth and high profits went hand in hand with socio-economic backwardness and the emergence of defective reproduction structures (the process of underdevelopment). Upsurges in the demand for the staple goods in question resulted in boom periods, and cyclical downturns in the world market led to local depressions. The affected economies were not flexible or adaptable enough to respond productively to changing world economic circumstances. Wherever such political and institutional conditions prevailed, diversified *national economic* development has as yet remained elusive. Transitions to other forms of production were the result of violent political upheaval (wars, civil wars, revolts).[131] Even though such periphery economies were integrated into the capitalist world economy, their growth dynamics were not at all characterized by the functional mechanisms crucial to the development of core capitalism—as, for example: the transition from extensive to intensive production by means of productivity-raising technological progress as well as organizational and institutional innovation; free wage labour in place of various forms of forced labour extracted from a tied labour force; pressure towards productive investment as a result of capitalist competition; and diversification of economic activity resulting in the broad-based development of economic regions.[132]

The slave-owners of the southern states profited no less from exporting in large quantities 'their' staple goods, cotton and tobacco, than did the Romanian boyars and the Hungarian landlords from grain exports.[133] For the self-preservation of the dominant classes an export-orientated economy, which operated at a low level of productivity but was still profitable, proved sufficient. And even in conditions of growing indebtedness extensive production methods were, as a rule, not abandoned. Rather, attempts were made to achieve a still more extensive mobilization of resources by means of political force. Where sections of such oligarchies turned into agents of agricultural modernization (as in Hungary), change of this kind remained confined to certain sectors so that the traditional *political status quo* was not undermined. The main interest of such rentier-capitalist classes lay in the securing of income increases as the material basis for conspicuous consumption rather than in the safeguarding and maximizing of profits as a result of an expanding industrial capitalism, whose non-oligarchic class structure would have threatened their own existence.[134]

A purely economic analysis cannot fully explain the behaviour of the rentier-capitalist classes.[135] Of course they were interested in increasing output. But such increases had to take place within a social framework that safeguarded the political dominance of the oligarchy. Productive investment in an expanding industrial capitalism tended, however, to result in social change, which could no longer be reliably controlled by the traditional oligarchy, and in the long run in their own replacement as the leading political force. Many instances of class conflict between the oligarchy and a rising industrial bourgeoisie in export economies point to deep-seated social antagonisms within the dominant classes. Where such conflicts were resolved in favour of the oligarchy, the development of export economies into peripheries was politically guaranteed and historically sealed.[136] In those circumstances, the accumulation potential that was hypothetically there could not be tapped for the development of industrial capitalism.

Spain: an untapped development potential

The preceding considerations also apply to cases where not just one single, quantitatively dominant staple commodity was produced for export, but several such commodities which were usually produced in different regions. Historical experience indicates that, in the presence of *oligarchic structures*, export earnings were as unlikely to be translated into diversified *national* economic development as they were in the case of export economies with only one staple commodity. In this connection one should consider the development of Spain which, in the nineteenth century, exported a whole range of goods to north-western Europe (e.g. olives, wheat, citrus fruits, cork, iron ore, lead, copper, zinc, sulphur, mercury), without using these diverse export activities for the establishment of an integrated and coherent national economy.[137] The reasons for this waste of a broad-based development potential go back to the period of the Reconquista, during which had emerged the dominant oligarchic structure of society that was to determine the course of Spanish development over the following centuries. From the very beginning Spanish development had a rentier-capitalist bias caused by the expansion of large estates, the predominance of extensive cattle-rearing and not least the spoils from predatory colonialism in the New World which, in the final analysis, proved devastating for the Spanish economy. For it led Spain into structural stagnation, nipping in the bud any solid proto-industrial development. According to a seventeenth-century Spanish commentator, Spain ought to consider herself lucky for not having to produce anything herself but for being able to import all manufactures from abroad, in view of the precious metals influx from the New World. 'The whole world serves Spain and Spain serves nobody.'[138] Today, Spain has still not recovered from the consequences of this self-delusion, which has become part of her social and economic structure.

From the beginning Spain developed in the fashion of a periphery economy, which is why it is misleading—as has recently been pointed out with justification—to talk about 'Spain's decline' since the seventeenth century, as she never shared the early characteristics of developed economies.[139] For centuries her agriculture remained characterized, according to region, by latifundia (e.g. Andalusia) or smallholdings (e.g. Galicia).[140] Where, as in Catalonia, agricultural modernization took place, it was based on medium-sized farms operating on capitalist lines. However, such developments remained regionally limited, exacerbating the regional disparities within the country.[141] The expropriation of Church land and the enclosures of the middle of the nineteenth century (desamortisaciones) resulted in increased concentration of land ownership and reinforced the political and economic power of the agrarian oligarchy. If, as in Spain, a narrowness of the domestic market rooted in the social structure combines with an unproductive agriculture and a deficient internal communications network and infrastructure, *broad-based* industrialization cannot happen, even if it is promoted by the state (which was hardly the case in Spain).[142] The probable outcome in these cases, as in all peripheries, is economic growth that is limited to certain regions and sectors and reinforces the structural heterogeneity of the society and the economy. Even today Spanish development is still hampered by centuries' old structural defects. Despite considerable industrialization impulses during the Franco regime and her reintegration into the world market since 1959, Spain has not overcome the status of a semi-periphery—otherwise the problems connected with her entry into the European Community would not have arisen.[143]

The strategic importance of long-term policy decisions in the development process: Australia versus Argentina

In the earlier discussion about the smaller agricultural exporters, like Denmark, New Zealand and Uruguay, the importance of *long-term political settlements* for the direction of the development process and the resulting economic structure was emphasized. This political dimension is also of strategic importance in the critical development phases of larger export economies. The differing development patterns of Australia and Argentina offer a particularly clear illustration of the process in question. Within social science literature this difference has provided the favourite subject-matter for comparative studies on export economies.[144] This is hardly surprising, since both societies occupy a roughly comparable position in the world economy of the nineteenth and early twentieth centuries, and, as in the late 1920s—at least according to Colin Clark's data—the per capita income of both countries ranged among the highest in the world (Argentina in fifth and Australia in sixth place after the United States, Canada, New Zealand, Britain and Switzerland);[145] while in 1977 the ratio of their per capita incomes was in the order of 1:4.5 (Australia, $7,340; Argentina, $1,730) (see Table 5).

As is only to be expected, even in the most recent literature on the subject the controversy continues to centre on this question: at what point in time did the discrepancy between the Argentine and Australian development paths begin? Dyster, for example, has recently located the start of the divergence in development in the late eighteenth and early nineteenth centuries.[146] He argues that even at this early stage Australia developed as a region with high wages and land prices, while in Argentina wages remained low and property-owners had to pay little for their land.

> In Australia the relatively high costs of labour and land were tolerable to capitalists because they underwrote purchasing power and forced rural proprietors to come to terms with urban investors. The magnates of Argentina, on the other hand, saw labour and land simply as costs that must be minimized so as to enlarge the margin of profit won from producing for non-Argentine consumption.[147]

Dyster bases his thesis on the contrasting development of Argentina and Australia in the early period of the late eighteenth and early nineteenth centuries. In the case of Argentina he diagnoses early peripheralization as a result of the open integration into 'Atlantic trade links', with the displacement competition that was introduced into the country by way of silver exports (silver sales in exchange for English goods) leading to the ruin of the industrially quite developed interior which, subsequently, provided for decades a pool of cheap labour. Moreover, on account of the civil wars in the middle of the last century and of dramatic inflation, the position of landowners was strengthened, with the result that the internal disseverance of Argentine society was accentuated and the domestic market remained limited. In the case of Australia, the present author identifies as early as in the period of the penal colony a group of producers and traders with an interest in the *local* production of goods for local consumption:

> Whereas the import trade into Argentina undermined local production, in Australia local production, growing from nothing, emerged as its complement. . . . The process of capturing silver to spend on imports to Argentina early in the nineteenth century 'unemployed' Argentinian resources, while the process of capturing treasury bills to spend on imports to Australia generated domestic activity there.[148]

According to Dyster, this initial constellation provided already the basis for two divergent development paths:

> An export-orientated economy has an interest in low wages, low land costs and a weakened currency. The interests of capital in Australia, however, had grown with a relatively high rate of consumption, widely distributed; the

most powerful interests were vested equally, or more, in trade and exchange as in export production. The Australian pastoralists' demand for cheap labour (convicts or indentured workers from Asia and the Pacific) and for cheap land conflicted with the merchants' demand for an expanding consumer market and capitalization of land. Australia's income, the merchants argued, must not be earned at the expense of the domestic market for goods and real estate. The merchants prevailed. The revival of convict transportation was successfully resisted, and Land Acts were passed which forced the occupants of grazing runs to pay for their use, and to pay again.[149]

Dyster reports how, around the turn of the century, Argentina, on account of her cheaper labour and land, was credited with better development prospects than Australia. In reality, development has taken a different course. 'High cost' Australia has become a well-differentiated, mature, capitalist economy, while 'low cost' Argentina has still not succeeded in overcoming certain development blocks.[150]

Whatever the significance of the early history of Australia and Argentina, there is no mistaking the different patterns of development policy that were set in this century.[151] In both countries new political forces had emerged in the wake of the economic crises at the end of the last century: in Australia, the Labour Party and, in Argentina, the Radical Party. As reform parties, both groups shared similar programmes aiming at *structural change.* They opposed the hegemony of the landed oligarchy and advocated some measure of nationalization, political reforms and decidedly national industrialization. Both parties came to power: the Labour Party in 1909 as the first Labour government in the world, the Radical Party in 1916. But, once in government, the two parties pursued completely different policies. In Australia, protectionist policies were adopted, aiming at a process of *national industrialization* designed to create an industry that was also internationally competitive.[152] The additional impulse towards import substitution industrialization, brought about by the First World War, spread in the 1920s into important areas such as that of the processing of minerals and the steel industry. Protection was employed as an instrument of industrial promotion. As with all export economies, Australia was greatly affected by the world economic crisis, but her ability to weather the crisis was far greater than that of Argentina on account of the preceding industrialization that had taken place under tariff protection but had been geared to the establishment of competitive industries. As a result of this crisis Australia witnessed a diversification of the basic and engineering industries, a process that continued under the impact of the Second World War. In this way Australia avoided the pitfalls of a short-lived 'light' phase of import substitution industrialization typical of Latin

America as a whole and also of Argentina after 1930.

Notwithstanding its political programme, the Radical Party of Argentina did not pursue a comparable purposive industrialization policy by means of protectionist measures.[153] Although the oligarchic interests were weakened politically by its policies, the *economic position of the agrarian oligarchy was eventually strengthened.* Tariffs served essentially a fiscal purpose, as there were no other ways of raising taxes, given the resistance of powerful oligarchic interests. Moreover, industrial protection received little backing from the supporters of the Radical Party, as they feared the emergence of unproductive and uncompetitive industries and high prices, which would have been to the disadvantage of the working class and the urban lower and lower-middle classes. Though Argentina, too, went through a process of import substitution industrialization as a result of the war, this produced much less of an impact than Australian industrial development and was reversed after 1920. Import substitution industrialization, which took off in response to the world economic crisis, therefore remained on the whole confined to the 'light' stage—that is, to the substitution of simple light industrial goods, without advancing at an early stage to the broad substitution of heavy industrial goods and equipment.

Despite a continuing bias towards the export of primary sector commodities, an integrated domestic economic structure emerged in Australia. This, moreover, was based upon a new constellation of political forces (the Labour Party, trade unions, national bourgeoisie, new middle classes). So far as Argentina was concerned, however, exports remained orientated towards agricultural products, and no comparable diversification of the domestic economic structure emerged. *The lack of integration of the economic structure is matched by political fragmentation which, for decades, has been a source of continuing political instability.*[154] The building up of basic and engineering industries, which started in the post-war period, was not the result of internal development processes but a consequence of the penetration by multinational companies whose activities to the present day have obviously not helped to solve the structural problems of the Argentine economy.[155] Industrial growth still depends on a single major source of foreign exchange, the export of agricultural commodities. In the agricultural sector the transition from extensive to intensive production methods has yet to take place. Despite the existence of medium-sized farms, the distribution of land remains persistently unequal, the industrial structure is fragmented into highly capital-intensive subsectors and undercapitalised, uncompetitive areas, and—as in the rest of Latin America—the tertiary sector is excessively bloated.[156]

The fact that statistics on present-day Argentina indicate that the manufacture of machinery, electrical engineering products and transport equipment contributes 24 per cent of the net industrial product, compared with 25 per cent in the case of Australian, while 10.4 per cent of Argentine exports, but only 4.4 per cent of Australian exports, consist of such goods (see Table 8, p. 118), could lead to the wrong conclusion that the Argentine economy is internally more integrated and, moreover, internationally more competitive, than the Australian one. In reality the Australian capital goods sector is much more closely integrated into the whole domestic economy, which also constitutes a much more potent force in terms of income distribution and, consequently, effective domestic demand. The share of wage income in the GDP, for example, amounts to 68 per cent in Australia, as compared with only 46 per cent in Argentina (see Table 7, p. 117). Even after allowing for the difference in the relative proportions of wage labour and self-employed producers in Australia and Argentina, the discrepancy should still be in the order of 15 per cent—as already argued at a comparable point in the analysis of Denmark and Uruguay.[157]

As outlined above, while the early development stage in Argentina during the first half of the nineteenth century resulted in the emergence of a pool of cheap labour in the hinterland of Buenos Aires, labour shortages developed in Australia at an even earlier stage. Furthermore, immigration laws prevented the influx of cheap labour from India, China and the rest of Asia—a policy that was adopted by the Labour government in order to prevent the erosion of the existing welfare standards. The conservative groups in Australia embraced this policy for ideological reasons. In this way Australia became a high-wage country.[158]

Together with New Zealand, Australia is numbered among those countries with a high per capita income whose export structure is marked by a persistently high proportion of primary commodity exports. Canada, too, falls into this category.[159] Exports of foodstuffs, agricultural raw materials, fuels and minerals accounted together for almost 85 per cent of the total exports in New Zealand, 82 per cent in Australia, and even in Canada they still amounted to 49 per cent. If one compares these three countries with Argentina, South Africa[160] and Uruguay, which also have a high proportion of primary goods exports (Argentina 77 per cent, South Africa 66 per cent, Uruguay 66 per cent),[161] the former are distinguished by having become, in each case for different reasons, high-wage countries, while the latter have remained relatively low-wage countries, despite their privileged position—compared with other Third World countries—in terms of income (as in the case of Argentina and Uruguay).[162] The pronounced bias towards primary commodity exports presents a problem in both groups of countries, since world economic crises can immediately translate themselves into domestic economic crises in *such highly* export-orientated countries. Nevertheless, a relatively integrated domestic economic structure makes it much easier to respond productively to such crises in the first-mentioned cases than in the case of primary commodity exporters without a diversified and coherent domestic economic structure.[163]

As with the preceding analysis of Denmark, Uruguay and New Zealand, a comparison of the world trade shares of Australian, Canadian, South African and Argentine exports shows to what extent these are linked to the maturity level of the respective domestic economies (see Table 6, p. 116). In the case of Australia (population 14 million), this share was 1.31 per cent in 1975; in that of Canada (23 million), 3.64 per cent. South Africa (27 million achieved a share of only 0.6 per cent, and Argentina (26 million) an even smaller share of 0.33 per cent. Kravis's observation that export opportunities are determined not only by world market demand, but by the development level of the productive forces in the respective societies (i.e. by the supply side), is therefore probably correct.[164] *Export shares in world trade increase in line with the growth in overall GDP and the rising maturity level of an economy.* The latter is a result of growing diversification of the domestic economic structure and rising overall productivity. However, in the case of export economies Kravis's observation that trade provides less an engine of growth than a supporting prop, applies probably to a lesser degree to the first development stage. In these cases growth usually started with the production and export of staple goods, but Kravis is certainly right with regard to the long-term development process, as has been demonstrated with both positive and negative outcomes by the examples discussed in the present chapter. Whether export economies—be they large or small, rich or poor in resources—developed successfully or unsuccessfully in the world economy of the nineteenth and twentieth centuries, depended mainly on the development of their domestic economic potentials, and consequently on a process that extended their capacity to adapt to changing world market conditions at the same time as it increased their ability to compete in changed conditions.'It seems unlikely that external demand conditions can account for the correlation between export performance and diversification. It is more probable that the reasons for the differences are to be found in the differences in internal factors that determine the mobility of resources and which therefore promote growth in general.'[165]

Some Theoretical Implications

The 'staple theory of economic growth'

The preceding illustrative case-studies have pointed to the crucial importance of a *broad-based* development of the domestic economic potential to complement the export activities of export economies. Such *broad-based development processes* generate important impulses towards a *qualitative deepening* of the export structure. In the majority of successful development cases the monostructure was overcome. But even where the export commodities' basket still remains characterized by a relatively high percentage of staple goods (as in the cases of Australia, Canada and New Zealand), the detrimental effects of an export bias of this kind were counterbalanced by domestic economic development that acquired its own dynamics. The development scenario was the same in that of populous export economies with abundant resources as in the case of small agriculture-orientated ones. The initial impulse emanated from the export of staple goods which had a different linkage potential[166] in each case. The distribution of resources and incomes determined the incentives for productive investment in light, basic and capital goods industries. Labour shortages and the concomitant rise in wage costs decided how early and how fast the development of the domestic market could advance by way of the growing demand from a growing number of people, with the result that the narrowness of the domestic market, which was usually prematurely diagnosed, did not materialize even in small export economies.

Many years ago Canadian economic historians provided decisive theoretical impulses for the analysis of such a development path. The *staple theory of growth*,[167] developed by Innis and others, outlined a growth and development scenario for Canada, which later continued to prompt other scientists to study further export economies from a comparable perspective.[168] From the outset, Canada's development was stimulated by the export to Europe (and later also to the United States) of specific staple goods: fish, pelts, timber and wheat from 1820 onward, and later meat, dairy products and minerals. This export-orientated economy was, however, complemented at a very early stage by domestic economic measures consciously promoted by the state (increased internal trade through the building up of infrastructure, railway construction, purposive immigration policy, the introduction of protective tariffs after 1879, etc.).[169]

What are the main propositions put forward by the Canadian 'staple theory of growth'? It conceives economic development as a diversification process evolving around an export base. 'The central concept of a staple theory, therefore, is the spread effects of the export sector— that is, the impact of export activity on the domestic economy and society. To construct a staple theory, then, it is necessary to classify these spread effects and indicate their determinants.'[170] The theory distinguishes:[171]

(a) backward linkages (infrastructural measures induced by staple goods production; manufacture of agricultural machinery, and so on, important for agricultural modernization);

(b) forward linkages (use of the staple commodity as input in local production processes—that is, the processing of wood into paper, milk into butter and cheese, etc.);

(c) final demand linkages (these depend on the distribution of the export receipts and the demand for capital and consumer goods induced by those export receipts); and

(d) fiscal linkages (opportunities for the state to raise revenues in the area of staple goods exports by way of taxes, tariffs and duties; revenues which, in their turn, are rechannelled into processes of domestic economic development).

For the economic 'deepening' of the export sector in the narrow sense, the two first mentioned linkage effects are essential. For the integration of the export sector into a domestic economy, which is diversifying beyond the export sector, the two last-mentioned processes are crucial. In this context even early contributions to the staple theory have documented the strategic role of distribution structures and their underlying socio-structural and institutional foundations—for example, Baldwin in his comparison of plantation economics and agrarian structures based on family-operated farms owned by economically independent farmers.[172]

Final demand linkages will tend to be higher, the higher the average level of income and the more equal its distribution. At a higher level of income, consumers are likely to be able to buy a range of goods and services that lend themselves to domestic production by advanced industrial techniques. Where the distribution is relatively unequal, the demand will be for subsistence goods at the lower end of the income scales and for luxuries at the upper end. The more equal the distribution, the less likelihood of opulent luxury importers and the greater the likelihood of a broad-based market for mass-produced goods.[173]

The preceding case-studies have confirmed these observations in both directions. In cases where, for various reasons, labour was scarce and the standard of living consequently relatively high, such a configuration induced not only a broad demand for capital goods at an early stage but a demand for consumer goods that rendered investment in a *local* capital and consumer goods sector attractive at an early stage.[174] This was quite different in the case of the export-orientated *plantation economy* investigated by Baldwin and in *societies with oligarchic structures* discussed in preceding paragraphs.[175] In these cases, as in those characterized by received development theory as *dualistically* fragmented into export sector and subsistence economy, *growth without development* took the place of broad-based domestic economic development processes. And in these cases there exists, for structural reasons, an inexhaustible supply of extremely cheap labour, making unlikely the broad development of the locally available economic potential.[176]

The 'staple theory of growth' loses its relevance where the export sector itself forfeits its growth-triggering role as dynamifier of the domestic economy and where the development of the domestic economy acquires its own dynamic impetus,[177] without the export bias as such being eliminated—as demonstrated by the concrete examples above. The relevance of the theory in question is thus limited to a specific development phase: it defines a number of important conditions which, in the case of export economies, help to translate exogenous growth impulses into broad-based development processes. Therein lies its continuing relevance for comparative-historical studies[178] and for current development policy analyses.

Critique of some aspects of the 'world system approach'

In the light of the facts presented in this chapter, a fundamental critique of certain causal assumptions of the so-called *world system approach*, which has rapidly spread in development research since the late 1970s, seems appropriate. In various publications Wallerstein, the main proponent of this approach, and a number of similar-minded scientists, have interpreted the capitalist world economy as a zero-sum game. Within the hierarchy of the international division of labour the rise of one society to a capitalist core country (metropole) necessarily leads—according to these authors—to the decline of another society. To use a concrete example, which has been discussed from this angle: if Scotland develops successfully, this is supposed to result in the peripheralization of Ireland or Portugal.[179]

It is never possible for *all* peripheral zones to move 'upward', even if all use the same modalities at the appropriate historical moments. Contrary pressures act against all but a very few of the upward-striving states (and their entrepreneurs). The space for the very few who do succeed is made by the fact that some others are not merely standing still but rather declining—not by intent, of course, but as a result of the operation of the world economy. In a sense, the stronger states within the world economy have a large share in deciding which of the weaker states improve their position at any given time, by extending their protection or minimizing their ferocity.[180]

The important recent critiques of the 'Wallerstein school' have focused on its questionable interpretation of the emergence of peripheries within the world economy since the early fifteenth century, especially on the underestimation, and hence misinterpretation, of the local political, socio-structural and socio-economic determinants that were present in each case.[181]

This critique, which is usually substantiated by historical examples from the sixteenth and seventeenth centuries, is also supported by the present study, which deals with a later stage of world economic development (the nineteenth and early twentieth centuries). For, according to the above-cited central thesis of the world system approach on the *modus operandi* of the capitalist world economy, Denmark, the Netherlands and New Zealand could become capitalist core countries ('by invitation')[182] only because other societies, such as those of Uruguay, Ireland and Romania, were turned into peripheries of the world economy.

There is, however, nothing to support such a thesis. The studies contained in the present chapter prove that in the cases examined which were not typical colonies under foreign control and which faced *comparable world market conditions*, the decision on autocentric development or peripheralization was taken *within the respective societies themselves*, and that this decision reflected different *internal* social conditions for the processing of the opportunities and restrictions which the world market offered to the development processes of individual societies. The causal relationship postulated by the world system approach between the *autocentric* industrial development of one group of societies and the *periphery* development of another group, does not exist at all. In order to locate the causes of autocentric development or peripheralization one should, therefore, look at the different transformation and innovation capacities of individual societies.[183]

Some statements of dependency theory qualified

In dependency theory the extent and quality of the world market orientation of export economies are under scrutiny. Factors such as a large share of exports, a high export commodity concentration, a high partner concentration in foreign trade, a large external debt and extensive foreign investment (dependence on foreign capital), a high degree of technology imports (technological dependence), unfavourable terms of trade with regard to particular commodities or particular development stages, are all regarded as causes of development blocks or of movement towards underdevelopment. Societies whose position within the world economic system can be described by means of such indicators are considered candidates for periphery development.

Statements of this kind have to be qualified in the light of the findings in development history presented in this chapter.[184] For a comparative historical analysis shows that, in the presence of a *development-promoting internal profile*, disadvantageous external economic and world market conditions could, if necessary, be internally processed so as not to block development. If, however, this internal profile were lacking or incomplete, as is nowadays the case in the majority of Third World countries, the very same factors, in conjunction with unfavourable socio-structural and politico-institutional conditions, usually proved development-impeding. Given the profusion of peripheralization processes that can be observed worldwide, it is the latter constellation on which the dependency theory has always focused.

In summary, the export orientation of export economies that were never or were no longer colonies (these have been the specific subject of our analysis) did not, as such, during the nineteenth and early twentieth centuries, determine the path to successful autocentric development or that to peripheralization. Autocentric development *or* peripheralization stemmed from different core structures – that is to say, from different social structures and from different outcomes of the struggles between traditional oligarchic interests and the rising sectors of the bourgeoisie, bourgeois middle classes and the working class. Given a comparable initial export orientation but different outcomes of political and social conflicts, some development processes could have taken a quite different course. Successful export economies and societies whose development is based on the dynamic impulse of the domestic market (Type I societies) have this in common: that a broad-based increase in agricultural productivity, subsequent industrialization and, resulting from both these processes, a gradual opening up of the domestic market, provided the basis for development.

The development chances of export economies thus did not really lie in the export sector, for its growth can be observed in both successful export economies and peripheries.[185] They lay in the export-led *development of the domestic market potential as the basis of a reasonable long-term utilization of, precisely, the export sector.* Where this domestic market potential remained undeveloped, the result was not only periphery development but the weakening of the external economic position *vis-à-vis* other trading nations.[186] From the viewpoint of development history, the development policy recommendation of W.A. Lewis is therefore inescapable: 'The most important item on the agenda of development is to transform the food sector, create agricultural surpluses to feed the urban population, and thereby create the domestic basis for industry and modern services. If we can make this domestic change, we shall automatically have a new international economic order.'[187] In certain conditions export growth can assist such development efforts. As a rule, it undermined them.

4 Elements of an Export-Orientated and Autocentric Development Path

In the two preceding chapters the conditions were examined in which societies that were (as export economies) particularly exposed to international competence differentials and displacement competition, have developed autocentrically or have become peripheries of the world economy.[1] In the section that follows, some general lessons will be drawn from these comparative historical analyses. Furthermore, some questions will be formulated which, inspired by the diagnosis derived from development history, may be relevant to the discussion of present-day cases of export-orientated development.

The term 'export-orientated countries' is usually used in the sense of small, sparsely populated societies whose initial economic growth and the dynamic development impetus deriving from it is based on the export of one or more locally produced products. Not always, but in most cases of export economies, those export goods comprise initially *unprocessed foodstuffs* or agricultural, forestry and mineral *raw materials*. One of many indicators of export economies is a high foreign trade share. As a rule, the foreign trade share is inversely proportional to the size of the country: the smaller the population of an export economy, the larger is the foreign trade share.[2] Usually it is attributable to the high propensity to export of one or a few sectors. This is the reason for the initial, exclave-like, dualistic structure of export economies. If this is not mastered, the outcome of export growth is the development of typically peripheral-capitalistic social structures, including the structural heterogeneity characteristic of them.

In contrast, where export economies followed an autocentric development path, the following development processes were of considerable importance:

Export Growth and Domestic Market Development

Export-orientated development begins with the onset of or increase in international demand for goods (foodstuffs, raw materials, services) which the country concerned is able to supply because natural conditions and/or the corresponding availability of factors (e.g. land, mineral deposits, forests, suitable labour) are given and enable production of such goods for export to be taken up. Such *international demand* originates chiefly in large countries (historically, Great Britain and Type I countries), in which progressive industrialization gives rise to additional needs for increasingly scarce or unavailable raw materials, foodstuffs and energy resources. In such situations, especially in periods marked by economic upswings, potential importing countries usually pursue a trade policy that is propitious for the export chances of potential supplier countries (abrogation of import bans and navigation acts, tariff cuts, preferential tariffs, etc.). Historically prominent examples are the reduction and abolition of the British grain and timber tariffs after 1840, and the temporary transition to free trade in Europe from the late 1850s onward. Apart from the removal of institutional impediments to trade, innovations in transport technology and the building up of an international communications structure constitute important preconditions for the expansion of trade between large industrial societies and export economies. Only these two processes make the transport of staple goods over long distances economically expedient. A development of this nature set in historically around the middle of the nineteenth century and gained impetus from the 1880s onward.

The already mentioned stimuli for demand and institutional preconditions result in countries that become export economies in the building up of export sectors in agriculture, animal husbandry, forestry or mining, in which connection an initial high capital participation on the part of importing countries can be observed relatively frequently. The export of unprocessed foodstuffs and raw materials sets in and attains an economically relevant order of magnitude. In cases of successful development, soon production facilities and infrastructures are built up at the stage preceding the production of the export goods (backward linkages).[3] They include the production of goods such as simple agricultural machinery, of equipment for sawmills and warehousing, of equipment for shipping, for railways and energy generation, of packaging material, and so on. Such production activities and associated services, which begin as a rule on a modest scale, gradually gain importance and in their turn induce other new production facilities at still earlier stages.

An important phase in an export-orientated and autocentric development scenario is the *transition to the processing and finishing of the main export goods in the country itself*. For instance, paper is made from wood and hardware from ores or metals, feed grain is used to produce animal products and leather goods. Such a *processing industry in the export sector* is a qualitative step beyond the production and export of unprocessed goods. Once again, activities are induced at an earlier stage in the equipment field. These new production facilities not only expand the structure of the domestic economy; after a time, particularly when capacities can cover domestic demand, -they lead to *diversification of the goods in the export basket*. This applies to both consumer and capital goods. For example, the export commodities' basket of an export economy which originally exported only timber is extended so that at a later date products of the woodworking and wood-processing industry, products of the paper industry and equipment for the wood-based and paper industry achieve a large share in exports. It is remarkable that even small export economies can become competitive internationally in specific fields of mechanical engineering, in which connection the *niche technologies* they develop are of decisive importance for the building up and further dynamic development of the processing industry concerned (e.g. sawmill equipment, specific ore smelting processes, milk centrifuging technology).

In step with the growing exports and growing export receipts of the producers, and with the wage income resulting in the export sectors, the *domestic demand* for consumer goods increases. This expanding domestic market makes investments in consumer goods industries worthwhile. In consequence, consumer goods imports can be replaced by local goods production (import-substitution industrialization). This consumer goods industrialization is mostly followed in selected spheres by import-replacing capital and industrialization of producers' goods, which partly satisfies the needs of the consumer goods industry for intermediate goods and machinery, and which produces goods for expanding the infrastructure.

All the activities mentioned, which extend over decades, eventually lead to a gradually improving maturity of the economy, which is characterized by increasing intrasectoral and intersectoral diversification and integration *(intermeshing)*. The export economy, whose growth was originally determined by an exclave-like, dualistic export sector, gains *internal coherence*. It becomes a national economy whose dynamic development impetus stems from within, in contrast with monocultures and plantation economies, even though the principal export sector or sectors are preserved or indeed have to be retained as 'leading sectors'.

This growth and diversification process, which is tantamount to a gradual, thorough capitalization of the export economy, sooner or later leads in individual cases to scarcity of economic factors, often first of all to scarcity of labour and land, and finally to scarcity of capital. Such a scarcity is by no means development-inhibiting, but development-promoting. Together with domestic and foreign competition, it compels investments which serve to improve the productivity of labour, land and capital. Following a prolonged, first period of extensive economic activity (capital extension), such *capital-intensification measures* deliver macro-economically dynamic impulses, because they lead to the building up of high-productivity sectors such as mechanical engineering, which promote productivity in other sectors, exert additional income effects and induce further intermeshing effects.[4]

Apart from this ideal type scenario, of which there are historical approximations, as for instance Sweden and Finland, several variants are conceivable and can be found in history. For example, it is conceivable that the initial, export-orientated production of foodstuffs and raw materials may be lacking for natural reasons and that the export sector starts out from the processing of *imported* raw materials (feeds, tropical products, etc.). The initial impetus is then the availability of abundant, initially *cheap labour*. An *export processing sector* that comes into being in this way is likewise capable of triggering the expansion effects outlined above, as can be demonstrated by the historical examples of Switzerland and Denmark, in the latter case after the transition to a processing economy.

It is also conceivable that *in special cases* no transition to the processing of export goods takes place, that they are exported for a relatively long period as *un*processed goods, but that nevertheless import-substituting industrialization at earlier stages takes place. The export commodity basket would then have a persistently high 'raw material content', without the countries concerned falling victim to a vertical international division of labour. Historical examples are some of the present OECD societies, the so-called 'regions of recent settlement', particularly Australia, Canada and, with certain limitations, New Zealand.

Although the foreign trade and domestic economic growth scenario (and its variants) set forth in the foregoing can be demonstrated for a number of European and non-European countries, historical and current examples show that, given the same initial world economic conditions, it is *not* a development path to be taken for granted. Export economies such as those of Argentina, Uruguay, Hungary, Romania and others likewise had good export chances in the late nineteenth and early twentieth centuries —that is to say, at the same time as the cited successful examples (Scandinavia, Netherlands, Switzerland, Canada, the United States, Australia, New Zealand). In their case, too, the usually persistent international demand gave rise to remarkable export growth. That growth, however, did not have the structural spill-over effects described above. Those export economies did *not* develop into coherent national economies.

Based on experience gained from development history, the following test questions can be formulated with regard to *economic* factors affecting autocentric development paths of export economies involving integration in the world market:

— Does world market demand for potentially available goods offer any chance of export-orientated development? Can export growth of a relevant order of magnitude be observed? Is a society capable of responding to such demand incentives—that is, of seizing export chances?

— Does the export growth have consequential, economic structural effects in the export sector *(backward linkages)*, and is there a gradual transition—however it may be caused—to the processing and finishing of goods originally exported unprocessed *(forward linkages)*?

— Does export growth result via income effects in incentives for import-substituting industrialization *(final demand linkages)*?

— Do the main economic factors become scarce and can productivity-improving investments (i.e. capital intensification) be observed? Can the 'Hoffmann sequence' be observed—that is, a step-by-step increase in the importance of the capital goods sector relative to the consumer goods sector, culminating eventually in greater importance of the former as an expression of capital intensification and growing maturity of the economy?[5]

— Are niche technologies developed in specific mechanical engineering fields and utilized for export?

— Does the export commodity basket become more diversified to an extent consonant with an inherently diversifying, intensifying and maturing domestic economy?

— To sum up, is the entire linkage potential (forward, backward, final demand, fiscal linkages) mobilized in consequence of export growth, and does an initially foreign-trade-dependent and tendentially dualistically structured export economy gain internal coherence (measurable *inter alia* with input-output tables).[6] That is, do widespread internal development processes take place despite persisting dependence on exports?

Socio-structural Foundations, Competence Levels and General Political Conditions

The observation of similar and simultaneous, *external* initial conditions for export growth with long-term, varying development results suggests the conclusion that evidently other factors governed the development chances of export economies—their development path to autocentric development *or* their peripheralization. In this connection, a fundamental factor is the prevailing social structure *at the beginning of export growth*. The following circumstances are relevant:[7]

(1) *Autocentric* development takes shape in export economies when the local social structure permits a relatively *broad distribution of export receipts*. In the case of exports of agricultural and forestry goods, such conditions are found, for example, where ownership of arable land, animal feed areas, pasture land (and hence animal husbandry) or forests is not highly concentrated, and where land fragmentation is also not too extreme. A distribution of property approximating the statistical normal distribution is a good precondition—and this can be demonstrated empirically—for export-orientated and autocentric development of export economies. Neither different variants of large real-estate holdings nor too widely dispersed smallholdings are favourable starting-points for such development. Medium-size, family-operated holdings have proved particularly conducive to development.

In the case of industrial or mineral export production, a high share of wages in the export income and high real wages may have the same effects.

Indicators of this are a moderate concentration index (Gini index) of land distribution and income distribution.

This distribution profile based on social structure is so fundamentally important because widely dispersed export receipts result in a demand profile that is orientated from the outset towards industrialization serving to produce widely accessible, simple equipment and mass-consumer goods. The opening up of a *broad domestic market for both types of goods* is an important prerequisite for import-substituting industrialization, especially if it is not to end up prematurely in a cul-de-sac pre-ordained by the social structure—that is, in 'narrowness of the domestic market' such as can be observed everywhere in peripheries.[8] For instance, in the case of plantation and latifundian economies of large-scale extensive animal husbandry and of share-cropping farming, there is a big concentration of export receipts which results in luxury consumption on the one hand and mass poverty on the other. Such agrarian economies are *extensive* in nature. As a rule, abundant land and/or labour is available, for which reason there are no incentives for agricultural modernization and intensification, and linkage effects between agriculture and industry remain lacking.[9] As is demonstrated by a great number of historical studies, the luxury consumption can be satisfied by imports, and the enduring mass poverty, together with the factors previously mentioned, prevents widespread, domestic economic development processes.[10] Furthermore, in contrast with well-capitalized agriculture, the pressure to maintain competitive market positions by productivity-increasing investments is extremely small.

Conversely, where predominantly fragmentation of the land in too small holdings prevails—that is, where the export income per producer is very low (the Balkan countries in the nineteenth century), dynamic development is inhibited despite broadly distributed landed property, because fragmented land does not allow the production of surplus, therefore remains undercapitalized and resembles a poor subsistence economy more than a commercialized farming one.

In cases where the main emphasis is on the export of industrial and mineral goods, high wage shares in export income and high real wages occur when the bargaining power of the labour employed in the export sector, which has to become scarce in the course of time, is great. From the socio-political standpoint, this demands its organization in labour unions and parties, a growing legitimacy of such organizations within the political system and the recognition of labour as an opposing power by private or state enterprises within varying forms of institutionalized conflict regulation.

(2) Nowadays, it is forgotten all too often that the dynamic development impulse for societies that are not yet industrialized or only beginning to be industrialized depends on their agricultural structure. This also applies, as outlined above, to export economies. What apart from those elementary socio-structural circumstances mentioned, determined the *gradudl, qualitative, higher development of the export economies?* What made possible the transition from the export of unprocessed goods to a processing and mature economy?

The development of successful export economies provides some information on this. One economic historian described Swedish development as that of an 'impoverished sophisticate',[11] and in so doing drew attention, over and above the Swedish case, to a factor that might be described in a general sense as *competence level.* The seizing of export chances and their productive handling in a society depend most decisively on the attained level of education and knowledge and on the resulting skills and competence.[12] In the case of Denmark, an illiterate and ignorant peasantry could never have achieved the transition from a bread-grain export economy to the import of feed grain with the object of converting to an export-orientated processing economy. And a peasantry without advanced education in village adult education schools would never have brought forth a decisive *institutional innovation*, namely the organization of family-operated farms in rural cooperatives. What the current development theory debate refers to as human capital or as invisible and intangible capital also played an outstanding role in the history of development of successful export economies. The big development of invisible capital—owing to the early, extensive spreading of literacy, the building up of institutions for advanced education, including vocational and technical colleges, technological universities and general universities, government and private research facilities and laboratories[13]—can be regarded as one of the reasons for the high adaptability and the innovative and transformative capabilities of such societies. The knowledge available in more highly developed societies is utilized; but local abilities are also developed, with the help of which foreign knowledge is transformed productively, and scientific and technological innovations are brought forth. The development of such competence can be regarded as one of the reasons for the growing improvements in productivity and the enduring competitive capacity particularly of small export-orientated societies which are often poor in natural resources. The material resources that were not available or became scarce were often made up for mobilizing immaterial resources.

(3) In all development paths of successful export economies, a significant shift in political power can be observed, which is linked up with economic development. In the case of successful European and non-European export economies, export growth was preceded as a rule by far-reaching de-feudalization which found expression in agricultural reforms and agrarian revolutions. This de-oligarchization was one of the prerequisites for agricultural modernization and for growing mobility and the commercialization of land, labour and capital.[14]

In step with export growth and its consequential effects for the domestic economy, *social change* is induced, which is evidenced by a higher urbanization rate, the transfer of the working population from the primary to the secondary and tertiary sectors, increasing horizontal and vertical mobility, the formation of new vocational groups. This social mobilization gives rise to new interest groups which gradually organize themselves politically and attempt to assert their interests in the political struggle. The observable, concomitant internal *shifts in power* correspond, at least in the long run, to the economic structural change originally induced from outside, which then spreads within the domestic economy. In the process, the self-steering capacity of such societies increases.[15]

This observation is impressively confirmed by those cases of export economies (e.g. Australia and New Zealand) in which the *economic power* of big landowners was preserved for a long time, but where they had to relinquish their *political* power to new urban-industrial power groups (entrepreneurs, labour, the urban middle class).[16] If large estates are preserved and if there is *no* dissociation of political and economic power, then—as can frequently be observed in 'underdeveloped' export economies right up to the present—typical peripheral development sets in. But a precondition for such dissociation is the building up of political institutions which become receptive to new social interests and aspirations, alternating political coalitions between old and new groups of forces proving conducive to such a political transformation process.

(4) In all cases of successful, export-orientated and autocentric development, the *sovereign power of self-determination*, especially in foreign economic policy and in reaction to crises of internal development policy caused by world economic conditions, is unmistakable. Although export growth presupposes increased integration into the world market (*associative* orientation), in normal foreign trade conditions nearly all successful export economies have adopted *selective-dissociative* behaviour (e.g. by imposing infant industry tariffs in the import-substitution sector). In times of crisis, these otherwise merely selective-dissociative components assumed massive dimensions. Thus with a mixture of foreign trade control (foreign exchange controls, etc.) and government-directed and forced development policy at home, it was possible to counteract development bottlenecks and development setbacks deriving from external pressures. This type of reaction to crises imparted a strong positive stimulus to autocentric development in successful export economies.[17]

History has also taught us that local resources suitable for export can be used in building up an economy only if national sovereignty rights are assured. For only then is domestic use of export income probable. The controversy in Norway before the First World War concerning national or foreign utilization of water power reserves as a basis for the electrochemical and electrometallurgical industries built up by foreign firms could be cited here as an example.[18]

In the light of historical experience, the following further test questions may, thus, be formulated:
— Does the prevailing distribution of property in the export sector permit a direct or indirect (mostly via government machinery) broad distribution of export income (concentration of property and distribution)?
— Is the structure of the society such that the *spread effects* initially deriving from export growth can have a dynamic impact on the rest of

society and contribute to thorough capitalization on the basis of growing mobility of land, labour and capital?

— What level of knowledge and competence has an export economy attained at the beginning of export growth? What immaterial prerequisites for adaptation to changing environmental conditions (world market) and what innovation capabilities have been developed?

— Is there a political, institutional framework for flexible political reaction to changing socio-economic conditions? Does a growing socio-economic complexity induced by the development of productive forces and social change coincide with an opening up of traditional political institutions, which makes it possible for new groups of social forces to organize lobbies and gain access to the political process for their interests?

— Does a society have sovereignty over its own resources? Are the foreign policy and foreign trade prerequisites for sovereign control of national development policy given?

The cited building blocks for a successful development scenario by no means always existed simultaneously in concrete cases, but in the final analysis they interacted with each other, though occasionally with time-lags, in such a manner that their high degree of interdependence had an extraordinarily dynamic impact on development. Wherever one or the other of those elements was less marked, development successes were achieved more slowly. Where those socio-structural conditions prevailed which are described above as detrimental, it is remarkable that also all other elements otherwise conducive to development hardly existed, or were even completely lacking. The aftermath of export growth was then peripheralization and peripheral development.

5 In Europe's Footsteps?
Far Eastern Development Paths

The Renaissance of a Development Theory Debate

The development of South Korea (and also Taiwan) provides a bone of contention in the present debate on development theory and policy. For some observers South Korea represents the prime example of successful *integration into the world market (associative development)*;[1] for others the South Korean development path is rather deterrent, not at all exemplary for other developing countries, and a blind alley for South Korea herself. Latterly this polarized debate has been enriched by another variant. With increasing frequency, scientists who consider themselves Marxists cite South Korea (together with Taiwan, Hongkong and Singapore) as an example of emerging *delayed* development under *capitalist* premise.[2] What is meant by this?

The development debate of the 1950s and 1960s, which was informed by modernization theory, saw the elimination of backwardness and underdevelopment as analogous to the development processes of European and extra-European 'forerunners'. In contrast, the more recent development theory debate of the late 1960s and 1970s emphasized the structural difference between the development processes of *metropolitan capitalism* and so-called *peripheral capitalism*.[3] While the development of metropolitan capitalism (i.e. the present OECD societies) was marked, from the middle of the eighteenth century onward, by growing coherence, that of peripheral capitalism has remained characterized until the present day by defective reproduction structures. In the former case increasingly differentiated social and economic structures emerged, which at the same time became more densely intermeshed, thus providing the basis of self-sustaining economic growth and continually expanding reproduction. In the latter case growth resulted in an increasing internal disseverance between highly pro-

168

ductive subsectors and areas with below-average productivity, mainly in the primary and tertiary sectors where the majority of the labour force has remained trapped. The more recent development theory debate has therefore diagnosed a *divergent long-term development dynamics* in the two cases: in the one, towards an increasing *homogenization* of society and economy; and in the other, increasing *structural heterogeneity.*[4] Despite all differences in detail and despite an historically determined dialectical relationship between the development of metropolitan and peripheral capitalism, the divide between the two structures was relatively well defined. Many reasons were given why, in present conditions, the transition from peripheral to metropolitan capitalism must be regarded as relatively unlikely if not completely impossible.[5] By questioning the thesis on the improbability or impossibility of fully-fledged delayed capitalist development in present conditions, more recent Marxist development theories attack (all minor qualifications notwithstanding) the dichotomous differentiation between metropolitan and peripheral capitalism, but also attempt to promote the revision of the dominant development theory of the 1970s.

According to this latest variant of the development theory debate, the symptoms that are today diagnosed all over the Third World are phenomena which have always characterized capitalist development. After all, was not the development of the societies in northern and north-western Europe during the nineteenth and early twentieth centuries characterized by fundamental structural change and the social upheaval resulting from it? Were there not famines, mass unemployment and even marginality in nineteenth century Europe— that is, phenomena which are, among others, associated with peripheral capitalism? And was not capitalist accumulation, between the middle of the eighteenth and twentieth centuries, based on penury and mass deprivation, no different from that which can nowadays be observed in the Third World, even in those export-orientated cases that are considered successful, like South Korea and Taiwan?

The development theory debate, which seemed to have run its course, has thus been reopened. Fundamental questions are raised afresh. The Far Eastern examples, South Korea and Taiwan, play a central role in this newly accentuated development theory debate, since both are considered (together with Hong Kong and Singapore) pertinent examples of fully fledged delayed development under capitalist premise.[6] In this respect, incidentally, the more recent overall assessment coincides with the view of conventional development theory, according to which these very examples demonstrate, in exemplary fashion, in what external and internal conditions national capitalist

development can still be repeated even today.[7] The weakness of the
very recent development theory debate lies, however, in the fact that it
tends globally to postulate the prospect of fully fledged delayed capitalist development with regard to the Far Eastern examples cited
above, while the relevant theory-orientated empirical analyses are still
lacking—in distinct contrast with conventional development theory
which, during the past ten years, has inspired a host of empirical
studies on the above-cited cases.

The Case of South Korea

Let us concentrate on South Korea (and, incidentally, Taiwan) and
pose this question: In which direction is this country going to develop?
Will she have arrived, as postulated by conventional theory *and* the
latest Marxist development theory, within ten to thirty years, as a
mature capitalist country at the lower level of the OECD countries and
be structurally a part of these? In other words, will she have achieved
autocentric development in spite of, or precisely because of, her decidedly world market-orientated development policy? Or will South
Korea in the twenty-first century still have to be legitimately classed
with the area of *peripheral* capitalism? In the first case South Korea
would be an example of a successful 'late late-modernizer'; in the latter
case she would, in typological terms, occupy a special position within
peripheral capitalism. For she is a relatively populous country (in 1980,
38 million inhabitants), basing her development path, after an initial
period of import substitution industrialization, on an extreme export
orientation which, to this degree, can usually be observed only in the
case of sparsely populated countries. If, for example, the Ivory Coast
with 7.8 million people (1978) and Tunisia with 6 million inhabitants
(1978) have export shares of 38 per cent and 31 per cent of the GDP
respectively, while South Korea with 38 million has attained an export
share of 34 per cent, then the first-mentioned cases are, in international
comparison, representative with regard to the proportion in question,
while South Korea represents an anomaly. If one compares Korea with
highly developed or peripheral societies of similar size, one would rather
expect an export share of between 25 per cent and 30 per cent.[8]

   The question regarding the further development of South Korea is
difficult to answer, for the South Korean profile differs in several
respects from the usual peripheral capitalist development profiles.
Whether such differences are of lasting importance is at present difficult

to judge, but it is possible that they might steer the development process in a different direction from that which can commonly be observed in the peripheral-capitalist Third World at present. Income inequality in present-day South Korea, for example, is less pronounced than in the remaining countries of the Third World (with the exception of Taiwan), for which data on income distribution are available. While in South Korea the most affluent 20 per cent of households command 45 per cent of the total income, the relative percentage of the total income earned by the same proportion of households in various other countries is as follows: Honduras, 67.8 per cent; Brazil, 66.6 per cent; Peru, 61 per cent; Turkey, 56.5 per cent; Mexico, 57.7 per cent; Philippines, 53.9 per cent; Venezuela, 54 per cent; Chile, 51.4 per cent; Argentina, 50.3 per cent; Spain, 42.2 per cent; Yugoslavia, 40 per cent. The share of the least affluent 20 per cent of households, in South Korea too, is more or less double the average (just under 6 per cent of the above-named countries.[9] The Gini index, which provides a numerical synthesis of the overall extent of inequality, stands at 0.36, with the extreme of 0 indicating total equality, and 1.0 total inequality.[10] Of all the developing countries for which figures on income distribution are available, only Taiwan presents an even more favourable picture: the top 20 per cent of households command 39.2 per cent of the total income, the lowest 20 per cent, 8.7 per cent, and the Gini index stands at 0.29. The same relatively favourable profile characterizes the distribution of land. Here the Gini index of concentration is 0.39 in the case of South Korea, a figure considerably lower than in other developing countries (Honduras, 0.75; Brazil, 0.84; Peru, 0.93; Turkey, 0.59; Mexico, 0.69; the Philippines, 0.53; Venezuela, 0.90; Argentina, 0.86; Spain, 0.79; Yugoslavia, 0.43).[11]

Whatever the margins of error in such data, on the whole they tend to point in the same direction. The share of the big and the biggest income and land ownership groups is likely to be understated, while that of the lowest income and ownership groups is likely to be exaggerated, if only because a number of data collection methods do not include the poorest small households. Will this lower degree of inequality compared with other developing countries in the South Korean (and Taiwanese) development process make any real difference in the long run? Will it be at all sustainable? It is clear that during the 1970s income inequality increased in South Korea; but, compared with the rest of the Third World, it was still relatively moderate. The comparative analysis of export economies[12] shows that a moderate degree of income inequality is one of the socio-structural prerequisites for domestic market development, despite export orientation. The wide distribution of export income provides the basis of a growing demand for locally produced consumer and capital goods—and consequently an additional dynamic impulse for the domestic economy in spite of continuing export orientation. The maturing process of the domestic economy, then, also results in the diversification of the export structure and in its qualitative evolution towards higher levels of processing. Historically, this was the development path of northern Europe, where, in the course of a few decades, export-orientated economies turned into fully-fledged, mature, capitalist metropoles.

There, a delayed sequence of export growth and domestic market development took place, while, at a later stage, domestic economic development acquired its own impetus, generating impulses towards the qualitative improvement of the export commodities basket.[13] In all cases where, by contrast, the internal structures were characterized by gross inequalities (compare Uruguay and Denmark, Romania and Finland, etc.), this spill-over effect between export growth and domestic market development was blocked. Seen from such a comparative historical perspective, it does make a difference whether an export-orientated South Korea (or Taiwan) is characterized by crass or only 'moderate' inequality.[14]

In spite of the fact that, during the 1950s and early 1960s, South Korean (and Taiwanese) development was orientated towards import substitution industrialization, and despite the fact that, even after development policy had been reorientated towards export diversification the domestic markets continued to expand, though less dynamically, the development of the domestic market potential remained incomplete. This is reflected in both the above-average export share of the GDP and the below-average wage share in national income. In South Korea the latter proportion amounts to 40 per cent, which is the same as in the rest of the Third World, but 25 per cent below the Japanese figure and 25 to 30 per cent below the level of the other highly industrialized societies.[15] Other Third World societies, like that of Argentina, which have passed through a relatively broad process of industrialization much earlier than South Korea, have never achieved the breakthrough to mature capitalist societies because a low wage share in national income, caused by political and socio-structural factors, has blocked a full development of the domestic market and, consequently, of the dynamics of capitalist reproduction.[16] In the case of Argentina, a persistent oligarchic social structure blocked, despite intermittent populism, any breakthrough to a broad-based development of the domestic market and, consequently, the emergence of mature metropolitan capitalism. In the case of South Korea, the export orientation on the basis of the very lowest wages—the imputed comparative advantage of this society—threatens to become a development trap. For how could South Korea's breakthrough to a mature capitalist society and economy be conceived?

Such a breakthrough can be conceived only as occurring in a relatively conventional pattern. The dynamic growth of the whole economy would have to be of such strength that, in the course of time, the potential labour reserve would be absorbed and labour shortages develop, with the result that the interplay between higher wage demands and growing productivity would lead to an increase in both wages and profits. This is the classic capitalist growth dynamics which, in the presence of labour shortages, is translated into development dynamics.[17] Where it is initially based on exports, it can, in specific conditions, still be directed towards the domestic market, even if exports continue to play a considerable role (possibly simply on account of the small population).[18] Is such a growth dynamics, translating itself into a broad-based development dynamics, to be expected in South Korea in the foreseeable future? In other words, are there any indications that labour is becoming scarce and expensive, and that consequently the foundations are being laid for an increase in mass-purchasing power which will lead to the development of the Korean domestic market?

Population growth in South Korea is just below 2 per cent, but in view of the demographic make up of society the economically active population is growing faster than the population as a whole. In terms of demographic change, the pool of labour is increasing rather than decreasing. There still exists, moreover, considerable surplus population in the agricultural sector. At the end of the 1970s 41 per cent of the labour force produced 24 per cent of GDP.[19] The Korean economy is, moreover, under pressure to 'deepen' the existing industrial structure. Import substitution industrialization in the area of intermediate and capital goods production is overdue. Whether such an industry is orientated towards the world market or the domestic economy, it is bound to be capital-intensive and thus less able to absorb labour than the markedly labour-intensive export industrialization of more recent years. Such an expansion of the local industrial structure is under way.[20] And it will possibly become inevitable even in the case of persistent export orientation, since other suppliers (like the People's Republic of China, as well as other Third World countries) will appear in the world market, able to produce still cheaper the same goods that South Korea has been selling latterly in the world market (e.g. as a result of even lower wages). In that case, South Korea could succeed against international competition only by introducing labour-saving investment into the traditional export-orientated sectors or by shifting to the production of high-value goods, namely capital-intensive, technology-intensive and skill-intensive products. Such a reorientation of economic policy would, without doubt, generate a new growth impulse within the South Korean economy. However, a proportional absorption of labour would be less likely.[21]

It is indeed also conceivable that, in conditions of continuing structural change in Korean society (increasing proletarianization and urbanization), the demands of the labour force for higher wages, which could hitherto be rejected and contained, could no longer be controlled. In that case, too, the export orientation could be sustained only if increased labour costs were offset by labour-saving investment.

Taking all these factors into consideration, it becomes apparent that the next stage of the Korean development path is not going to lead to the impending drying up of a still 'unlimited supply of cheap labour', even in favourable world market conditions. The dynamic impulse of the domestic market will therefore remain of secondary importance, without even taking into consideration all the other problems of the existing development path, such as the large foreign debt, insufficient capitalization of companies, and so forth.

South Korea is thus caught in a dilemma. Her growth success in the past has been based to a considerable extent on the exploitation of extremely cheap labour. But a nationally integrated economy cannot be constructed on the basis of cheap labour remaining cheap. A comparative analysis of the early phases of capitalist development in the present OECD countries shows that, after the first growth spurts in the export sector or the domestic economy, the maturing process of capitalist societies depended crucially on the fact that labour shortages developed, that labour began to organize politically, that the wage share in national income increased, and that *the conflict between capital and labour resulted in the deepening of the capitalist maturing process through a dialectical relationship between inexorably increasing productivity and a rising share of wages*. This dialectical process does not take place, or remains incomplete, if the supply of cheap labour fails to dry up. And it is fatal for *overall* economic development if, in order to remain internationally competitive, labour costs are kept down, with the result that the domestic market, too, is not developed to its full potential.[22]

In the current development theory debate, outlined at the beginning of this chapter, it is rightly emphasized that capitalist development depends on the elimination of pre-capitalist relationships of production, and that the proletarianization of labour is one of the essential factors in the emergence of an economy based on division of labour and, consequently, in the development of the domestic market.[23] In this debate it is also correctly postulated that low wages are one of several prerequisites for capital accumulation to take off. *What is being overlooked is the long-term dialectic of capitalist development dynamics.*[24] This dialectical process depends on cheap labour becoming expensive through getting scarce, whereby the growing scarcity of labour is itself often a reflex of an increasing capitalization of the economy. Not least, it is crucially important that the process is accelerated by the political organization of labour (cooperatives, trade unions, labour parties, farmers' parties).

Given a 41 per cent share of the agricultural labour force (1978) and an urbanization rate of 55 per cent (1980), the disintegration of pre-capitalist relationships of production is far advanced, even though in the agricultural sector one cannot yet speak of an unchallenged dominance of agrarian capitalism in view of an extremely fragmented structure of land tenure. Compared with a decade ago, the share of gross domestic savings in gross domestic investment has increased considerably, and the local element in capital formation is thus much larger than previously (up to 90 per cent). But is South Korea not getting caught in a dilemma which is, strangely enough, similar to that of many socialist developing countries? In those countries, as in South Korea, a considerable production potential is being established which is insufficiently linked to the agricultural sector and the dynamics of the domestic market.[25] In South Korea the production potential is developed for the sake of export industrialization and everything is subordinated to this objective. In present-day conditons such an orientation can have fatal consequences—with the result, for example, that international competitiveness can be achieved only through low production costs, which, in the case of products with a high labour content, implies above all low labour costs, which in turn can be achieved and sustained only if basic foodstuffs are cheap and remain cheap. This results in the absurd situation that agriculture has to produce goods at prices which will allow a large part of the urban population to live at subsistence level. In this way agriculture is deprived of the incentive to modernize, intensify and, consequently, increase its production. The resulting structural weakness of agriculture has a damaging impact on the whole economy, even though the numbers employed in agriculture are falling and industry's contribution to the GDP has by now surpassed that of agriculture.[26] A development path does not become any less perverted if the competitiveness of the export industry is achieved at the expense of agriculture than if, as in the case of socialist developing countries, heavy industrialization for its own sake is excessively promoted at the expense of agriculture.[27]

South Korea's Development in Historical Perspective

Are there any historical precedents for the South Korean development path?[28] So far as I can see, none of today's highly industrialized, *populous* capitalist (and socialist) countries has attempted to develop by way of export industrialization—not even Japan, which is often mentioned in this connection.[29] The only country where, from the very start, export industrialization based on the export of *processed* goods (textiles) took place, was Switzerland after 1780, which at the time had slightly more than 2 million people. It is interesting that (with the partial exception of the Netherlands since the second part of the nineteenth century) the history of industrialization knows no second truly Ricardian development path. Above all, no *populous* country of the size of present-day South Korea has ever attempted to follow such a development path. One should keep in mind that in 1860 what was later to become Germany had 36 million inhabitants, Austria-Hungary 35 million, France 37 million, Italy 25 million, and Spain 16 million. Their development was, as can only be expected, primarily *based on the dynamic impulse of the domestic market*, while the export side played a complementary rather than a leading role. Those highly industrialized societies of the day, whose exports were of essential importance, were (with the exception of Great Britain, the industrial pioneer) small European and non-European ones of between 2 million and 5 million (1860). This also applies to those countries endowed mainly with agricultural resources (like Denmark, Finland and New Zealand), where the growth impulse originated in the export of initially unprocessed agricultural commodities and later shifted, by way of structural diversification and economic deepening, to the export of processed agricultural commodities and to the development of the domestic market. In typological terms, South Korea is actually trying to retread the development path of resource-starved Switzerland in much more difficult world market conditions, even though the former is a populous territorial state, while the latter—given a continent whose industry was still scarcely developed—was able directly to compete in certain niche areas with Britain which, apart from exporting machinery, flooded the markets with above all cheap mass-produced goods. Despite all the differences between nineteenth century and present-day industrialization processes, it is in every respect exceptional that a populous territorial state of South Korea's size should once again attempt delayed capitalist development by way of world market integration. This, incidentally, also applies to Taiwan with her population of almost 18 million.[30]

The further development of South Korea will, over the next two decades, help reveal the validity or otherwise of the current postulates of development theory which, as has been described above, point in one or the other direction. In this respect South Korean (and Taiwanese) development presents just as lasting a challenge as do the questions surrounding the *newly industrializing countries* which will continue to occupy the development theory debate well into the next decade.[31]

6 Socialism: an Interpretation from the Perspective of Development History and Theory

Socialist Expectations and the Reality of Socialism

A transition from capitalism to socialism has been expected and practically striven for since the second half of the nineteenth century by critics who challenged capitalist society as a matter of principle. If anywhere socialist policy seemed to have a real chance and objective only in 'mature' capitalist societies. The more dynamic the capitalist development of a society, and hence the development of productive forces, the sooner should internal inconsistencies be aggravated and the more unavoidable would a revolutionary upheaval in favour of socialism appear. In the light of human history, socialism seemed a new and higher stage of social development.[1]

Since socialist criticism of capitalism related to real human needs—the consequences of early capitalist development—it was able, through the medium of socialist parties and trade-union organizations, to grow into an historically powerful force. Its long-range effect, however, by no means consisted in overcoming capitalism. Nowhere in the history of advanced capitalist societies has the antagonism between capital and labour led to the political breakthrough of socialism. On the contrary, it can be shown that it is precisely the institutionalized antagonism between the owners of capital and the proletariat that has contributed in the long run to dynamification (and stabilization) of capitalist development.[2] Without an antagonist, initially predominant capital would have been wrecked by sweated labour—one of a number of early means to cut production costs—and the resulting 'accumulation of pauperism'.[3] Without pertinacious opposing forces, capital-owners, adhering to profit calculations necessarily constrained

by short-term business considerations, would have been able to ac-
cumulate a great deal, but without potent, domestically developed
national economies coming into being. Capitalist growth requires
accumulatable surplus value and an adequate aggregate demand.[4] If
capitalism, which is a decentrally organized 'anarchic' economic system, is not to be shattered by its inherent inconsistencies, paradoxically
it needs for its self-stabilization politically organized and pertinacious
opposing forces. It is not surprising, therefore, that societies with a
well-organized labour movement and/or high real wages were the
earliest to overcome the symptoms of early capitalism and to pass
through a dynamic development process on their way to becoming
'mature' capitalist economies.[5]

If socialism in the principal countries with a capitalist development
did not result from the ever more aggravated inconsistencies in the
capitalist mode of production, how can socialism, under which a
third of the world population currently turns out a bare fifth of the
gross world product, be assigned a location in developmental history?

From the developmental standpoint, socialism must be assigned a
different rank than that envisaged in the traditional (socialist) theory
which criticizes capitalism. In that theory, socialism was regarded as a
step beyond the positively and negatively assessed 'abundance' of
capitalism. In reality, however, tasks on this side of the abundance of
capitalism devolved upon it. Where socialism became a societal deter-
minant (and did not remain just one political force among others
within capitalist societies), it was the basis and motive force of accelerated, delayed development in adverse internal and international
conditions which, as a rule, make successful delayed development
under the banner of capitalism improbable.[6] This observation calls for
an explanation.

The Problems of Delayed Development

In an increasingly intermeshed world economy, the development
problems of latecomers are aggravated by the fact that, on average,
the economies of the forerunners of development, the early modern-
izers, are more productive.[7] An international competence gap opens up
between forerunners and latecomers, because the former's economies
(like those of north-eastern Europe after 1750) are more efficient in all
fields: their average agricultural and industrial productivity exceeds
that of potential latecomers; their infrastructure is more highly devel-

oped; private and public services are more efficient; finally, the human capital that has matured in them is greater and more highly differentiated, for which reason dormant productive forces can be mobilized more rapidly and greater proficiency in the control of development processes is on tap. If, in a relatively interdependent, international economy, such forerunners come face to face with latecomers, extensive displacement competition ensues, in which latecomers are at a disadvantage unless protective action is taken. This competition is much in evidence, not only in the exchange of goods, in which merchandise made by more productive methods outrivals the products of latecomers, but also in the services sector, and it lames development of the latecomers' intellectual and organizational competence. While among the forerunners research and development flourish and management knowledge spreads, on the other side proficiencies are stunted. Latecomers face the danger of peripheralization, consequently being robbed of the chance to achieve comprehensive development comparable to that of the forerunners.[8]

Since the middle of the eighteenth century, only a few latecomers have succeeded in escaping threatening peripheralization and in attaining comprehensive development. What was still possible in the nineteenth and early twentieth centuries—that is, the successful, delayed development of most of the present OECD countries by way of capitalism—has not, as a general rule, been repeated under the capitalistic premise in the twentieth century.[9] Successful, delayed development leading to the overcoming of the symptoms and structures of peripheralization in the twentieth century, has taken place in the majority of cases under the premise of socialism.

In the nineteenth century and still at the beginning of the twentieth century, societies developed along many different capitalist development paths.[10] The first was characterized by competitive-capitalist dynamification of domestic consumer goods markets, without the competence gap assumed for delayed development being too deleterious. This development profile is characteristic particularly of densely populated countries of a large area with a comparatively favourable infrastructure, which derived from preceding development phases during mercantilism and enlightened absolutism (for example, in France, and the principal Austro-Hungarian countries). The second development path is characterised by successful integration from the outset in the world market in accordance with the liberal Ricardian principle of comparative advantages (Switzerland)—an exceptional case which, in the current developmental debate, is raised to the status of a paradigm. What is interpreted in the theory, of imminent peripheralization as the pressure of exogenous problems, is regarded here in practice as an opportunity. In part this applies also˙ to typical cases of a third development path. On this path, development takes place partly through integration into the world market by way of marked export orientation and partly through dissociation for the purpose of local industrialization (for example, Denmark, Sweden, Australia). In the world market, advantage is taken of opportunities. On the other hand, the described competence differential is evaded where it is felt most, in the building up of a self-reliant, differentiated industry. This development path calls for adroitness and flexibility. Consequently it can be observed only where relatively highly developed human capital was already available at the onset of delayed development. In cases assignable to the fourth development path, it is not so much dynamification of private consumption that plays a strategic developmental role, or a combination of integration into the world market and selective dissociation, but rather accumulation imperatives laid down by state classes[11] and, derivable therefrom, the investment activities with respect to industrial development, infrastructural measures and public-sector consumption (for example, Japan). Typically, densely populated, large-area countries with problematical development conditions are assignable to this development path.

In all the named cases of successful delayed development, socio-economic structures were built up, which are characterized by increasing division of labour and intrasectoral and intersectoral differentiation coupled with simultaneous, closer intermeshing of domestic economic activities. Productive forces are developed in all essential spheres: in agriculture, the mass-consumer goods industry, the producers' goods industry, in the invention and production of technology, and in the field of private and public services. The political and administrative system, too, gains efficiency, as a result of which the social-cybernetic capacity for self-control and self-steering is increased.[12] Parallel with the formation of domestically developed national economies, there evolved from formerly socially and culturally fragmented small societies, those with their own political culture and independent cultural identity. In such autocentric societies and economies, factor mobility increases, which accelerates the spreading of technical progress. Societies and economies which develop along autocentric lines gain over the long run in internal (structural) cohesion. They are subject to constant social change and their differentiated structure facilities adaptation and innovation, as compared with the sluggishness of traditional societies. A factor of substantial importance is their capacity to cope successfully within an interdependent world society with potentially efficient and more competent economies and to participate selectively in the international division of labour.

Only a few societies, in which moreover only a minority of the world population lives, have achieved such autocentric development.[13] The majority of the world population lives at present in societies which for various reasons were peripheralized in the past decades and centuries: in consequence of their transformation from tolerably viable subsistence economies to monocultures during the colonial and imperial periods; in consequence of displacement competition which (although they were not, or are no longer, colonized areas) they were unable to stand up to; and in consequence of their being thrust into the role of geographically peripheral undeveloped structures in which the stagnative forces of traditional social systems won out over potentially new and dynamic forces. Most societies passed through a process of structural peripheralization on account of their transformation into agricultural monocultures and mineral exclave economies.

In peripheral economies, defective development processes can be observed.[14] No broad-based, comprehensive increase in productivity can be observed in agriculture; expansion in the industrial sector is orientated towards a restricted demand, though with high purchasing power; the production of means of production remains undeveloped or underdeveloped; and the infrastructure is, as a rule, export-orientated and little suited to help open up local, domestic markets. These development processes cause the structural defects of peripheral economies, lacking as they do the interlinkage between agriculture and industry, and depth of production. The consequence is imperfect economic circuits, since peripheral economies constitute exclaves for the metropolitan-capitalistic economies, and part of their reproductive structure is to be found in the metropolitan economies. Such defects and a lack of internal balance, which becomes accentuated as a result of peripheralization processes, find expression, even in large-area societies with large populations, in a chronic artificial 'narrowness of the domestic market'. In the course of growth processes, in peripheral economies the internal gap widens between relatively productive sectors within growth poles and economic spheres of below-average productivity in the urban and rural 'hinterland'. Unlike autocentric development, what ensues is not homogenization, but disseverance of domestic economic areas (structural heterogeneity).

Such societies become incapable of integrating the mass of their population productively into the economy. Many of them lose the capacity to supply their own population with sufficient locally produced farm goods; demographic trends in them become uncontrollable—a result of socio-economic disruption. As a consequence of peripheralization, the ability is lost to invent and produce equipment and technologies of their own and to adapt such goods that are available elsewhere to local needs. From the dialectics of misguided growth and spreading mass penury, considerable food for social conflict is derived, which nourishes the advocates and recipients of an alternative, socialist policy.[15]

In such a situation, it devolves upon socialism to save peripheralized societies from further peripheralization and, by developing coherent productive forces, to make possible once again an accelerated, delayed development. Socialism becomes a development policy without alternatives in conditions in which capitalism failed. Its function is that of a midwife and pacemaker for a differentiated and well-proportioned development of productive forces. It was not abundance but privation, and, what is more, usually privation aggravated by war, which was the ground in which socialism was able to take root and become a decisive societal force.

Prehistory of Socialist Development

In the international society of the present day, many countries call themselves socialist. The following deliberations apply to only a few of them. The present writer has chosen two categories of countries: on the one hand, the Soviet Union and the socialist countries of eastern and south-eastern Europe (GDR, CSSR, Hungary, Poland, Romania, Yugoslavia, Bulgaria); and on the other, four socialist developing countries (China, North Korea, Cuba and Albania), which, with the exception of Cuba, have three to four decades of experience with socialist development policy like the eastern and south-eastern European socialist countries. In the case of Cuba, the experience now covers two decades.

In their history prior to the radical change to socialism, varying degrees of peripheralization can be observed in ten of the twelve cases cited. The exceptions are the GDR and the CSSR.

Prehistory of socialist development in eastern and south-eastern Europe

Prior to the partition of Germany, the GDR was part of a quite highly industrialized country and by no means a peripheral economy. The same is true, though not so manifestly, of the Czech part of Czechoslovakia. Even under the Austro-Hungarian monarchy, the Bohemian Crownlands belonged to the relatively highly industrialized centres. So far as their industrial and agricultural structure was concerned, they lagged behind development in northern and western Europe quantitatively (e.g., per capita income), but, unlike the other countries of eastern and south-eastern Europe, by no means in terms of structural profile. Development problems arose only as a result of the combination of 'Czechy', a quite highly developed economic area, and Slovakia, a former periphery of Hungary,[16] which in its turn exhibited typical peripheral characteristics.

The remaining six countries of eastern and south-eastern Europe cannot readily be reduced to a common denominator.[17] Her size alone makes imperial Russia stand out from the rest; she was by far the most densely populated country in Europe in the nineteenth century (in 1860, 81 million inhabitants). Hungary and Poland were further developed than the Balkan countries—Serbia (and later Yugoslavia), Bulgaria and Romania. While for the history of Poland and Hungary the phase of the 'second serfdom' from the sixteenth century onwards was of momentous course-setting importance, it was, above all, the centuries of integration in the Ottoman Empire that left their mark on the Balkan countries.

Reviewing the history of eastern and south-eastern Europe in the nineteenth and early twentieth centuries, we find that for all the differences in details there are substantial similarities, which are briefly depicted below:

(1) In the period mentioned, the stagnation of the traditional society was partially overcome. Serfdom was abolished and a capitalistic agricultural system came into being; an initial phase of industrialization began, earlier and to a greater extent in Hungary and Poland than in the Balkan countries. From time to time, economic growth reached remarkable orders of magnitude, for example at the turn of the century and up to the outbreak of the First World War.

(2) Despite dynamification in terms of growth and social change, the development of these countries did not follow an autocentric course. The causes are to be found in the agricultural structure, the type of industrialization and the class structures that characterized society. The latifundism of Hungary was no more suitable than the peasant smallholding system of the Balkans (Serbia, Bulgaria) for helping to increase the efficiency of the agricultural sector. Where there was a mixture of latifundial and small-scale peasant farming (as in Romania and, tendentially, in Poland), the evils of both were cumulative. Where land reforms were carried out, they mostly brought little

change in the actual, social power relationships and, in particular, no increases in productivity. To achieve the latter, structural reforms would have had to result in efficient farms and a differentiated rural infrastructure (banking system, marketing organization, etc.). Without them, the rural areas were still characterised in the 1930s by gross inequality and/or rural pauperism.

The structural weakness of industry was no less grave than that of the rural sector. The one hinged on the other and they were mutually aggravating. The intermeshing of agriculture and industry (linkage effects), which is important for autocentric development, occurred, if at all, in only a fragmentary processing industry in Hungary. Part of the industrial structural weakness resulted from the cut-throat competition practised by the centres of industrial concentration in western Europe and the Austro-Hungarian monarchy.[18] If the classical theory of foreign trade and development were right, within the Austro-Hungarian monarchy, which was a unified customs area, the differences between the more highly developed areas of the Czech region and Austria and the less developed areas ought to have been smoothed out, whereas in reality they became more marked.

Further industrial structural weaknesses derived from the high degree of monopolization of eastern and south-eastern Europe's industry.[19] Before competitive capitalism could begin to play a decisive role, monopolized capital structures gained a firm footing. In contrast with the situation in the principal capitalist countries, however, the latter were not the outcome of a protracted process of centralization and concentration, but were superimposed on traditional crafts and trades structures. In the Balkan countries, industrialization long remained exclave-like in nature; essentially it served the development of export-orientated transport networks and the opening up of mineral deposits. An initially weak import-substitution industrialization set in only in reaction to the world economic crises of the 1920s and 1930s.

Although, on the outbreak of the Second World War, industry in the countries mentioned had attained a share of between 20 and 35 per cent in the GNP, those countries were still essentially of agrarian structure as far as the distribution of the active population was concerned. In the most advanced case, Hungary, slightly more than 50 per cent of the work force was employed in the agricultural sector, while the figure was still 65 per cent in Poland, 76 per cent in Yugoslavia, 78 per cent in Bulgaria and an unchanged 80 per cent in Romania.[20] Both proportions—the share of the industrial sector in the GNP and the share of the working population in agriculture—show, in line with current experience in the Third World, the discrepancy between the

sectors of the economy with respect to technical equipment and productivity. This is a sign of structural heterogeneity.

The traditional class structures were not conducive to forced and
comprehensive development either in the eastern European or Balkan
variant.[21] Except in Serbia and Bulgaria, political and social life were
under the sway of the aristocracy and the landed oligarchy. A bourgeoisie and middle class developed only in Hungary and Poland, but
they remained weak and politically of secondary importance. The general weakness of the Balkan countries was linked to a numerically
smaller and economically more fragile middle class. The high degree of
monopolization in industry went hand in hand with a relatively small
proletariat, which faced tremendous difficulties in getting organized,
either illegally or legally. In rural areas, pauperism was rife among
farm workers, peasants and the landless.

(3) In such political, social, and economic conditions, the domestic
market remained undeveloped and hence could impart no accumu-
lation-promoting impetus. Foreign trade with agricultural goods,
raw materials and energy was regarded by political and economic
leaders as a lever for the dynamification of their societies. But their
structure prevented any development of coherent productive forces
in both the Hungarian-Polish and the Serbian (Yugoslavian), Bulgarian and Romanian variant. Up to the outbreak of the Second World
War, the development profile of Hungary and Poland is similar in
many respects to that of Latin American countries during their export-
orientated and their import-substitution phase; the Balkan countries, on the other hand, can be compared with exclave economies of
the Third World in which import-substitution industrialization is
playing an inceptive role at present. In both cases, there is a lack of
well-proportioned internal development of agriculture and industry—
and, within the industrial sector, a lack of heavy industry and consumer goods production. Foreign trade activities consequently assume
disproportionately great importance. Such countries suffer cyclical
fluctuations, and not only in times of world economic crises. Being of
inherently unstable fabric, they find themselves in a persistent structural crisis.

Prehistory of socialist development in Albania, China, Cuba and North Korea

In the cases of Albania, China, Cuba and North Korea, the type of pre-
revolutionary social configuration can be briefly characterized as follows.

The pre-revolutionary Albanian society is characterised by incipient
peripheralization.[22] The period in which penetration took place from

outside chiefly from Italy, was relatively short, and its extent was relatively limited. But the development that took shape from the 1920s onward amounted to an embryonic form of peripheral capitalism. Compared with this onset of development, paramount importance attaches to the endogenous factors of socio-economic stagnation. Both in the phase of her integration in the Ottoman Empire and after the attainment of independence in the present century, pre-revolutionary Albania was more an *un*developed than an *under*developed country. Development of productive forces was lacking everywhere so that, in spite of such stagnation, and in contrast with the well-marked exclave economies, there could be no comprehensive formation of defective reproduction structures. When considering the initial penetration of Albania into the Italian economic area and subordinating it to Italy's geostrategical interests, it becomes clear how even such an undeveloped country did not escape the threat of peripheralization.

In the case of China, peripheralization was not only latent, but from the middle of the nineteenth century also acute. But on account of its size, China was spared geographically sweeping peripheralization.[23] Direct penetration by foreign powers and economic forces took place in the large urban agglomerations near the coast and in the estuary and hinterland areas of the big rivers. In these economic areas, typical peripheral-capitalistic structures came into being, while the rest of China, the vast hinterland inhabited by the mass of the people, remained relatively stagnant. In China, both dualistic and peripheral-capitalistic structures can be observed as the outcome of development since the middle of the nineteenth century. This profile has had a profound impact on socialist development policy in post-revolutionary China.

In the case of Cuba, we find neither a merely imminent nor just a partial peripheralization. On the contrary, it was total.[24] It began with Spanish colonial rule and resulted in the nineteenth century in Cuba's definitive transformation into a monocultural 'sugar island', a prototype exclave economy.

The transformation of Korean society into a peripheral economy was limited to the decades preceding the outbreak of the Second World War, but it had no less serious consequences than in the case of Cuba.[25] The Japanese had colonized Korea in order to procure from that country goods and people which they needed for the expanded capitalist reproduction of Japan. Thus in South Korea an agrarian exclave economy came into being (rice production), and in North Korea, where there are abundant mineral deposits, a relatively broad-based, heavy-industry exclave economy. Infrastructure was built up by the Japanese to the extent that it served mobilization, to a slight extent processing and, above all, the outward transportation of agricultural and mineral goods. With the beginning of Japan's imperialist wars in Asia, the Korean economy was subordinated completely to the requirements of Japan's war economy. The mobilization of Korean resources by the Japanese resulted in a typical peripheral-capitalist reproduction structure: The export-oriented sectors were developed hypertrophically without establishing the linkages with other economic activities which are necessary for coherent development. Japan was not interested in promoting well-proportioned, national economic development in Korea, but in exploiting Korean resources for Japan's own benefit (war economy).

Two of the countries mentioned, Cuba and Korea, are ideal-type cases of peripheral development. The other two, China and Albania, exhibit specific features that have already been described in the foregoing. Where stagnation no longer prevailed and productive forces were mobilized, the development of those forces led to deformed economic and social structures. As in the eastern and south-eastern European countries, socialist development policy in the post-revolutionary societies of the four cases named set itself the task of mobilizing dormant productive forces and giving balanced proportions to defectively developed structures.[26]

Tasks of Socialist Development Policy in the First Structural Reorganization and Building-up Phase

Compared with the experience made with delayed capitalistic development in the nineteenth century and the early twentieth century, the development-policy tasks of delayed development have not only become individually greater during the twentieth century, but greater *in toto*.[27] Slight, flanking government investments in infrastructure by no means sufficed; nor did merely selective protective measures for foreign trade *vis-à-vis* more competent forerunners on the lines of protective tariff policy. The later delayed development sets in and the more it is staged against a peripheral-capitalist or an underdeveloped-stagnative background, the more dramatic are the development tasks—and the more impossible is a renewed, comprehensive, delayed development. Yet these are precisely the circumstances in which delayed development is attempted with socialist development policy. It is a *tour de force* beyond compare. One might say, a radical social cure, the result of which is the overcoming of underdevelopment and for which, as a rule, there is but one alternative: the sort of development that can currently be observed in the Third World.[28]

With what tasks is delayed socialist development confronted? The following four are the chief ones:

(1) After political revolution has been accomplished, new, political and administrative structures have to be built up. The social-revolutionary change of social structure is imperative, since the traditional social order blocks balanced development of productive forces—even when remarkable growth rates are attained in individual, mostly export-orientated sectors and in the field of import substitution. Since socialist development proceeds according to bureaucratic plans, the new political organizations assume strategic importance for the guidance of society and the economy.[29] This primacy of the political domain is linked with chances and dangers. The chances lie in the mobilization and allocation of resources to serve long-range development objectives, the dangers in the oligarchization of the new political leadership groups and their bureaucratic machinery.[30]

(2) Revolutionary changes can lay the political foundation for delayed socialist development. They cannot conjure up overnight the lacking infrastructural prerequisites, the legacy of the pre-revolutionary society.[31] It is necessary, for instance, to eliminate illiteracy where it is still widespread, to build up a health system accessible to the masses, and to develop further the communications and transport system that has often been distorted by colonialism. In cases of delayed capitalist development, in many instances, such infrastructures were already available at the onset of agro-industrial revolution as a result of previous mercantilistic and absolutist policy. In cases of delayed socialist development, they must first be developed with high priority in addition to all the other tasks.

(3) The third task is development of agriculture, the consumer goods and heavy industries. In the pre-revolutionary societies of the cases mentioned, development in these fields was fragmentary and uncohesive. Some subsectors were hypertrophically developed (the enclaves), others were often completely lacking (e.g. equipment goods industry). Thus a not very efficient agriculture was paired with a not very efficient, fragmentary industry. This sort of economic structure was the characteristic of traditional class relationships, the elimination of which removed development barriers, but without enabling the creation of a balanced economic structure at short notice.

(4) Foreign trade relations, too, had to be newly regulated. Since the traditional relations to the world market, from which a substantial

share of the growth impetus of the pre-revolutionary society derived, were interrupted in consequence of the radical socialist change, and socialist countries were additionally subjected to politically motivated embargoes imposed by capitalist metropolitan economies, in a first development phase only other socialist countries were available as potential economic partners. Since they were all in the same critical situation, little could be expected from an activation of foreign trade relations in the socialist camp. These countries were therefore constrained to pursue an economic course that was autarchic in tendency and, moreover, was ideologically justified by the Soviet development doctrine.[32] But even without such justification, the majority of socialist countries would have been left to themselves in the early phase of their development.

The tasks that socialist development policy set itself were many and varied; their simultaneous financing was a sheer impossibility.[33] Where is capital for industrial development to be drawn off, if not from agriculture? But agriculture itself was marked by considerable structural weaknesses. Simultaneous development of agriculture and industry at short notice—what is more, against a background of defectively developed, or even entirely undeveloped, infrastructures—how could such a task be dealt with? Moreover, socialist policy sets out to abolish the pauperism of the pre-revolutionary society and improve the lot of the masses: to banish hunger, eliminate illiteracy, provide housing, make an extensive public health system possible, build up advanced education institutions, establish new communication channels and organizational structures.

Delayed capitalist development in the nineteenth and early twentieth centuries was difficult, but how much more difficult it was to finance delayed socialist development. As a rule there was no alternative to self-sacrificing accumulation locally. Redistribution measures were suitable only for dealing with initial problems in the first few years. Then the burden of forced accumulation fell upon the mass of the population—that is, in these countries, usually on the peasant population. Where an industry, however fragmentary, already existed, the industrial workers, too, must be numbered among those who bore the burden of initial socialist accumulation.[34]

The mobilization of financial resources to finance socialist development policy was both a political and a technocratic task in an environment fraught with political conflict. The so-called industrialization debate in the Soviet Union demonstrated in exemplary manner in the 1920s the political problems that arise.[35] How great a burden can be imposed on what social groups without their refusing to participate in

socialist development and without their obstructing it? What sectors
must be rigorously planned in building up a socialist economy, and
what sectors can be left to the free play of forces without undermining
socialist development? Can a reasonable solution be found to the conflict between long-range development objectives and short-range consumption interests? The attainment of long-range development goals
requires substantial investments in a differentiated production potential (with high start-up costs and long maturing periods), the magnitude of which cannot be translated into an immediately perceptible,
short-term improvement of the standard of living. How many sacri-
fices is a generation prepared to make if their fruits can be harvested
only by later generations?[36]

The Soviet industrialization debate, like all comparable debates in
socialist countries after 1945, demonstrated that such political questions can only be answered politically, in which connection no socialist
body of leaders can be sure that it has not made wrong, fundamental
and/or day-to-day policy decisions which adversely affect socialist
development for years if not for decades.

In addition to the cited difficulties, there is the further factor that in
no case of socialist assumption of power has the internal and international question of power been clearly settled in favour of the new
socialist leaders. Up to now, socialist societies have come into being
during international wars and/or in the train of civil wars.[37] Such
unclarified power relationships and the sum of all development policy
tasks to be performed result, following the revolutionary change, in
autocratic political regimes coming into being, which, in the critical
early phases of socialist development, have hitherto embodied, almost
without exception, variations of Stalinist rule. Attempts have been
made to interpret such regimes as the heritage of 'Asiatic despotism'.[38]
Although there may be links in individual cases between 'Asiatic
despotism' and socialist development despotism of the Stalinist kind,[39]
it is by no means necessary to resort to the theory of Asiatic despotism
to grasp the autocratic character of socialist development. Even without that theory it can be explained why socialist development in the
conditions mentioned took place within an autocratically repressive
framework.[40]

Incidentally, it should not be forgotten in this connection that capitalist development, too, did not occur in participatory conditions.
In both capitalist and socialist conditions, accumulation means the
production of a surplus product and investment of surplus in expansion
of the productive basis of the society and economy. In the conditions of
both political systems, at the beginning development processes are

similar to a zero-sum game. To the conditions of delayed socialist development, this is far more dramatic than in earlier stages of development history. In these early phases, authoritarian regimes have the function of modernization agencies that compel abstinence from consumption and divert the unconsumed surplus product into productive investments. This function is particularly marked in the early history of socialist development, but it is likewise evident in the capitalist development of latecomers such as Prussia, Tsarist Russia and Japan.[41] Incidentally, autocratic regimes do not guarantee a development path that leads automatically to autocentric social structures. In peripheral-capitalist societies, the dialectic of relatively great economic growth and spreading mass penury leads sooner or later to militarization, which finds expression in repressive authoritarian regimes and military dictatorships. It can be demonstrated by current examples in the Third World and by the history of eastern and south-eastern European societies in the period between the wars that without prior changes in social structure, authoritarian regimes are incapable of bringing about long-term, well-proportioned development. Even the authoritarian, corporative, fascist regimes of southern Europe, in which the class structures typical of peripheral-capitalist societies were firmly consolidated, failed to attain well-proportioned development, although in some of them (as in Spain and Italy) the production potential was considerably enlarged in the period of fascism.[42]

Results of the First Phase of Socialist Development

What are the accomplishments of socialist development policy, which has been interpreted here as an instrument for accelerated, delayed development?

Monographic and comparative studies of socialist countries,[43] which proceed from different theoretical premises, come to the conclusion that, even in an international comparison, socialist development policy is capable of mobilizing remarkable economic growth on the basis of a high accumulation rate, concentrated and purposive investments, and an often enormous labour input. The chronic unemployment (marginality) which characterized the pre-revolutionary societies tends to be eliminated, although particularly in densely populated countries not all forms of underemployment were eliminated at the first attempt. Socialist development policy can boast considerable accomplishments in the way of establishing and expanding the educational system and health protection, also in the sphere of social security, but much less in the domain of housing construction. The once crippled domestic market, where the needs of a few could be satisfied at the expense of many and without the many having any realistic prospect of a fair share, is a thing of the past. Its place has been taken by an homogenized domestic market, the development impetus of which serves three principal objectives: building up and improving the efficiency of differentiated agro-industrial structures, whose development rhythm in a first development phase lags behind short-term profitability calculations and is the result of long-range development planning; the building up of infrastructures capable of interlinking economic areas; and satisfaction of the basic needs of the masses by a growing supply of initially simple, and only in the long run more complex goods. In this first development phase, 'egalitarianism' gains the day. It is the decisive instrument of economic policy to remedy the heterogeneity of the peripheral society, and pave the way for homogeneity of the domestic market—a homogeneity which the forerunners of capitalist development achieved for the most part step by step as far back as in the age of mercantilism and absolutism and in a first protracted phase of thorough capitalization.[44]

In all cases of socialist development, important building blocks for a well-proportioned economy have been created up to the present without the economy itself meriting classification as a well-proportioned economy. The structural gaps typical of peripheral-capitalistic societies have been narrowed everywhere. This is particularly true of the building up of heavy industry and a producer's goods sector. Meanwhile the overdue shifting of priorities in favour of agriculture and the consumer goods sector, which would be essential for proper proportioning of the economy, has not taken place to an adequate extent. In this economic disproportionateness, which also has political causes, lies one of the unremedied structural problems of the socialist society.[45]

The accomplishments of socialist development policy can also be outlined with the help of hypothetical scenarios. What would have happened to the countries mentioned without any socialist transformation? Viewed in comparative developmental perspective, it is not difficult to picture their political, social and economic situation. They would also belong to the problem cases of international development policy and would still have the characteristics of peripheral-capitalist societies.

China would not differ fundamentally from Brazil and India, and if we take into account the potential mass penury that would exist in China in peripheral-capitalist conditions, the World Bank's statistics on the extent of absolute poverty in the world would have to be raised by over 50 per cent from the listed 800 million people to a figure of between 1.2 and 1.5 billion. And a replica of what the north-east of the country is for Brazil, an enormous poverty-stricken region, would be found in the entire, non-coastal hinterland of China as opposed to the maritime, urban growth centres. Moreover, China would have by no means been spared the ever more grave problems of overpopulation and slum formation in the urban centres, whereas in actual fact the relationship between the urban and rural population has been preserved tolerably well in the past decades. The traditional, coastal agglomeration centres of China would be popular investment terrain for multinational firms and, as in Brazil, the latter would preferably produce for a small sector with high demand (which, however, would run into millions) those consumer durables with which they promise to spread technical progress in the Third World, although such production fails to meet elementary development requirements (macro-economic structural policy, organic development of the entire domestic economy). Without socialist transformation, China's agriculture would be disaster-prone as in the past, and the mass of the farmers would be ever less capable of securing their own subsistence. For without new inputs, subsistence farming erodes—the Chinese learnt that lesson in the 1950s. In view of the fact that the mass of the population still lives in rural areas, it is not difficult to imagine the extent of imminent and acute starvation. Like other governments in Asia, the Chinese government would resort to the expedient of the Green Revolution. True, this would enable agricultural yields to be increased, but would involve substantial social costs such as the further marginalization of already marginal peasant strata. Such a scenario could well be terrible reality.[46]

But what seems particularly dramatic in the case of China in view of the billion people involved, would be no less dramatic in smaller countries in which socialist development policy has meanwhile been practised and which now by no means still number among the acute problem cases of international development policy. As an aftermath of Japanese colonial policy, North Korea could even now still be an exclave economy specializing in the export of minerals, dependent on considerable food imports, broken down into mineral growth centres and a stagnant, penurious agricultural hinterland, and passing through a first phase of import-substitution industrialization. Albania would certainly be numbered among the least developed countries, whose development chances are ever more frankly declared to be hopeless in international documents. It would have sunk more or less to the status of a recipient of charitable development aid. And Cuba would still have to be classified as one of the monocultural exclave economies of the Caribbean. Had they not undergone socialist transformation, Romania, Bulgaria, Yugoslavia and Hungary would now still be representative cases of peripheral-capitalist development midway between a Latin American and a 'Turkish-Greek' development profile.[47]

Socialist development cannot work wonders. Appreciation of its accomplishments is not synonymous with playing down the costs of the socialist development path. But peripheral capitalism is no alternative to the socialist development of former peripheral-capitalist societies. And what social results was capitalistic development able to present in the space of twenty to forty years in the nineteenth and early twentieth centuries?[48]

Socialist Development Policy in the Second Development Phase

The development history of socialist societies demonstrates that peripheral-capitalist and undeveloped, stagnant societies can be transformed by socialist development policy into societies with economic structures that tend to be coherent. By means of such structural reorganization, the foundation is laid for further dynamic development.

As soon as socialist societies have got through the first development phase, however, new problems arise. In societies which (like the GDR and CSSR) were never peripheralized, they present themselves at an early stage.[49] In other societies which had a bigger development backlog they arise later. What is their nature? Rulership-structure and economy-immanent problems, which in reality are closely interrelated.[50] They are outlined briefly below.

The developmental causes of the emergence of autocratic regimes in the case of delayed socialist development have been dealt with in the foregoing. Wherever power is monopolized, there is an imminent risk of self-isolation of leadership groups from their own societies. It is precisely in a society without private enterprise that the resulting social distance has considerable negative consequences with respect to the effectiveness of self-steering mechanisms. Such self-isolation results in the weakening of reality-testing, as is shown theoretically by social cybernetics and in practice by socialist societies. Without participation, publicly relevant communication atrophies, information sources run dry and motivations wither. In consequence, the basis for a down-to-earth assessment of reality by leadership groups shrinks and their chance of controlling political, social and economic processes rationally is impaired.[51] The more they lay claim to infallibility, the more their loss of reality is translated into pathological learning. How uncertain such leadership groups are objectively, or feel subjectively, is revealed by the expansion of the internal security machinery and the militarization of society.[52]

The reaction of the population to such political conditions consists, perfectly rationally, in withdrawal into their private sphere, in a consumption orientation geared to private wants and in political apathy. As a result, the control problems in ever more complex socialist societies become more profound. Prerequisites for their dynamic change, particularly in the narrower economic sphere, are the cutting back of executive bureaucracies, decentralization and the building up of participatory control mechanisms and, in particular, forms of open, institutionalized conflict settlement between the principal groups of society.[53] In such conditions, individuals would have sufficient opportunities for self-fulfilment, which are also a prerequisite for the overdue improvement of the productivity of labour.

Up to the present, even the most advanced socialist societies have not overcome the difficulties involved in the transition from an extensive to an intensive economy. The unsolved problems are evidenced by declining efficiency of investments (declining capital productivity) and by the chronic inter-industry supply bottlenecks with effects extending right along the line to the consumer.[54] The lack of efficiency in the economy, which results from a hypertrophic planning bureaucracy, from no longer expedient priorities and probably even now from inadequate division of labour among socialist societies, prevents adequate satisfaction of accumulated consumption wants and thus undermines the economic legitimation of socialist development. In view of the impossibility of finding a purely technocratic solution to the economic structural bottlenecks during transition from an extensive to an intensive socialist economy, the danger of mutual aggravation of the political and economic legitimation crises is acute.

Up to the present, the leadership groups of socialist societies have managed to take the edge off pent-up conflicts by a mixture of concessions and repressions. The economic crises, which have led to occasional reshuffling of priorities, and the political crises, which have mostly brought nothing more than rotation of the top leadership teams, have not resulted, either individually or in combination, in reforms and structural changes that might form a sound basis for dynamic socialist development following a by now completed, extensive building-up phase.[55] The reform capacity of individual social systems admittedly varies, depending on the type of regime.[56] Experience over the past two decades, however, shows that already initiated reforms are as a rule reversed, sometimes step by step and occasionally abruptly.[57] while in countries (such as Hungary) where economic reforms were carried through fairly consequentially, new social conflicts threaten to arise in consequence of growing social inequality.[58] If reforms are not carried out, the effectivity trend of the economy further declines. If they are carried out, new and hitherto unusual forms of open conflict settlement are necessary, which conflict with the present, political-institutional character of socialist societies. Here lies the acute structural dilemma of present socialist societies.[59]

If we accept as the only realistic assumption that the new leadership groups of socialist societies (the new classes) will not relinquish voluntarily the political and social supremacy they have attained and that, on the other hand, reforms are unavoidable, the question arises of the direction in which such societies will develop in the long run. A transition from the despotic phase of socialist development to a 'social-emancipatory socialism'[60] would seem improbable *in the condition which has just been formulated*. It would seem more reasonable, in the long run, that a class society develops in which social conflicts among the classes are carried out, as in a mature capitalist society, by way of open, institutionalized conflict settlement.[61] A scenario of this sort presupposes that the contradictions of a socialist society are frankly admitted and that the political organization of differing interests is conceded to be legitimate. The obstacle to such a development is the dogma that, by definition, socialist systems embody the interests of the workers, the farmers and the intelligentsia, for which reason any political interest organization, not to mention any opposition is officially interpreted as an attack on the foundations of socialist society.

It is repugnant to traditional theories of socialism to see in the open political organization of class structures and institutionalized conflict settlement based thereon (e.g. between party and bureaucracy, on the one hand, and union organization of wage-earners, on the other) a way out of the structural crisis of *socialist* societies during the transition from their extensive development phase to an intensive one. If it is impossible to continue along the traditional development path without detriment and if social-revolutionary changes are improbable (these are the conditions that precede the argument), the development path depicted here is by no means unrealistic and improbable. It was recently described as attractive for the power élite and, for lack of an alternative, for the wage-earners, in the following words:

Regardless of the institutional structure of an industrial society, transformation from an extensive to an intensive growth phase is inevitable and a precondition therefore is a shift from coercive mechanisms to institutionalized conflict settlement. The reason for this lies in the fact that intensive growth cannot be commanded, but can only be achieved by releasing potential human resources by the use of incentive systems congruent with existing value systems. Under the conditions prevailing in a class society, such value systems cannot be expected to be based on collectivistic perspectives; on the contrary, they are based on self-interest and, in this sort of constellation, efficient incentive systems must leave room for conflicting interests. Consequently, the logic of an industrial society works towards the introduction of institutionalized conflict settlement. The problem of intensive growth is important for industrial society, because such growth permits the increase of profits and wages simultaneously. Intensive growth is therefore the stabilizing factor of an industrial class system, because it brings the classes of a society into balance. But intensive growth involves more than that: It reduces the tension between capital accumulation (and hence productive investment) and consumption. This means that additional productivity and an improving standard of living can be attained simultaneously.[62]

Uncertain ruling classes are little inclined to make political concessions. Self-assured ruling classes can make concessions without objectively endangering their supremacy or subjectively feeling it is endangered.[63] Up to the present, the leadership groups in socialist societies have not managed to achieve self-assurance by the political opening of the regime, by resetting economic priorities and by way of the positive effects for economic development deriving from these two steps.[64] And up to the present, all attempts at open political organization of varying interests have been forestalled. Autocratic regimes, it was argued above, have a propensity for pathological learning. And the handling of economic and political crises so far seems rather to have resulted in "illusionary learning' that sets economic disequilibrium to rights for a short time and reduces political tensions, but without eliminating the structural causes of unbalanced growth and political tension.[65] Despite this experience in the past years, it is probably also true of socialist societies that the few lose their grip on dispositive power monopolies which they control and that the latter are thus 'socialized'.

Wherever the division of functions is marked and, in addition, still growing, the few who, in ever new waves, lay monopolistic claim to opportunities for themselves alone, find themselves sooner or later in difficulties and at a disadvantage relative to the many, due to the fact that they have to rely on the services of all others and are therefore functionally dependent on them.[66]

Since wage-earners in socialist societies live in relative social security and are not exposed to the capitalist competition mechanism, there is a concrete chance of 'socialization of the monopoly', for without them not even the economy can be further developed. This fact is expressed simply and clearly by a statement that comes from workers in eastern Europe: 'As long as the bosses pretend they are paying us a decent wage, we shall pretend that we are working.'[67]

The Reinterpretation of Socialism in the Light of Development Experience

Against the background of the preceding reflections on development history, the function of socialism in the development process can be characterized as follows.

In the *capitalist core countries* (OECD) the development dynamics of capitalism resulted in the inevitable transformation of socialism, based on a critique of capitalism, into *social democracy*. The debate as to which concrete socialist programme might lead to the elimination of capitalism remained to a large extent without consequence, as the development dynamics of maturing capitalism undermined any socialist programme aiming at the elimination of capitalism. The above-mentioned dialectical relationship between anti-capitalist movements, which organized themselves politically, and the deepening of the capitalist development dynamics, which was partly a response to those movements, has found the clearest expression in these cases.

Socialism was development-promoting where the issue at stake was the elimination of *peripheral-capitalist* structures. But with increasing complexity, namely when such a development policy began to show results, socialist development moved into a fundamental systems' crisis whose outlines have been sketched in the previous chapter.

In those cases where socialist development policy was grafted on to advanced capitalist countries (East Germany, Czechoslovakia), the symptoms of such crises showed up first. In such a context, in conditions of a command economy and political autocracy, socialism is tantamount to social regression. For, as is extensively documented by the theoreticians of *reform socialism*,[68] the social and economic development potential is stifled, human resources remain untapped and considerable material resources are wasted. In such conditions, socialist development runs, from the very outset, into the kind of bottlenecks which, in the case of the socialist transformation of peripheral-capitalist societies, become apparent only in a second development stage.

According to more recent development theory, so-called *semi-peripheries* are located between capitalist metropoles and as yet little developed peripheral-capitalist societies. In contrast with metropoles, they are characterized by a considerable degree of structural heterogeneity, while—in contrast to typical peripheries—they have achieved a broader development of the productive forces, especially in the secondary sector, which secures them an intermediate position between metropoles and peripheries within the hierarchy of the international division of labour (exports of traditional commodities to the metropoles, exports of processed goods, including capital goods, to the peripheries).

It is no accident that *eurocommunism* is a typical product of semi-peripheries. The main issue in these countries is the elimination of development blocks. This would require a broad political coalition, a so-called 'historic compromise'—a coalition for which there is no call in typical capitalist core countries. This is one of the reasons why euro-communism as a variant of socialism emerged in its original and earliest form in Italy and Spain, while its French version appeared artificial and inspired by opportunistic considerations of day-to-day politics. Since France is not a semi-periphery, this different role of eurocommunism follows directly from the historical location of social-ism in the development process that has been presented here.

Finally, there are the many forms of socialism in the Third World that have emerged where revolutionary social change remained elusive, and socialism has more often than not turned into an ideology of domination within a persistent peripheral-capitalist social framework. Even though such variants of socialism ('Arab', 'African', 'Indonesian' socialism, etc.) tend to disappear as quickly as they appear, socialist rhetoric does nevertheless reflect the objective requirements of delayed development which, as a rule, is unlikely to occur in peripheral-capitalist conditions. The development blocks which are characteristic of peripheries, and which cannot usually be overcome within the existing political structure, give rise to conflict potentials which often provide the basis for the ascendancy of *corporatist regimes* (left-wing and right-wing juntas). Quite often, as in the first decades of this century in southern and south-eastern Europe, these have recourse to socialist and nationalist ideologies in order to legitimize their rise to power and their development projects.

There appears, then, to exist a direct relationship between specific development profiles and specific variants of socialism. The positive, or negative, aspects of socialist development, by way of delayed development, should be seen in clear correlation with the development level of productive forces.

The greater and the more differentiated the existing development of the productive forces, the more damaging for further socio-economic progress are the typical instruments of delayed socialist development. The more undeveloped and underdeveloped the productive forces, the more inevitable delayed socialist development (peripheries). In countries such as Italy and Spain, which constitute a sort of semi-periphery, eurocommunism takes the role which in periphery societies is played by socialist development policy. In capitalist core societies, socialist movements are gradually transformed into social democratic parties. A capitalist metropole, like Czechoslovakia before 1945, upon which a socialist development path was imposed, became the place where the 'third way between capitalism and socialism' was most clearly articulated, and grew into a relevant political force.

Since the nineteenth century, socialist programmes directed against capitalism have been based on the assumption that socialism could be politically justified only when it is founded on democratic structures, and when it guarantees individual freedom. Has there ever been a socialist development path based on grass-roots democracy? And if so, what course did it take? The only case in development history that might be relevant in this connection, is the development of Israel. If one forgoes purist standards—during the past three decades the non-Jewish population in Israel have lacked equal opportunities—then, despite such qualifications, the Israeli development path can be characterized as democratic. For all her particularities, Israel is today no less 'capitalist' than the OECD societies. In comparative historical perspective, as employed in the present chapter, such a development path is merely consistent. For, if delayed development takes place under socialist colours in a democratic context, one or the other variant of a mature capitalist society should emerge.

Such a 'counter-productive' experience in development history was no more foreseen in classical socialist theory than was the role of socialism this side of the 'abundance' of capitalism. From the viewpoint of development history, socialism has until now functioned as a crutch for development policy in the pursuit of delayed development in capitalist peripheries. Without a shift towards decentralized administrative structures and increased political participation, the resulting 'socialist reality' remains a preliminary stage of capitalism which, in the final analysis, can be suppressed only by force.

In terms of development policy, herein lies the explosive nature of the latent and manifest conflicts of the state-socialist societies in Europe—an experience that could be of considerable benefit to socialist late-developers outside Europe.[69]

7 Is There an Alternative Development Policy for the Third World?

Introductory Remarks

This chapter is based on an article that was written in 1977, and first published in 1978. The piece was designed to summarize the development policy arguments advanced in *Weltwirtschaftsordnung und Entwicklungspolitik—Pädoyer für Dissoziation* (1977) for a wider public. Because the reflections on development history presented here are connected with the studies on development theory and policy undertaken at that time, the author considers it useful to reprint unchanged the article in question at this point in the present work.

The article was concerned with certain basic features of an autocentric development model. This model was derived, by way of a contrast analysis, from an examination of peripheral-capitalist societies and from a tentative assessment of the development dynamics of metropolitan capitalism (particularly Type I societies) and of delayed socialist development. The various autocentric *development paths* which, in recent development history, have led to the emergence of autocentric accumulation structures, were not considered, since their different make-up and historical sequence were at the time still unknown. The present book attempts to fill this particular gap.

Rather than being undermined by such a detailed examination of autocentric development paths—an opinion recently voiced by a critic—the model of autocentric accumulation is positively vindicated by it. The main contentions of the article which, at the time, flowed from considerations of development theory, could today be substantiated with diagnoses derived from development history. Thus, for example, the strongly emphasized need *coherently* to develop in each case the

203

existing domestic market potential as the basis of successful delayed development. The analyses of export-orientated and autocentric development paths and the studies of contrasting cases, namely periphery development in Europe, also underline this diagnosis.

Whether delayed development is today probable only under dissociative auspices—a central contention of the earlier book (1977)—continues to remain, as in the development policy debate of the last few years, a controversial question. The answer depends nowadays mainly on the assessment of the 'newly industrializing countries'. In this context one has to bear in mind that none of the current conceptual approaches to the question of the newly industrializing countries attaches any importance to the two dimensions of successful delayed development that are central to the programmatic considerations contained in earlier publications and in the present book—that is, the linking of the development of the productive forces in agriculture and industry—and, based on this, the nature of domestic market development. Whether a few fast-growing peripheries whose *industrial sector* (including the capital goods industry) is unquestionably expanding, resulting in increasing *exports* of *finished* manufactures, are approaching a 'threshold', thus gradually becoming, in qualitative-structural terms, *developed* (autocentric) societies, cannot be judged on the basis of these indicators alone. This, to the present writer, seems an apt conclusion to draw from the diagnoses of development history presented in this book. These indicators could, however, be of value in the attempt to provide a theoretical foundation for a sensible conceptual approach to the newly industrializing countries.

When this contribution was originally written, the analysis of peripheral societies focused on typical 'colonial countries', which resulted in specific theses on the connection between the international division of labour and periphery development. The role of colonial countries—in the beginning, usually that of an exclave of their respective metropoles—was imposed on them from outside. They were forcibly integrated into a vertical or asymmetrical system of exchange. Only political independence created the opportunity to pursue an alternative development policy directed towards the development of the domestic productive potential. However, only in the rarest of cases was this opportunity seized.

In contrast, the reflections on development policy contained in the present volume have focused—so far as peripheries are concerned—on those peripheral societies which, despite their relative political sovereignty, aspired on their own accord to world economic roles similar to those of colonial countries and which, as suppliers of foodstuffs, agricultural and mineral raw materials, in the course of time grew into such roles. For them, integration into the world market became a structural trap, not because there was no alternative, but because export orientation without a broad-based development of the domestic market was the self-inflicted consequence of domestic political struggles. To overstate the point: these societies pursued a policy of self-colonization. For them, the integration into an unequal international division of labour was the result of national domestic and foreign economic policies that were deemed lucrative at the time. As demonstrated in Chapter 2 (pp. 75–86), the crucial factor was not what was exported in each case, but how the export opportunities were processed within each of the societies in question.

Both cases—colonization without development alternative and self-colonization—call for comparative studies that would deal with the history of those societies which have become peripheries of the world economy, and particularly with the extent of autonomy or foreign control present in each case.

The Problem

This study has been conceived as a contribution to the current development theory and policy debate. That debate focuses on the Third World's demand for the replacement of the old world economic order by a 'New International Economic Order'. The study does not deal directly with the struggle over this new world economic order that is taking place between the Western industrial nations and the Third World. Rather, it advances a number of theses designed to stimulate reflection on a reorientation of development policy. The underlying debate on development theory and policy can be summarized as follows.

Until now the development policy of the industrial societies and the Third world in programme and practice has amounted to an increased integration of all the parties into the world economy. Increased trade (imports/exports), increased private investment and public aid, improved conditions for technology transfer and increased cooperation in many other areas are all expected to bring a rapid solution to the acute problems of the Third World. The strengthening of the Third World's integration into the international economy thus provides the guiding principle for development policy, thought and action. Contrary to this, it will be argued in the following pages that only through a limited period of de-coupling can the societies and economies of the Third

World come to stand on their own feet, in order to achieve in the long run a fruitful cooperation with other societies and economies within the international economic system. Not integration, but varying degrees of selective de-coupling and dissociation, constitute the rationale of this kind of development policy programme. It is not the intention behind this contribution to present dissociative development policy as a simple panacea. Rather, it is to provide a thought-provoking thesis, whose plausibility is suggested by both sound historical experience and recent studies of those social and economic structures of the Third World and the international economy that give rise to the acute difficulties and problems of the Third World.[1]

After a short discussion of the economic foundations of viable economies and of some essential structural characteristics of Third World economies, the conclusions arising from those analyses, which recommend de-coupling or dissociation as the proper course for development policy, will be presented.

Economic Foundations of Viable Economies

Comparative historical studies show that a precondition for successful economic and social development is the shaping of a specific structure and dynamic process of capital formation (capital accumulation) in a society and economy. From a purely *economic* standpoint, the combination of the following factors is of fundamental importance:

(*a*) a positive *increase in agricultural productivity*, by which the basic food supply for the domestic population and supplies of agricultural raw materials for industry are ensured;

(*b*) industrial *production of consumer goods* that are within the reach of the mass of the population (*mass*-consumer goods as opposed to luxury consumer goods);

(*c*) industrial *production of means of production*: equipment for agriculture; means of producing consumer goods (e.g. light mechanical engineering); means of producing intermediate products (e.g. heavy mechanical engineering); means of producing other means of production (machine tools, computers, telecommunication, control technology);

(*d*) *production of intermediate products*: intermediates for *consumer goods* (iron and steel industry, chemicals, energy); intermediates for *producers'* goods (iron and steel industry, energy, non-ferrous metals); and

(*e*) creation of an *infrastructure* and *goods for collective consumption* (transport and communications systems, training facilities, public health system, etc.).

The history of viable economies builds up on differentiated development and gradual mutual interlinking of the above-mentioned sectors and subsectors. The high degree of differentiation of the production structure and the growing extent of interrelationships and intermeshing tend to lead in such an economy to structural cohesiveness and to interlinkages that enable such economies to become economic and social entities of *high coherence*. In principle, different degrees of such coherence are measurable by analyses of intrasectoral and intersectoral intermeshing (input-output analyses). Such economies have the following basic capabilities:

(1) The mass of the people in them are integrated productively into the economy. People find work, receive incomes and become consumers, in consequence of which needs can be satisfied to varying degrees, depending on the level of development.

(2) In these economies there is an inherent interrelationship (congruence) among the production facilities, level of employment, income distribution and structure of consumption (consumption profiles).

(3) Such congruence results—in the long run—in an organic development process from the simple to the complex, in which at the development level reached at any given time, the complexity of the consumption profiles matches the organically evolved complexity of the production facilities and technology. There tends to be feedback between the rise in the level of productive capacity and the level of real wages.

(4) Such economies are distinguished by high innovative capacity; technical progress determines the dynamics of development to a considerable extent.

(5) Structural change is a persistent concomitant of such economies (high transformability), different degrees of active and passive transformability (also combined with differing degrees of innovativeness) being observable.

(6) Successful development processes are characterized by the growing homogenization of the production level of the various sectors, though perfect homogenization is unattainable on account of technical and social change. The acid test is whether a society and economy become more fragmented (heterogeneous) or more homogeneous in consequence of the development of productive forces. The *tendency* towards homogeneity is apparent in the never complete, but nevertheless far-reaching correspondence of the costs of factors such as land, capital and labour *within* the various sectors and in the unbridgeable, but also never wide gap of such factor costs between the various sectors. The pertinent, absolute and relative differences can be determined empirically by a study of real wage levels, interest rates, profit rates,

productivity levels, and so on.

Up to now, every successful development process has been marked by specific successions of stages and accentuations, which were dependent in each case on the initial situation within the stage of development reached by the international economy. In this connection, recent systematic, historical development theory has drawn attention to the constraints imposed by the structure of the modern world system on the nature and form of *internal* development. However, it has also pointed out the compass-bearing influence of internal political and socio-economic constellations on the nature and form of individual development processes. The historical variablity of development processes attributable to the two factors named is impressive. For the current development policy debate, however, it is more remarkable that the development of metropolitan capitalism in the present OECD countries as well that of socialist economies in the Soviet Union and in eastern European societies, although enacted by capitalist methods in the one case and staged by socialist methods in the other, have led to the same configuration of burgeoning productive forces that has been outlined above. Furthermore, it is remarkable that those developing countries which—in contrast with a few decades ago—no longer number among the acute problem cases in the specific regions respectively of the Third World (such as China, North Korea, Albania, Cuba), are now aspiring to a systematic development of their productive forces in all the cited subsectors of a viable economy, with the predictable attainment of a comparable depth structure: by the encouragement of agricultural productivity, by the building up of industrial sectors for the manufacture of producer's goods and the creation of technologies, for making intermediate products and mass-consumption goods, and by the systematic expansion of their infrastructure.

All three of the above-mentioned case—metropolitan capitalism, metropolitan socialism, socialist developing countries—*are characterized by an identical coherent structure of capital formation*, although the precedent social conditions exhibit most striking differences, not only as between capitalist and socialist development processes, but within capitalist and socialist systems. None of these processes is free from crises; each of them develops specific symptoms. Some symptoms are all-embracing (e.g. the ecological problems), but in all cases there is the potential—at completely different development levels—of attaining the above-mentioned basic economic accomplishments, which in their turn constitute the essential basis for social accomplishments.

Structural Characteristics of Third World Economies

The societies and economies of the Third World (peripheral economies) are characterized by exactly the opposite of what has been outlined above as a viable economy and its basic accomplishments:

(1) Only the *export-orientated* segment of agriculture is marked by some degree of dynamic impetus; for the most part, no substantial increase in agricultural productivity occurs on a broad basis. Hence, an essential precondition for a successful development process is unfulfilled. The same applies to the raw materials sector. True, in many places this sector is highly productive, but it is no more than an *exclave* of metropolitan economies and is therefore not integrated into a coherent, intermeshed domestic economy.

(2) The industrial production of *mass*-consumer goods is *stagnant* compared with the import of industrially produced, luxury consumer goods or, in some instances, with local production of luxury consumer goods. This structural distortion reflects the wide, and in most cases still increasing, income differentials in peripheral capitalist societies. . . . This phenomenon, too, reflects the incapability of such economies of integrating the mass of the population productively into the capital-forming process.

(3) As a rule, a sector for domestic *production of means of production* is completely *lacking*, and its development has been prevented by asymmetrical division of labour between metropolitan and peripheral economies. Hence, peripheral economies are systematically deprived of vital development impulses. In the few cases in which such production facilities are built up, they are typically orientated towards the dominant growth poles (and thus, for example, towards the production of equipment for manufacturing luxury consumer goods and the related infrastructure).

(4) The *production of intermediate goods* is but *little developed*, and this, together with the lacking production of equipment and technologies, is the cause of the far-reaching, technological dependence of peripheral capitalist economies on the industrial societies, which is turning to an increasing extent into hopeless financial dependence.

5. The *collective consumer goods* (education, health, etc.) and the development of the infrastructure have not, as a rule, contributed towards homogenizing the society of the Third World, but towards *accentuating the disparities* between growth poles and the hinterland.

Peripheral economies lack the vital production sectors (productive agriculture, mass-consumer goods industry, equipment industry, broad infrastructure) that are essential for a viable society, and they lack interlacement of those sectors. They may therefore be described as *structurally crippled*.[2] Their basic problems lie not in the fact that no productive forces develop in them. In the period 1950–75, for instance, the economic growth of the developing countries attained orders of magnitude never achieved by the industrial societies in any comparable period prior to 1950. As a general rule, the peripheral economies are decidedly high-growth economies, or, to be more accurate, growth-pole economies. Their problem lies in the fact that their growth is concentrated on a few, mostly export-orientated sectors, and that even where domestic industrialization processes have made good headway, the growth processes orientated towards the home market are strictly limited sectorally and in terms of stratification. The result is structure-conditioned fragility of such economies. Their *lack of coherence* is attributable to:

(*a*) a *lack of intermeshing* of agriculture and industry (no deep forward or backward linkages);

(*b*) *lacking depth of production*—that is to say, the lack of complete economic cycles: Part of the capital-forming process, especially the production of technologies and equipment, and to a substantial extent that of intermediate products and consumer goods, takes place in the industrial societies; the economic spin-off effects of such reproduction are continually lost to the peripheral economies and find expression in the structural crippling already mentioned;

(*c*) the inherent, sociologically conditioned tendency of industrialization stages up to the present to satisfy the *demand of high-income strata* (landowning oligarchy, import-export oligarchy, the urban middle class, members of the services sectors, the public administration, the military, segments of the better-paid workers in urban centres), while the production of *mass*-consumer goods remains relatively stagnant on account of the only less-than-average or even negative growth of the purchasing power of the masses (farmers, informal sector, workers); and

(*d*) the consequent, by no means natural, narrowness of the domestic market, which has been brought about by historical and socio-economic processes, and which is the logical outcome of incomplete economic cycles and of a non-coherent reproduction dynamics.

Problems of Third World Economies

Underdevelopment has nothing to do with traditional backwardness and it is not the outcome of inadequate development of productive forces (for then the economies in question would be *un*developed). Underdevelopment is, rather, a manifestation of *misguided development of productive forces*.[3] The problem of the economies of the Third World lies not in their incapacity to form capital, but in a wrongly structured accumulation, which has detrimental effects for the majority of the people. The capital formation is not designed to open up a country's domestic market. It is orientated towards the metropolitan economies, whether through the high-pressure production of goods for the world market or through taking over metropolitan consumer goods, consumption patterns and technologies, all of which reflect a far higher and more complex (and hence more capital-intensive, more energy-intensive and also more costly and centralized) development level, the products of which must necessarily act as structure-deforming foreign bodies in economies with less advanced and distorted development of productive forces.

This conventional structure of misdirected capital formation is the result of integrating the societies of Latin America, Africa and Asia into a system of *unequal international division of labour* during the phase of colonialism and imperialism. It is remarkable that, right up to the present day, the current debate on development theory still has no concept of *unequal* division of labour. As a rule, it adheres to the classical, free-trade dogmas of foreign trade theory. According to that theory's prevailing doctrine of comparative advantages, all participants in international trade benefit, provided they specialize in the production of those goods for which they can make the best use of locally available factors (land, natural resources, capital, labour, technological know-how, etc.). In this context, in the theory the question has never been consequentially raised of what specific effects specialization conforming to the postulates of the doctrine of comparative advantages will exert on production structure, income distribution, consumption profiles, labour market and infrastructure in the case of trading partners on *unequal* initial levels. If this question had been raised, the fundamental difference between trading structures of a *symmetrical* and an *asymmetrical* nature would have become evident. The above-diagnosed effects on a peripheral economy are manifestly the consequence of integrating the economies of Latin America, Africa and Asia into an *asymmetrically* structured international economy, which is permeated and dominated by metropolitan capitalism. That metropolitan capitalism is marked by relatively productive, viable economies; its dynamic vigour stems from a gradual, systematic opening up of the countries' *own* domestic markets. However, the viability of these economies was facilitated by relations with the overseas economies: by the plundering of large areas of the Third World in the phase of primitive accumulation; and by the possibility of importing cheap agricultural and mineral products, cheap energy and cheap labour from the colonies, or of using cheap labour there for the local production of mineral and agricultural raw materials and, later on, of finished goods requiring little processing—factors which have all contributed and still contribute to the reduction of production costs in metropolitan economies.

In the course of this process, not only was locally accumulated capital drawn off from the southern continents. A much more radical result was the transformation of fairly viable, subsistence economies into *defective and crippled peripheral economies*, the dynamic reproduction process of which brings specific effects:

(1) The incapability of integrating the mass of the population productively into the economic production process.

(2) The growing incapability of feeding the mass of the population with locally produced agricultural goods.

(3) The incapability of inventing and manufacturing their own means of production, equipment, hand tools and technologies, and of adapting existing goods of these types to local needs.

(4) The incapability of originating technical progress geared to local problem situations (innovative incapacity) and of changing traditional structures (transformative incapacity). These latter disabilities reflect the lack of structural differentiation, which in extreme cases takes the form of a monocultural economy.

(5) The structural crippling is evidenced by a striking and growing heterogeneity of peripheral societies and peripheral economies. If homogeneity or heterogeneity is measured operationally with indicators such as labour productivity, wage levels, qualification of labour, degree of organization of capital and labour, capital intensity and labour intensity of production, and so on, it can hardly be denied that in the peripheries the fissures between 'modern' growth poles and the rest of the economy have widened during the past decades. This is equally true of the primary, secondary and tertiary sectors. The relevant differences, for instance between the by no means disappearing minifundium and the capital-intensive agro-business groups which produce as a rule for the world market, but in the meantime also for the domestic, urban luxuries and semi-luxuries market, are undoubtedly more marked than the traditional differences between minifundium and latifundium. In other spheres, comparable hierarchization can be observed—for example, between groups with multinational operations, local undertakings, local crafts and trades, and the informal sector.

(6) This heterogeneity and hierarchization matches up with a very

unequal distribution of political organization: the mass of the population remains or is placed under political tutelage, notwithstanding intermediate phases of a different stamp (e.g. populism). This phenomenon is in contrast with the growing political structuring of all levels of metropolitan societies, and particularly with the increasing degree of political organization of labour—a result of a long-drawn-out and wearisome struggle of the union labour movement.

(7) The dialectics of misguided growth and mass penury generate a substantial amount of conflict potential which is the background for the growing internal militarization of societies of the Third World. The danger of such internal militarization being the basis of classical, international and intersociety conflict fronts is becoming ever more manifest.

Many years ago, Karl Schiller described the development path of the countries of the Third World under the present system of division of labour as follows:

> In the raw material countries overseas, on their coming into touch with the capitalist world, the process began, so to speak, with the second act. (Some proponents of the theory of comparative costs often forget that in Ricardo's example, of course, before the inception of foreign trade, both countries, Portugal and Britain, can produce both products, wine and cloth, and *after* its inception specialize in wine or cloth, each country maintaining its respective national employment volume. So in that case, attainment of a stage where productive forces are developed even *before* specialization is presupposed.) Modern production processes were transferred to the various countries, which, according to the 'law', were appropriate there for participation in world trade. The first act of step-by-step 'education' of the whole economy towards a modern mode of operation was omitted. Thus an overseas economy came into being, which has very modern production facilities, but on the whole only in those lines in which it is a specialized exporter. The overseas economy was developed in its modern segment—that is to say, not across the full breadth of its structure as, for instance, in the principal European-American countries, but at 'focal points' that were complementary 'counter-structures' to these latter countries. The 'tendency of production to spread' did not even start to take effect across the full breadth of overseas economies. . . . So up to now, in the case of many overseas countries, we have only lopsided or top-heavy integration into the modern economy,' so to speak, which is geared solely to 'world-wide division of labour'.[4]

The question of what would have happened to the countries of the Third World without any integration into the international division of labour dominated by the metropolitan economies can hardly be of any interest today. All that remains for us is to record the lack of total development across the board which was diagnosed by Schiller, namely, the lacking 'full-breadth development' or the lacking development of a 'full-breadth structure'. The task of development theory and development policy is to consider the preconditions and measures that make development in breadth possible.

A clear conception of the structural make-up of a peripheral economy is essential in order to arrive at meaningful, development policy guide-lines. If, as is conventionally assumed, the economies of the Third World are regarded as *traditionally* backward in contrast with metropolitan *modern* economies, if they are conceived as embyronic, miniature editions of early phases of metropolitan economies to which it is only necessary to impart dynamic impetus, the failure of development policy strategies based on such conceptions is already built into the initial interpretations, as has meanwhile been demonstrated incontestably by the abortive development policy in the past decades.

Three Imperatives of Development Policy

What, then, are the implications resulting from the preceeding analysis? Three imperatives for a sound development policy will be spelled out: the imperative of *dissociation*, the imperative of *internal restructuration*, and the imperative of a *new division of labour* among economies of the Third World.

The imperative of dissociation

In the long run, the Third World has a chance of building up self-reliant and viable economies and societies only if it dissociates itself temporarily from the prevailing international economy—that is, the metropolitan economies. As Karl Schiller correctly analysed, the developing countries lack 'the first act of in-breadth development' necessary for a successful development process. Historical experience of capitalist *and* socialist development processes which resulted in more or less viable structures shows that, without a period of self-centredness, the duration of which may vary from case to case—that is to say, *without protection motivated by development policy, a balanced development of productive forces is hardly possible*. Mercantilism, phases of purposive protective policy, enforced or voluntarily self-imposed autarchy, constitute, in the light of these systematic aspects, merely variations of one and the same requirement. And is it just coincidence or of more fundamental significance that in that area of western and central Europe in which the development processes of our modern age began, development was determined by 'temporary severance from the main arteries of previously prevailing trade'?

> In the Carolingian age, an important area did, in fact, centre itself for the first time upon a focal point lying very far inland. Society was confronted with the task of developing inland communications more intensively. As it succeeded in doing so in the course of the centuries, in this respect, too, the heritage of antiquity had new conditions imposed upon it. The foundation was laid for configurations unknown to antiquity. It is from this standpoint that certain differences between the integrated units of antiquity and the others which slowly evolved in the occident must be considered: states, nations, or whatever those units may be called, comprised for the most part ethnic groups clustered around inland centres or capital cities and linked with each other by inland arteries.[5]

Is it not precisely the growth of inland interlacement as the nucleus for political control capacities, development of economic productive forces and cultural identity which peripheral societies typically lack and which they cannot attain as long as they remain integrated in the traditional world market structures as they have been in the past decades and centuries?

Self-centredness of this sort, with the goal of intensive development of productive forces in a country's own area, need not necessarily be identical with autarchy, although in the light of history it would seem scarcely to be a coincidence that, in view of the ever greater differences between the average productivity level of economies within the international economy, protection is being built up more comprehensively on all fronts—that is to say, variable extents of autarchy are gaining importance as an instrument of development policy. Since, as mentioned above, peripheral economies are characterized by a lack of innovative and transformative capacity, such a course of development, quite apart from the political circumstances, is considered to bring heavy losses in respect of short-term cost-benefit assessments. However, such an assessment changes nothing in the sound development policy thesis that development can be brought to fruition only by one or the other form of selective dissociation.

Even premising dissociation, trade with the more productive, dominant metropolitan economies is possible, *but that trade is a consequence of an inward-orientated dynamic accumulation process* in the sense that it is merely expedient and does not determine the dynamic impetus of the entire reproduction process. Trade must be pursued *selectively*, and only that form of *selective cooperation* should be practised which benefits the building up fo a viable internal structure in the countries of the southern continents. Hence, what is involved, as shown in a study on such widely differing cases as the development of Japan and that of the Soviet Union, is calculated isolation coupled with selective utilization of the world market,[6] in which connection it should be pointed out that present-day China, more than any other country, seems to be repeating this scenario 'of calculated isolation, insistence on the vitality and superiority of strategies internally developed, and selective borrowing'.

For the majority of countries of the Third World, *dissociation* nowadays means in particular: a break with the traditional, export-orientated economy and instead mobilization of their *own* resources, with the goal of making such resources utilizable for their *own* purposes. This would mean particularly: a break with the production of raw materials, which are processed mainly in the metropolitan economies; a break with export-orientated industrialization, which will very soon prove to be very costly and a new cul-de-sac in the traditional development process; and also a break with misguided industrialization geared to import substitution, which, where it was pursued, patently satisfied chiefly the demand of high-income strata and was not orientated towards the potential demand of the impoverished masses.

The imperative of socio-economic restructuring

The second imperative relates to the *building up of coherent accumulation structures* in the countries of the Third World themselves. This sort of autocentric development is hardly conceivable without organic linking of the following activities:
— renewed prospecting of locally available resources;
— local utilization of local resources;
— building up of a domestic industrial sector for the production of means of production and intermediate goods;
— invention and reinvention of suitable technologies, and further development and adaptation of existing technologies to local needs;
— in-breadth productivity improvement in agriculture;
— industrial production of mass-consumer goods designed to satisfy the basic needs of the masses;
— building up of a broadly effective infrastructure.

Only the convergence of these activities permits *step-by-step opening up of the domestic market*, by which the mass of the population is integrated into productive activities, purchasing power can be achieved, and dynamic impetus imparted to the demand for agricultural and industrial equipment and mass-consumer goods, and for private and public services on the spot, all *orientated towards the satisfaction of local needs.*

Though individual requirements of such a guide-line may meanwhile have gained acceptance also in traditional development programmes, there can be no doubt that a development programme that would further the realization of all named factors in combination is opposed. The reason is that such a programme is not conceivable without far-reaching repudiation of the traditional doctrine of comparative costs and advantages. What does this mean?

In an international economy in which national economies of differing development levels and average degrees of productivity coexist, goods of every type (consumer goods, machinery, technology, etc.) can be purchased by less productive economies in economies with higher productivity at less than the cost of producing them themselves. If trade is carried on within an asymmetrical structure, for example between a metropolitan economy and a peripheral economy, comparative cost calculations result in peripheralization of the less productive economy. *The less productive economy buys on the world market in more productive economies at lower cost—and in return, if it does not follow first and foremost an autocentric development path, it suffers fundamental structural defects.* It saves itself the *learning costs* that are indispensable for building up a viable economy, only to be divested in the end of its capacity to invent, develop, adapt and produce its own or foreign tools, equipment and technology. This is the reason why those Third World countries that possessed relatively abundant capital (e.g. Venezuela), are marked by much more profound structural distortions than those that manage to acquire foreign exchange only with the greatest difficulty (e.g. neighbouring Colombia).[7]

The consequence is that foreign machines and foreign technologies, and the more complex consumer goods of an economy with higher average productivity, are transferred as *finished* products to a less, and moreover defectively, developed economy and there necessarily act as economic foreign bodies with distorting socio-economic effects.

If the countries of the Third World are really to develop, it is essential for them to break away from an unequally structured international division of labour and the doctrine of comparative costs. The costs necessary for building up a coherent economic structure must be classified, as in the case of every viable economy, as *inevitable learning costs*. They are a burden; but unwillingness to bear them would only mean carrying over the present structural defects and their social consequences into the future (unemployment, marginality, uncontrollable population growth, wide inequality of incomes, etc.).

Industrialization means . . . step-by-step development of production capability by a steady, slow and patient process of learning by doing. It means much more than just setting up certain production capacities, which if need be, of course, can be imported from abroad. If the broad mass of the population is given a part to play in production and is to receive income via that production, suitable conditions must be created for the integration of the broad masses into the ever more differentiated process of division of labour. To this end it is essential that basic knowledge of alphabetization, technology and organization be imparted and furthered systematically. Similarly, the organizational prerequisites for industrial production must be created and all involved familiarized with `appropriate organizational know-how. It is precisely these things which no country can import, but must accomplish itself. It is possible to import ideas, certain finished solutions to problems, which can then be adapted in every country concerned. But the adaptive capacity itself must exist or be systematically built up and developed.[8]

It is not against the doctrine of comparative costs *per se* that criticism is levelled. That doctrine appears to be fairly meaningful in development planning and assessment of trade processes when the economies concerned are in fairly similar situations (e.g. France and the Federal Republic of Germany at the present time), because in such a case the comparable initial situation permits expectation of a fair benefit for all involved. If peripheral economies follow the doctrine of comparative benefit and hence allocation calculi of the *international* economy, optimal allocation of a given stock of factors from a *cosmopolitan* standpoint can be expected (e.g. input of cheap labour for export-orientated production of finished goods in free production zones), *but not the building up of domestic development potential, the gaining of depth of production and coherence.* Friedrich List emphatically drew attention to this fact in the debate with the proponents of classical English economics (theory of value). He enumerated his arguments relating to the building up of domestic development potential in a *theory of the production of productive forces.*

In dealing with the demands of the Third World, the Western capitalist societies now resort, in the final analysis, to the doctrine of free trade. As demonstrated by Friedrich List more than 140 years ago, that is a doctrine which caters to the interests of highly productive economies. In such pleas it is forgotten that in the history of most capitalist metropolitan economies, regardless of whether they were those of densely or more sparsely populated societies, there were phases in which only by disregarding free-trade economic and development policy—that is, by *disregarding the price mechanism as a means of controlling development processes*, could an untapped development potential be opened up with the object of opening up an economy's domestic market, expanding it and making it into an integrative structure.[9]

It is remarkable that the development-policy debate on, academically speaking, the theory of value and the theory of the production of productive forces not only played an important role in the development process of the capitalistic, metropolitan economies (as is evidenced by the theory and agitation of Friedrich List, to cite just one example); the same problems played a comparable role also in the debate on the international division of labour and foreign trade cooperation *among socialist societies with differing development levels.*

The Sino-Soviet altercation on the appropriate development path for China in the second half of the 1950s and early 1960s related *inter alia* to this controversy.[10] And the dispute between the Soviet Union and North Korea, a case made interesting by the differences in size and development level, revolved in the second half of the 1950s around the issue of whether a developing country like North Korea could afford to pursue a development path intended to build up a heavy industry designed to stimulate light industry and agriculture—or whether it would not be more expedient to arrange a far-reaching division of labour between the Soviet Union, which is productive in every respect, and a North Korean economy in which only subsectors should be built up and become specialized on the division-of-labour principle.[11] In 1965, in a lecture given in Indonesia, Kim il Sung described the controversy in retrospect as follows:

> The anti-Party elements lurking within the Party, and the revisionists and dogmatists both at home and abroad, loudly protested against the line of ensuring the priority growth of heavy industry while simultaneously developing light industry and agriculture. According to their arguments, everything should have been directed to the daily need of consumption, leaving the future out of account. *Their purpose,* in the final analysis, *was to prevent our country from building its economic foundations.*[12]

In autumn 1963, the official party organ of North Korea stated:

> Today some people . . . have unilaterally repealed their agreements with fraternal countries and have virtually cut off the relations of economic and technical cooperation. They brand the construction of an independent national economy a 'nationalistic tendency'. . . . Those who oppose the building of an independent economy advocate, instead, the establishment of an 'integrated economy' of the socialist countries. . . . Under the signboard of 'integrated economy' they want to stamp out the economic independence of fraternal countries . . . and make them subordinate to others. . . . It goes without saying that the loss of independence in economy will make it

impossible for any country to maintain its genuine independence and sovereignty. . . . 'Aid' with strings attached, or 'aid' given as a precondition for interference in others' internal affairs, as practised among capitalist countries, cannot exist and must not exist among socialist countries.[13]

Elsewhere, Kim il Sung depicts the same facts systematically as follows:

> We do not intend by any means to oppose the economic cooperation of countries and to build up socialism in isolation. What we do oppose is the trends pursued by the Great Powers which, under the guise of 'economic cooperation' and 'international division of labour', amount to no less than impeding the independent and complex development of the economy of a country and subjugating that economy. We are of the opinion that every country must cooperate with others on the basis of developing its own national economy, and that only then can economic cooperation among countries be unremittingly expanded and further developed according to the principle of completely equal rights and mutual benefit. Today, our country is building up its economy with its own technology, with its own resources, with the strength of its own cadres and its own nation, and covers domestic demand for the products of heavy and light industry and for agricultural products largely from domestic production.[14]

The debate on the international division of labour and economic cooperation within COMECON is likewise an indication of the problems raised here, which are of importance also in relations among socialist countries.[15] Faced with the alternative of far-reaching international, socialist division of labour, on the one hand, or the relatively expensive building up of a broad-based agricultural and industrial structure, on the other, the countries of eastern Europe have evidently decided in favour of List's solution, which is evidenced, among other things, by the relatively small degree of integration in COMECON. Particularly the south-eastern European states, which were characterized up to the First World War by all the attributes of peripheral-capitalistic social formations, regard international specialization of production as a process which, though important, does not have to be given priority in all circumstances and in all spheres of production. Hence, the concentration on mobilization and utilization of domestic resources and efforts serves also within the framework of international division of labour among socialist societies a *protective function* similar to that which List provided for in his strategy of temporary dissociation.

The empirical examples cited here from the domain of development of capitalist *and* socialist metropolitan economies, and of socialist developing countries, underline an observation recently formulated by

Paul Streeten. In a paper on self-reliance, he writes that the new argument is tantamount to *protection* (if not to autarchy)—at least in principle—*of all economic activities*:

> By opening up a society indiscriminately and too widely, we reduce the incentives and opportunities to develop indigenous processes and products appropriate for the low-income groups in developing countries, for their small and low-income markets, for their scarcity of physical and human capital and for their desire for the wide spread of the benefits of development. The educational, psychological and institutional arguments against a move towards world free trade, for capital flows and general openness, point to the need to protect all activities from the eroding influences of the advanced world economy and, more important, they point to the need for constructive indigenous efforts, which, of course, do not result automatically from looking towards like-minded countries, but which may be hampered by an excessively outward-looking strategy and by emulation of the style of the rich.
>
> Something like this also underlies the distinction between self-reliance and dependence, between autonomy and domination. Countries and groups of countries that generate their own technological capability, their own social institutions and organizations (not only in technology and industry but in land tenure and rural institutions), will be able to mobilize their efforts more effectively than those that always look at how they order these things in the metropolis.[16]

New forms of an international division of labour

Another, third imperative of development policy relates to evolving *new forms of division of labour among the economies of the Third World itself*. Nowadays the term 'collective self-reliance' is used to describe this imperative. But an international division of labour in the subregional, regional and continental domains—and also among the three southern continents—will have little success without dissociation of the peripheries from the dominant industrial societies. If they remain integrated in the world market as it is structured today, the idea of collective self-reliance is interesting, but without any real significance for development policy, as new market arrangements (e.g. free-trade zones and the like) extending beyond individual economies would very easily prove to be nothing more than enlarged areas providing enhanced possibilities for penetration by the metropolitan economies.

Dissociated from the world market, the peripheries would have the chance of developing their economies in relation to each other—that is, by mutually complementary processes. In this connection, importance would attach not merely to division of labour in the pure economic sense, but also to the *building up of subregional, regional and continental infrastructures* with provision for common transport and communication systems, means of transport, insurance companies, news agencies, and so forth. This would contribute towards the *de-hierarchization* of the present, grossly hierarchical international society and hence to the formation of effective counterweights to the so-called metropolitan economies.

If we proceed from the primary requirements of development policy—namely, satisfaction of the basic needs of the masses—the translation of this third imperative into practice in a first stage of meaningful development policy is less dramatic than it seems at first.

> This building 'from the ground up' involves a basic fabric of economic activities which are needed by all mankind and can be pursued nearly everywhere. It involves the production of and demand for 'local goods'. Determination of the necessary assortment—for instance, according to the balanced growth principle—is not an unsolvable problem, especially in the early development stages, and above all, production of and demand for such goods are relatively independent of the world economy. The problem of coordination is not really acute. There is good reason to believe that in this apparently unpretentious sphere, which, however, would embrace the great mass of the non-integrated population, lie the best development chances for nearly all developing countries.[17]

The imperative of *collective self-reliance* involves two specific lines of march.

First, the building up of *structures of reciprocal relations* among societies and economies with similar development problems, which can never be achieved by the traditional type of asymmetrical integration of such economies into the world economy. This sort of *horizontalization* of the relations among the societies of the Third World would lead to repression or elimination of the metropolitan economies as mediation agencies. *New institutions* through which mutual aid could be given would have to supplement these more close-meshed structures of relations.

Secondly, strengthening the basis for Third World solidarity, above and beyond rhetorical proclamations, could bring a significant increase in the *political weight* of the Third World *vis-à-vis* the metropolitan economies and enable a change in the international division of labour to be achieved, both of which would lead to a new, *essentially multicentrically structured international economy* (a really *new* international economic order.[18] The grossly biased, traditional hierarchy of the international economy, based on the division of labour between the metropolitan economies and the peripheries, would give way to a structure in which there were more independent, if not self-sufficient, viable economic areas with their own autonomous communication and decision-making systems. Whether such economic areas would be possible only where especially dense populations are to be found, as suggested by spatial economic theories, is a question that would have to be examined thoroughly.[19] Collective self-reliance among the countries of the Third World would undoubtedly have repercussions affecting the metropolitan economies, which in the latter would result in structural adjustments which ought also to raise the degree of self-reliance in these economies, too. It is the function of a theory of a multicentric world economy, prompted by considerations of development policy and spatial economic analysis, to reflect on these relationships, our view of which has hitherto been obstructed by one-sided concentration on liberal free-trade theory and its underlying, generally accepted allocation calculi.[20]

W. Arthur Lewis, the well-known economist, expressed the practical philosophy underlying this imperative in 1969, when he wrote:

> It is true that the prosperity of underdeveloped countries has in the past depended on what they could sell to the industrial countries, but there is no reason why this should continue. The underdeveloped countries have all the resources needed for their own development. Taken together they have a surplus of fuel, fibres, iron ore, copper, bauxite, and practically every other raw material. In agriculture they are perfectly capable of feeding themselves, through exchange with each other, and do not have to beg the United States to buy more tea and coffee so that they can pay for American grain, when they could produce more grain for themselves. The underdeveloped countries are short of skills, but these can be learnt, so they could do all their own manufacturing. Apart from skills, the development of Asia, Africa and Latin America could continue even if all the rest of the world were to sink under the sea. If this is so, it must mean that these countries have the solutions to their problems in their own hands, and should stop thinking all the time only in terms of what they can sell to or buy from the industrial countries.[21]

Conclusions for a Development Programme of Autocentric Development

From the foregoing arguments we can draw several general conclusions for a development programme that would lead in the short run to considerable structural changes, but in the long run—if pursued energetically—would offer the chance of a solution to the development problems currently under discussion. Three of them should be given special emphasis:

(*a*) a well-balanced accumulation structure;

(*b*) the intermeshing of resource mobilization and resource utilization in the domestic sphere; and

(*c*) the organic development of structures ranging from the simple to the complex.

As regards (1), according to currently received development theory, it is necessary for the developing countries to specialize in their foreign and domestic trading behaviour within the international economy in line with their 'natural factor endowment'. Autocentric development, however, presupposes differentiated development of productive forces and balanced capital formation. If, as in many countries of the Third World, sufficient natural resources are available, this sort of strategy would assign priority to the building up of a domestic heavy industry, in so far as it would contribute *simultaneously* to the dynamification of agriculture, light industry and mining.

> . . . it is erroneous to neglect the rehabilitation of heavy industry and the re-enforcement of the country's economic base; but it is no less erroneous not to establish a light industry, which is called for to ameliorate the people's living standard, by putting emphasis only on heavy industry. To improve the people's livelihood, it is necessary to increase rapidly the production in its totality, increase production of necessity goods and systematically lower prices.[22]

What appears to be nonsensical from the profitability standpoint, because it is uneconomical—that is, the building up of production facilities which, in the initial phase, are capable only of producing goods at greater cost than if they were bought on the world market— gains strategic significance in a process of autocentric development. The problem is illustrated graphically by the observations of two North Korean economists:

> When the Party had set out this line [of building heavy industry simultane-ously with light industry and agriculture], factionalists within the Party were against it. Some foreign friends also interfered with the policies of our Party. The factionalists said we were putting too much emphasis on heavy industry. 'How can machines produce rice?' they asked. In other words, they wanted us to eat up all resources and foreign aid, living well for a short period and then have nothing. Our Party rejected this line, because without giving priority to heavy industry, we should have been unable to stabilize the people's livelihood, our defence power would have suffered, and we should have been unable to lay the foundation of an independent national economy. As a matter of fact, machines can also produce rice! Heavy industry is the foundation for agricultural and light industrial development. When we make more agricultural machines, we produce more rice; when we make building equipment, we produce many more houses; and with vessels we catch more fish.[23]

This example is cited in this context because at that time, in the second half of the 1950s and the early 1960s, the North Korean administration was advised to import more consumer goods instead of machinery and equipment, and on the other hand to concentrate on the production of raw materials. The rejection of this recommendation and the will to oppose received allocation calculi were the basis for the pursuance by the administration of a course of *independent development* borne by confidence in its own strength. This is one of the few cases in which the development slogan 'confidence in one's own strength' (self-reliance or, as the North Korean say, *juche*) really assumed operative significance.

The principle of balanced development extends also to a balance between the requirements of massive capital formation, on the one hand, and the requirements of steady improvement of the material and cultural living conditions of the mass of the population, on the other. The setting of wrong—that is, one-sided—priorities in this respect may have disastrous consequences for the entire dynamic development process.

The principle of balanced development applies also to the technology mix (within the spectrum range from labour-intensity to capital-intensity), in which connection 'balanced' does not mean uniform in all sectors. Especially in industries producing preliminary products for further processing in subsequent production stages, it is possible, even in an economy with a low average productivity level, for a more capital intensive production to impart substantial dynamic impetus, if only because it enables such products to be turned out at lower cost, if appropriate allowance is made for economies of scale.[24] Such products can then be further processed by less capital-intensive methods, so that the labour-saving effects of the first stage can be offset by work-creating effects in the second and subsequent stages. A prerequisite for this, however, is growing coherence of the local economy, which, in its turn, is enduringly strengthened by such an association of heavy industry, light industry and agriculture. In the relevant, more recent, planning debates in China and North Korea since 1955, the practical problems encountered have been formulated. In particular, they demonstrated the dubiousness of the distinction drawn in the traditional development debate between a development programme with balanced growth and one with unbalanced growth. Although, in an unbalanced, crippled economic structure, a strategy of unbalanced growth leads to further dynamification of already existing growth focuses—and thus to the further disruption of already disrupted structures—elements of that strategy nevertheless have a positive and constructive role in a balanced development process in which new 'disproportional' emphasis is placed temporarily on further dynamification of what is in essence a balanced economic structure.

As regards (2), such a development path is marked by the convergence of resource mobilization and resource utilization geared to priorities in a country's *own* economy. This is exactly the opposite of what can be observed in present-day peripheral economies, whose outward orientation continually cuts the ground from under any such development design. Linked with this is the fact that equilibration of needs and demand occurs. This form of intermeshing is likewise lacking at present in the peripheral economies, as the effective demand is extremely top-heavy, and on account of the lack of a broad-based economic structure, the satisfaction of the needs of the masses does not provide a sound basis for the economy. As a result, not only is the development of productive forces distorted and misdirected. In addition, considerable latent—that is, mobilizable—development potentials remain untapped in such crippled development processes.

As for (3), successful development processes proceed essentially and in line with priorities from the simple to the complex. An organic process of this sort lays the foundation for sound growth and broad-based effectiveness. The fact that in the course of such processes it is possible, as mentioned above, for disproportional development impulses (e.g. by the selective input of a technology that is more complex than the average achieved level of technological development) to have a substantial impact on the remainder of the economy and exert a dynamifying effect on it, makes it clear that this development principle is not a plea for linear, unbroken development. An organic process complying with a definition of that sort presupposes an income distribution that stimulates demand for standardized, mass-consumer goods. The top-heaviness of the demand profiles in the existing peripheral economies, with their bias towards complex, capital-intensive and energy-consuming consumer durables for the respective upper stratum and urban middle class, contradicts this development principle.

The operational test of whether there is autocentric development in a specific case depends on the answers to the following questions:

— Does the coherence of an entire economy improve in the course of the development process?

— Can such an economy provide certain, above-defined basic services for the mass of the population as a result of development?

— Is there an improvement in the capability for selective cooperation which can be made to benefit a country's own development?

The learning costs of political, administrative, economic and technological experimentation cannot be set at a low level even in a process of autocentric development. But in the long run those costs bring a pay-off in the shape of increased independence, a fairly coherent economic structure, and satisfaction of the basic needs of the mass of the population.

The Third World must now start out from the empirical fact that in the past 300 years there has not been a single case of successful development in which central determinants of autocentric development did not have a combined effect:

(*a*) the *differentiated development of productive forces* in all important spheres—agriculture, capital goods industry, production of intermediate goods, invention and production of technology, mass-consumer goods industry, private and public services—with the goal of attaining depth of production and interlinking effects;

(*b*) the *growing capacity for independent self-control and self-steering* of politics, society, the economy and culture[25]—that is, the attainment of autonomy;

(*c*) the achievement of individual and collective *specific identities*, and thus also of a specific identity of the political culture; and

(*d*) *exchange* with social units beyond a country's own frontiers, initially on a strictly *selective* basis, and in later development phases on a more widespread one.

As can easily be seen from this enumeration, the current development scene is topsy-turvy:

(*a*) Exchange processes under unequal international division of labour result in

(*b*) deformed development of productive forces, which

(*c*) keeps the potential for independent self-control and self-steering limited and

(*d*) does not permit a country to find its own identity.

Consequently, autonomy, self-control, skills and learning capacities are structurally distorted and remain limited.

Concluding Remarks

Every thought-provoking proposition generates more questions than it can answer. This also applies to the plea for a dissociative development policy, which has been offered in this book. Such questions as there are relate less to the validity of the underlying diagnosis of the Third World; rather, they relate to the political, social and economic feasibility of development strategies. In this respect, however, they do not differ in principle from questions which should also be directed at the present practical development policy. After all, are the alternatives to autocentric development really feasible? Do the development policies which are pursued at present really succeed in their aims? Obviously not! And why should considerations that aim at elaborating a new development programme be considered illusory simply because at the moment they admittedly lack political backing in the majority of cases?

After all, the historical experience of the development of Western-capitalist industrial societies, as well as the experiences of socialist industrial societies—and of those few socialist developing countries that have overcome within a few decades the starkest characteristics of underdevelopment—support the rationality and practicability of an autocentric development path. The argument that history does not repeat itself is correct, but carries little conviction in this context. No two cases of autocentric development are completely comparable. This applies as much to differences among Western or Eastern industrial societies as to the fundamental structural divide between capitalist development and socialist development after 1917. The British development path could not be repeated in Japan any more than that of the Soviet Union was slavishly copied in North Korea. But, despite all the differences, countries like Britain, Japan, the Soviet Union and North Korea share similar features which were described above as core characteristics of viable economies and societies. Should not development theory and policy benefit from such a common experience? It is at this point that the discussion of a dissociative development policy becomes relevant. Even though the considerations underlying such a policy are old (see the references to Friedrich List[26] above), it is not at an end but still in its beginnings.

Notes

Preface

1. Dieter Senghaas (ed.), *Imperialismus und strukturelle Gewalt. Analysen über abhängige Reproduktion*, Frankfurt, 1972; *idem* (ed.), *Peripherer Kapitalismus. Analysen über Abhängigkeit und Unterentwicklung*, Frankfurt, 1974; *idem* (ed.), *Kapitalistische Weltökonomie. Kontroversen über ihren Ursprung und ihre Entwicklungsdynamik*, Frankfurt, 1979; *idem*, 'Multinational Corporations and the Third World', *Journal of Peace Research*, 12, No. 4 (1975), 257–74.
2. My own approach was then clearly influenced by the issues raised by peace research. See D. Senghaas, 'Peace Research and the Third World', *Bulletin of Peace Proposals*, 5, No. 2 (1974), 158–72.
3. D. Senghaas, *Weltwirtschaftsordnung und Entwicklungspolitik. Plädoyer für Dissoziation*, Frankfurt, 1977. A summary can be found in Chapter 7 of the present book as well as in my contribution, 'Dissociation as a Development Rationale', in Dieter Ernst (ed.), *The New International Division of Labor, Technology and Underdevelopment*, Frankfurt and New York, 1980, pp. 564–74.
4. D. Senghaas, 'Friedrich List and the New International Economic Order', in Kirsten Worm (ed.), *Industrialization, Development and the Demands for a New International Economic Order*, Copenhagen, 1978, pp. 237–53.
5. See the references in note 10 of the preface to the German edition.
6. An early contribution in which these questions are systematically examined is Dieter Senghaas and Ulrich Menzel, 'Autocentric Development despite International Competence Differentials: Why Did the Metropolitan Economies Become Metropolitan and Not Peripheral Economies?', *Economics* (published by the Institute for Scientific Cooperation, Tübingen), 21 (1980), 7–35.
7. See Ulrich Menzel, *In der Nachfolge Europas. Autozentrierte Entwicklung in den ostasiatischen Schwellenländern Südkorea und Taiwan*, Munich, 1985.

Foreword

1. Senghaas, *Weltwirtschaftsordnung*.
2. The more recent classic literature on European development usually concentrates on the highly developed part of north-western and central Europe, e.g. Norbert Elias, *Über den Prozeß des Zivilisation*, 2 vols, Frank-

229

furt, 1976; Maurice Dobb, *Studies in the Development of Capitalism,* London, 1946; David Landes, *The Unbound Prometheus,* Cambridge, Mass., 1968; Karl Polanyi, *The Great Transformation,* Vienna, 1977. Symptomatic of this state of affairs also is the *Cambridge Economic History of Europe,* Vol. 7, 2 parts (Cambridge, 1978), which deals with Great Britain, France, Germany, the United States, Japan and Russia, as well as Scandinavia. For a useful source on the older literature covering the period up to the early 1970s, see the bibliographies in Rudolf Braun *et al.* (eds), *Industrielle Revolution,* Cologne, 1972; Hans-Ulrich Wehler (ed.), *Geschichte und Soziologie,* Cologne, 1972; *idem* (ed.) *Geschichte und Ökonomie,* Cologne, 1973). On the theoretical and methodological questioning of the literature on European economic history, see F. Crouzet, 'The Economic History of Modern Europe', *Journal of Economic History,* 31 (1971), 135–52; Richard and Charles Tilly, 'Agenda for European Economic History in the 1970s', ibid., 184–98; Richard Tilly, 'Das Wachstumsparadigma und die europäische Industrialisierungsgeschichte', *Geschichte und Gesellschaft,* 3 (1977), 93–108 (a discussion of the *Fontana Economic History of Europe* quoted in note 4 below).

3. See, for example, Dudley Seers *et al.* (eds), *Underdeveloped Europe: Studies in Core-Periphery Relations,* London, 1979; Seers *et al.* (eds), *Integration and Unequal Development: The Experience of the EEC,* London, 1980; Seers *et al.* (eds), *The Second Enlargement of the EEC: Integration of Unequal Partners,* London, 1982; Juan Antonio Payno *et al.* (eds), *The Second Enlargement of the EEC: The Prospective New Members,* (London, 1982; Kjell Öström and Dudley Seers (eds), *The Crises of the European Regions,* London, 1982. See also the studies by the Deutsches Institut für Entwicklungspolitik, Berlin, for a summary of which, see Stefan A. Musto, 'Die Süderweiterung der Europäischen Gemeinschaft', *Kyklos,* 34 (1981), 242–72.

4. Especially A. Milward and S.B. Saul, *The Economic Development of Continental Europe, 1780–1870,* London, 1973; *idem, The Development of the Economies of Central Europe, 1850–1914,* London, 1977; Sidney Pollard, *Peaceful Conquest: The Industrialization of Europe, 1760–1970,* Oxford, 1981; also the extensive empirical studies by Irma Adelman and Cynthia Taft Morris, 'A Typology of Poverty in 1850', *Economic Development and Cultural Change,* 25, supplement (1977), 314–43; *idem,* 'Growth and Impoverishment in the Middle of the Nineteenth Century', *World Development,* No. 6 (1978), 245–73; *idem,* 'Patterns of Market Expansion in the Nineteenth Century: A Quantitative Study', *Research in Economic Anthropology,* No. 1 (1978), 231–324; *idem,* 'The Role of Institutional Influences in Patterns of Agricultural Development in the Nineteenth and Early Twentieth Centuries: A Cross-Sectional Quantitative Study', *Journal of Economic History,* 39 (1973), 159–76; *idem,* 'Patterns of Industrialization in the Nineteenth and Early Twentieth Centuries: A Cross-Sectional Quantitative Study', *Research in Economic History,* 5 (1980), 1–83. In addition, see Paul Bairoch, *Commerce extérieur et développement économique de l'Europe au XIXᵉ siècle,* Paris, 1976; W. Arthur Lewis, *Growth and Fluctuations, 1870–1913,* London, 1978; also *Fontana Economic History of Europe,* ed. Carlo M. Cipolla, 6 vols, London, 1972 *et seq.;* Eric J. Hobsbawm, *The Age of Capital, 1848–1875,* London, 1975. On the 'pre-history' of the more recent history of European development, see Jerome Blum, *The End of the Old Order in Rural*

Europe, Princeton, N.J. 1978; Peter Kriedte, *Peasants, Landlords and Merchant Capitalists*, Leamington Spa, 1983; more systematic, Walt W. Rostow, *How It All Began: Origins of the Modern Economy*, London, 1975; Douglas C. North and Robert P. Thomas, 'An Economic Theory of the Growth of the Western World', *Economic History Review*, 23 (1970), 1–17; *idem, The Rise of the Western World: A New Economic History* (Cambridge, 1973).

5. For exceptions to this rule, see the studies by W.A. Lewis, as well as Adelman and Morris, quoted in note 4 above. See also Paul Bairoch, *Die Dritte Welt in der Sackgasse*, Vienna, 1973; Immanuel Wallerstein, *The Modern World System*, Vol. 1, London, 1974, Vol. 2, London, 1981; André Gunder Frank, *L'Accumulation mondiale, 1500–1800*, Paris, 1977; Hartmut Elsenhans, *Geschichte und Ökonomie der europäischen Welteroberung*, Frankfurt, 1985; Samir Amin, *Class and Nation, Historically and in the Current Crisis*, New York, 1979. An account of my own thoughts can be found in 'Autocentric Development'.

6. There are at present only a few contributions to this subject. See especially R. Cameron, 'Economic Development: Some Lessons of History for Developing Nations', *American Economic Review*, 57 (1967), 312–24; Simon Kuznets, 'Underdeveloped Countries and the Pre-industrial Phase in the Advanced Countries' in A.N. Agarwala and S.P. Singh (eds), *The Economics of Underdevelopment*, London, 1979 pp. 135–53; Knut Borchardt, 'Europas Wirtschaftsgeschichte—Modell für Entwicklungsländer' in Rudolf Braun *et al.* (eds), *Gesellschaft in der Industriellen Revolution*, Cologne, 1973, pp. 343–66; Wolfram Fischer, 'Die Basis war noch immer das tägliche Brot. Entwicklungsländer und Entwicklungspolitik im Lichte der Wirtschaftsgeschichte', *Franfurter Allgemeine Zeitung* (4 Apr. 1981) (reprinted in *BMZ—Entwicklungspolitik. Spiegel der Presse*, 11 (1981), 422ff.); David Landes, 'Wirtschaftshistorische Thesen zur Unterentwicklung', *Neue Züricher Zeitung* (31 Aug. 1978) (reprinted in *NZZ—Schriften zur Zeit*, 41 (1979), 28ff.); Eckart Schremmer, 'Das 18. Jahrhundert, das Kontinuitätsproblem und die Geschichte der Industrialisierung. Erfahrunge für die Entwicklungsländer?', *Zeitschrift für Agrargeschichte und Agrarsoziologie*, 29 (1981) 58–78.

7. On the role of eurocentrism, see Hans Magnus Enzensberger, 'Eurozentrismus wider Willen', *Trans Atlantik* (Oct. 1980), 62–7.

8. See Jeffrey B. Nugent, 'What Has Orthodox Development Economics Learned from Recent Experience?', *World Development*, 7 (1979), 545–54.

9. For a discussion that is interesting as well as stylizing the situation, see Johan Galtung and Fumiko Nishimura, *Von China lernen?* (Opladen, 1978), among a host of other literature on the subject.

10. See especially Volker Mathies, *Neue Weltwirtschaftsordnung*, Opladen, 1980; Hans-Jürgen Harborth, 'Dissoziation—mit welchem Ziel?', *Entwicklung und Zusammenarbeit*, No. 718 (1977), 17–18; Detlef Lorenz, 'Weltwirtschaft zwischen Arbeitsteilung und Abkopplung', *Konjunkturpolitik*, 23 (1977), 196–215; Peter Richter, 'Die Neue Internationale Arbeitsteilung und die deutschen Direktinvestitionen', *Konjunkturpolitik*, 24 (1978), 98–122; Ward Moorehouse, *Technological Autonomy and Delinking in the International System: An Alternative Economic and Political Strategy for National Development*, New York (UNITAR), 1979; John H. Adler, 'The Political Economy of Delinking', *Inter-economics* (May/June 1980), 136–43; Urs

Heierli, *Abkopplung, Freihandel oder Entwicklung nach innen,* Diessenhofen, 1979; Sung-Jo Park, *Gemeinschaftsunternehmen und Indigenizationsstrategie in der Dritten Welt,* Bochum, 1979; Mohammed Massarat and Rainer Schweers, 'Weltwirtschaftsordnung und Dritte Welt—eine Kontroverse', *Berliner Hefte, Zeitschrift für Kultur und Politik,* 10 (1979), 38–46; the review by Antonio Carlos in *Telos,* 36 (1978), 197–206; Silvio Borner, 'Kritische Fragen an die Außenhandelstheorie', *Schweizerische Zeitung für Volkswirtschaft und Statistik,* 116, No. 3 (1980) 231–4; *idem,* 'Die Internationalisierung der Industrie', *Kyklos,* 34 (1981), 14–35; El-Shagi el-Shagi, 'Weltwirtschaftliche Dissoziation zwischen Industrie-und Entwicklungsländern? Eine kritische Auseinandersetzung mit der These von Senghaas', *List-Forum,* 10, No. 2 (1979/80), 112–30; Jörn Altmann, 'Definitiveness and Operationality of Dissociation', *Inter-economics* (July/Aug. 1981), 166–70; A. Basler, 'Neuere entwicklungspolitische Theorieansätze und ihre Bewertung im Hinblick auf Nahrungsversorgung und Weltagrarhandel', *Agrarwirtschaft,* 28 (1978), 217–26; Thomas Hurtienne, 'Peripherer Kapitalismus und autozentrierte Entwicklung. Zur Kritik des Erklärungsansatzes von Dieter Senghaas', *Prokla,* 11, No. 3 (1981), 105–36; Andreas Buro, *Autozentrierte Entwicklung durch Demokratisierung. Lehren aus Vietnam and anderen Ländern der Dritten Welt,* Frankfurt, 1981.

11. See the book quoted in note 1 above and my contribution, 'Dissoziation und autozentrierte Entwicklung. Eine entwicklungspolitische Alternative für die Dritte Welt', in Senghaas, *Kapitalistische Weltökonomie,* pp. 376–412, as well as ch. 7 of the present volume.

12. A summary of the attempts to provide an analytical differentiation can be found in Klaus Esser and Jürgen Weimann, *Schwerpunktländer in der Dritten Welt,* Berlin, 1981.

13. On this topic, from a growing body of literature, see Kushi M. Khan and Volker Matthies, *Collective Self-Reliance. Programme und Perspektiven der Dritten Welt,* Munich, 1978; Kushi M. Khan, *Nord-Süd-Dialog und die Solidarisierung innerhalb der Dritten Welt,* Hamburg, 1981.

14. See the important study by Ulrich Menzel, *Auswege aus Abhängigkeit. Die entwicklungspolitische Aktualität Europas,* Frankfurt, 1985. That study, which originated from the same context as the present volume, includes case-studies of the export-orientated development of Switzerland, Denmark, Sweden and Canada.

15. Dieter Senghaas and Ulrich Menzel, 'Entwicklung und Unterentwicklung? Untersuchung über die Wahrscheinlichkeit nachholender Entwicklung von Schwellenländern am Beispiel Südkoreas und Taiwans' (ms), Bremen, 1981, publ. as *In der Nachfolge Europas. Ein Problemaufriß,* Munich, 1985.

16. See the as yet unpublished study by Georg Simonis (Constance University).

17. On Israeli development from a democratic-socialist start to a 'maturing' capitalist society, see Part III of the present volume.

18. See the book quoted in note 1 above, especially pp. 75ff., and Part I of the present volume. See also the studies by Alexander Gerschenkron, *Economic Backwardness in Historical Perspective,* Cambridge, 1962, and *Continuity in History and Other Essays,* Cambridge, 1968.

19. Such different emphases can be found in studies that focus to a greater degree on the process of political development, e.g. Barrington Moore,

Social Origins of Dictatorship and Democracy, Boston, 1966; Perry Anderson, *Lineages of the Absolutist State*, London, 1974; Reinhard Bendix, *Kings or People*, 2 vols, London 1978; Hans-Ulrich Wehler (ed.), *Klassen in der europäischen Sozialgeschichte*, Göttingen, 1979; Karl W. Deutsch, *Nationalism and Social Communication: An Inquiry into the Foundations of Nationality*, Cambridge, 1966 (2nd ed.). They can also be found in studies that focus on the theory of modernization, comprehensively covered in Hans-Ulrich Wehler, *Modernisierungstheorie und Geschichte*, Göttingen, 1975; Peter Flora, *Modernisierungsforschung. Zur empirischen Analyse der gesellschaftlichen Entwicklung*, Opladen, 1974; *idem, Indikatoren der Modernisierung. Ein historisches Datenhandbuch*, Opladen, 1975. See also the studies by Stein Rokkan which are summarized in Peter Flora, 'Stein Rokkans Makro-Modell der politischen Entwicklung Europas. Ein Rekonstruktionsversuch', *Kölner Zeitschrift für Soziologie ind Sozialpsychologie*, 33 (1981), 397–436. For an emphasis on the theory of democracy, see Goran Therborn, 'The Rule of Capital and the Rise of Democracy', *New Left Review*, No. 103 (May/June 1977), 3–41. And for an emphasis on the theory of revolution, see Theda Skocpol, *States and Social Revolutions: A Comparative Analysis of France, Russia and China*, Cambridge, 1979.

20. On theoretical and methodological problems, see Theda Skocpol and Margaret Somers, 'The Uses of Comparative History in Macrosocial Enquiry', *Comparative Studies in Society and History*, 22 (1980), 174–97; Victoria E. Bonnell, 'The Uses of Theory, Concepts and Comparisons in Historical Sociology', 156–73. Both these contributions also discuss important recent comparative historical publications. See also Charles P. Kindleberger, *Economic Response: Comparative Studies in Trade, Finance and Growth*, Cambridge, Mass., 1978. For a recent study which is of exemplary methodological importance, see Patrick O'Brien and Caglar Keyder, *Economic Growth in Britain and France 1789–1913: Two Paths to the Twentieth Century*, London, 1978. An excellent comparative historical study not considered in the above-mentioned two articles is Iván T. Berend and György Ranki, *Economic Development in East-Central Europe in the 19th and 20th Centuries*, New York and London, 1974; see also *idem, The European Periphery and Industrialization 1780–1914*, Cambridge, 1982.

1 Autocentric Development despite International Competence Differentials: Problem and General Diagnosis

1. On this, see the impressive *Times Atlas of World History*, ed. Geoffrey Barraclough (London, 1978), one of the few atlases on world history avoiding misguided eurocentrism.
2. See, for example, Samir Amin, *The Arab Nation: Nationalism and Class Struggle*, London, 1978.
3. See, for example, Diethmar Rothermund, *Europa und Asien im Zeitalter des Merkantilismus*, Darmstadt, 1978.
4. The so-called *world system approach* is connected mainly with the studies of Immanuel Wallerstein. See particularly *The Modern World System*, Vols 1–2, New York, 1974, 1980 (a further two volumes are in preparation). See also *idem, The Capitalist World Economy*, Cambridge and Paris 1979.
5. See particularly the discussion published in the year-book that is regu-

larly edited by Immanuel Wallerstein, *Political Economy of the World System Annuals*, Vols 1 *et seq.*, London, 1978 *et seq.*, and Albert Bergesen (ed.), *Studies of the Modern World System*, London, 1980.

6. See the interesting discussion taking place in the journal *Past and Present* since the publication of a study by Robert Brenner, 'Agrarian Class Structure and Economic Development in Pre-Industrial Europe', No. 70 (1976), 30–76; also Kriedte, *Peasants*; *idem*, 'Spätmittelalterliche Agrarkrise oder Krise des Feudalismus?', *Geschichte und Gesellschaft*, 7 (1981), 42–68; and also the comprehensive study by Bendix, *Kings or People*.

7. See Paul Bairoch and M. Lévy-Leboyer (eds), *Disparities in Economic Development since the Industrial Revolution*, New York, 1981; also the earlier study by Simon Kuznets, *Modern Economic Growth*, London, 1966.

8. For a qualification of this frequently raised question, see Rostow, *How It All Began*; N.F.R. Craft, 'Industrial Revolution in England and France: Some Thoughts on the Question "Why Was England First?" ', *Economic History Review*, 30 (1977), 429–41. Also, for a critical analysis of the more recent discussion, Michael Fores, 'The Myth of a British Industrial Revolution', *History*, 66 (1981), 181–98; and Malcolm E. Falcus, 'Modern British Economic Development: The Industrial Revolution in Perspective', *Australian Economic History Review*, 19 (1979), 42–64.

9. On this, see the excellent studies in A.E. Musson (ed.), *Wissenschaft, Technik und Wirtschaftswachstum im 18. Jahrhundert*, Frankfurt, 1977.

10. An excellent summary and a detailed evaluation of the more recent literature on the industrialization of England and Europe are contained in the study by Pollard, *Peaceful Conquest*. See also Rudolf Braun *et al.* (eds), *Industrielle Revolution. Wirtschaftliche Aspekte*, 2 vols, Cologne, 1972, and Braun *et al.* (eds), *Gesellschaft in der industriellen Revolution*, Cologne, 1973 (all three volumes contain excellent literature lists); also the classic study by Landes, *Prometheus*.

11. See the excellent works on economic history by A. Milward and S.B. Saul, *The Economic Development of Continental Europe, 1780–1870*, London, 1973 (from now on cited as Milward/Saul 1) and *The Development of the Economies of Continental Europe, 1850–1914*, London, 1977 (from now on cited as Milward/Saul 2).

12. See William Woodruff, *Impact of Western Man: A Study of Europe's Role in the World Economy*, 1750–1960, New York, 1966; Mildward/Saul 2, ch. 9, including references to further literature; and see especially Douglas C. North, 'Ocean Freight Rates and Economic Development, 1750–1913', *Journal of Economic History*, 18 (1958), 537–55.

13. See ch. 6, on socialist development policy in historical perspective.

14. See Senghaas, *Weltwirtschaftsordnung*; also the theoretical studies by Jochen Röpke, which are of fundamental importance to the problem to be discussed. And see Röpke, 'Der Einfluß des Weltmarkts auf die wirtschaftliche Entwicklung', H. Giersch *et al.* (eds), *Weltwirtschaftsordnung und Wirtschaftswissenschaft*, Stuttgart, 1978, pp. 30–52; *idem*, 'Probleme des Neuerungstransfers zwischen Ländern unterschiedlicher Entwicklungsfähigkeit', *Ordo*, 29 (1978), 245–79; *idem*, 'Weltwirtschaftliche Arbeitsteilung bei internationalem Kompetenzgefälle. Eine entwicklungstheoretische Analyse der Wirkung von Freihandel und Protektionismus auf Außenhandel und wirtschaftliche Entwicklung' in A. Schiller

and U. Wagner (eds), *Außenwirtschaftspolitik und Stabilisierung von Wirtschaftssystemen*, Stuttgart, 1980, pp. 81–97. From the viewpoint of systems analysis, the following studies are of particular interest: Tom Baumgartner *et al.*, 'Unequal Exchange and Uneven Development: The Structuring of Exchange Patterns', *Studies in Comparative International Development*, 2 (1976), 51–72; *idem*, 'Towards a Systems Theory of Unequal Exchange: Uneven Development and Dependency Relationship', *Kybernetes*, 5 (1976), 15–23. See also Paul Krugman, 'Trade Accumulation and Uneven Development', *Journal of Development Economics*, 8 (1981), 149–61.

15. See especially the studies by Röpke cited in note 14 above.

16. See my book cited in note 14 above and, for a summary, Senghaas, 'Dissoziation' in *Kapitalistische Weltökonomie*, pp. 376–412; see also chapter 7 below.

17. First arguments on these lines can be found in Senghaas and Menzel, 'Autocentric Development'.

18. On this, see the statements on the development of export economies in Part II of the present volume.

19. On this, one could cite any number of studies dealing with certain aspects of the question. See, for example, Wilhelm Treue, *Gesellschaft, Wirtschaft und Technik Deutschlands im 19. Jahrhundert*, Stuttgart, 1975, pp. 19, 21, 105, 144, 151–8, 163, 171, 177–8, 249 and 274; also in general Milward/Saul 1–2.

20. See for a summary Pollard, *Peaceful Conquest*, as well as W.O. Henderson, *Britain and Industrial Europe, 1750–1870: Studies in British Influence on the Industrial Revolution in Western Europe*, Liverpool, 1954, and *idem*, *The Industrialization of Europe, 1870–1914*, London, 1969; also R.E. Cameron, *France and the Economic Development of Europe 1800–1914*, Princeton, N.J., 1961.

21. See the study by F. Crouzet, 'Western Europe and Great Britain: Catching up in the First Half of the 19th Century' in A.J. Youngson (ed.), *Economic Development in the Long Run*, London, 1972, pp. 98–125, which is still worth reading.

22. On the following, see the classic study by Paul Bairoch, *Commerce extérieur et développement économique de l'Europe au XIXᵉ siècle*, Paris, 1976, particularly ch. 7.

23. Kuznets, op. cit., (note 7 above), p. 306.

24. By Bairoch, op. cit. (note 22 above), pp. 168ff.

25. See especially Pollard, *Peaceful Conquest*; also the earlier contribution by *idem*, 'Industrialization and the European Economy', *Economic History Review*, 26 (1973), 636–47.

26. On the data concerning England and France, see the study by Bairoch cited in note 22 above. On the Scandinavian data, see the sources in ch. 2 on Scandinavian development.

27. The vital role of a domestic market based on the production of goods for mass consumption is rightly stressed by Hartmut Elsenhans, 'Grundlagen der Entwicklung der kapitalistischen Weltwirtschaft' in Senghaas (ed.), op. cit. (note 16 above), pp. 103–48.

28. See Kindleberger, *Economic Response*, ch. 2.

29. See the analysis of the different development paths of export economies in Part II.

30. See, for a summary, the study by Bairoch cited in note 22 above.

31. On this, see Menzel, *Auswege aus Abhängigkeit*, ch. II, 1.
32. Correspondingly complex were usually the constellations of political alliances with regard to this question. On this, see Peter Alexis Gourevitch, 'International Trade, Domestic Coalitions and Liberty: Comparative Responses to the Crisis of 1873–96', *Journal of Interdisciplinary History*, 8 (1977), 281–313.
33. On England, see Ralph Davis, 'The Rise of Protection in England, 1689–1786', *Economic History Review*, 19 (1966), 306–17; Jochen Röpke, 'Außenhandelstheorie und wirtschaftliche Entwicklung aus theoretischer und wirtschaftsgeschichtlicher Sicht' (unpublished manuscript, Marburg, 1980).
34. See the early deliberations of Friedrich List, *Das nationale System der politischen Ökonomie*, Tübingen, 1959 (1st ed. 1841); also Friedrich von Wieser, 'Theorie der gesellschaftlichen Wirtschaft', section 1, part II of *Grundriß der Sozialökonomik*, Tübingen, 1924, pp. 317ff.
35. On this, see also Ulrich Menzel, 'Autozentrierte Entwicklung in historischer Perspektive. Dogmengeschichtliche und typologische Aspekteteines aktuellen Konzepts' in Khushi M. Khan (ed.), *Self-Reliance als nationale und kollektive Entwicklungsstrategie*, Munich, 1980, pp. 33–65. Further references can be found there.
36. An explicit reference to List can be found in my study, *Weltwirtschaftsordnung*, pp. 75ff.
37. A pleasing exception is the recent study by Silvio Borner, 'Kritische Fragen an die Außenhandelstheorie', *Schweizerische Zeitschrift für Volkswirtschaft und Statistik*, 116, No. 3 (1980), 231–4; also implicitly *idem*, 'Die Internationalisierung der Industrie', *Kyklos*, 34 (1981), 14–35.
38. Mihail Manoilesco, *Die nationalen Produktivkräfte und der Außenhandel*, Berlin, 1937; *idem*, *Une Nouvelle conception du protectionisme industriel*, Bucharest, 1931; *idem*, *L'Équilibre économique européen*, Bucharest, 1931; and *idem*, 'Die theoretische Problematik des Außenhandels. Synthese, Beweisführung, Polemik', *Weltwirtschaftliches Archiv*, 51 (1940), 1–82. On the Romanian background to Manoilesco's deliberations, see Henri H. Stahl, 'Théories de C.D. Gherea sur les lois de la pénétration du capitalisme dans les pays retardataires', *Review*, 2, No. 1 (1978), pp. 101–14.
39. On North Korea, see the relevant self-description, *The Building of an Independent National Economy in Korea*, Pyongyang, 1977; also on the political relevance of North Korean development, my preface to Juttka-Reisse, *Agrarpolitik*, pp. i–x. In that study a description summarizing the so-called *dschutsche* doctrine will be found.
40. See the important, study by Uwe Stehr, *Sozio-ökonomische Bedingungen des Außenverhalten der RGW-Staaten*, Frankfurt, 1977 (HSFK-Studie 17).
41. See Sandro Sideri, *Trade and Power: Informal Colonialism in Anglo-Portuguese Relations*, Rotterdam, 1970; *idem*, 'International Trade and Economic Power' in *Towards a New World Economy*, Rotterdam, 1972; Urs von der Mühll, *Die Unterentwicklung Portugals. Von der Weltmacht zur Halbkolonie Englands*, Frankfurt, 1978, pp. 58ff.; also Miriam Halpern Pereira, *Livre câmbio e desinvolvimento economico. Portugal na segunda metade do século XIX*, Lisbon, 1971; *idem*, *Asimetrias de crecimento e dependência externa*, Lisbon, 1974.
42. This observation can be brought into accord with Gerschenkron's delib-

erations on development history. See Gerschenkron, *Economic Backwardness*; *idem*, *Continuity in History*.

43. See the study quoted in note 17 above.
44. On this, see Karl W. Deutsch and Ingo A. Schwarz, *Bewertung der abnehmenden Tendez von Außenhandel zu Bruttosozialprodukt mit der Größe von Nationen auf der Basis neuester Daten*, Berlin, 1980 (Publications of the International Institute for Comparative Social Research, WZX No. 109).
45. This is the reason why in the following chapters (Part II) the development paths of export economies are given prominence.
46. On this, see my study, *Weltwirtschaftsordnung*.
47. On other attempts at elaborating a typology see Gerschenkron, 'The Typology of Industrial Development as a Tool of Analysis' in *idem*, *Continuity in History*, pp. 77–97; Bert F. Hoselitz, *Wirtschaftliches Wachstum und sozialer Wandel*, Berlin, 1969, pp. 54ff.; also the studies by Irma Adelman and Cynthia Taft Morris, particularly 'Growth and Impoverishment in the Middle of the Nineteenth Century', *World Development*, 6 (1978), pp. 245–73. For an early pertinent study which is still worth reading see Walther G. Hoffmann, *Stadien und Typen der Industrialisierung*, Jena, 1931. In the following section detailed annotation is omitted, as easily accessible modern studies contain excellent bibliographies on the particular countries dealt with ; thus notably Milward/Saul 1–2 as well as the *Fontana Economic History of Europe*, in this context mainly Vols 4–5. On the following discussion, see Ulrich Menzel and Dieter Senghaas, 'Autozentrierte Entwicklung im Weltsystem. Versuch einer Typologie' in Jochen Blaschke (ed.), *Perspektiven des Weltsystems*, Frankfurt, 1982. In this article short biographies of seventeen currently highly industrialised OECD societies can be found.
48. See particularly Pierre Lebrun *et al.*, *Essai sur la révolution industrielle en Belgique, 1770–1847*, Brussels, 1979; and on more recent literature Joel Mokyr, 'Industrialization in Two Languages', *Economic History Review*, 34 (1981), 143–9.
49. See Hoffmann, *Stadien*.
50. On the United States, see Sigrid Meuschel, *Kapitalismus oder Sklaverei. Die langwierige Durchsetzung der bürgerlichen Gesellschaft in den USA*, Frankfurt, 1981. See also Christopher Chase-Dunn, 'The Development of Core Capitalism in the Antebellum United States: Tariff Politics and Class Struggle in an Upward Mobile Semi-Periphery' in Bergesen *Studies*, pp. 189–230.
51. See, for example, Rolf Horst Dunke, 'Die wirtschaftlichen Folgen des Zollvereins' in Werner Abelshauser und Dietmar Petzina (eds), *Deutsche Wirtschaftsgeschichte im Industriezeitalter* Königstein, 1981, pp. 242–73.
52. See, for example, O'Brien and Keyder, *Economic Growth*; Alexander Gerschenkron, *An Economic Spurt That Failed: Four Lectures in Austrian History*, Princeton, N.J., 1977; Knut Borchardt, *Grundriß der deutschen Wirtschaftsgeschichte*, Göttingen, 1978, especially pp. 46ff.
53. See the article by Menzel cited in note 35 above.
54. See Milward/Saul 2.
55. Hoffmann, *Stadien*.
56. Bairoch, *Commerce extérieur*, p. 177.
57. See Menzel, *Auswege aus Abhängigkeit* which deals in detail with the Swiss

development path.
58. This is documented in detail *ibid.*
59. Milward/Saul 2, pp. 182ff.
60. In contrast with Switzerland, the Netherlands could, to a modest degree, fall back on her colonies.
61. For more detailed references, see the chapters on the development paths of export economy in Part II of the present volume.
62. See Menzel, op. cit. (note 35 above).
63. Milward/Saul 2, ch. 7, on the development of Russia. On Japanese development, see my study *Weltwirtschaftsordnung*, pp. 88ff; also the article by Ian Inkster, which discusses the more recent literature, 'Meiji Economic Development in Perspective: Revisionist Comments upon the Industrial Revolution in Japan' in *The Developing Economies*, 17 (1979), 45–68; and the earlier interesting article by Ippei Yamazawa and Akira Hirata, 'Industrialization and External Relations: Comparative Analysis of Japan's Historical Experience and Contemporary Developing Countries Performance', *Hitotsubashi Journal of Economics*, 18, No. 2 (1978), 33–61. On development prior to the Meiji restoration, see Susan Hanley and Koto Yamamura, *Economic and Demographic Change in Preindustrial Japan, 1600–1868*, Princeton, N.J., 1977. On the literature in Japanese, see the excellent summaries by Mikio Sumiya and Koji Taira, *An Outline of Japanese Economic History, 1603–1940*, Tokyo, 1979.
64. Milward/Saul 2, ch. 4.
65. Cyril Black *et al.*, *The Modernization of Japan and Russia: A Comparative Study*, London, 1975.
66. See ch. 6 on socialism from the viewpoint of development history and the literature cited there from a research project on the subject.
67. Menzel, *In der Nachfolge Europas*.
68. Borner (op. cit., note 37 above) regards the newly industrializing countries as special cases, while other studies tend to come to more optimistic conclusions regarding the possibilities for delayed development. See, for example, Jürgen B. Donges and Lotte Müller-Ohlsen, *Außenwirtschaftsstrategien und Industrialisierung in Entwicklungsländern*, Tübingen, 1978.
69. On this, see Jochen Röpke, 'Entrepreneurship and Economic Development in Indonesia', *Prisma* (Djakarta), No. 13 (June 1979), 51–66, especially p. 66, and Fernando Fajnzylber, 'Sobre la restructuración del capitalismo y sus repercusiones en América Latina', *El Trimestre Económico*, 46 (1979), 889–914, especially 900ff.
70. But also of Italy and Hungary, two cases which, with certain qualifications, could be subsumed under this type.
71. See, on the contrast between Japanese and Chinese development, Frances V. Moulder, *Japan, China and the Modern World Economy*, London, 1977.
72. On this, see particularly Hartmut Elsenhans, 'Zur Rolle der Staatsklasse bei der Überwindung von Unterentwicklung' in Alfred Schmidt (ed.), *Strategien gegen Unterentwicklung*, Frankfurt, 1976, pp. 250–65; *idem*, *Abhängiger Kapitalismus oder bürokratische Entwicklungsgesellschaft*, Frankfurt, 1981.
73. This point has also been made by Gerschenkron in *Economic Backwardness and Continuity in History*.

74. On this, see James R. Kurth, 'The Political Consequences of the Product Cycle: Industrial History and Political Outcomes', *International Organization*, 33 (1979), 1–34; *idem*, 'Industrial Change and Political Change: A European Perspective' in David Collier (ed.), *The New Authoritorianism in Latin America*, Princeton, N.J., 1979, pp. 319–62.

75. Hans F. Illy *et al.*, *Diktatur—Staatsmodell für die Dritte Welt?*, Freiburg and Würzburg, 1980.

76. An early study on this subject, still worth reading, is George B. Curtiss, *Protection and Prosperity: An Account of Tariff Legislation and Its Effect in Europe and America*, London, 1896. On the whole question, see also Pollard, *Peaceful Conquest*, and Kindleberger, *Economic Response*, ch. 3.

77. On this explicitly, see List, *Nationale System*, *passim*. Such a leading position reflects the high development level of the domestic economy; foreign trade has only a supporting role and free trade can prove a thoroughly two-edged sword, as is evidenced by Donald N. McCloskey in the case of England, 'Magnanimous Albion: Free Trade and British National Income, 1841–1881', *Explorations in Economic History*, 17 (1980), 303–20.

78. H. Kitamura, *Zur Theorie des internationalen Handels*, Weinfelden, 1941, pp. 250ff.

79. Milward/Saul 2, pp. 66ff.

80. For a summary, see Volker Matthies, *Neue Weltwirtschaftsordnung. Hintergründe—Positionen—Argumente*, Opladen, 1980.

81. On these questions, see Bairoch, *Commerce extérieur*.

82. On this see also especially *ibid.*

83. Although in individual cases such an integration was quite controversial, the political struggles tended to end in favour of local oligarchic interests advocating free trade. On this, see for example the study by Kurt-Peter Schütt, *Externe Abhängigkeit und periphere Entwicklung in Lateinamerika. Eine Studie am Beispiel der Entwicklung Kolumbiens von der Kolonialzeit bis 1930*, Frankfurt, 1980, ch. 4; also Charles Issawi, 'De-Industrialization and Re-Industrialization in the Middle East', *International Journal of Middle East Studies*, 12 (1980), 469–79. On the whole question, see Rudolf von Albertini, *Europäische Kolonialherrschaft*, Munich, 1982.

84. Without collaboration European powers would have had far less success in the southern continents than turned out to be the case. On this, see Ronald Robinson, 'Non-European Foundations of European Imperialism: Sketch for a Theory of Collaboration' in Roger Owen and Bob Sutcliffe (eds), *Studies in the Theory of Imperialism*, London, 1972, pp. 117–42.

85. See the studies by Manoilesco, op. cit. (note 38 above), and also the discussion of the relevant debate on development policy in south-eastern Europe in Kenneth Jowitt (ed.), *Social Change in Romania, 1860–1940: A Debate on Development in a European Nation*, Berkeley, Calif., 1978. See also the exposition in Milward/Saul 2, chs 4 and 8.

86. For an exemplary study on Romanian development since the early nineteenth century, see Stefan Welzk, 'Entwicklungspolitische Lernprozesse. Rumänische Erfahrungen' in *Befreiung, Zeitschrift für Politik und Wissenschaft*, Nos 19/20 (1980), 70–118; also the studies in Jowitt, op. cit. (note 85 above). On Hungarian development, see Andrew C. Janos, *The Politics of Backwardness in Hungary, 1825–1945*, Princeton, N.J., 1981.

87. An interesting study on the Italian case is A. James Gregor, *Italian*

Fascism and Developmental Dictatorship, Princeton, N.J., 1979; also Anthony James Joes, 'On the Modernity of Fascism', *Comparative Political Studies*, 10, No. 2 (1977), 259–68. An earlier appraisal of this kind can be found in Franz Borkenau, 'Zur Soziologie des Faschismus' in Ernst Nolte (ed.), *Theorien über den Faschismus*, Cologne, 1967. On the pre-history of the Italian development path, see Ruggiero Romano et al., *Die Gleichzeitigkeit des Ungleichzeitigen. Fünf Studien zur Geschichte Italiens*, Frankfurt, 1980, especially pp. 22–75; Gino Luzzatto, *L'economia italiana dal 1861 al 1894*, Turin, 1974; Giorgio Mori (ed.), *L'industrializazione in Italia*, Bologna, 1977; Volcker Hunecke, 'Soziale Ungleichheit und Klassenstrukturen in Italien vom Ende des 18. bis zum Anfang des 20. Jahrunderts' in Wehler, *Klassen*, pp. 210–32.

88. On the terminology, see Gregor, *Italian Fascism*, and Jowitt, *Social Change in Romania, passim*.

89. Daniel Chirot, 'The Corporatist Model and Socialism', *Theory and Society* 9, No. 2 (1980), 363–81. For an attempt in this direction, see Walter L. Goldfrank, 'Fascism and World Economy', *Political Economy of the World System Annuals*, 1 (1978), 75–117.

90. Cf. A. James Gregor, 'Nazionalfascismo and the Revolutionary Nationalism of Sun Yat-sen', *Journal of Asian Studies*, 39, No. 1 (1979), 21–37.

91. See the early publication by John H. Kautsky (ed.), *Political Change in Underdeveloped Countries, Nationalism and Communism*, New York, 1962.

92. On the whole question, see ch. 6, on the role of socialism in the development process.

93. On this correlation, see especially Milward/Saul 1–2. See also Adelman and Taft-Morris, 'Role of Institutional Influences', *Journal of Economic History*, 39 (1979), 159–76; Tom Kemp, *Historical Patterns of Industrialization*, London, 1978, ch. 3. Regarding the discussion of concrete cases, special references to literature are from now on given only when the developing societies in question are not treated in more detail in later chapters of the present volume.

94. On this, see particularly Lewis, *Growth and Fluctuations*, pp. 159ff. See also E.L. Jones, 'Agricultural Origins of Industry', *Past and Present*, No. 40 (1968), 58–61; *idem, Agriculture and the Industrial Revolution*, Oxford, 1974; *idem* and S.J. Woolf (eds), *The Agrarian Change and Economic Development*, London, 1974.

95. On this connection, see the reflections on economic history by Bairoch, *Dritte Welt*, part I; *idem*, 'Die Landwirtschaft, der für die Einleitung der Entwicklung bestimmende Faktor' in Hermann Kellenbenz *et al.* (eds), *Wirtschaftliches Wachstum im Spiegel der Wirtschaftsgeschichte*, Darmstadt, 1978, pp. 83–99. A comprehensive analysis, including an excellent examination of all the relevant modern literature, can be found in Hartmut Elsenhans, 'Agrarverfassung, Akkumulationsprozeß und Demokratisierung' in Hartmut Elsenhans (ed.), *Agrarreform in der Dritten Welt*, Frankfurt, 1979, pp. 505–652. A brief discussion of the subject can now be found in Hermann Priebe and Wilhelm Hankel, 'Der Agrarsektor im Entwicklungsprozeß', *Entwicklung und Zusammenarbeit*, No. 5 (1981), 9–12, and Peter Mathias, 'A Concept or Two about Industrialization' in Jürgen Schneider (ed.), *Wirtschaftskräfte und Wirtschaftswege*, Vol. 4, Stuttgart, 1978, pp. 695–706. An interesting treatment of this question from

the viewpoint of economic and doctrinal history can be found in Rolf Steppacher, *Surplus, Kapitalbildung und wirtschaftliche Entwicklung*, Liebefeld and Bern 1976, ch. 2. How little pre-capitalist agrarian structures enabled steady development to take place is shown by their cyclical nature up to the middle of the nineteenth century (so-called crises of *type ancien*). On this see Wilhelm Abel, *Massenarmut und Hungerkrisen im vorindustriellen Deutschland*, Göttingen, 1977 (2nd ed.); *idem, Stufen der Ernährung*, Göttingen, 1981, as well as the excellent comprehensive study by Kriedte, *Peasants*.

96. For an early tentative typology see Mogens Boserup, 'Agrarstruktur und take-off' in Rudolf Braun *et al.* (eds), *Industrielle Revolution*, Cologne, 1972, pp. 309–30. Boserup distinguishes four main types of agrarian structure—the British, Eastern, French and Mediterranean—each of which provides different opportunities and restrictions for industrialization.

97. See Milward/Saul 2, ch. 8.

98. See data in Lewis, *Growth and Fluctuations*, pp. 296–7, table A16.

99. The data are taken from Lewis, *ibid.*, p. 163; Colin Clark, *The Conditions of Economic Progress*, London, 1940, pp. 246, 41/2, as well as Bairoch, *Commerce extérieur*, p. 172.

100. *Ibid.*

101. See the more detailed exposition on the development paths of export economies in Part II of the present volume.

102. On the following discussion, see O'Brien and Keyder, *Economic Growth*, especially ch. 5; François Caron, *An Economic History of Modern France*, London, 1979. On France, see now Colin Heywood, 'The Role of the Peasantry in French Industrialization, 1815–80', *Economic History Review*, 34 (1981), 359–76.

103. On this, see also Blum, *End of the Old Order*, ch. 12 and *passim*; also the interesting article by Kozo Yamamura, 'Preindustrial Landholding Patterns in Japan and England' in Albert Craig (ed.), *Japan: A Comparative View*, Princeton, N.J., 1979, pp. 276–323, especially pp. 302ff.

104. See also Adelman and Taft-Morris, op. cit. (note 47 above), 245–73.

105. On this see Menzel, *Autozentrierte Entwicklung*, ch. II, 2, where Danish development between 1870 and 1940 is covered in detail.

106. See Pollard, *Peaceful Conquest*; also *idem* (ed.), *Region und Industrialisierung*, Göttingen, 1980. See also Otto Büsch *et al.* (eds), *Industrialisierung und europäische Wirtschaft im 19. Jahrhundert*, Berlin, 1976.

107. See Milward/Saul 1–2. Also still worth reading on the subject is M. Weber, 'Kapitalismus und Agrarverfassung', *Zeitschrift für die gesamte Staatswissenschaft*, 108 (1952), pp. 431–52, and commenting on it W. Schluchter, *Rationalismus der Weltbeherrschung. Studien zu Max Weber*, Frankfurt, 1980, especially p. 159; also the discussion between Johannes Nichtweiss and Jürgen Kuczynski, The 'Prussian Path', *Zeitschrift für Geschichtswissenschaft*, 1 (1953), 687–717 and 2 (1954), 467–76.

108. See Milward/Saul 2, ch. 5; Alfred Hoffman, 'Grundlagen der Agrarstruktur der Donaumonarchie' in Alfred Hoffmann (ed.), *Österreich-Ungarn als Agrarstaat. Wirtschaftliches Wachstum und Agrarverhältnisse in Österreich im 19. Jahrhundert*, Vienna, 1978, pp. 11–65; Karl Dinklage, 'Die landwirtschaftliche Entwicklung' in Alois Brusatti (ed.), *Die wirtschaftliche Entwicklung. Die Habsburger Monarchie 1848–1918*, Vol. 1, Vienna, 1973,

pp. 403–61.

109. See Berend and Ránki, *Economic Development*; also particularly the earlier article by Nicolas Spulber, 'Changes in the Economic Structure of the Balkans, 1860–1960', in Charles and Barbara Jelavich (eds), *The Balkans in Transition*, Berkeley, Calif., 1963, pp. 346–75.

110. Menzel, *Auswege aus Abhängigkeit*, ch. II, 1.

111. See T. Bergh *et al.*, *Growth and Development: The Norwegian Experience, 1830–1980*, Oslo, 1980, especially ch. 2 and p. 19.

112. Johan de Vries, *The Netherlands' Economy in the Twentieth Century*, Assen, 1978; also the studies by Joel Mokyr, especially 'Industrialization and Poverty in Ireland and the Netherlands', *Journal of Interdisciplinary History*, 10, No. 3 (1980), pp. 429–58, and *idem, Industrialization in the Low Countries, 1795–1850*, London, 1966.

113. See the analysis of the development paths of export economies in Part II of the present volume.

114. On Greece, see the study by Kostas D. Lambos, *Abhängigkeit und fortge-schrittene Unterentwicklung dargestellt am Beispiel der Landwirtschaft Griechenlands*, Frankfurt, 1981; and that by Nicos Mouzelis, *Modern Greece: Facets of Underdevelopment*, London, 1978.

115. See Milward/Saul 2, pp. 446ff.

116. See Blum, *End of the Old Order*; also Rainer Schweers, *Kapitalistische Entwicklung und Unterentwicklung* Frankfurt, 1980, *passim*.

117. Irma Adelman, 'Economic Development and Political Change in Developing Countries', *Social Research*, 47, No. 2 (1980), 213–34; Erik Thorbecke, 'Agricultural and Economic Development', ibid., 290–304; Ozay Mehmet, *Economic Planning and Social Justice in Developing Countries*, London, 1978, especially part 1; and Gary S. Fields, *Poverty, Inequality and Development*, Cambridge, 1980.

118. See Ernest Feder, *Erdbeer-Imperialismus. Studien zur Agrarstruktur Lateinamerikas*, Frankfurt, 1980, pp. 233ff.; also the case-study on such agrarian reform in Sicily by Anton Blok, *Die Mafia in einem sizilianischen Dorf, 1860–1960*, Frankfurt, 1981, pp. 96ff.

119. See also H.H. Herlemann, 'Technisierungsstufen der Landwirtschaft. Versuch einer Erweiterung der Intensitätslehre Thünens', *Berichte über Landwirtschaft*, new series, 32 (1954), 335–42; William Nicholls, 'Development in Agrarian Economies: The Role of Agricultural Surplus, Population Pressures and Systems of Land Tenure' in Clifton R. Whalton (ed.), *Subsistence Agriculture and Economic Development*, Chicago, Ill., 1969, pp. 296–319.

120. For an interesting study on Asian societies, see Masao Kikuchi and Yujiro Hayami, 'Agricultural Growth against a Land Resource Constraint: A Comparative History of Japan, Taiwan, Korea and the Philippines', *Journal of Economic History*, 38, No. 4 (1978), pp. 839–64.

121. See Blum, *End of the Old Order*; Douglas North and Robert Paul Thomas, 'An Economic Theory of the Growth of the Western World', *Economic History Review*, 23, No. 1 (1970), pp. 1–17; also Henri Lepage, *Der Kapitalismus von morgen*, Frankfurt, 1979, chs. 3–4.

122. See Schweers, op. cit. (note 116 above). See also Philip Ehrensaft and Warwick Armstrong, 'Dominion Capitalism: A First Statement', *Australian and New Zealand Journal of Sociology*, 14 (1978), 353–63, esp. 358ff.

123. See the interesting case-study by Carville Earle and Ronald Hoffmann, 'The Foundation of the Modern Economy: Agriculture and the Cost of Labor in the United States and England, 1800–1860', *American Historical Review*, 85 (1980), 1055–94. On the general question, see Arbeitsgruppe Bielefelder Entwicklungssoziologen (ed.), *Subsistenzproduktion und Akkumulation*, Saarbrücken, 1979, as well as Schweers, *Kapitalistische Entwicklung*.

124. See W. Arthur Lewis, 'The Dual Economy Revisited', *Manchester School of Economic and Social Studies*, 47, No. 3 (1979), pp. 211–29; Joan Robinson, *Aspects of Development and Underdevelopment*, London, 1979, p. 8; Hartmut Elsenhans, 'Grundlagen der Entwicklung der kapitalistischen Weltwirtschaft' in Senghaas, *Kapitalistische Weltökonomie*, pp. 103–48.

125. Exceptions are familiar cases such as those of Argentina, Brazil, Mexico and India. But even here a considerable technological dependency on highly industrialized societies continues to characterize this sector. On this question, see M.R. Bhagavan, *Technological Transformation of Developing Countries*, Stockholm, 1980 (Economic Research Institute, School of Economics, Stockholm).

126. See Menzel, *Auswege aus Abhängigkeit*, ch. II, 3.

127. See Gabriel Tortella-Casares, *Banking, Railroads and Industry in Spain, 1829–1874*, New York, 1977; Miguel Artola (ed.), *Los ferrocarriles en Espana*, 1844–1943, 2 vols., Madrid, 1978.

128. Milward/Saul 2, ch. 8.

129. See William Beranek and Gustav Ranis (eds), *Science, Technology and Economic Development: A Historical and Comparative Study*, New York and London, 1978.

130. See Gourevitch, 'International Trade', *Journal of Interdisciplinary History*, 8 (1977), 282–313.

131. See Kemp, *Historical Patterns*, ch. 9.

132. This line is taken by Iida Tsuneo in 'Prerequisites for Asia's Modernization', *Japan Echo*, 8 (1981), 38–44.

133. Comparative historical analysis fully confirms the statement by Ehrensaft and Warwick that the maturing process of capitalism occurred only in those societies where the owners of capital (bourgeoisie) were successfully challenged politically by trade unions, labour parties and labour governments (and, one should add, where labour shortages emerged). 'Without a powerful historical challenge from below, individual sections of the bourgeoisie would be able to pursue but short-term interests, which could undermine the long-term foundations of the very bourgeoisie' (op. cit., note 122 above), 361.

134. See David Landes, 'The Creation of Knowledge and Technique, Today's Task and Yesterday's Experience', *Daedalus*, 109, No. 1 (1980), 11–120; also in general on the role of 'human capital' Richard A. Easterlin, 'Why Isn't the Whole World Developed?', *Journal of Economic History*, 41 (1981), 1–19, and Peter Lundgreen, *Bildung und Wirtschaftswachstum im Industrialisierungsprozeß des 19. Jahrhunderts*, Berlin, 1973.

135. See Karl W. Deutsch, 'National Integration: Some Concepts and Research Approaches', *Jerusalem Journal of International Relations*, 2, No. 4 (1977), 1–19, especially 12ff. Deutsch uses the image of 'a rather badly organized conveyor belt on the basis of stochastic processes'. In this

context, the time factor and the particular circumstances of delayed development are of considerable importance in the long term, as indicated by the continuing debate on the differences between western European/northern American and Japanese development. See *inter alia* Ronald P. Dore, 'The Late Development Effect' in Hans-Dieter Evers (ed.), *Modernization in South-East Asia*, London, 1973, pp. 65–80; Robert Cole, 'The Late-Developer Hypothesis: An Evaluation of Its Relevance for Japanese Employment Practises', *Journal of Japanese Studies*, 4, No. 1 (1978), 247–65; Ronald P. Dore, 'More about Late Development', ibid., 5, No. 10 (1979), 137–51.

136. See the references in notes 4 and 5 above.

137. On the following see Paul Bairoch, 'Geographical Structure and Trade Balance of European Foreign Trade from 1800 to 1970', *Journal of European Economic History*, 3, No. 3 (1974), 557–608; David S. Landes, 'The Great Drain and Industrialization: Commodity Flows from Periphery to Centre in Historical Perspective' (paper [69 pages] for the fifth world congress of the International Economic Association, Tokyo, 1967); Wolfram Fischer, 'Die Rohstoffversorgung der europäischen Wirtschaft in historischer Perspektive' in Jürgen Schneider *et al.* (eds), *Wirtschaftskräfte und Wirtschaftswege*, Vol. 4 (Übersee-und allgemeine Wirtschaftsgeschichte), Stuttgart, 1978, pp. 675–94; William Woodruff, 'The Emergence of an International Economy, 1700–1914', *Fontana Economic History of Europe*, Vol. 4 (2), London, 1973, ch. 11. Additionally, see Woodruff, *Impact of Western Man*; Milward/Saul 2, ch. 9; Walt W. Rostow, *The World Economy: History And Prospect*, London, 1978; Wolfram Fischer, *Die Weltwirtschaft im 20. Jahrhundert*, Göttingen, 1979.

138. On the following data see Bairoch, op cit. (note 137 above).

139. See Arghiri Emmanuel, 'White-Settler Colonialism and the Myth of Investment Imperialism', *New Left Review* (1972), 35–57.

140. This applies both to analyses dating from the brief period of free trade after 1860 (e.g. Marx) and to the theories of imperialism which, without due care, generalized from the imperialist endeavours of the turn of the century.

141. On the composition of the trade between Europe and the 'Third World', see particularly the studies by Landes and Fischer cited in note 137 above.

142. For example, copper from Chile, tin from Malaysia and Indonesia, wolfram from Burma, vanadium from Peru.

143. See especially Lewis, *Growth*, pp. 199ff.

144. Bairoch, op. cit. (note 137 above), p. 581.

145. See Lewis, *Growth and Fluctuations*; also *idem*, *Aspects of Tropical Trade, 1883–1965*, Stockholm, 1969.

146. On this, see above all Robert Brenner, 'The Origins of Capitalist Development: A Critique of Neo-Smithian Marxism', *New Left Review*, No. 104 (1977), 25–92; *idem*, 'Agrarian Class Structure and Economic Development in Pre-Industrial Europe', *Past and Present*, No. 70 (1976), 30–75; *idem*, 'Dobb on the Transition from Feudalism to Capitalism', *Cambridge Journal of Economics*, 2 (1978), 121–40.

147. A highly differentiated position has recently been developed by Kriedte, *Peasants*. On this, see also the assessment by Max Weber: 'The accumula-

tion of wealth produced by colonial trade—this must be emphasized in contrast with W. Sombart—was of little importance for the development of modern capitalism. Though colonial trade facilitated to a considerable extent the accumulation of wealth, it did not promote the specifically occidental pattern of work organization, since it was itself based on the principle of looting, and not on market-orientated profitability calculations. . . . However important sixteenth- to eighteenth-century slavery was for the accumulation of wealth, its impact on European economic organization was negligible. It bred a large number of rentiers, but contributed very little to the development of industrial production and capitalist organization' (*Wirtschaftsgeschichte*, Berlin, 1958, pp. 258/9). The same line is taken, from a comparative perspective, by Kindleberger, *Economic Response*, ch. 5, on 'Commercial Expansion and the Industrial Revolution'.

2 Growth and Equity: The Scandinavian Development Path

1. Statements of this kind can be found in recent dependency theory as well as in theories of peripheral capitalism, and also—even though differently argued—in the theoretical tradition of authors such as Prebisch, Singer and Myrdal.
2. Settler colonies face different conditions of development. Notable among these are factors such as a larger per capita resource endowment (land and raw materials), a lower population density and, often, skilled labour owing to immigration.
3. The following economic history literature is especially useful as an introduction to the Scandinavian development path: Milward/Saul 1, ch. 8; K.G. Hildebrand, 'Labour and Capital in the Scandinavian Countries in the Nineteenth and Twentieth Centuries', *Cambridge Economic History of Europe*, Vol. 7, part 1 (Cambridge, 1978), pp. 590–628; Lennart Jörberg, 'The Industrial Revolution in the Nordic Countries', *Fontana Economic History of Europe*, Vol. 4, part 2 (London, 1973), pp. 375–485; Lennart Jörberg and Olle Krantz, 'Scandinavia 1914–1970', *Fontana Economic History of Europe*, Vol. 6, part 2 (London, 1976), pp. 377–459.
4. Clark, *Conditions*, pp. 41/2.
5. *World Development Report 1979*, published by the World Bank, Washington, D.C., 1979.
6. On Finnish development, see in addition to the literature mentioned in note 3 above: Eino Jutikkala, *Geschichte Finnlands*, Stuttgart, 1976 (2nd ed.); D.G. Kirby, *Finland in the Twentieth Century: The History and an Interpretation*, London, 1979; E. Jutikkala, 'Industrialization as a Factor in Economic Growth in Finland' in *First International Conference of Economic History*, Stockholm, 1960, pp. 149–61; E. Jutikkala, 'Industrial Take-Off in an Underdeveloped Country: The Case of Finland', *Weltwirtschaftliches Archiv*, 88 (1962), 52–65; Helmut Witmaack, 'Finnlands Industrialisierung', *Jomsburg*, 3 (1939), 294–303; Timo Helelä *et al.*, 'Some Reflections on the Nature of the Growth Process in the Finnish Economy', *Weltwirtschaftliches Archiv*, 92 (1964), 222–31; Riitta Hjerppe and Erkki Pihkala, 'The Gross Domestic Product of Finland in 1860–1913: A Preliminary Estimate', *Economy and History*, 20, No. 2 (1977), 59–68; Kimmo Kiljunen,

'Finland in the International Division of Labour' in Seers, *Underdeveloped Europe*, pp. 279–302. See also Jussi Raumolin, 'Development Problems in the Scandinavian Periphery' (unpublished manuscript, Helsinki, 1979), Antonio D. Vittorio, 'The Scandinavian Economic History Review and the Economic Development of Finland', *Journal of European Economic History*, 5, No. 2 (1976), 485–94, provides an insight into the Scandinavian literature on Finnish development. An interesting comparison can be found in E. Allardt and W. Wesolowski, *Social Structure and Change: Finland and Poland. Comparative Perspective*, Warsaw, 1980. The following data are taken from the literature below. Data on the sectoral distribution of the work-force and the composition of the GDP in the late 1970s are drawn from the *World Development Report 1979* issued by the World Bank; the foreign trade data of the late 1970s can be found in *UNCTAD Handbook of International Trade and Development Statistics*, New York, 1979. These sources are not repeated at a later stage.

7. See also Hans Brems, 'Great-Power Tension and Economic Evolution in Finland since 1809', *Journal of Economic Issues*, 5 (1971), 1–19.

8. On these questions, see also Deutsch, *Nationalism*, pp. 196ff. In general, Robert Schweitzer, *Autonomie und Autokratie. Die Stellung des Großfürstentums Finnland im Russischen Reich in der zweiten Hälfte des '19. Jahrhunderts (1863–1899)*, Marburg, 1978.

9. On this, see above all the study by Kirby, *Finland*.

10. See A. Kieskinen, 'Regional Economic Growth in Finland, 1880–1952', *Scandinavian Economic History Review*, 9 (1961), 83–104.

11. On this, too, see the study by Kirby cited in note 6 above and Max Jacobson 'Substance and Appearance: Finland', *Foreign Affairs*, 58 (1980), 1034–44.

12. See the as yet unpublished manuscripts by Sven-Erik Aström, 'Commercial and Industrial Development in the Baltic Region in Relation to the Other Areas of Europe' and 'Foreign Trade and Forest Use in North-Eastern Europe and Finland, 1660–1860' (University of Helsinki, 1977–8).

13. On this development dynamics and the underlying problem, see Jaleel Ahmad, 'Import Substitution: A Survey of Policy Issues', *The Developing Economies*, 16, No. 4 (1978), 355–72.

14. See, for example, Jorma Ahvenainen, 'The Competitive Position of the Finnish Paper Industry in the Inter-War Years', *Scandinavian Economic History Review*, 22 (1974), 1–24.

15. On this, see in particular the studies by Jutikkala mentioned in note 6 above.

16. See the interesting contribution by Christine Hartinger, 'Wie Finnland zur Schwerindustrie kam', *Süddeutsche Zeitung*, (27 Dec. 1979). The following data are taken from this contribution and from the brochure 'Finnland stellt sich vor' (Helsinki, 1978).

17. On Norwegian development see, in addition to the general literature mentioned in note 3 above, Fritz Hodne, *An Economic History of Norway, 1850–1970*, Bergen, 1975; Sima Lieberman, *The Industrialization of Norway, 1800–1920*, Oslo, 1970; Edvard Bull, 'Industrialization as a Factor in Economic Growth' in *First International Conference of Economic History* (Stockholm, 1960), pp. 261–71; Fritz Hodne, 'Growth in a Dual Economy: The Norwegian Experience 1814–1914', *Economy and History*, 16

(1973), 81–110; T. Bergh *et al.*, *Growth and Development: The Norwegian Experience, 1830–1980*, Oslo, 1981. On development after 1945, see Bela Balassa, 'Industrial Development in an Open Economy: The Case of Norway', *Oxford Economic Papers*, new series, 21 (1969), 344–59.

18. On the Danish development path see particularly, in addition to the literature cited in note 3 above, Sevend Aage Hansen, *Early Industrialization in Denmark*, Copenhagen, 1970 (see also the detailed review of a book on Danish economic history by Hansen, which is available only in Danish, in *Economy and History*, 18 [1975], 83ff.). See also Kristof Glamann, 'Industrialization as a Factor in Economic Growth in Denmark since 1700' in *First International Conference in Economic History*, (Stockholm, 1960), pp. 115–28; Jens Warming, 'Die Industrialisierung Dänemarks unter besonderer Berücksichtigung der Landwirtschaft', *Weltwirtschaftliches Archiv*, 43 (1936), 441–71. Explicitly from the standpoint of development theory, see Menzel, part II, 2.

19. See the classic contribution by Kindleberger, *Economic Response*, pp. 19ff. On the general link between the configuration of political forces and the economic reaction to the world economic crisis of the 1870s and 1880s, see Gourevitch, 'International Trade', *Journal of Interdisciplinary History* 8 (1977), 281–313.

20. On the Swedish development path see, in addition to the general literature cited in note 3 above, Lennart Jörberg, *Growth and Fluctuation of Swedish Industry 1869–1912: Studies in the Process of Industrialization*, Stockholm, 1961; *idem*, 'Structural Change and Economic Growth: Sweden in the 19th Century', *Economy and History*, 8 (1965), 3–46; also Menzel, *Auswege aus Abhängigkeit*, part II, 3.

21. Hoffmann, *Stadien*, 121, 154/5.

22. For such a comparative study, see the following chapter.

23. On the present intra-Scandinavian discussion, see the articles in the two important English language periodicals, *Scandinavian Economic History Review* and *Economy and History*. Latterly, excellent studies can also be found in the periodical *Scandinavian Political Studies*, which has a rather more political science bias.

24. On Hirschman's linkage theory, see Albert O. Hirschman, 'A Generalized Linkage Approach to Development, with Special Reference to Staples', *Economic Development and Cultural Change*, 25, supplement (1977), 67–98 (Festschrift for Bert S. Hoselitz). See also John T. Thoburn, *Primary Commodity Exports and Economic Development*, London, 1977, especially chs. 1–2.

25. On this, see the article by J. Ahmad, op. cit. (note 13, above), which emphasizes the *structural* prerequisites for successful or unsuccessful import substitution industrialization.

26. On this, referring to western Europe in general, including Denmark, see Blum, *End of the Old Order*. More specifically on Scandinavia, see Øyvind Østerud, *Agrarian Structure and Peasant Politics in Scandinavia: A Comparative Study of Rural Response to Economic Change*, Oslo, 1978.

27. The structure of such inequality can be described as follows: 5 per cent of the population control 35 per cent of specific resources (e.g. land or income), 40 per cent control 60 per cent of resources, and 55 per cent control 5 per cent. Inequality is thus mitigated by the existence of a

sizeable middle class. The data cited correspond more or less with the distribution pattern in Danish agriculture in 1901. Quoted from Blum, *End of the Old Order*, p. 437.

28. See for example on Sweden, Lars G. Sandberg, 'The Case of the Impoverished Sophisticate: Human Capital and Swedish Economic Growth before World War 1', *Journal of Economic History*, 39 (1979), 225–41. Data on the high literacy rate of Scandinavia can be found in Peter Flora, *Modernisierungsforschung*, p. 170.

29. Also on Sweden, see *inter alia* Lars G. Sandberg, 'Banking and Economic Growth in Sweden before World War 1', *Journal of Economic History*, 38 (1978), 650–80.

30. See the study, translated from the Russian, by A.S. Kan, *Geschichte der Skandinavischen Länder*, Berlin 1978, chs 10 *et seq.*

31. In this connection autochthonous technological inventions and the growing importance of the engineering sector—outlined in the figures above—played of course an important role.

32. On this model, see P.F. Leeson, 'The Lewis Model and Development Theory', *Manchester School of Economic and Social Studies*, 47, No. 3 (1979), 196–210. That issue contains further contributions on Lewis's model on the occasion of the twenty-fifth anniversary of Arthur Lewis's famous study 'Economic Development with Unlimited Supplies of Labour', ibid., 22 (1954), 139–91. In this Lewis symposium the author himself provides a reappraisal: 'The Dual Economy Revisited', ibid., pp. 211–29. Explicitly on Lewis's model from the standpoint of development theory, see the studies by Fritz Hodne cited in note 17 above.

33. See Ingrid Semmingsen, 'Emigration from Scandinavia', *Scandinavian Economic History Review*, 20 (1972), 45–60; and, referring to Sweden, Claudius H. Riegler, 'Emigrationsphasen, Akkumulation und Widerstandsstrategien. Zu einigen Beziehungen der Arbeitsmigration von und nach Schweden 1850–1930' in Hartmut Elsenhans (ed.), *Migration und Wirtschaftsentwicklung*, Frankfurt, 1978, pp. 31–79.

34. Particularly in the inter-war period high unemployment constituted, of course, a retarding factor in the elimination of a large labour reserve, which is crucial for development.

35. On this see, for example, Erik Lundberg, 'Crisis of the Capitalist Economic System?' in Ulrich Gärtner and Jiri Kosta (eds), *Wirtschaft und Gesellschaft. Kritik und Alternativen*, Berlin, 1979, especially pp. 108ff.

36. On this see particularly Hans-Gerhard Voigt, *Probleme der weltwirtschaftlichen Kooperation*, Hamburg, 1969, and Alfons Lemper, *Handel in einer dynamischen Weltwirtschaft*, Munich, 1974.

37. See the comparative study by Blum, *End of the Old Order*, especially the passages on the de-oligarchization and de-feudalization of Danish agriculture. Cases where forest resources have resulted in a less marked development of the productive forces are covered in several as yet unpublished studies on Finland, the United States, Quebec and others by Jussi Raumolin (Helsinki, Finland).

38. On this see *inter alia* Berend and Ránki, *Economic Development*; and, *idem*, 'Foreign Trade and Industrialization of the European Periphery in the XIXth Century', *Journal of European Economic History*, 9, No. 3, (1980), 539–84.

39. On the role and dimensions of such an identity finding, see Deutsch, *Nationalism*.
40. See *inter alia* Montek Ahluvalia, Nicholas Carter and Holly Chenery, 'Growth and Poverty in Developing Countries', *Journal of Development Economics*, 6 (1979), 299–341; *World Development Report 1979*, Washington, D.C., 1979, ch. 7; David Morawetz, *Twenty-five Years of Economic Development, 1950–1975*, Baltimore, Md., 1978, and *idem*, 'Economic Lessons from Some Small Socialist Developing Countries', *World Development*, 8 (1980), 337–70.
41. On this problem, see Hartmut Elsenhans, 'Grundlagen der Entwicklung der kapitalistischen Weltwirtschaft' in Senghaas (ed.), *Kapitalistische Weltökonomie*, pp. 103–48.
42. On this, see also the article by Berend and Ránki, op. cit. (note 38 above).

3 Alternative Development Paths of Export Economies

1. The analysis is limited to countries which are not or are no longer colonies and whose export growth usually started at the end of the nineteenth century. Cases where political de-colonization happened after the Second World War will not be considered.
2. The term 'export economy' used here is derived from the important study by Jonathan V. Levin, *The Export Economies* (Cambridge, Mass., 1960), which has, however, been largely ignored in the development theory debate. With regard to their position within the international division of labour, such export economies correspond with the associative-dissociative type of autocentric development analysed in Part I.
3. On these data, see the literature on Denmark and Uruguay cited below.
4. On this theorem, see Johan Galtung, 'A Structural Theory of Imperialism', *Journal of Peace*, 8 (1971), 81–118.
5. See for example G. Pendle, *Uruguay: South America's First Welfare State*, London, 1963 (3rd ed.).
6. On Danish development, see the comprehensive study by Menzel, *Auswege aus Abhängigkeit*, ch. II, 2. On earlier literature, see particularly Svend Aage Hansen, *Early Industrialization in Denmark*, Copenhagen, 1970; Kristof Glamann, 'Industrialization as a Factor in Economic Growth in Denmark since 1700' in *First International Conference of Economic History* Stockholm, 1960), pp. 115–28; Jens Warming, 'Die Industrialisierung Dänemarks unter besonderer Berücksichtigung der Landwirtschaft', *Weltwirtschaftliches Archiv*, 43 (1936), 441–71.
7. Menzel, *Auswege aus Abhängigkeit*, chap. II.2.
8. *Ibid.*
9. On the positive function of Protestantism in populous territorial states during the second half of the nineteenth century, see Bairoch, *Commerce extérieur*.
10. Kindleberger, *Economic Response*, pp. 19ff. On the general connection between the configuration of political forces and economic reaction to the world economic crisis of the 1870s and 1880s, see Gourevitch, 'International Trade', *Journal of Interdisciplinary History*, 8 (1977), 281–313.
11. Menzel, *Auswege aus Abhängigkeit*, chap. II.2.

12. Clark, *Conditions*, p. 246.
13. Menzel, *Auswege aus Abhängigkeit*, chap. II.2.
14. See the data in the previous chapter.
15. On this, see the literature cited in note 10 above.
16. See Flora, *Modernisierungsforschung*, pp. 170ff.
17. On these problems, see the interesting study by Bruce F. Johnston; 'Agricultural Development and Economic Transformation: A Comparative Study of the Japanese Experience', *Food Research Institute Studies*, 3, 1962/3, 223–76, which compares the agricultural development of Japan, Taiwan and Denmark.
18. Menzel, *Auswege aus Abhängigkeit*, chap. II.2.
19. On the important role of increasing self-organization in successful development processes, see Deutsch, *Nationalism, passim*.
20. On the role of innovation in the development process, see Jochen Röpke, 'Innovation, Organisationstruktur und wirtschaftliche Entwicklung. Zu den Ursachen des wirtschaftlichen Aufstiegs von Japan', *Jahrbuch für Sozialwissenschaft*, 21 (1970), 203–31.
21. Menzel, *Auswege aus Abhängigkeit*, chap. II.2.
22. On the early industrialization phase in Denmark, see Hansen, *Early Industrialization*.
23. Menzel, *Auswege aus Abhängigkeit*, ch. II,2.7.
24. On the Uruguayan development path, see Dieter Nohlen, 'Uruguay' in *Handbuch der Dritten Welt*, Vol. 3 (Hamburg, 1976), pp. 444–60. See also L. Benvenuto *et al.*, *Uruguay hoy*, Buenos Aires, 1971; and the important article by Peter Winn, 'British Informal Empire in Uruguay in the Nineteenth Century', *Past and Present*, No. 73 (Nov. 1976), 100–26, which is based on a doctoral thesis.
25. Nohlen, op. cit. (note 24 above), p. 445.
26. See also Fernando H. Cardoso and Enzo Faletto, *Abhängigkeit und Entwicklung in Lateinamerika*, Frankfurt, 1976, pp. 56ff.
27. See Winn, op. cit. (note 24 above), 103.
28. The following exposition is based largely on the article by Winn, op. cit. (note 24 above).
29. Ibid., p. 110.
30. Ibid., p. 112.
31. Ibid., p. 113.
32. Nohlen, op. cit. (note 24 above), p. 446.
33. Winn, op. cit. (note 24 above), pp. 113/14.
34. Ibid., p. 114.
35. This term is derived from Levin, *Export Economies*. In relation to the Latin-American context, see the important study by Andreas Boeckh, *Interne Konsequenzen externer Abhängigkeiten*, Meisenheim am Glan, 1979, ch. II.
36. Winn, op. cit., (note 24 above), p. 120.
37. Nohlen, op. cit., (note 24 above), p. 447.
38. Ibid., pp. 447/8.
39. *UNCTAD 1979 Handbook*, p. 266.
40. The linking of agriculture and industry is crucially important for this process, which makes it problematic to disregard the agricultural sector when analysing import substitution industrialization and export diversification. For an analysis that fails to take the agricultural sector into

account, see Juergen Donges and Lotte Müller-Ohlsen, *Außenwirt-schaftsstrategien und Industrialisierung in Entwicklungsländern*, Tübingen, 1978. On this, see my review 'Um eine Kieler Studie von innen bittend' in *epd-Entwicklungspolitik*, Nos. 9–10 (1979), pp. 5–8 (reprinted in English translation in *Law and Society*, 13 [1980], No. 1, 58–64).

41. One could say of Uruguay what Sideri once said of Portugal—that this country which is dominated by agriculture has not even had the chance to become a proper agrarian nation. See Urs von der Mühll, *Die Unterentwicklung Portugals. Von der Weltmacht zur Halbkolonie Englands*, Frankfurt, 1978, p. 87. On a present-day agricultural export economy based on extensive production methods and on its limited development potential (in spite of high growth rates), see Eddy Lee, 'Export-led Rural Development: The Ivory Coast', *Development and Change*, 11 (1980), 607–42.

42. The data are taken from the *UNCTAD 1979 Handbook*, p. 461.

43. On the analysis of such defects, see Senghaas, 'Dissoziation' in *Kapitalistische Weltökonomie*, pp. 376–412.

44. See the data contained in Nohlen, op. cit. (note 24 above), pp. 449ff.

45. Ibid.

46. In 1972 the proportion of this sector in various countries (as a percentage of net industrial product) was as follows: Australia, 25 per cent; Austria, 22 per cent; Belgium, 29 per cent; Canada, 26 per cent; Finland, 25 per cent; France, 35 per cent; FRG, 33 per cent; Great Britain, 32 per cent; Italy, 27 per cent; Japan, 36 per cent; Netherlands, 22 per cent; Norway, 26 per cent; Sweden, 35 per cent; Switzerland, 42 per cent; United States, 31 per cent. These data are taken from the *World Development Report 1979*, p. 155.

47. The figures are taken from the *UNCTAD 1979 Handbook*, pp. 210, 261.

48. Ibid., pp. 293–5.

49. See Osvaldo Sunkel, 'La dependencia y la heterogeneidad estructural', *El Trimestre Económico*, 45/1, No. 177 (1978), 3–20; and Wassily Leontief, 'The Structure of Development', *Scientific American*, 209, No. 3 (1963), 148–66.

50. On this, see the contribution by Carter Goodrich, 'Argentina as a New Country', *Comparative Studies in Society and History*, 7 (1964/5), 70–88, especially 73ff.

51. See pp. 143–4 below.

52. On the distribution structure in Danish agriculture see Menzel, *Auswege aus Abhängigkeit*, chap. II.2.

53. On the distribution structure in Uruguayan agriculture, see Nohlen, op. cit. (note 24 above), p. 451. For a general study, see Ernest Feder, *Erdbeer-Imperialismus. Studien zur Agrarstruktur Lateinamerikas*, Frankfurt, 1980.

54. See also the study by Levin, *Export Economies*.

55. The historical experience of import substitution industrialization being blocked as a result of gross inequalities in the domestic structures is today being repeated in the Third World. On this, see the study by Jaleel Ahmad, *Import Substitution, Trade and Development* (Greenwich, 1978), as well as the summary *idem*, 'A Survey of Policy Issues', *The Developing Economy*, 16, No. 4 (1978), 355–72. Ahmad rightly emphasizes the socio-structural and institutional factors limiting broad-based import substitu-

tion industrialization.

56. See Hoffmann, *Stadien*; also Arghiri Emmanuel, 'Myths of Development versus Myths of Underdevelopment', *New Left Review*, No. 85 (1974), 61–82.
57. This term has been suggested by K.W. Deutsch.
58. See Senghaas, *Weltwirtschaftsordnung*, pp. 65ff.
59. On the different agricultural development patterns in Europe and the resulting differences in the realization of the development potential, see Blum, *End of the Old Order*. On the differing class constellations and their crucial influence on the development process, see Wehler, *Klassen*.
60. This was the situation typical of eastern Europe and Romania. On this, see the later section on Hungary and Romania, pp. 218–21.
61. Bairoch, *Commerce extérieur*.
62. On the concept of over-determination in the analysis of social structures, see Karl W. Deutsch and Dieter Senghaas, 'A Framework for a Theory of War and Peace' in Albert Lepawsky *et al.* (eds), *The Search for World Order*, New York, 1971, pp. 23–46 (Festschrift for Quincy Wright).
63. See Walt W. Rostow, *The World Economy: History and Prospect*, London, 1978.
64. Nohlen, op. cit. (note 24 above), p. 460; also *inter alia* Klaus Esser, *Lateinamerika. Industrialisierungsstrategien und Entwicklung*, Frankfurt, 1979, pp. 218ff.
65. On the development of New Zealand, see W.B. Sutch, *The Quest for Security in New Zealand, 1840–1966*, London, 1966; Keith Sinclair, *A History of New Zealand*, Harmondsworth, Middx, 1969; Muriel Lloyd Prichard, *An Economic History of New Zealand to 1939*, Oakland, Calif., 1970.
66. See the study by W. Plügge, *Innere Kolonisation in Neuseeland*, Jena, 1916. It is still worth reading.
67. Ibid., p. 124.
68. Ibid., p. 38.
69. Ibid., p. 61. See also J.D. Gould, 'The Twilight of the Estates, 1891–1910', *Australian Economic History Review*, 10, No. 1 (1970), 1–26.
70. In this context New Zealand's development strongly calls to mind that of Australia at the time. On this, see Richard N. Rosecrance, 'The Radical Culture of Australia' in Louis Hartz, *The Founding of New Societies*, New York, 1964, pp. 275–318.
71. See G.R. Hawke, 'Acquisitiveness and Equality in New Zealand's Economic Development', *Economic History Review*, 32, No. 3 (1979), 376–90. On the same question, see also Warwick Armstrong, 'Land, Class, Colonialism: The Origins of Dominion Capitalism' in *New Zealand and the World* (Festschrift for Wolfgang Rosenberg), Canterbury, N.Z., 1980, pp. 28–44.
72. In this respect, too, there are numerous parallels with Australian development. See, for example, the article by Rosecrance cited in note 70 above.
73. See the data in Plügge, *Innere Kolonisation*, p. 126.
74. Ibid. See also Lewis, *Growth*, p. 196. Here New Zealand is reported as having in 1913—after Canada and Australia—the third highest per capita consumption of manufactures in the world. On the high per capita production of manufactures in New Zealand, see ibid., p. 163. Moreover, it should be pointed out here that as early as the turn of the century New

Zealand was renowned for active state-interventionist policies, especially
in the sphere of social security, through which minimum wages, standardized wages and employment protection were implemented. In order
to study these achievements, the Webbs and André Siegfried travelled to
New Zealand at the beginning of the century. On this, see *inter alia* André
Siegfried, *Neu-Seeland, eine sozial- und wirtschaftspolitische Untersuchung*, Berlin, 1910.

75. On the following, see W. Lutz, 'Neuseeland', in *Fischer Länderkunde
    Südostasien—Australien*, Frankfurt, 1975, pp. 418ff.

76. See Clark, *Conditions*, p. 246.

77. Lutz, op. cit. (note 75 above), p. 428.

78. Which is the reason why the New Zealand government is still exploring
    possibilities for further diversifying the local economy. For an interesting
    document in this connection, see *New Zealand in an Enlarged EEC*, Wel-
    lington (*New Zealand Monetary and Economic Council Report*, No. 19), 1970,
    especially pp. 12ff. On the lack of coherence, though greatly over-
    emphasized, see Warwick Armstrong, 'New Zealand: Imperialism, Class
    and Uneven Development', *Australian and New Zealand Journal of Sociology*,
    14(1978), 297–303.

79. In addition to the countries referred to below, Finland should be men-
    tioned. Her development was based mainly on wood products, while in
    only a few parts of the country agricultural modernization had led to the
    emergence of dairy farming (butter exports). An analysis of Finland has
    been made in ch. 2 of the present volume. Another interesting case of
    agriculture-based export development is Israel. For, on the one hand, the
    agricultural resource endowment of that country was initially not at all
    favourable and the agricultural potential had to be wrested from nature;
    and, on the other hand, the Israeli development path points in the same
    direction as that of Denmark, the Netherlands and New Zealand, namely
    in the direction of diversification and productivity increases across the
    whole economy, accompanied by the emergence of highly specialized
    sectors of production orientated towards the domestic market as well as
    the world market. On Israeli development, see for a summary Christiane
    Busch-Lüty, 'Entwicklungsphänomen Israel. Vom Kibbuz zum Kapi-
    talismus?', *Aus Politik und Zeitgeschichte, Beilage zum Parlament*, No. 4/1979
    (27 Jan. 1979), 3–29; also Haim Barkai, *Growth Patterns of the Kibbutz
    Economy*, Amsterdam, 1977. On the data see Tables 5–8, pp. 115–18.

80. On the data on Iceland, see *World Development Report 1979*, p. 195; also in
    general T.K. Berry, *A History of Scandinavia*, London, 1979, p. 370, as well
    as Jussi Raumolin, 'Development Problems in the Scandinavian Per-
    iphery' (unpublished manuscript, Helsinki, 1979).

81. On the development of the Netherlands, see Milward/Saul 2, pp. 182ff.;
    see also Vries, *Netherlands Economy*; J.A. de Jonge, 'Industrial Growth in
    the Netherlands, 1850–1914', *Acta Historiae Neerlandica*, 5(1971), 158–212;
    I.J. Brugmans, 'The Economic History of the Netherlands in the 19th
    and 20th Century', ibid., 2(1967), 260–98; of the older literature particu-
    larly, Ernst Baasch, *Holländische Wirtschaftsgeschichte*, Jena, 1927. On early
    Dutch development, see Joel Mokyr, *Industrialization in the Low Countries
    1795–1850*, New Haven, Conn., 1976.

82. Milward/Saul 2, p. 184.

83. Ibid.
84. On the economic history literature on Ireland, see L.A. Clarkson, 'The Writing of Irish Economic and Social History since 1968', *Economic History Review*, 33, No. 1(1980), 100–11. See above all L.M. Cullen (ed.), *The Formation of the Irish Economy*, Cork, 1969.
85. On the following, see particularly Raymond Crotty, 'Capitalist Colonialism and Peripheralization: The Irish Case' in Seers, *Underdeveloped Europe*, pp. 225–35.
86. The Irish experience, incidentally, led Marx to abandon his anti-Listian stance with regard to free trade and/or protectionism in favour of a protectionist position. On this, see the informative article by Kenzo Mohri, 'Marx and Underdevelopment', *Monthly Review*, 30, No. 11(1979), 32–42. That article reveals the extent to which the later comments of Marx on the Irish question contradict his early euphoric characterization of the consequences of the expansion of British capitalism in India.
87. Crotty, op. cit. (note 85 above), p. 228.
88. Bernard Schaffer, 'Regional Development and Institutions of Favour: Aspects of the Irish Case' in Seers, *Underdeveloped Europe*, pp. 237–56, figs. p. 237.
89. Ibid., *passim*.
90. On the role of such external conditions, including that of export fluctuations, see John R. Hanson, 'Export Instability in Historical Perspective: Further Results', *Journal of Economic History*, 40, No. 1(1980), 17–23.
91. For a comparable assessment, see the interesting article by J.W. McCarty, 'Australia as a Region of Recent Settlement in the Nineteenth Century', *Australian Economic History Review*, 13(1973), 148–67.
92. See Kuznets, *Economic Growth*, ch. 3.
93. See Hoffmann, *Stadien*.
94. On Belgian development, see Lebrun, *Essai sur la révolution*.
95. On Swiss development, see Menzel, *Auswege ous Abhängigkeit*, ch. II, 1. On Switzerland's present position in the world economy, see Peter J. Katzenstein, 'Capitalism in one Country? Switzerland in the International Economy' (Paper No. 13 of the Western Societies Program, Cornell University, Ithaca, N.Y., 1980).
96. On this question, Beranek and Ranis, *Science, Technology*.
97. Sutch reports on New Zealand that as early as the turn of the century that country began to export simple capital goods, e.g. wool presses to South America, ploughs and harrows to South Africa, refrigeration equipment to Australia. See Sutch. *Quest*, p. 74.
98. With regard to the distribution of the labour force and GDP between the primary, secondary and tertiary sectors, such a profile is reflected in a ratio of about 8:37:55.
99. See, however, the special cases of New Zealand, Australia and Canada which continue to have a high percentage of agricultural and mineral raw materials exports. These cases are further discussed from this angle below.
100. David Morawetz, *Twenty-five Years of Economic Development, 1950–1975*, London, 1977, p. 41.
101. See pp. 72–9.
102. See Douglas C. North and Robert Paul Thomas, 'An Economic Theory of the Growth of the Western World', *Economic History Review*, 23(1970),

1–17, and, *idem, The Rise of the Western World.* See for a summary Lepage, *Kapitalismus,* ch. 4; also Rondo Cameron, 'Pourquoi l'industrialisation européenne fut-elle inégale?' in Pierre Léon *et al., L'Industrialisation en Europe au XIXme siècle,* Paris, 1972, pp. 524-31; and the article by Röpke, op. cit. (note 20 above).

103. On this see Boeckh, *Interne Konsequenzen,* in which the whole question is discussed using the examples of Peru, Colombia and Venezuela.

104. See Sutch, *Quest,* in which these conflicts, as they developed in New Zealand, are described in detail.

105. Gunnar Myrdal, *Ökonomische Theorie und unterentwickelte Regionen,* Frankfurt, 1974, especially ch. 2.

106. Fabian, *Kubanische Entwicklungsweg.* In the same book, see also my preface (pp. v–xxiii) on the importance of the Cuban development path from the perspective of development history.

107. See the following chapter on socialism.

108. Among the countries rich in resources but low in population, Sweden should also be mentioned. See Menzel, *Autozentrierte Entwicklung,* ch. II, 3.

109. Data on Hungarian and Romanian grain production and Argentine grain exports can be found in Lewis, *Growth,* pp. 290ff.

110. I.T. Berend and G. Ránki, *Hungary: A Century of Economic Development,* New York, 1974, p. 42.

111. Milward/Saul 2, p. 448.

112. On Hungarian development, see above all Berend and Ránki, *Hungary*; further, Wilhelm Offergeld, *Grundlagen und Ursachen der industriellen Entwicklung Ungarns,* Jena, 1914; Berend and Ránki, 'Ungarns wirtschaftliche Entwicklung 1849–1918' in Alois Brusatti (ed.), *Die wirtschaftliche Entwicklung,* Vol. 1 of *Die Habsburger Monarchie 1848–1918,* Vienna, 1973, pp. 462–567; *idem, Economic Development*; Andrew C. Janos, *The Politics of Backwardness in Hungary, 1825–1945,* Princeton, N.J., 1981; and Joseph Held (ed.), *The Modernization of Agriculture: Rural Transformation in Hungary, 1848–1975,* Boulder, Colo., 1980.

113. Berend and Ránki, *Hungary,* table 12.

114. Ibid.

115. Ibid., p. 62.

116. See especially the studies by Berend and Ránki as well as L. Katus, 'Economic Growth in Hungary during the Age of Dualism, 1867–1913' in *Sozial-ökonomische Forschungen zur Geschichte von Ost-Mitteleuropa* (Budapest, 1970), pp. 35–87.

117. On Romanian development in the nineteenth and early twentieth centuries, see Milward/Saul 2; further, Jowitt, *Social Change in Romania*; and Stefan Welzk, 'Entwicklungspolitische Lernprozesse: Rumänische Erfahrungen', *Befreiung,* Nos. 19/20(1980), 70–118.

118. Feder, *Erdbeer-Imperialismus.*

119. See Blum, *End of the Old Order.*

120. In this connection we use the example of Thailand, well aware that, in geographical-ecological and climatic terms, it is not comparable with the cases discussed above or with those which will be discussed later. In this context it is, however, the refutation of a potential objection with which we are concerned.

121. On Thai development, see J.C. Ingram, *Economic Change in Thailand,*

1850–1970, Stanford, Calif., 1971 (2nd ed.); David B. Johnston, 'Rice Cultivation in Thailand: The Development of an Export Economy by Indigenous Capital and Labour', *Modern Asian Studies*, 15, No. 1 1981, 107–26.

122. See David Feeny, 'Paddy, Princes and Productivity: Irrigation and Thai Agricultural Development, 1900–1940', *Explorations in Economic History*, 16(1979), 132–50.

123. This agrarian structure can still be observed today. See Friedrich W. Fuhs and Karl E. Weber, 'Thailand' in *Handbuch der Dritten Welt*, Vol. 4 (Hamburg, 1978), pp. 663–89: 'Agriculture is still based on medium-sized and small farms. About 75 per cent of all farms are smaller than 5 hectares [12 acres]. Large landholdings exist only in small numbers—mainly in the form of rubber plantations in the southern part of the country. Roughly two-thirds of the agricultural units are worked by owner-farmers. The proportion of tenant farmers is said to be rising fast, however. Moreover, it has to be taken into consideration that some provinces of the central region are dominated by large landholdings which, however, are worked by small farmers. In those regions tenant farming is so widespread that it is becoming a social problem' (p. 686). See also Pasuk Phongpaichit, 'The Open Economy and Its Friends: The "Development" of Thailand', *Pacific Affairs*, 53, No. 3(1980), 440–60.

124. See Levin, *Export Economies*; Boeckh, *Interne Konsequenzen*, and Giovanni Caprio, *Haiti—wirtschaftliche Entwicklung und periphere Gesellschaftsformation*, Frankfurt, 1979.

125. Stephen A. Resnick, 'The Decline of Rural Industry under Export Expansion: A Comparison Among Burma, Philippines, and Thailand, 1878–1938', *Journal of Economic History*, 30, No. 1(1970), 51–73.

126. Ibid.

127. David Feeny, 'Competing Hypotheses of Underdevelopment: A Thai Case Study', *Journal of Economic History*, 39(1979), 113–27.

128. Ibid., p. 122.

129. Lewis, *Growth*, pp. 221ff.

130. The debate relates to different interpretations of slavery in the southern states of the USA. A cliometrical position which has neo-classical roots can be found in Robert William Fogel and Stanley L. Engermann, *Time on the Cross*, 2 vols, Boston, 1974. This study explains why the plantation economy was profitable in capitalist terms: it represented a form of organization comparable to the factory system which allowed the reaping of economies of scale. The counter-position can be found in Eugene D. Genovese, *The Political Economy of Slavery*, New York, 1961; *idem, The World the Slaveholders Made*, New York, 1969; *idem, Roll Jordan, Roll: The World the Slaves Made*, New York, 1976. In Genovese's view slavery was a profitable but inefficient system. For a discussion of both positions, see Wallerstein, *Capitalist*, pp. 202ff; and Christopher Chase-Dunn, 'The Development of Core Capitalism in the Antebellum United States' in Albert Bergesen (ed.), *Studies of the Modern World System*, London, 1980, pp. 189–230.

131. See the seminal article by Eugene D. Genovese and Elizabeth Fox-Genovese, 'The Slave Economies in Political Perspective', *Journal of American History*, 65, No. 4(1979), 7–23. See also Sigrid Meuschel, *Kapitalismus oder Sklaverei*, Frankfurt, 1981.

132. On this, see the equally seminal article by Jonathan M. Wiener, 'Class

Structure and Economic Development in the American South, 1865–1955', *American Historical Review*, 84, No. 4(1979), 970–92.

133. On the favourable external terms of trade enjoyed by the staple goods from the southern states, see Thomas F. Huertas, 'Damnifying Growth in the Antebellum South', *Journal of Economic History*, 39, No. 1(1979), 87–100. The article demonstrates how, from a comparative-static perspective, the South's specialization on the production of its typical staple goods could become a structural trap of the same kind as was to be found in many export economies between the mid-nineteenth century and the end of the First World War as a result of favourable terms of trade. See, for example, on the Brazilian coffee export economy the contribution by Carlos Manuel Pelaez, 'The Theory and Reality of Imperialism in the Coffee Economy of 19th Century Brazil', *Economic History Review*, 29(1976), pp. 276–90.

134. On this question see Boeckh, *Interne Konsequenzen*, pp. 99f., and, *idem*, 'Grundrente und Staat. Argentinien und Venezuela im 19. und 20. Jahrhundert' in Rolf Hanisch und Rainer Tetzlaff (eds), *Historische Konstitutionsbedingungen des Staates in Entwicklungsländern*, Frankfurt, 1980, pp. 47–98.

135. See particularly the studies by Genovese cited in notes 130 and 131 above; also Héctor Pérez Brignoli, 'The Economic Cycle in Latin American Agricultural Export Economies (1880–1930)', *Latin American Research Review*, 15, No. 2(1980), 3–33, especially pp. 18ff. On Max Weber's early treatment of this question, see Wolfgang Schluchter, *Rationalismus der Weltbeherrschung*, pp. 165ff.

136. On the (in my view) first European case of far-reaching peripheralization and the underlying class struggles between agrarian oligarchy, commercial capital and the Church on the one hand, and a rising industrial bourgeoisie on the other, see the study on Portugal by Urs von der Mühll, cited in note 41 above, especially ch. 10 on 'Portugal's Second Attempt to Develop Autonomously' under Marques de Pombal. On the question in general, see André Gunder Frank, *Abhängige Akkumulation und Unterentwicklung*, Frankfurt, 1980.

137. On Spanish development, see Jordi Nadal, *El fracaso de la revolución industrial en España 1814–1913*, Barcelona, 1975; Niclas Sáchez-Albornoz, *España hace un siglo. Una economía dual*, Madrid, 1977; Gabriel Tortella-Casares et al., *Ensayos sobre la economía española a mediados del siglo XIX*, Madrid, 1970. A good overview of the literature is provided by Angus McKay, 'Recent Literature on Spanish Economic History', *Economic History Review*, 31, No. 1(1978), 129–45; also by Rafael Aracil and M. Garcia Bonafé, 'Aportaciones historiográficas sobre la economía española contemporánea', in *idem* (eds), *Lecturas de historia económica de España*, Vol. 2, (Barcelona, 1977), pp. 379–491.

138. See Henry Kamen, 'The Decline of Spain: A Historical Myth?', *Past and Present*, No. 81(Nov. 1978), 24–50, quotation pp. 30/1. On this, see also Carlo M. Cipolla, *Before the Industrial Revolution: European Society and Economy, 1000–1700*, London, 1976, pp. 244ff.

139. See the article by Kamen, op. cit. (note 138 above).

140. See Joseph Harrison, *An Economic History of Modern Spain*, Manchester, 1978, ch. 1.

141. Juan J. Linz and Armando de Miguel, 'Within-Nation Differences and Comparisons: The Eight Spains' in Richard L. Merritt and St. Rokkan (eds), *Comparing Nations*, New Haven, Conn., 1966, pp. 267–319; further, Juan J. Linz, 'Early State-Building and Late Peripheral Nationalisms against the State: The Case of Spain' in S.N. Eisenstadt and St. Rokkan (eds), *Building Nations and States*, Vol. 2 (London, 1973), pp. 32–116.

142. See Gabriel Tortella-Casares, *Banking, Railroads and Industry in Spain, 1829-1974*, New York, 1977; as well as in general on this question, I.T. Berend and G. Ránki, 'Die Rolle des Staats in der wirtschaftlichen Entwicklung des 19. Jahrhunderts' in Jürgen Schneider (ed.), *Wirtschaftskräfte und Wirtschaftswege*, Vol. 3: *Auf dem Wege zur Industrialisierung*, Stuttgart, 1978, pp. 325–46 (Festschrift for H. Kellenbenz).

143. On recent development, see Juergen Donges, *La industrialisación en España*, Barcelona, 1976; *idem*, 'From an Autarchic towards a Cautiously Outward-Looking Industrialization Policy: The Case of Spain', *Weltwirtschaftliches Archiv*, 107(1971), 33–75; Alison Wright, *The Spanish Economy 1959-1967*, New York, 1977; Stefan A. Musto, *Spanien und die Europäische Gemeinschaft. Der schwierige Weg zur Mitgliedschaft*, Bonn, 1977.

144. See *inter alia* Carter Goodrich, 'Argentina as a New Country', *Comparative Studies in Society and History*, 7(1964–5), 70–88; Arthur Smithies, 'Argentina and Australia', *American Economic Review*, 55, No. 2(1965), 17–30; Aldo Ferrer and E.L. Wheelwright, *Industrialization in Argentina and Australia: A Comparative Study*, Buenos Aires, 1966 (Instituto Torcuato di Tella. Centro de Investigaciones Económicas, mimeographed); Theodor H. Moran, 'The Development of Argentina and Australia', *Comparative Politics*, No. 1(1970), 71–92; McCarty, op. cit. (note 91 above); Barrie Dyster, 'Argentine and Australian Development Compared', *Past and Present*, No. 84 (Aug. 1979), 91–110; and especially John Fogarty et al. (eds), *Argentina y Australia*, Buenos Aires, 1979.

145. See the data in Clark, *Conditions*, pp. 41–2.

146. Dyster, op. cit. (note 144 above).

147. Ibid., p. 96.

148. Ibid., p. 106.

149. Ibid., p. 110.

150. See also Arghiri Emmanuel, *Unequal Exchange: A Study of the Imperialism of Trade*, London, 1972, pp. 357ff. (appendix IV).

151. On the following, see above all Moran, op. cit. (note 144 above). See also Philip Ehrensaft and Warwick Armstrong, 'Dominion Capitalism: A First Statement', *Australian and New Zealand Journal of Sociology*, 14(1978), 352–403, especially 358ff.

152. On Australian development, see R.V. Jackson, *Australian Economic Development in the Nineteenth Century*, Canberra, 1977; James Griffin (ed.), *Essays in Economic History of Australia*, Milton, N.S.W., 1970. For an excellent overview of the present state of the economic history literature, see C.D. Schedvin, 'Midas and the Merino: A Perspective on Australian Economic Historiography', *Economic History Review*, 32, No. 4(1979), 542–56.

153. On this, see the important study by Atilio Alberto Boron, 'The Formation and Crisis of the Liberal State in Argentina, 1880–1930', (mimeographed manuscript, dissertation, Harvard University, Cambridge, Mass., 1976).

154. The correspondence between politically coherent development and econ-

omically coherent development and politically and economically defective development is pointed out by Moran, op. cit. (note 144 above). See also Philip McMichael, 'Settlers and Primitive Accumulation: Foundations of Capitalism in Australia', *Review*, 4, No. 2(1980), 307–34.

155. On the structural foundations of Argentine development, see Jonathan C. Brown, *A Socioeconomic History of Argentina 1776–1860*, Cambridge, Mass., 1979; Laura Randall, *An Economic History of Argentina in the Twentieth Century*, New York, 1978; Carlos F. Diaz-Alejandro, *Essays on the Economic History of the Argentine Republic*, New Haven, Conn., 1970. On the current problems, see *inter alia* Moisés Ikonicoff, 'La industrialización y el modelo de desarrollo de la Argentina', *El Trimestre Económico*, 47, No. 185(1980), 159–92; Marcos Kaplan, *Social Change and the Political System in Argentina*, Ebenhausen, 1979 (publication of the *Stiftung Wissenschaft und Politik*); *idem*, '50 anos de historia Argentina (1925–1975). El labyrinto de la frustración' in Pablo Gonzalez Casanova (ed.), *América Latina. Historia de medio siglo*, Mexico, 1977, pp. 1–73; Lawrence A. Alschuler, 'The Struggle of Argentina within the New International Division of Labour' (paper for the Conference of the International Peace Research Association, Königstein, 1979). See also the important study by Alain Rouquié, *Pouvoir militaire et société politique en République Argentine*, Paris, 1977.

156. On this, see also Peter Waldmann, 'Argentinien', in *Handbuch der Dritten Welt*, Vol. 3(Hamburg, 1976), pp. 13–36, especially pp. 16ff.

157. See Goodrich, op. cit. (note 144 above), pp. 73ff. In an important article, Aldo Ferrer pointed out that, since the military take-over in the mid-1970s, the share of wages and salaries in the GDP dropped from 47 per cent (1975) to 34 per cent (1979), while the investment share rose by only 1.2 per cent. The military *coup* obviously brought about a shift in the income distribution in favour of higher income groups and their luxury consumption. See Aldo Ferrer, 'The Argentine Economy, 1976–1979', *Journal of Interamerican Studies and World Affairs*, 22, No. 2(1980), 131–62, especially 147; also Adolfo Canitrot, 'Discipline as the Central Objective of Economic Policy: An Essay on the Economic Programme of the Argentine Government since 1976', *World Development*, 8, No. 11(1980), 913ff.

158. On this, see also the article on radical culture in Australia by Rosecrance, op. cit. (note 70 above).

159. On Canadian development, see W.T. Easterbrook and M.H. Watkins (eds) *Approaches to Canadian Economic History*, Toronto, 1967; also, for a summary, Kemp, *Historical Patterns*, ch. 9; and Menzel, *Auswege aus Abhängigkeit*, ch. II,2.4.

160. On South African development, see Philip Ehrensaft, 'Polarized Accumulation and the Theory of Economic Dependence: The Implications of South African Semi-Industrial Capitalism' in Peter Gutkind and Immanuel Wallerstein (eds), *The Political Economy of Contemporary Africa*, London, 1976, pp. 58–89. See also Ruth Milkman, 'Contradictions of Semi-Peripheral Development: The South African Case' in Walter Goldfrank (ed.), *The World System of Capitalism: Past and Present*, London, 1978, pp. 261–84.

161. The 'verticality indicator' with regard to the trade structure devised by Galtung (op. cit., note 4 above) is therefore very high in these cases: Argentina, 0.91; Australia, 0.86; New Zealand, 0.97; South Africa, 0.58.

162. Of course, this applies particularly to the segregation and apartheid policy in South Africa. Two excellent articles describe how in South Africa labour is obtained in the cheapest possible way: Harold Wolpe, 'Capitalism and Cheap Labour-Power in South Africa: From Segregation to Apartheid', *Economy and Society*, 1, No. 4(1972), 425–56; and Martin Legassick, 'South Africa: Capital Accumulation and Violence', *Economy and Society*, 3, No. 3(1974), 253–91.
    On the question in general see Emmanuel, *Unequal Exchange*; Goodrich, op. cit. (note 144 above.)

163. It is obvious that the density of the domestic economic structure, and consequently its transformation and innovation capacity, depend on the political and technological autonomy of local economic groups. The growing internationalization of capital and labour has brought considerable problems in a number of the above-mentioned economies. This has recently led Michel Chossudovsky to comment that Canada is a high-wage periphery. On the present problems of countries like Canada, Australia and New Zealand, see for example, Michel Chossudovsky, 'Is the Canadian Economy Closing Down?' in Fred Caloren *et al.*, *Is the Canadian Economy Closing Down?*, Montreal, 1978, pp. 131–61.

164. Irving B. Kravis, 'Trade as a Handmaiden of Growth: Similarities between the Nineteenth and Twentieth Centuries', *Economic Journal*, 80(1970), 850–72.

165. Ibid., p. 869. For a similar assessment, see also T.C. Smout, 'Scotland and England: Is Dependency a Symptom or a Cause of Underdevelopment?', *Review*, 3(1980), 601–30.

166. On the different linkage potential of staple goods, see Albert Hirschman, op. cit. (ch. 2, note 24 above).

167. See for a summary M.H. Watkins, 'A Staple Theory of Economic Growth' in Easterbrook and Watkins, *Approaches*, pp. 49–73.

168. See, for example, J.W. McCarty, 'The Staple Approach in Australian Economic History', *Business Archives and History*, 4(1964), 1–22; D.G. North, *The Economic Growth of the United States 1790–1860*, Englewood Cliffs, N.J., 1961. For a discussion of the relevant literature of the past two decades, see Thoburn, *Commodity Exports*, part I.

169. See Kemp, *Historical Patterns*, as well as Menzel, *Autozentrierte Entwicklung* ch. II,2.2.

170. Watkins, op. cit. (note 167 above), pp. 53–4.

171. Based on early studies by Albert Hirschman.

172. Robert Baldwin, 'Patterns of Development in Newly Settled Regions', *Manchester School of Economic and Social Studies*, 24(1956), 161–79; *idem*, 'Export Technology and Development from a Subsistence Level', *Economic Journal*, 73(1963), 80–93. On the strategic importance in the development process of domestic distribution structures for the actualization of a linkage potential, see K.P. Raj, 'Linkages in Industrialization and Development Strategy: Some Basic Issues', *Journal of Development Planning*, No. 8(1975), 105–19.

173. Watkins, op.cit., (note 167 above), p. 56.

174. This observation derived from export economies coincides with the general one formulated by Hartmut Elsenhans with regard to populous territorial states. See Elsenhans, 'Grundlagen der Entwicklung der kapi-

talistischen Weltwirtschaft' in Senghaas, *Kapitalistische Weltökonomie*, pp. 103–48.

175. On the structure and mode of reproduction of plantation economies, see George L. Beckford, *Persistent Poverty: Underdevelopment in Plantation Economies of the Third World*, New York, 1972.

176. This thesis is explicitly elucidated through the example of an export economy in Nathaniel H. Leff, 'Tropical Trade and Development in the Nineteenth Century: The Brazilian Experience', *Journal of Political Economy*, 81(1973), 678–96, especially 692ff.; Boeckh, *Interne Konsequenzen*, pp. 101f. On the question in general, see Emmanuel, *Unequal Exchange*; Samir Amin, *Die ungleiche Entwicklung*, Hamburg, 1975; *idem*, *L'Échange inégal et la loi de la valeur*, Paris, 1973; W. Arthur Lewis, *The Evolution of the International Economic Order*, Princeton, N.J., 1978; *idem*, *Growth*, chs 7–8.

177. It is quite conceivable that domestic economic growth derives from endogenous impulses, without necessarily being linked with the boom phases of export production. On this question, see Edward Chambers and Donald Gordon, 'Primary Products and Economic Growth', *Journal of Political Economy*, 74(1966), 315–32. In that article the authors tried to prove that autonomous productivity increases, which came to determine growth across the whole Canadian economy, materialized outside the staple goods sector. By contrast, for a study which emphasizes the role of the export sector, see Jeffrey G. Williamson, 'Greasing the Wheels of Sputtering Export Engines: Midwestern Grains and American Growth', *Explorations in Economic History*, 17(1980), 189–217.

178. Albert Hirschman has recently made a plea for such studies (op. cit., ch. 2, note 24 above), which he as a non-Marxist economist wants to have understood as a call for 'micro-Marxist investigations'. Detailed studies conforming to Hirschman's plea become more and more numerous, irrespective of whether or not they can be labelled 'micro-Marxist'. Of decisive importance is the detailed historical-genetic and structural analysis of the link between external and internal factors as a basis of export-orientated development. In addition to the many studies cited in the present chapter, see for example Albert Bill, *An Essay on the Peruvian Sugar Industry, 1880–1920*, Norwich, 1976; Rosemary Thorp and Geoffrey Bertram, *Peru—1890–1977: Growth and Policy in an Open Economy*, London, 1978; also Kurt-Peter Schütt, *Externe Abhängigkeit und periphere Entwicklung in Lateinamerika. Eine Studie am Beispiel der Entwicklung Kolumbiens von der Kolonialzeit bis 1930*, Frankfurt, 1980.

179. The *locus classicus* for Wallerstein's position is his debate with the historian T.C. Smout on Scottish development: T.C. Smout, 'Scotland and England: Is Dependency a Symptom or a Cause of Underdevelopment?', *Review*, 3, No. 4(1980), 601–30; and Wallerstein's reply, 'One Man's Meat: The Scottish Great Leap Forward', ibid., 631–40. See also Wallerstein, *Capitalist*, especially ch. 4 and pp. 73ff.

180. Wallerstein, ibid., p. 636.

181. See above all Robert Brenner, 'Agrarian Class Structure and Economic Development in Pre-Industrial Europe', *Past and Present*, No. 70(1976), 30–75; *idem*, 'The Origins of Capitalist Development: A Critique of Neo-Smithian Marxism', *New Left Review*, No. 104(1977), 25–92. See also Peter Worsley, 'One World or Three? A Critique of the World System

Theory of Immanuel Wallerstein' in *Socialist Register 1980* (London, 1980), pp. 298–338; Peter Gourevitch, 'The International System and Regime Formation', *Comparative Politics* (Apr. 1978), 419–37; Jairus Banaji, 'Modes of Production in a Materialist Conception of History', *Capital and Class*, No. 3(1977), 1–44; Wallerstein Symposium Review with contributions by T. Skocpol, M. Janowitz and J. Thirsk in *American Journal of Sociology*, 82, No. 5(1977), 1075–1102; Hilton Root, 'The Debate on the Origins of the Modern World System: The Ottoman Example', *Comparative Studies in Society and History*, 20, No. 4(1978), 626–9; Angus McDonald, 'Wallerstein's World Economy: How Seriously Should We Take It?', *Journal of Asian Studies*, 38, No. 3(1979), 535–40; Ellen Kay Trimberger, 'World Systems Analysis: The Problem of Unequal Development', *Theory and Society*, 8(1979), 127–37; Philip McMichael, 'Settlers and Primitive Accumulation: Foundations of Capitalism in Australia', *Review*, 4, No. 2(1980), 307–34; Giovanni Arrighi, 'Peripheralization of Southern Africa', *Review*, 3, No. 2(1979), 161–91, especially 184ff.; Stanley Aronowitz, 'A Metatheoretical Critique of Immanuel Wallerstein's The Modern World System', *Theory and Society*, 10, No. 4(1981), 503–20; Sidney Mintz, 'The So-Called World System: Local Initiative and Local Response', *Dialectical Anthropology*, 2, No. 4(1977), 253–70. On the discussion on the peripheralization of the Ottoman Empire, see Hans Michael Trautwein, 'Der Niedergang des Osmanischen Reiches und die neuere Kontroverse um die Bedeutung des Handels für die Peripherisierung' (thesis, Bremen University, 1981).

182. Wallerstein calls this process 'development by invitation'. On this, see his comments in *Capitalist*, pp. 76ff.

183. On the terminology, see Hans-Gerhard Voigt, *Probleme der weltwirtschaftlichen Kooperation*, Hamburg, 1969; and Detlef Lorenz, *Dynamische Theorie der internationalen Arbeitsteilung*, Berlin, 1967, pp. 136ff.

184. This observation leads to a correction of Galtung's verticality thesis (note 4 above)—a thesis that is correct in the case of unfavourable sociostructural conditions for growth, without being necessarily correct in the case of different development promoting conditions.

185. See the seminal study by W. Arthur Lewis (ed.), *Tropical Development, 1880–1913: Studies in Economic Progress*, London, 1970.

186. On this see Lewis, *Growth*, especially chs 7–8. For a summary, see *idem*, 'The Diffusion of Development', in Thomas Wilson and Andrew Skinner (eds), *The Market and the State: Essays in Honour of Adam Smith*, Oxford, 1976, pp. 135–65, as well as Amin, *L'Échange*; further, Amit Bhaduri and Joan Robinson, 'Accumulation and Exploitation: An Analysis in the Tradition of Marx, Sraffa and Kalecki', *Cambridge Journal of Economics*, 4 (1980), 103–15, especially 11. For a general analysis see Joan Robinson, *Aspects of Development and Underdevelopment*, Cambridge, 1979.

187. Lewis, *Evolution*, p. 75; *idem*, *Aspects*; also Graciela Chichilnisky, 'Terms of Trade and Domestic Distribution: Export-led Growth with Abundant Labour', *Journal of Development Economics*, 8 (1981), 163–92, especially 181f.; and, *idem*, 'North-South Interdependence: Development and Trade', *IFDA-Dossier*, No. 18 (1980), 59–74 (reprinted in *Socialist International Women Bulletin*, No. 3 [1981] 46–50).

4 Elements of an Export-orientated and Autocentric Development Path

1. In the general debate on development theory and economics the controversy over this question is continuing. See Sheila Smith and John Toye (eds), *Trade and Poor Economies*, London, 1979 (first published in *Journal of Development Studies*, 15, No. 3 [1979], special issue); Richard E. Caves, Douglas C. North and Jacob M. Price, 'Exports and Economic Growth', introduction to case-studies in *Explorations in Economic History*, 17, Nos 1 and 3 (1980); John W. Meyer and Michael T. Hannan (eds), *National Development and the World System*, London, 1979. For a thorough discussion of the problem, see Menzel, *Autozentrierte Auswege aus Abhängigkeit*.

2. K. W. Deutsch and I. A. Schwarz, *Bewertung der abnehmenden Tendenz von Aussenhandel zu Bruttosozialprodukt mit der Grösse der Nationen auf der Basis neuester Daten*, Berlin, 1980 (duplicated, Publications of the International Institute for Comparative Social Research, WZB, No. 109).

3. The linkage theory has proved particularly important in this connection. See Hirschman, op. cit. (ch. 2; note 24 above); also K. P. Raj, 'Linkages in Industrialization and Development Strategy: Some Basic Issues', *Journal of Development Planning*, No. 8 (1975), 105–19.

4. See the study by Lewis, 'Dual Economy', *Manchester School of Economic and Social Studies*, 47, No. 3 (1979), 211–19.

5. Hoffmann, Stadien. See also J. Cornwall, *Modern Capitalism: Its Growth and Transformation*, London, 1977, pp. 130ff.

6. On this, see W. Leontief, 'The Structure of Development', *Scientific American*, 209, No. 3 (1963), 148–66.

7. The following assessment of historical cases corresponds to observations on current cases by I. Adelmann in 'Economic Development and Political Change in Developing Countries', *Social Research*, 47, No. 2 (1980), 213–34.

8. On this see J. Ahmad, 'Import Substitution, Trade and Development', Greenwich, 1978; and the comprehensive article *idem*, 'Import Substitution—a Survey of Policy Issues', *The Development Economy*, 16, No. 4 (1978), 355–72.

9. How important the transition from extensive to intensive agriculture is, particularly in the case of export-orientated agricultural growth, has been demonstrated recently by a study on the Ivory Coast where that transition has not taken place and corresponding linkage effects have not been induced despite high growth. On this specific example see E. Lee, 'Export-led Rural Development: The Ivory Coast', *Development and Change*, 2 (1980), 607–42.

10. On this see *inter alia* Levin, *Export Economies*.

11. L. G. Sandberg, 'The Case of the Impoverished Sophisticate: Human Capital and Swedish Economic Growth before World War I, *Journal of Economic History*, 39 (1979), 225–41.

12. On this, see the study by E. Hagen, 'Why Economic Growth Is Slow', *World Development*, 8 (1980), 291–8; S. Kuznets, 'Driving Forces of Economic Growth: What Can We Learn from History?', *Weltwirtschaftliches Archiv*, 116 (1980), 409–30.

13. See *inter alia* P. Lundgreen, *Bildung und Wirtschaftswachstum im Industriali-*

sierungsprozess des 19 Jahrhunderts, Berlin, 1973; also R. A. Easterlin, 'Why Isn't the Whole World Developed?', *Journal of Economic History*, 41 (1981), 1–19.

14. Our observations agree with the studies of Adelman and Morris: see *inter alia* 'Patterns of Market Expansion in the Nineteenth Century: A Quantitative Study, *Research in Economic Anthropology*, 1 (1978), 231–324; Patterns of Industrialization in the Nineteenth and Early Twentieth Century', *Research in Economic History*, 5 (1980), 1–83. On this, see also as *locus classicus* W. Sombart, 'Kapitalismus' in *Handwörterbuch der Soziologie*, Stuttgart, 1959 (2nd ed.), pp. 258ff.

15. The term is used here in the sense of Deutsch, *Nationalism*. On the other dimensions, see Flora, *Modernisierungsforschung*. Regarding the process of democratization, see the instructive article by G. Therborn, 'The Rule of Capital and the Rise of Democracy', *New Left Review*, No. 103 (May–June 1977), 3–41.

16. See the forthcoming study by W. Dinkloh (Bremen) on the Australian development path.

17. This circumstance is the reason why the export economies integrated in the world market (with the exception of Switzerland and the Netherlands) are to be classified as *associative-dissociative* cases.

18. The same also applies to the nationalization of ore mining in Sweden. On this, see Menzel, *Auswege aus Abhängigkeit* ch. II, 3.

5 In Europe's Footsteps? Far Eastern Development Paths

1. Kwangsuk Kim and Michael Römer, *Growth and Structural Transformation: Studies in the Industrialization of the Republic of Korea, 1945–75*, Cambridge, Mass., 1979. This study is representative of many others on Korea that have been published over the past decade.

2. See in particular Rainer Schweers, *Kapitalistische Entwicklung und Unterentwicklung. Voraussetzungen und Schranken der Kapitalakkumulation in ökonomisch schwach entwickelten Ländern*, Frankfurt, 1980, pp. 201ff. and *passim*. Pointing in the same direction but arguing more generally: Bill Warren, 'Imperialism and Capitalist Industrialization', *New Left Review*, No. 81 (1973), 3–44; also the posthumously published book with contributions *idem*, *Imperialism: Pioneer of Capitalism*, London, 1980, particularly chs 7–8; Wolfgang Schoeller, *Weltmarkt und Reproduktion des Kapitals*, Frankfurt, 1976, pp. 258–75; Thomas Hurtienne, 'Peripherer Kapitalismus und autozentrierte Entwicklung. Zur Kritik des Erklärungsansatzes von Dieter Senghaas', *Probleme des Klassenkampfs* 11, No. 44 (1981), 105–35.

3. See Senghass, *Weltwirtschaftsordnung*.

4. See Senghass, 'Dissoziation' in *Kapitalistische Weltökonomie*, pp. 376–412.

5. Folker Fröbel, for example, who is close to the above-mentioned position, has, however, recently written: 'The conclusion that the marginality and marginalization of the developing countries are permanent and irremovable within the context of the capitalist world system raises theoretical as well as empirical doubts. It becomes apparent that the possibility can no longer be dismissed that, in the foreseeable future, and on the basis of foreseeable development trends within the capitalist world system, at least some of the present-day developing countries could transform

themselves into industrial-capitalist societies with a corresponding accumulation model by way of world market-orientated partial industrialization and progressive capitalization', ('Zur gegenwärtigen Entwicklung der Weltwirtschaft', *Starnberger Studien*, 4 [Strukturveränderungen in der kapitalistischen Weltwirtschaft], Frankfurt, 1980, p. 16). A more cautious assessment has recently been given by Amin: 'Are we dealing with an illusion or with an embryonic exception which would have to be explained with Confucian ideology? The crucial question to be answered is whether the accumulation by monopolistic enterprises finances the local economy, or the other way round' (*Class and Nation*, p. 149).

6. It is, therefore, not surprising that basic assumptions of the so-called dependency theory have been critically tested on the two examples of South Korea and Taiwan, although with differing analytical competence. Less impressive in analytical terms is Myung Hwa Han's attempt in relation to South Korea, 'Dependency Theory and Its Relevance to Korean Development', *Korea and World Affairs*, 3, No. 3, 385–97. On Taiwan, see Alice H. Amsden's exceptionally enlightening article, 'Taiwan's Economic History: A Case of Etatism and a Challenge to Dependency Theory', *Modern China*, 5, No. 3 (1979), 341–79.

7. See, for example, Donges and Müller-Ohlsen, *Außenwirtschaftsstrategien*.

8. On the data, see the statistical appendix in *World Development Report 1980*, published by the World Bank, Washington, D.C., 1980.

9. Ibid., table 4.

10. The Gini index figures are taken from Volker Bornschier and Peter Heintz (eds), *Compendium of Data for World-System Analysis*, Zürich, 1979, pp. 216/17.

11. Ibid., pp. 257f.

12. On this see the preceding chapters in the present volume.

13. On the Scandinavian development path, see ibid.

14. In this connection the discussion on growth and distributive equity generated by the World Bank should be mentioned. Many of the more recent publications have drawn attention to the development dynamics of Korea and Taiwan which differ from the usual development profile, especially with regard to the different extent of the increase or lack of increase in absolute poverty within the Third World, according to the differing distribution structures at the beginning of the growth process. For a summary, see Morawetz, *Economic Development*; and Parvez Hasan, 'Wachstum und Gerechtigkeit in Ostasien', *Finanzierung und Entwicklung*, 15, No. 2 (1978), 28–32; Hollis B. Chenery, 'Armut und Fortschritt—Alternativen für die Dritte Welt', ibid., 17, No. 2 (1980), 12–16; Montek S. Ahluwalia *et al.*, 'Growth and Poverty in Developing Countries', *Journal of Development Economics*, 6 (1979), 299–341. On the relevance of the difference made by initial moderate or gross inequality in different societies in relation to the type of growth process, see the comparative analysis by Geoffrey B. Hainsworth, 'Economic Growth and Poverty in Southeast Asia: Malaysia, Indonesia and the Philippines', *Pacific Affairs*, 52, No. 1 (1979), 5–41.

15. The data are quoted from the *Yearbook of National Account Statistics 1978*, published by the United Nations, New York, 1979. So far as the quoted comparison is concerned, it must however be taken into account that the

number of independent economic units in South Korea is bound to be higher than in highly industrialized societies. This means that the wages share must be lower than in highly developed countries. Taking this into account, a difference of about 15 per cent would still remain.

16. See the previously mentioned studies in the present volume.
17. On this, see Lewis, 'Dual Economy', *Manchester School of Economics and Social Studies*, 47, No. 3 (1979), 211–19 (as well as the other contributions in this issue, which was published on the occasion of the twenty-fifth anniversary of Lewis's famous study, *Economic Development with Unlimited Supplies of Labour*).
18. See the previously mentioned studies in the present volume.
19. Data taken from the *World Bank Report 1980*.
20. On this, see *inter alia* Suleiman Cohen, 'Industrial Performance in South Korea: A Descriptive Analysis of a Remarkable Success', *Developing Economies*, 16, No. 4 (1978), 385–407.
21. In this connection the example of Japanese development in the 1920s and 1930s is of interest. Although, compared with South Korean development, Japan's development from the turn of the century onward was much more balanced—that is, geared at the same time to the domestic market and export-orientated—the growth impulse which resulted from the building up of heavy industry during the 1920s and early 1930s produced development-retarding repercussions, given a still considerable surplus population in the rural sector (in addition to other factors). Japanese development at that time was not geared to 'capital extension' but 'capital intensification', a development pattern that was brought about—among other factors—by the search for continuing and increasing competitiveness in the world market. On this, see Bruce F. Johnston, 'Agricultural Development and Economic Transformation: A Comparative Study of the Japanese Experience', *Food Research Institute Studies*, 3 (1962/3), 223–76, particularly 246ff.
22. On this see also Lewis, *Evolution*.
23. See the studies cited in note 2 above.
24. See Elsenhans, 'Grundlagen' in Senghaas, *Kapitalistische Weltökonomie*, pp. 103–48.
25. On this, see the study in note 26 below.
26. See Arghiri Emmanuel, 'Myths of Development versus Myths of Underdevelopment', *New Left Review*, No. 85 (1974), 61–82.
27. This is evidenced by developments in eastern Europe, including the Polish crisis of 1980/1. These problems are also clearly articulated in the discussion currently taking place in China. On this, see D. Senghaas, 'Kontinuität und Wandel in der chinesischen Entwicklung'. Der Modernisierungskurs im Lichte der Theorie autozentrierter Entwicklung', *Internationales Asienforum*, 2(1980), 45–59; *idem*, 'China auf der Suche nach einer proportionierten Wirtschaft', *Leviathan*, 9 (1981), 195–210. On the question of the agricultural sector in South Korean development, see Samuel P.S. Ho, 'Rural-Urban Imbalance in South Korea in the 1970s', *Asian Survey*, 19, No. 7 (1979), 645–59; also Eddy Lee, 'Egalitarian Peasant Farming and Rural Development: The Case of South Korea', *World Development*, 7 (1979), 493–517. However, it should be pointed out in favour of South Korea that, compared with all other peripheral-

capitalist Asian countries, her per capita food production has shown surprisingly high (even though fluctuating) growth rates since 1967/8. On this see *UNCTAD 1979 Handbook*, p. 529.

28. On the historical background to the following considerations, see the preceding chapters.

29. In this connection some differences between Japanese development during this century and the recent development path of South Korea should be pointed out. The Japanese development path was characterized by the fact that foreign trade before the Second World War did not grow faster than the economy as a whole. At the most 25 to 35 per cent of the manufactures produced in Japan were exported at that time, and the export share of the GDP was usually no higher than 20 per cent. Today it is 11 per cent, according to the *World Bank Report 1980*; while the figure for South Korea is 34 per cent, as already cited above. The wages share of the GDP was 40 per cent in Japan before the Second World War, by now it has grown to more than 65 per cent. Military defeat and the elimination of the traditional, extremely autocratic, political regime and of the power élites behind it have encouraged such a shift. The defeat of 1945 also ushered in the process of democratization without which, according to historical experience, increasingly complex industrial societies cannot be run efficiently. Particularly in comparison with Japan, it becomes apparent how problematic in political and economic terms is the present development in South Korea. On Japanese development, see the study by William W. Lockwood, *The Economic Development of Japan: Growth and Structural Change, 1868–1938*, Princeton, N.J., 1968 (2nd ed.); Kazushi Ohkawa and Miyohei Shinohara (eds), *Patterns of Japanese Economic Development*, New Haven, Conn., 1979; also Ippei Yamazawa and Akira Hirata, 'Industrialization and External Relations: Comparative Analysis of Japan's Historical Experience and Contemporary Developing Countries' Performance', *Hitotsubashi Journal of Economics*, 18, No. 2 (1978), 33–61.

30. On Taiwanese development, which should always be examined in relation to South Korean development, see Samuel P.S. Ho, *Economic Development of Taiwan, 1860–1970*, New Haven, Conn., 1978; John Fei, Gustav Ranis and S. Kuo, *Growth with Equity: The Taiwan Case*, London, 1980; Gustav Ranis, 'Equity with Growth in Taiwan: How Special Is the Special Case?', *World Development*, 6, No. 3 (1978), 397–409; Samuel P.S. Ho, 'Decentralized Industrialization and Rural Development: Evidence from Taiwan', *Economic Development and Cultural Change*, 28 (1979), 77–96; Shirley W.Y. Kuo, Gustav Ranis and John C.H. Fei, *The Taiwan Success Story: Rapid Growth with Improved Distribution in the Republic of China, 1952–1979*, Boulder, Colo., 1981.

31. This also applies to the completely different development path of North Korea, which is based on a dissociative-autocentric strategy. On this, see *inter alia* Juttka-Reisse, *Agrarpolitik*; also Rainer Knoblauch, *Industrialisierungsprozeß und gesamtwirtschaftliche Entwicklung Nordkoreas* (in preparation).

6 Socialism: an Interpretation from the Perspective of Development History and Theory

1. Herbert Marcuse, *Gesellschaftslehre des sowjetischen Marxismus*, Neuwied,

1964, ch. 1. For a critical view see Iring Fetscher, 'The Changing Goals of Socialism in the Twentieth Century', *Social Research*, 47, No. 1 (1980), 36–62. See also D.M. Nuti, 'Socialism on Earth', *Cambridge Journal of Economics*, 5 (1981), 391–403.

2. On this, see the preceding chapters as well as Mark Kesselman, 'Continuity and Change on the French Left', *Social Research*, 47, No. 1 (1980), 93–140.
3. Fritz Sternberg, *Marx und die Gegenwart*, Cologne, 1955, *passim*.
4. See Elsenhans, 'Grundlagen' in Senghaas *Kapitalistische Weltökonomie*, pp. 103–48; Arghiri Emmanuel, *Le Profit et les crises*, Paris, 1974.
5. By 'mature capitalism' we mean a capitalist society whose primary, secondary and tertiary sectors have undergone tendentially thorough capitalization, where labour productivity is high and where the owners of capital and their employees confront each other within an institutionalized bargaining system.
6. Among the different interpretations of the function of socialism which can be found in literature, those based on an explicit modernization theory approach are closest to the interpretation offered below. However, I am not aware of any interpretation which explicitly links the theory of peripheral capitalism and that of delayed socialist development. Such a link forms the basis of the interpretation proposed below. In the more recent literature, important modernization theory approaches can be found above all in Charles Gati (ed.), *The Politics of Modernization in Eastern Europe: Testing the Soviet Model*, New York, 1974; Mark G. Field (ed.), *Social Consequences of Modernization in Communist Societies*, London, 1976 (particularly the contribution by Anthony Jones, 'Modernization Theory and Socialist Development', pp. 19–49); Kenneth Jowitt, *The Leninist Response to National Dependency*, Berkeley, Calif., 1981. Among the important early literature are: John Kautsky, *Communism and the Politics of Development*, New York, 1968; *idem, Patterns of Modernizing Revolutions: Mexico and the Soviet Union*, London, 1975; *idem, The Political Consequences of Modernization*, New York, 1972: Charles K. Wilber, *The Soviet Model and Underdeveloped Countries*, Chapel Hill, N.C., 1969; Chalmers Johnson (ed.), *Change in Communist Systems*, Stanford, Calif., 1970. For a more recent study, see Gerd Meyer, *Sozialistische Systeme. Theorie und Strukturanalyse*, Opladen, 1979, pp. 207ff., especially the report and the critical discussion on the studies by Alfred G. Meyer. According to Meyer, communism appears to a large degree 'a function of economic, political and cultural underdevelopment' (p. 247). Within the socialist debate itself, too, reflection on socialism as an agency of delayed development has always been of importance. See René Ahlberg, *Die sozialistische Bürokratie. Die marxistische Kritik am etablierten Sozialismus*, Stuttgart, 1976, pp. 63ff.; *Richta Report. Zivilisation am Scheideweg*, Prague, 1968; and, for a later contribution, Rudolf Bahro, *Die Alternative. Zur Kritik des real existierenden Sozialismus*, Cologne, 1977; also *Bahro-Kongreß. Aufzeichnungen, Berichte und Referate*, Berlin, 1979, pp. 132ff.; Charles Bettelheim *et al.*, *Zurückforderung der Zukunft. Macht und Opposition in den nachrevolutionären Gesellschaften*, Frankfurt, 1979. In this connection, see also the special issues of *Theory and Society*, 9, No. 2 (1980), and *Social Research*, 47, No. 1 (1980), which are devoted to the question of socialism. See also the topical issue of *Leviathan*

edited by me, including my editorial, as well as the special issue of *World Development*, 9 (1981), Nos 9/10 on 'Socialist Models of Development'. Among the more recent interpretations those based on a 'world system approach' (Wallerstein) are of particular interest. See especially Christopher Chase-Dunn, 'Socialist States in the Capitalist World Economy', *Social Problems*, 27, No. 5 (1980), 505–25, and the symposium following that article in *Social Problems*, 28, No. 3 (1981), 509–32. See also various studies in *Political Economy of the World System Annuals*, Vols 1 *et seq.*, London, 1978 *et seq.* For a critique of the interpretation of socialism by means of the world system approach see Peter Worsley, 'One World or Three?' in *Socialist Register 1980*, pp. 298–338. Of particular interest is Amin, *Class and Nation*; *idem*, *L'Avenir du maoisme*, Paris, 1981.

7. On this, see the preceding chapters as well as Senghaas, *Weltwirtschaftsordnung*.

8. On this, see the preceding chapters.

9. The Israeli development path occupies an intermediate position. It was based on socialist premises, but shifted increasingly towards a far-reaching integration into the capitalist world market. See Christiane Buch-Lüty, 'Entwicklungsphänomen Israel: Vom Kibbuz zum Kapitalismus?', *Aus Politik und Zeitgeschichte*, supplement to *Parlament*, No. 4 (27 Jan. 1979), 3–29. Another special case is Taiwan. Her development was never founded on socialist premises. It is, however, based on two agrarian reforms which were far more than just symbolic, on a first phase of domestic-market-orientated industrialization, a later stage of export-orientated industrialization and on a moderate degree of internal inequality. Together, these factors can provide a sound basis for national-capitalist development. On Taiwan, see Gustav Ranis, 'Equity with Growth in Taiwan: How Special Is the Special Case?', *World Development*, 6, No. 9 (1978), 397–409.

10. On the typology, see the preceding chapters.

11. On the role of state classes as a substitute for private entrepreneurs in processes of delayed development, see Hartmut Elsenhans, 'Zur Rolle der Staatsklasse bei der Überwindung von Unterentwicklung' in Alfred Schmidt (ed.), *Strategien gegen Unterentwicklung. Zwischen Weltmarkt und Eigenständigkeit*, Frankfurt, 1976, pp. 250–65.

12. On these processes, see the study by Deutsch, *Nationalism*, which retains its relevance; also *idem*, 'National Integration: Some Concepts and Research Approaches', *The Jerusalem Journal of International Relations*, 2, No. 4 (1977), 1–29.

13. On the theory of autocentric development, see Senghaas, 'Dissoziation' in *Kapitalistische Weltökonomie*, pp. 376–412.

14. See for a summary Senghaas, *Weltwirtschaftsordnung*, ch. 1, and the literature cited there.

15. See James Petras, 'Towards a Theory of Twentieth Century Socialist Revolutions', *Journal of Contemporary Asia*, 8, No. 2 (1978), pp. 167–95; and, *idem*, 'Socialist Revolutions and Their Class Components', *New Left Review*, No. 11 (1978), 17–44. On socialism in the Third World, see Helen Desfosses and Jacques Levesque, *Socialism in the Third World*, New York, 1975; also the studies in *World Development*, Nos 3–4 (Apr. 1975), with case-studies on Egypt, India and Tanzania. In the present study such

cases of 'socialist development' are not considered, as they do not represent a sufficiently clear break with peripheral-capitalist development dynamics. A more recent study of such cases (Burma, Sri Lanka, Tanzania, Chile, Portugal) can be found in David Morawetz, 'Economic Lessons from Some Small Socialist Developing Countries', *World Development*, 8 (1980), 337–70.

16. For an historical analysis of the socio-economic and socio-cultural development of Czechoslovakia, see Milward/Saul 2, pp. 284ff.; Jiri Kosta, *Abriß der sozialökonomischen Entwicklung der Tschechoslowakei 1945–1977*, Frankfurt, 1978, pp. 10ff.; Galia Golan, 'Nationale Traditionen und Sozialismus in Osteuropa. Das Beispiel der Tschechoslowakei und Jugoslawiens' in S.N. Eisenstadt und Yael Azmon (eds), *Sozialismus und Tradition*, Tübingen, 1977, pp. 45–85, especially pp. 45–65.

17. On the socio-economic development of eastern and south-eastern Europe, see from a development theory and development policy perspective Berend and Ránki, *Economic Development*; Milward/Saul 2, chs 5 and 8; 'Die wirtschaftliche und soziale Entwicklung Südosteuropas im 19. und 20. Jahrhundert', *Südosteuropa Jahrbuch*, Vol. 9, Munich, 1969; Wolfgang Zorn, 'Umrisse der frühen Industrialisierung Südosteuropas im 19. Jahrhundert', *Vierteljahresschrift für Social- und Wirtschaftsgeschichte*, 57 (1970), 500–33; Nicolas Spulber, 'Changes in the Economic Structure of the Balkans, 1860–1960' in Charles and Barbara Jelavich, *The Balkans in Transition*, Berkeley, Calif., 1963, pp. 346–75; John R. Lampe, 'Varieties of Unsuccessful Industrialization: The Balkan States before 1914', *Journal of Economic History*, 35 (1975), 56–85. William Ashworth, 'Typologies and Evidence: Has Nineteenth-Century Europe a Guide to Economic Growth?', *Economic History Review*, 30 (1967), pp. 140–58; also Alois Brusatti (ed.), *Die wirtschaftliche Entwicklung*, Vol. 1 of *Die Habsburger-Monarchie 1848–1918*, Vienna, 1973. An early development policy study on this question is Kurt Mandelbaum, *The Industrialization of Backward Areas*, Oxford, 1945. In the Festschrift for Mandelbaum, Hans Singer has recently drawn attention to this study. See his contribution in *Plus ça change . . . Essays in Honour of Kurt Martin*, special issue of *Development and Change*, 10, No. 4 (Oct. 1979).

18. On the extent of displacement competition and its impact on the economic structure illustrated by the example of the disproportionate development of the food processing industry and the underdevelopment of the textile industry in Hungary, see for example I.T. Berend and G. Ránki, *Hungary: A Century of Economic Development*, New York, 1974, part 1.

19. The countries of eastern and south-eastern Europe together with the Third World have in common this early high degree of monopolization and cartelization of the economy. On the damaging consequences of such economic structures, see for a general analysis Meir Merhav, *Technological Dependence, Monopoly, and Growth*, London, 1969.

20. On the data, see Berend and Ránki, *Hungary*, pp. 303ff.

21. On the class structure and social stratification in pre-revolutionary societies, see Walter D. Connor, *Socialism, Politics and Equality: Hierarchy and Change in Eastern Europe and the USSR*, New York, 1979, ch. 2.

22. On Albania, see Ruß, *Entwicklungsweg Albaniens*, part 1.

23. On peripheralization in the case of China see Menzel, *Chinesische Entwicklungsmodell*, part 1. See also the recent symposium on China's

economic history with contributions by Victor Lippit, Albert Feuer-
werker, André Gunder Frank, Keith Griffin and Carl Riskin in *Modern
China*, 4, No. 3 (July 1979), especially the contribution by Victor Lippit,
'The Development of Underdevelopment in China' (251–330).

24. On Cuba, see Fabian, *Kubanische Entwicklungsweg*; Jorge L. Dominguez,
Cuba: Order and Revolution, Cambridge, 1978.

25. On Korea, see Gerd Wontroba and Ulrich Menzel, *Stagnation und Unterentwicklung in Korea* (with an introduction by D. Senghaas), Meisenheim am Glan, 1978; also Sang-Chul Suh, *Growth and Structural Changes in
the Korean Economy, 1910–1940*, Cambridge, 1978; Ingeborg Göthel, *Geschichte Koreas*, Berlin, 1978. See also the interesting comparative article by
Seizaburo Sato, 'Response to the West: The Korean and Japanese Patterns'
in Albert Craig (ed.), *Japan: A Comparative View*, Princeton, N.J., 1979,
pp. 105–29.

26. In addition to the four socialist countries cited above one ought to
mention the Mongolian People's Republic, as it represents—apart from
the Soviet Union—the oldest socialist society (since 1924). Information
on the Mongolian People's Republic is, however, extremely scarce, and
its pre-revolutionary history would certainly have to be included with the
undeveloped-stagnant type of society rather than with a clear-cut type of
peripheral capitalism. A short description can be found in Bernhard
Roßmann, 'Mongolische Volksrepublik' in *Handbuch der Dritten Welt*, Vol. 4,
part II (Hamburg, 1978), pp. 463–71; further, Robert Rupen, *How
Mongolia Is Really Ruled*, Stanford, Calif., 1979; Sechin Jagchid and Paul
Hyer, *Mongolia's Culture and Society*, Boulder, Colo., 1979; also the report-
age by Thomas E. Ewing, 'The Mongolian People's Republic Today',
Asian Affairs, 2(1980), 309–21.

27. On this, see also Stein Rokkan, 'Dimensions of State Formation and
Nation Building: A Possible Paradigm for Research on Variations within
Europe' in Charles Tilly (ed.), *The Formation of National States in Western
Europe*, Princeton, N.J., 1975, pp. 562–600, especially p. 573.

28. On peripheral-capitalist development dynamics, see Senghaas, *Peripherer
Kapitalismus*; Samir Amin, *Le Développement inégal*, Davis, 1973.

29. See the literature cited in note 6 above. See also the study by Skocpol,
States and Social Revolutions, and Elmar Altvater, 'Der Primat der Politik in
nachrevolutionären Gesellschaften' (paper for the Conference on Post-
Revolutionary Societies, Milan, 4–7 Jan. 1979; unpublished manuscript).

30. Buro, *Autozentrierte Entwicklung*. On socialist critiques of such auton-
omization tendencies, see for a summary Ahlberg, *Sozialistische Bürokratie*.
See also for a recent discussion of Stalinism relevant to this question, W.
Süß, 'Bürokratische Rationalität und gesellschaftliche Synthesis in der
Konstitutionsphase des sowjetischen Systems', *Probleme des Klassenkampfs*,
9, No. 35 (1979), 133–70. Süß criticizes functionalist interpretations
according to which the socialist modernization dictatorship derives from
rational economic requirements of accumulation. Opposing the thesis
that Stalinism represents an unchecked implementation of economic
rationality, he maintains that the Stalinist system of institutionalized
terror and political despotism should be interpreted as an attempt to
protect the rule of the party—'especially in those areas where it could no
longer be reconciled with economic rationality and an expansionist econ-

omic policy' (166).

31. On the following, see the literature cited in notes 22, 23 and 24 above. To complement the book on pre-revolutionary Korea cited in note 25, see the study on North Korea by Juttka-Reisse, *Agrarpolitik*; Ellen Brun and Jacques Hersh, *Socialist Korea*, New York, 1976; Youn-Soo Kim (ed.), *The Economy of the Korean Democratic People's Republic (1945–1977)*, Kiel, 1979; Ellen Brun, 'The Korean Example of Self-Centered Accumulation', *Marxistisk Antropologi* (Denmark), 3, No. 4(1978), 133–210. See also the enlightening book from North Korea, *The Building of an Independent National Economy in Korea*; and John Halliday, 'The North Korean Model: Gaps and Questions', *World Development*, 9(1981), 889–906. See for a complementary study on Albania, Michael Kaser and Adi Schnyther, 'Albania—A Uniquely Socialist Economy' in *East-European Economies Post-Helsinki: A Compendium of Papers*, ed. Joint Economic Committee, Congress of the United States, Washington, D.C., 1977, pp. 567–608; Bernhard Tönnes, *Albanien. Inver Hoxhas 'eigener Weg' und die historischen Ursprünge seiner Ideologie*, Munich, 1980.

32. On the problematic interaction between the Soviet Union and eastern Europe after 1945 with regard to the socio-economic development of eastern Europe, see the contributions by Gati, Aspaturian, Gitelman and Kanet in Gati, *Politics of Modernization*, part III ('Eastern Europe and the Soviet Union: Interaction and Influences'). See also, from the viewpoint of development theory, Stehr, *Sozio-ökonomische Bedingungen*.

33. On these questions see, for example, the early industrialization debate in the Soviet Union, particularly the contribution by E. Preobraschenski, *Die neue Ökonomik* (Berlin, 1971), in which the problems of primary socialist accumulation are clearly spelled out. See also Alexander Erlich, *Die Industrialisierungsdebatte in der Sowjetunion 1924–1928*, Frankfurt, 1971; Peter Hennicke (ed.), *Probleme des Sozialismus und der Übergangsgesellschaft*, Frankfurt, 1973; Peter W. Schulze (ed.), *Übergangsgesellschaft. Herrschaftsform und Praxis am Beispiel der Sowjetunion*, Frankfurt, 1974 (especially the contribution by P. Hennicke); Richard Lorenz, *Sozialgeschichte der Sowjetunion 1 (1917–1945)*, Frankfurt, 1976. On the continuing importance for delayed socialist and capitalist development of the problems discussed in this industrialization debate, see the contribution by Hans-Bernd Schäfer, 'Forcierte Industrialisierung in der dualistischen Wirtschaft', *Jahrbuch für Sozialwissenschaft*, 30, No. 1 (1979), 1–26. In this connection see also Alec Nove, 'Socialism and Development: Some Observations of the Soviet Contribution', published in the Festschrift for Mandelbaum, op. cit., (note 17 above), pp. 553–65. For a general study, see Robert W. Campbell, *Soviet Type Economies*, London, 1974; also Alec Nove, *The Soviet Economic System*, London, 1978 (3rd ed.); Marie Lavigne, *Les Economies socialistes soviétiques et européennes*, Paris, 1979.

34. This fact has been clearly illuminated in the recent debate on Soviet industrialization in the late 1920s and the 1930s. While the traditional view was based on the assumption that Stalinist collectivization of Soviet agriculture provided the institutional framework for a forced transfer of surplus from agriculture to industry, recent literature emphasizes the considerable contribution of the industrial workers towards achieving high accumulation rates—an achievement payed for by drastically falling

living standards among the urban population. On this debate, which elaborates the studies by Barsov, and which is crucial for a theory of delayed socialist development, see the controversy between James Miller and Alec Nove, 'A Debate on Collectivization: Was Stalin Really Necessary?', *Problems of Communism* (July/Aug. 1976), 49–62. For a summary and further elaboration, see Arvind Vyas, 'Primary Accumulation in the USSR Revisited', *Cambridge Journal of Economics*, 3(1979), 119–30; also the monograph by A. Vyas, *Consumption in a Socialist Economy: The Soviet Industrialization Experience (1929-1937)*, New Delhi, 1978. On the question in general, see the study by Ashok Mitra, *Terms of Trade and Class Relations: An Essay in Political Economy*, London, 1977.

35. Irrespective of his position in the above-mentioned debate, see the important contribution by Nikolai Bucharin, *Ökonomik der Transformationsperiode*, Reinbek b. Hamburg, 1970; also the literature cited in note 33 above. On this, see Keith Smith, 'Introduction to Bukharin: Economic Theory and the Closure of the Soviet Industrialization Debate', *Economy and Society*, 0 (1979), 440–72.

36. On this, see for example the study by Peter Knirsh, *Sowjetwirtschaft zwischen Anspruch und Realität*, Hanover, 1977 (publication of the State Centre for Political Education of Lower Saxony). In this connection one should bear in mind that in the case of delayed socialist development, even more than in the case of delayed development under state-capitalist auspices (Japan *et al.*), the sequence of industrialization reverses the original competitive-capitalist development path. The latter began with the building up of final demand consumer goods industries (particularly textiles) to be complemented during a second stage by heavy industry and engineering, until finally, in a third stage, capital goods industries outstrip consumer goods industries in size. In the two first-mentioned cases, particularly in the case of delayed socialist development, considerable priority was given to heavy and capital goods sectors in the building up of industry. On the early cases see Hoffmann, *Stadien*; on socialist development, Arghiri Emmanuel, 'The Socialist Project in the Disintegrated Capitalist World' in *Socialism in the World* (Cavtat, 1977), Vol. 2, pp. 21–38.

37. See the contributions by James Petras cited in note 15 above.

38. The crucial contribution to this question has come from Karl August Wittfogel, particularly in his main work *Oriental Despotism*, New Haven, Conn., 1957. On the evolution of Wittfogel's seminal studies, which in the recent debate have frequently been suppressed for political reasons, see the biography of Wittfogel by G.L. Ulmen, *Toward an Understanding of the Life and Work of Karl August Wittfogel*, New York, 1978; also my review of the latter book, 'Wittfogel redivivus', *Leviathan*, 8 (1980), 133–41.

39. See Bahro, *Alternative*, pp. 98ff.; also Rudi Dutschke, *Versuch, Lenin auf die Füße zu stellen*, Berlin, 1974. For a critique of the latter study, see Reinhard Kößler, 'Zur Kritik des Mythos vom "asiatischen" Rußland', *Probleme des Klassenkampfs*, 9, No. 35 (1979), 105–31. Wittfogel has restated his position in 'Einleitung zu "Marx Enthüllungen zur Geschichte der Diplomatie im 18. Jahrhundert" ' in Karl Marx, *Enthüllungen zur Geschichte der Diplomatie im 18. Jahrhundert*, Frankfurt, 1981, pp. xxiiiff.

40. The main difference between Asiatic despotism and delayed socialist

development lies in the fact that the former is founded on a stagnating society and economy, while the function of delayed socialist development lies in the dynamification of the productive forces.

41. On this see the study by Bendix, *Kings or People*.
42. On the connection between peripheral capitalism, corporatism and fascist structures of domination, see for example the recent studies on the case of Romania, especially Jowitt (ed.), *Social Change in Romania*; and Daniel Chirot, 'The Corporatist Model and Socialism: Notes on Romanian Development', *Theory and Society*, 9 (1980), 363–82. On Italy, see Gregor, *Italian Fascism*.
43. Janos Kornai, 'Some Properties of the Eastern European Growth Pattern', *World Development*, 9 (1980), 965–70. Comparative and systematic data collections can be found in the following studies: Jiri Kosta, *Sozialistische Planwirtschaft. Theorie und Praxis*, Opladen, 1974; Klaus v. Beyme, *Ökonomie und Politik im Sozialismus. Ein Vergleich der Entwicklung in den sozialistischen Ländern*, Munich, 1975; David Lane, *The End of Inequality? Stratification under State Socialism*, Baltimore, Md., 1971; *idem*, *The Socialist Industrial State: Towards a Political Sociology of State Socialism*, London, 1976; Connor, *Socialism, Politics and Equality*; Gerhard Lenski, 'Marxist Experiments in Destratification', *Social Forces*, 57, No. 2 (1978), 364–83. Lenski emphasizes as positive factors the ability to promote growth and the relatively low degree of inequality, and as negative factors the almost total lack of political participation, political inequality, working conditions not at all different from the Western factory system, the persisting inequality between man and woman, the gap between town and country, and the failure to achieve the real aim of socialism: 'socialist man'. Lenski is right in pointing out a dialectical relationship between positive and negative factors. Political inequality is a consequence of the efforts during the first development stage to reduce existing inequalities, to promote growth and to reproportion the economy. See also John M. Echols, 'Does Socialism Mean Greater Equality?', *American Journal of Political Science*, 25, No. 1 (1981), 1–31. Studies that are written explicitly from a development theory viewpoint are available on the following cases of delayed socialist development: on Albania, the study by Ruß, *Entwicklungsweg Albaniens*; on China, the study by Menzel, *Theorie und Praxis des chinesischen Modells*; on Cuba, the study by Fabian, *Der kubanische Entwicklungsweg*; on North Korea, the study by Juttka-Reisse, *Agrarpolitik*; and in the near future a complementary study on industrialization in North Korea by Rainer Knoblauch (in preparation). On the Soviet Union, see Basile Kerblay, *La Société soviétique contemporaine*, Paris, 1977. The available studies on eastern and south-eastern Europe are mainly informed by the modernization theory. See the contributions by Gati, *Politics of Modernization*; on Romania, see particularly John Montias, *Economic Development in Communist Rumania*, Cambridge, Mass., 1977; Kenneth Jowitt, *Revolutionary Breakthroughs and National Development: The Case of Romania, 1944–1965*, Berkeley, Calif., 1971; Trond Gilberg, *Modernization in Romania since World War II*, New York, 1975; also the important summary by Daniel Chirot, 'Social Change in Communist Rumania', *Social Forces*, 37, No. 2 (1978), 457–99; further, Amalendu B. Guha, 'Rumania as a Development Model', *Journal of Peace Research*, 11, No. 4 (1974), 297–323; Stefan Welzk, 'Ent-

wicklungspolitische Lernprozesse. Rumänische Erfahrungen', *Befreiung*, Nos 19/20 (1980), 70–118; Andreas Tsantes and Roy Pepper, *Romania: The Industrialization of an Agrarian Economy under Socialist Planning*, Baltimore, Md., 1979; on Hungary, see Berend and Ránki, *Hungary*, part III; on Bulgaria, J.F. Brown, *Bulgaria under Communist Rule*, New York, 1970; George Feiwel, *Growth and Reforms in Centrally Planned Economies: Lessons of the Bulgarian Experience*, New York, 1977; idem, 'A Socialist Model of Economic Development: The Polish and Bulgarian Experiences', *World Development*, 9 (1981), 929–50; on Yugoslavia, see Peter Jambrek, *Development and Social Change in Yugoslavia*, Lexington, Mass., 1975; Charles R. Chittle, *Industrialization and Manufactured Export Expansion in a Worker-Managed Economy: The Yugoslav Experience*, Tübingen, 1977; Branko Horvat, *Die jugoslawische Gesellschaft*, Frankfurt, 1969; on Czechoslovakia, Kosta, *Abriß der Sozialökonomischen Entwicklung*, as well as Otto Ulc, 'Some Aspects of Czechoslovak Society since 1968', *Social Forces*, 57, No. 2 (1978), 419–35; on Czechoslovakia as a non-periphery, on to which the Soviet development model was imposed, see *idem*, 'Czechoslovakia, the Great Leap Backward' in Gati, (*Politics of Modernization*; on Poland, see Dennis C. Priages, *Modernization and Political Tension Management: A Socialist Society in Perspective—Case Study of Poland*, New York, 1972; Stan Tellenback, 'The Logic of Development in Socialist Poland', *Social Forces*, 57, No. 2 (1978), 436–56; Joseph Fiszmann, *Revolution and Tradition in People's Poland*, Princeton, N.J., 1972.

44. 'Egalitarianism', defined in operational terms, means the elimination of structural heterogeneity and the homogenization of domestic economic regions—prerequisites for efficient consumer goods production.

45. See various contributions in the book *East European Economies Post Helsinki*, (note 31 above), as well as in Zbigniew M. Fallenbuch (ed.), *Economic Development in the Soviet Union and Eastern Europe*, Vols 1–2, New York, 1975–6. See also Michael Ellman, 'Agricultural Productivity under Socialism', *World Development*, 9(1980), 979–89.

46. On this, see the contributions in *World Development*, 7, Nos 4–5(1979), devoted to the topic 'Capitalist and Socialist Agriculture in Asia'.

47. On the analysis of such concrete periphery cases in Europe, see the studies in Seers, *Underdeveloped Europe*.

48. Even though such an assessment is based on value judgements, it does not entail a blanket preference for socialism as opposed to capitalism—as should become clear from the present contribution. It is hardly surprising that precisely in advanced peripheral-capitalist societies like Brazil, where the structural deficits typical of such societies are by no means overcome but manifest themselves in increased structural heterogeneity, politically relevant debates tend to surface in which socialist development policies are recommended for the solution of those problems that cannot be solved within the existing framework. On this, see Paul Singer, 'Alternative Scenarios of the Brazilian Future', *IFDA-Dossier* (International Foundation for Development Alternatives), No. 13(Nov. 1979), 59–70.

49. With regard to the German Democratic Republic and Czechoslovakia, it is not difficult to argue that under capitalist auspices their development would have been better proportioned and more successful than has actually been the case during the past twenty years or so. The question as

to how socialist development would have fared in such relatively highly developed industrial societies if the Soviet model had not been forced on to them, cannot be answered with certainty. But it is not self-evident that such alternative socialist development would have promoted social development any more than capitalist development on the western European pattern would have done.

50. See Teresa Rakowska-Harmstone (ed.), *Perspectives for Change in Communist Societies*, Boulder, Colo., 1979; and the so-called 'System Remodelling Debate' in the periodical *Soviet Studies*, 30, No. 1 *et seq.* (1978). See also the important contributions in the Festschrift for Ota Sik, ed. Ulrich Gärtner and Jiri Kosta, *Wirtschaft und Gesellschaft. Kritik und Alternativen*, Berlin, 1979; and on this book, see my review 'Wirtschaft, Gesellschaft, Sozialismus', *Leviathan*, 8(1980), 273–8. At this point a consideration of method may be permitted. The development paths of socialist societies have been quite different. It is doubtful that such differences (e.g. the Soviet Union/China) will lead to alternatives in the long run. The differences during the first development stage resulted from different resource endowments. Past experience suggests that, in the course of internal development by way of delayed socialist development, the development profiles tend to converge towards the prototype of the 'Soviet economy'. See *inter alia* Bernard Michael Frolic, 'Comparing China and the Soviet Union', *Contemporary Communism*, 2, No. 2(1978), 24–42; Jan S. Prybyla, 'Changes in the Chinese Economy: An Interpretation', *Asian Survey*, 19, No. 5(1979), 409–35, especially 432ff.

|51. Karl W. Deutsch, *The Nerves of Government*, New York, 1963; D. Senghaas, 'Sozialkybernetik und Herrschaft' in Claus Koch and Dieter Senghaas (eds), *Texte zur Technokratiediskussion*, Frankfurt, 1970, pp. 196–217. With regard to socialist societies, see the important article by Jadwiga Staniszkis, 'On Some Contradictions of Socialist Societies: The Case of Poland', *Soviet Studies*, 31, No. 2(1979), 167–87.

52. See in particular Staniszkis, op. cit. (note 51 above); W. Brus *et al.*, *Polen. Symptome und Ursachen der politischen Krise*, Hamburg, 1981; special issue, 'Polen—realer Sozialismus', of *Sozialismus*, Extra 3(Hamburg, Aug. 1981).

53. On the connection between structures of domination, legitimation and the requirements of technological rationality and economic efficiency in advanced socialist societies, see Richard Loewenthal, 'The Ruling Party in a Mature Society', in Field, *Social Consequences*, pp. 81–118; also Gerd Meyer, *Bürokratischer Sozialismus. Eine Analyse des sowjetischen Herrschaftsystems*, Stuttgart, 1977, especially ch. 7; W. Arthur Lewis, *Socialism and Economic Growth*, London, 1971, especially p. 7. On the problem as a whole, see Paul Sweezy, *Post-Revolutionary Society*, New York, 1980.

54. On this, see for example Jiri Kosta, *Abriß der sozialökonomischen*, pp. 99ff., and further literature cited in note 45 above as well as the exemplary analysis in Iván Berend, 'Hungary's Road to the Seventies', *Acta Oeconomica*, 25(1980), 1–17. The table on the facing page conveys information on the above-mentioned question. On the problem as a whole see also George Feiwel, 'Economic Problems of Eastern Europe: Current Problems and Perspectives', *Rivista Internazionale di Scienze economiche e commerciali*, 26, No. 7(1979), 773–86 (part 1) and No. 9, 891–904 (part 2). On the supply problem as a structural problem, see Jean Marczewski, 'The

Investment fund (as % of national income) and industrial growth (in %) in eastern Europe

	1950		1960		1970	
	IF	IG	IF	IG	IF	IG
Bulgaria	20.0	13.7	27.4	15.9	29.2	10.9
Czechoslovakia	17.1	10.9	17.6	10.5	27.0	6.7
GDR	8.5	13.7	18.1	8.7	24.0	6.5
Poland	21.1	16.2	24.2	9.9	27.9	8.3
Romania	23.0	15.1	20.1	10.9	29.2	11.9
Hungary	23.1	13.2	23.1	7.6	27.2	6.2
Soviet Union	23.9	13.2	26.8	10.4	29.5	8.5

IF = Investment Fund   IG = Industrial Growth

Source: COMECON Bulletins quoted from Silviu Brucan, 'The Strategy of Development in Eastern Europe', *IFDA Dossier*, No. 13 (Nov. 1979), 71–82, reprinted in *Review*, 5 (1981), 95–112.

Problem of Consumption in Soviet-Type Economies', *Soviet Studies*, 31, No. 1(1979), 112–17; also the literature on the hidden or 'second' economy: Dennis O'Hearn, 'The Consumer Second Economy: Size and Effects', *Soviet Studies*, 32(1980), 218–34 (also containing references to further literature).

55. On this, see also Renate Damus, *Der reale Sozialismus als Herrschaftssystem am Beispiel der DDR. Kritik der nachkapitalistischen Gesellschaft*, Giessen, 1978; and D.M. Nuti, 'The Contradictions of Socialist Economies' in *Socialist Register 1979* (London, 1979), pp. 228–73.

56. See Peter Christian Ludz, *Ideologiebegriff und marxistische Theorie*, Opladen, 1976, pp. 319ff. ('Formen und Alternativen sozialistischer Entwicklungen'), where the author distinguishes between the Yugoslav, Czechoslovak and East German models as representing different ways of solving the problems of advanced socialist societies.

57. On the economic reforms, see J. Wilczynski, *Socialist Economic Development and Reforms*, London, 1972; Radoslav Selucky, *Economic Reforms in Eastern Europe*, New York, 1972; as well as the literature cited in note 45 above. See also Wlodzimierz Brus, 'The East European Reforms: What Happened to Them?', *Soviet Studies*, 31, No. 2(1979), 257–67.

58. See the illuminating article by Ivan Volgyes, 'Modernization, Stratification and Elite Development in Hungary', *Social Forces*, 57, No. 2(1978), 500–21; also Henryk Flakierski, 'Economic Reform and Income Distribution in Hungary', *Cambridge Journal of Economics*, 3(1979), 15–32. On the Polish problem, see the interesting article by Henryk Szlajfer, 'Nachzuholende Entwicklung unter Bedingungen des Weltmarkts. Das Beispiel der polnischen Entwicklung', *Probleme des Klassenkampfs*, 7, No. 27(1977), 7–24; also Stefan Horton, 'Die Revolution der Hoffnung und ihre Ergebnisse—einige Bemerkungen zur gegenwärtigen Situation in Polen', ibid., 25–39.

59. On this, see especially the contribution by Loewenthal, op. cit. (note 53 above). See also the contributions from eastern and south-eastern Europe

in Udo Bermbach and Franz Nuscheler (eds), *Sozialistischer Pluralismus. Texte zur Theorie und Praxis sozialistischer Gesellschaften*, Hamburg, 1973. See also Radoslav Selucky, 'Detente and Economic Reforms in Eastern Europe: The Old Dilemma Revisited' in Gärtner and Kosta, *Wirtschaft und Gesellschaft*, pp. 147–61. On new literature on this subject, see the report by Antonin J. Liehm, 'East Central Europe and the Soviet Model', *Problems of Communism*, 30, No. 5(1981), 50–5. For a thorough discussion of these problems, see Gunnar Heinsohn and Otto Steiger, 'Geld, Produktivität und Unsicherheit im Kapitalismus und Sozialismus', *Leviathan*, 9(1981), 164–94; also the seminal studies by János Kornai: *Anti-Equilibrium*, London, 1971; *Economics of Shortage*, Amsterdam, 1980; and 'The Dilemma of a Socialist Economy: The Hungarian Experience', *Cambridge Journal of Economics*, 4(1980), 147–57. On one of the earliest debates, see Kurt Mandelbaum and Gerhard Meyer, 'Zur Theorie der Planwirtschaft', *Zeitschrift für Sozialforschung*, 3(1934), 228–62.

60. This term is used by Willfried Spohn in *Bahro-Kongreß*, p. 136.

61. Such a development is by no means certain, but there seems to be no alternative to it in the long term—that is, within the coming decades. What socialist societies have achieved is delayed development (= avoidance of further peripheralization and the establishment of integrated production structures); what they are lacking is 'the delayed development of a labour movement'. This seems paradoxical for 'workers' and farmers' states', but it explains their crux. The dilemma was pointed out by Max Weber as early as 1918 in his reflections on state socialism, when he observed that strikes against the state were impossible, with the result that the dependence of the worker was greatly increased under this kind of state socialism—and that the fusion of economic and state bureaucracies into one single body with unified interests made bureaucracy uncontrollable. See Weber, 'Der Sozialismus', *Gesammelte Aufsätze zur Soziologie und Sozialpolitik*, Tübingen, 1924, pp. 503–4.

62. Sten, Tellenback, 'The Logic of Development in Socialist Poland', *Social Forces*, 57, No. 2(1978), 436–56, quotation on pp. 452–3.

63. *Ibid*.

64. What they have achieved has been labelled 'consultative authoritarianism' or 'centralized pluralism'. Both are quite different from an open system of institutionalized political bargaining between organized interest groups. On the relevant discussion, see Gerd Meyer, *Bürokratischer Sozialismus*; *idem*, *Sozialistische Systeme*; Alec Nove, *The Soviet Economic System*, London, 1977; and, for a summary, Darrel P. Hammer, 'Bureaucratic Pluralism' (paper for the IPSA Congress in Moscow, 12–18 Aug. 1979).

65. This point is made by Staniszkis, op. cit. (note 51 above). Concrete proposals on how to solve these structural problems are developed by Jadwiga Staniszkis in 'On Remodelling the Polish Economic System', *Soviet Studies*, 30, No. 4(1978), 547–52.

66. Norbert Elias, *Über den Prozeß der Zivilisation*, Frankfurt, 1976, Vol. 2, p. 152.

67. Or: 'Ils font semblant de nous payer, nous faisons semblant de travailler' (quoted from a report on Romania in *Le Monde* [19 Nov. 1979], p. 4.

68. On this, see above all the studies by Ota Sik: *Plan und Markt im Sozialismus*, Prague and Vienna, 1967; *Der Dritte Weg*, Hamburg, 1972; *Das*

kommunistische Machtsystem, Hamburg, 1976; *Humane Wirtschaftsdemokratie*, Hamburg, 1979. See also, for a general assessment, Radoslav Selucky, *Marxism, Socialism, Freedom*, London, 1979.

69. See the report on the reception given to Ota Sik's ideas in China by Rosemarie Fiedler-Winter, 'Auf der Suche nach dem Dritten Weg. Werden Ota Sik's Reformideen im Fernen Osten verwirklicht?', *Die Zeit*, No. 47(13 Nov. 1981), p. 20. See also, for a pragmatic assessment, Martin Irion, 'Beobachtungen in China 1980—interpretiert am Beispiel anderer sozialistischer Gesellschaften' in Theodor Bergmann, Barbara Hasard and Dieter Senghaas (eds), *Wiedersehen mit China nach zwei Jahren*, Breitenbach, 1981, pp. 279–88. Against the backcloth of the problems referred to in the previous paragraph, studies on the efficiency profiles of socialist as opposed to capitalist, even peripheral-capitalist societies, are not only of increasing analytical interest but of growing political explosiveness. See, for example, Nicholas Burakow, 'Romania and Greece—Socialism versus Capitalism', *World Development*, 9(1980), 909–29.

7   Is There an Alternative Development Policy for the Third World?

1. This contribution picks up the thread of development theory and policy studies that I published in *Weltwirtschaftsordnung*.
2. List, *Das nationale System*, p. 164.
3. On this, see *inter alia* Senghaas, *Peripherer Kapitalismus*.
4. Karl Schiller, 'Zur Wachstumsproblematik der Entwicklungsländer', *Kieler Vorträge*, new series, No. 15 (Kiel, 1960), p. 89.
5. Elias, *The Civilizing Process*, 2 vols., Oxford, 1978, 1982, Vol. 2, p. 74.
6. Cyril Black *et al.*, *The Modernization of Japan and Russia: A Comparative Study*, London, 1975, especially pp. 233ff., 243ff.; quote from p. 235.
7. According to traditional development theory, which treats underdevelopment as being the result of scarcity of capital, this should not be the case.
8. Alfons Lemper, 'Collective Self-Reliance. Eine erfolgversprechende Entwicklungsstrategie?', *Mitteilungen des Verbands-Stiftung Deutsches Überseeinstitut*, No. 4 (Hamburg, 1976), 61–88; quoted from 75/6.
9. See Voigt, *Kooperation*, pp. 7ff., 121ff. and *passim*.
10. On this, see Menzel, *Theorie und Praxis des Chinesischen Entwicklungsmodells*, pp. 293ff.
11. On this, see Ellen Brun and Jacques Hersh, *Socialist Korea: A Case Study in the Strategy of Economic Development*, New York, 1976, pp. 180ff.
12. Ibid., p. 181; also Wayne S. Kiyosaki, *North Korea's Foreign Relations*, New York, 1976, pp. 69ff.
13. Quoted by Brun and Hersh, ibid., p. 184.
14. Kim il Sung, *Reden und Aufsätze*, Frankfurt, 1971, Vol. 1, p. 289. That this self-portrait reflects socio-economic reality is demonstrated by Joseph Sang-Hoon Cung in *The North Korean Economy*, Stanford, Calif., 1974.
15. See Stehr, *Sozio-ökonomische Bedingungen*.
16. Paul Streeten, 'Self-Reliant Industrialization' (manuscript for the Conference of the International Studies Association in St Louis, Mo., 1977, p. 22).
17. Hans Jürgen Harborth, 'Anforderungen an eine revidierte Integrations-

theorie für Entwicklungsländer', *Integration der Entwicklungsländer in eine instabile Weltwirtschaft*, Schriften des Vereins für Sozialpolitik, new series, 90 (Berlin, 1976), 65–88; quoted from pp. 84/5.

18. In what respects spatial economic considerations may be a potential help in this connection was indicated several years ago by Hans Jürgen Harborth in his essay 'Zur Rolle der Entwicklungsländer in einer multi-zentrischen Weltwirtschaft', *Jahrbuch für Sozialwissenschaften*, 22, No. 2(1971), 244–56. Harborth's arguments should be developed further from the standpoint of the theory of autocentric development.

19. Hans Jürgen Harborth, 'Dissoziation—Mit welchem Ziel?', *Entwicklung und Zusammenarbeit*, Nos 7/8 (1977), 17–18.

20. For first attempts in this direction, see Johan Galtung, 'Alternative Life Styles in Rich Societies' in Marc Nerfin (ed.), *Another Development: Approaches and Strategies*, Uppsala, 1977, pp. 106–21.

21. W. Arthur Lewis, *Some Aspects of Economic Development*, Accra, 1969.

22. Kim il Sung, quoted from Brun and Hersh, *Socialist Korea*, p. 154.

23. Ibid., pp. 168/9.

24. Economies of scale arise from mass production and long production runs resulting in lower unit costs.

25. On the possibility of analysing these dimensions, see the still seminal study by Deutsch, *Nationalism*.

26. Which is why the position advanced in this book could be characterised as 'neo-Listian'.